Priority of Needs?

Bernhard Kittel • Stefan Traub
Editors

Priority of Needs?

An Informed Theory of Need-based Justice

Springer

Editors
Bernhard Kittel
Department of Economic Sociology
University of Vienna
Wien, Austria

Stefan Traub
Department of Economics
and Social Science
Helmut Schmidt University
Hamburg, Germany

ISBN 978-3-031-53050-0 ISBN 978-3-031-53051-7 (eBook)
https://doi.org/10.1007/978-3-031-53051-7

This work was supported by Deutsche Forschungsgemeinschaft.

This Springer imprint is published by the registered company Springer Nature Switzerland AG
The registered company address is: Gewerbestrasse 11, 6330 Cham, Switzerland

Paper in this product is recyclable.

Preface

This edited volume presents the results of several years of research by the research group "Need-Based Justice and Distribution Procedures" (FOR 2104) funded by the German Research Foundation (DFG), the Austrian Science Fund (FWF), and the Swiss National Fund (SNF). It is conceived as a follow-up on the edited volume *Need-Based Distributive Justice—An Interdisciplinary Perspective*, also published with Springer Nature in 2020 (editors: Stefan Traub and Bernhard Kittel), which first reviews the state of research on need-based justice from the perspectives of philosophy, psychology, sociology, political science, and economics and then outlines a framework for a theory of distributive justice based on the satisfaction of recognized needs. In the present volume, we elaborate the theoretical and experimental results of FOR 2104's subprojects and synthesize them into an *informed theory of need-based justice* within this research framework. The central result of these joint efforts is the proposition that the satisfaction of socially or politically recognized needs in a solidarity community should be prioritized over other principles of distribution ("Lexineed Principle").

The principal investigators of FOR 2104 come from psychology (Adele Diederich, Carl von Ossietzky University Oldenburg), philosophy (Mark Siebel, Carl von Ossietzky University Oldenburg), sociology (Bernhard Kittel, University of Vienna), political science (Tanja Pritzlaff-Scheele and Frank Nullmeier, University of Bremen; Kai-Uwe Schnapp, Universität Hamburg; Markus Tepe, University of Bremen), and economics (Andreas Nicklisch, University of the Applied Sciences of the Grisons Chur; Stefan Traub, Helmut-Schmidt University Hamburg). In eight subprojects, they all employed theoretical and laboratory experimental research designs in order to understand the various aspects of need as a principle of justice. The URL of FOR 2104's website is https://www.hsu-hh.de/bedarfsgerechtigkeit/en/.

Apart from the principal investigators and our Mercator Fellow Thomas Schramme (University of Liverpool), who engaged in the discussion of the initial ideas and the writing of the proposals, the postdoc members and PhD students employed in the project made it flourish as they developed fresh ideas out of the initial outline. We would like to take this opportunity to thank them all: Alexander

Max Bauer, Meike Benker, Marina Chugunova, Brian Dietrich, Sebastian Finkler, Helena Hagauer, Hermann Helke, Georg Kanitsar, Ann-Katrin Kienle, Jan Philipp Krügel, Maximilian Lutz, Christine Meemann, Frauke Meyer, Sabine Neuhofer, Fabian Paetzel, Manuel Schwaninger, Nils Springhorn, Réka Szendrő, Lilla Tolnai, Marvin Waibel, Arne Weiß, Marc Wyszynski, and Patricia F. Zauchner.

Besides the members of FOR 2104, we are also indebted to many people who have contributed at different stages and in various ways to the success of the project, in alphabetic order: André Bächtiger, Dagmar Borchers, Wulf Gaertner, Stefan Gosepath, Peter Hammond, Guillermina Jasso, James Konow, Dorothea Kübler, Claudia Landwehr, Stefan Liebig, Christian List, Jan Lorenz, Wolfgang J. Luhan, David Miller, Joe Oppenheimer, Ilana Ritov, David Rueda, Christian Seidl, and Susumu Shikano. We are also indebted to the officials at the Deutsche Forschungsgemeinschaft, in particular Dr. Eckard Kämper and his team, who were available for all questions in the preparatory process. Our research findings were presented to the wider public at a symposium on March 22, 2022, at the University of Hamburg with the support of the DFG and the German Institute for Interdisciplinary Social Policy Research (DIFIS). We would particularly like to thank the participants of the discussion panel, Claudia Czernohorsky-Grüneberg (Jobcenter Frankfurt/Main), Petra Lotzkat (Hamburg Social Welfare Authority), and Klaus Wicher (Sozialverband Deutschland) as well as the moderator Kolja Rudzio (*Die Zeit*). Last but not least, we thank the team at Springer, in particular Martina Bihn, Niko Chtouris, and Parthiban Gujilan Kannan.

Wien, Austria — Bernhard Kittel
Hamburg, Germany — Stefan Traub
March 2024

Contents

Part IV Differentiation

List of Figures

List of Tables

Chapter 1
Why Prioritize Needs?

Bernhard Kittel and Stefan Traub

Abstract The presumption underlying the scientific engagement with need-based justice is that neither the principle of equity nor the principle of equality safeguards a distribution that ensures the preservation of human dignity through the satisfaction of needs as a fundamental proviso of human sociality. In this introductory chapter, we first show that in the context of other principles of distributive justice, the satisfaction of needs takes a prominent position both empirically and in political philosophy. We then proceed to discussing fundamental contributions to the theory of need-based justice and outline the perspective that the present volume adds to the literature. At the core is a process model of need-based justice that conceptually differentiates the identification of needs, the social and political recognition of needs, and the consequences of need-based distributions. We suggest that these empirical questions are associated with normative claims about the consistency, the legitimacy, and the sustainability of need-based justice. The chapter concludes with a brief outline of the following chapters.

1.1 Introduction

The nineteenth and twentieth centuries have witnessed philosophical and political struggles over the prioritization of one of two principles of distributive justice: equity and equality. Equity means allocating a share of a common resource to an individual strictly proportional to that individual's contribution to the production of the resource. Equality means allocating the same amount of a resource to each member of the community.

B. Kittel (✉)
University of Vienna, Department of Economic Sociology, Wien, Austria
e-mail: bernhard.kittel@univie.ac.at

S. Traub
Helmut-Schmidt University, Department of Economics, Hamburg, Germany
e-mail: traubs@hsu-hh.de

B. Kittel, S. Traub (eds.), *Priority of Needs?*,
https://doi.org/10.1007/978-3-031-53051-7_1

The equity principle is liberal in the sense of allowing each individual to decide how much to contribute to the production of the resource and thus to autonomously determine her share. If she desires more, she contributes more. However, if allocations depend on contributions alone, as the equity principle mandates, all those who, for whatever reason, cannot contribute sufficiently to obtain a life-preserving share of the resource will perish. Equity has no inherent provision, for example, for the elderly, the sick, the heavily disabled, those who are in education, or those who are jobless.

In contrast, equal distributions of a shared resource neglect individual heterogeneity in both contributions and the required amounts of the resources. Even if those who require a larger amount of the resource contribute a larger share, they will obtain no more than an equal fraction of the community's overall output. Thus, contributing more does not pay off for the individual, and, as a consequence, the equality principle incorporates a stimulus to free ride on the efforts of others. The socially disruptive effect of ignoring individual contributions when distributing a resource produced by a joint effort has experimentally been shown in many variants of the public goods game (Chaudhuri 2011; Ledyard 1995). In the end, both principles of justice that constituted the philosophical foundation of the organizational forms dominating twentieth century societies—capitalism and communism—may produce outcomes that must be considered unjust from a humanistic perspective.

Taking the rallying cry of the French revolution—liberté, égalité, fraternité—as a point of departure, Pomfret (2011, vii) interprets the nineteenth century as the age of liberty—and thus equity—and the twentieth century as the age of equality. Extending this metaphor, perhaps fraternité, represented by the need principle, will come to characterize the twenty-first century. Does the need principle provide a better foundation for a legitimate social order than equity or equality? Does a focus on needs solve societal problems more fundamentally than the appeal to alternative principles of justice?

In this volume, we explore the conditions and implications of need-based justice in distributive decisions by developing hypotheses from theoretical arguments developed in psychology, sociology, political science, economics, and philosophy (Traub and Kittel 2020), and by empirically testing hypotheses derived from theories developed in these disciplines, predominantly using laboratory experimental methods. This introductory chapter sketches the context in which our argument is set. We first discuss the principles of equity, equality, and entitlement with a specific focus on the inherent limits of these principles. Then we elaborate on the theory of need and propose four areas that require more detailed scrutiny: How can we identify needs? When are individual need claims recognized by others? How sustainable are distributions that are based on needs? And what are the scope conditions of need-based distributions?

1.2 Entitlement, Equity, and Equality

The modern formulations of equity and equality were established as principles of distributive justice during the development of the humanistic ideal in the age of enlightenment. As radically new conceptions of society, they challenged the aristocratic principle of entitlement, which legitimized the claim to power and relative allocations of resources by divine providence, lineage, and inheritance (Spicker 2006, p. 66). As late as in the Austrian constitution of 1869, the title of the Austrian emperor Franz Joseph I still referred to the divine legitimacy of his inherited status: "Seine Kaiserliche und Königliche Apostolische Majestät [...] von Gottes Gnaden Kaiser von Österreich, [...]."[1]

Nowadays, European societies do not rank entitlement as a principle of justice particularly highly. According to data from the European Social Survey 2018, 69% of Europeans disagree or disagree strongly with the statement "A society is fair when people from families with high social status enjoy privileges in their lives" (see Fig. 1.1, upper-left panel, in European Social Survey 2018). While a clear majority rejects privilege by birth, the fact that 18% is ambivalent on this question and another 12% actually agree with the statement suggests that the entitlement principle has not completely died out as an idea of social order in Europe.

The equity principle, next, is both a logical implication of the bourgeois worldview and a legitimization of the wealth accumulated by the ideologically hegemonic groups in society, that is, merchants and traders. It gives precedence to income earned through effort over inherited property, the latter being the income source of the landed gentry. For example, Adam Smith (1790, Part IV, Section I) described the virtuous man as a prudent, industrious, skilled, frugal, and modest person, "who sacrifices the ease and enjoyment of the present moment for the probable expectation of the still greater ease and enjoyment of a more distant but more lasting period of time." The equity principle took up the ancient Greek concept of proportionality with relative merit, suggested by the philosopher Aristoteles as the criterion for a just distribution (Aristoteles 350bc, book V, p. 3):

> [...] for all men agree that what is just in distribution must be according to merit in some sense, though they do not all specify the same sort of merit, but democrats identify it with the status of freeman, supporters of oligarchy with wealth (or with noble birth), and supporters of aristocracy with excellence. [...] The just, then, is a species of the proportionate [...] For proportion is equality of ratios. [...] This, then, is what the just is—the proportional; the unjust is what violates the proportion.

The idea that merit is determined by a virtuous life, which, as the quote by Adam Smith above illustrates, means hard work and acquired skills, was explicitly turned against the aristocracy by the early socialist thinker Henri de Saint-Simon, who,

[1] https://de.wikipedia.org/wiki/Gro%C3%9Fer_Titel_des_Kaisers_von_%C3%96sterreich.

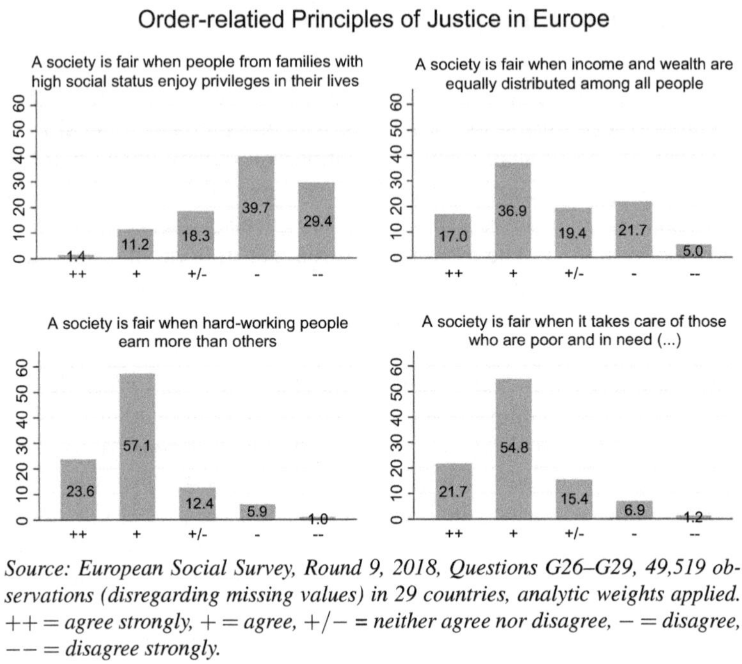

Fig. 1.1 Attitudes toward order-related principles of justice in Europe

advocating a meritocratic society, attacked the "idle class" by writing (Saint-Simon 1975 [1790], pp. 158–159):

> We regard society as the ensemble and union of men engaged in useful work. [. . .] But there is surrounding society, there circulates in its bosom a throng of parasites who, although they have the same needs and desires as the others, have not been able to overcome the natural laziness common to all men, and who, although they produce nothing, consume or seek to consume as though they did produce. These men use force to live off the work of the rest, either off what they are given or what they can take. In short, they are idlers, that is, thieves.

The equity principle is well-supported in modern societies. 81% of the European population agree or agree strongly with the statement "A society is fair when hard-working people earn more than others" (Fig. 1.1, lower-left panel).

Equality, the third principle, represents the humanistic ideal of the equal dignity of human beings, which has subsequently inspired socialist thought. The principle of equality is postulated as a legal and political idea in Jean-Jacques Rousseau's (2013 [1762], p. 32) treatise on the social contract:

> By whatever path we return to our principle we always arrive at the same conclusion, viz. that the social compact establishes among the citizens such an equality that they all pledge themselves under the same conditions and ought all to enjoy the same rights.

However, Rousseau (2013 [1762], p. 43) is reluctant to extend this formal notion of equality before the law and with respect to citizenship to the sphere of economics and settles on a much weaker conception:

> With regard to equality, we must not understand by this word that the degrees of power and wealth should be absolutely the same; but that, as to power, it should fall short of all violence, and never be exercised except by virtue of station and of the laws; while, as to wealth, no citizen should be rich enough to be able to buy another, and none poor enough to be forced to sell himself, which supposes, on the part of the great, moderation in property and influence, and, on the part of ordinary citizens, repression of avarice and covetousness.

For the most prominent philosopher of justice of modern times, John Rawls, equality enters the scene as the condition behind the veil of ignorance in which no one knows the position they will hold in the societal structure (Rawls 1971). This ignorance entails the risk of ending up at the lower end of the distribution and thus guarantees, according to Rawls, that people will choose a society in which the overall level of inequality will be minimized. As soon as people know their position, their preferences shift toward the interests induced by their position in the social strata (Kittel et al. 2017).

In the world of democratic governance, the distributive and redistributive implications of justice principles are a contested topic in political debates and policy-making. In election campaigns, parties select platforms such that their social policy issues bridge their partisan voters' and the general electorate's positions (Pinggera 2020). Under the present condition of rising inequalities, parties on the left typically emphasize economic issues and call for redistributive policies, whereas parties on the right focus more on values (Tavits and Potter 2015). In this vein, parties representing the liberal spectrum often propagate meritocratic justice conceptions (Mulligan 2017), a demand that is rooted in the equity principle. In contrast, parties on the left articulate egalitarian claims (Bremer 2018). For example, in the 2009 German elections, the liberal Freie Demokratische Partei (FDP) used the slogan "Work must pay off again," whereas the leftist party Die Linke propagated "Wealth for all" (Fig. 1.2).

In modern European societies, attitudes toward the principle of equality, measured by the item "A society is fair when income and wealth are equally distributed among all people" in the European Social Survey, are mixed. While about 54% of Europeans agree with this statement, 27% disagree (Fig. 1.1, upper-right panel).

While this "prima facie principle of equal distribution for all goods" (Gosepath 2015, p. 167) is a major tenet among political parties on the left, it is qualified in various respects in modern political philosophy (Gosepath 2003, 2011). For the present purposes, the most relevant qualification is that the universalistic idea of equal dignity as a human being does not mandate an equal distribution of goods but only rejects any departure from equal treatment that is not grounded in a reasonable, logically deducible principle (Gosepath 2015, p. 176), that is,

> [e]veryone must be treated numerically or strictly equally irrespective of their descriptive differences, unless certain [types] of difference[s] are presently relevant and successfully justify, through generally acceptable reasons, unequal treatment or unequal distribution.

"Wealth for all" (Reichtum für alle.) vs. "Work must pay off again" (Arbeit muss sich wieder lohnen).

Fig. 1.2 Electoral confrontation of equity and equality in election campaigns, Germany 2009

Applying the equality principle in distributive decisions, each individual should be allocated R/N with R being the total resource and N the number of community members, while individual contributions are disregarded. Here, universalism enters as the principle of equal provision taken literally, and every member of the community can legitimately claim an equal share in the resource produced by the joint effort (Phillips 2004).

For equity, in contrast, the proportionality rule $A_x/C_x = A_y/C_y$ holds, with A representing an individual's allocation and C that individual's contribution, whereby x and y are members of the same community (Adams 1965). The principle is universalistic in the sense of being fundamentally open: Every individual is assumed to have an equal opportunity to participate, and those who do contribute to the joint effort can legitimately claim a proportionate share in the resulting resource. Apart from the contribution, no other criterion enters the equation. The equity principle encompasses equality as the limiting case in which "persons are equal in distributionally relevant respects" (Gosepath 2015, p. 169). $A_x = A_y = R/N$ if $C_x = C_y$ for all $x, y \in N$ and $R = \sum C_i$. When it is impossible to determine C in sufficient detail, which is difficult and subject to controversy when contributions vary in kind, groups often resort to assuming that $C_x = C_y$.

The particular universalist ideas underlying equity and equality have specific implications that threaten their applicability as distributive principles in real-world societies. In both cases, two flaws undermine the practical implementation of the principle. First, the heterogeneity of individual "doings and beings" (Sen 1990, p. 113) is not accounted for by a principle that is exclusively guided by universalism.

If the fundamental idea of the enlightenment, the equal dignity of all human beings, has any bearing, both equity and equality fail in doing justice to those who do not fulfill their criteria. Variation in their physical or mental condition or their social and economic circumstances may prevent people from contributing to the joint effort and may cause differences in the resources that are required to attain equal dignity. This problem was noticed by Karl Marx, who rejected equality as a bourgeois ideal (Wood 2014, p. 253):

> Right by its very nature can consist only in the application of an equal standard; but unequal individuals (and they would not be different individuals if they were not unequal) are measurable by an equal standard only insofar as they are brought under an equal point of view, are taken from one definite side only, for instance [...] are regarded only as workers and nothing else is seen in them, everything else being ignored (Marx 1975, 24, p. 86).

For this reason, modern theories of equality are careful to specify the meaning of equality. For example, Ronald Dworkin (1981a, pp. 191–192) distinguishes equality of "success in fulfilling one's preferences, goals and ambitions" from distributions that "attempt to leave people as equal as possible in some aspect or quality of their conscious life" but rejects both of these definitions due to the heterogeneity of preferences and because of the improbability of reaching a distribution that satisfies all. Instead, he proposes a third definition, which is to think about equality in terms of resources privately owned by individuals. Unlike Rawls', Dworkin's thought experiment combines an initial condition of no private property with individuals who are informed about their own preferences in an auction of these resources. This process eventually generates inequalities that result from the individuals' own intentional actions. These inequalities are addressed by a correction mechanism that includes an envy test and an insurance scheme (Dworkin 1981b, p. 284).

One of the most outspoken defenders of the equality principle, Stefan Gosepath, puts forward the notion of moral equality as a right to equal recognition and safeguarding of individual autonomy, a right to equal dignity, and a ban on discrimination that assumes the unequal worth of humans (Gosepath 2003, p. 288). As we will argue below, these provisions point toward the need principle.

Evaluated from the universalistic perspective, there is no reason to restrict the vision of equal dignity to particular groups. However, humans form and live in social groups that are constituted by some sentiment of belonging to a "we" group based on experiences of common destiny, such as families, clans or nations (Schutz 1967 [1932]) or on a shared imagination of commonality (Anderson 1991). Redistribution necessarily requires the definition of a border between those who are entitled to a share of the resource and those who are not. Thus, the larger is the social distance thus generated between "me" and "the other," the less salient are the other's "doings and beings"—people know less about the other's situation and develop less empathy.

The fall of the communist regimes in Eastern Europe between 1989 and 1991 has shown the inherent contradictions of an economic system that is based on egalitarianism but realized inequality, social hierarchy, and dysfunctional political and economic processes (Maier 1997). And the increasing instability of the capitalist economic system over the last thirty years, with rapidly rising inequality in income and wealth in the rich countries (Piketty 2014) and increasing numbers of people who are unable to maintain their living standard also in Western countries (Atkinson 2019; Ravaillon 2016), marks the limits of the equity principle as a fundament of the organization of society.[2]

1.3 Need-Based Justice

The main proposition motivating this volume is that a major challenge of the twenty-first century will be the question of whether it is possible and advisable to give priority to needs in distributive and redistributive politics. In terms of the French revolutionaries' rallying cry, the question is whether fraternity can play any role in the new century despite the fact that we observe increasingly disintegrating societies and polarized politics.

> In the twenty-first century the world is moving on to address issues related to life in a common space. The challenge will be to find a political system that can respond at many levels while retaining the achievements of the last two centuries in the form of a market-based global economy modified by effective measures to promote equality of opportunity (e.g., through accessible education) and equality of outcome (e.g., through targeted assistance to those unable to benefit from or unavoidably hurt by the market economy and through more equal health outcomes). (Pomfret 2011, pp. 12–13)

Although the extreme poverty of large parts of the world's population has been a major driving force of revolutions and political reform in the last two centuries, the academic and political debates over the relative merits of equity and equality have implicitly assumed that the satisfaction of needs is no issue.

> Quite often, advocacy of egalitarianism is based less on an argument than on a purported moral intuition: economic inequality just seems wrong. It strikes many people as altogether apparent that, taken simply in its own right, the possession by some of more money than others is morally offensive. I suspect that people who profess to have this intuition concern manifestations of inequality are actually not responding to the inequality they perceive but to another feature of the situations they are observing. What I believe they find intuitively to be morally objectionable in circumstances of economic inequality is not that some of the individuals in those circumstances have less money than others. Rather, it is the fact that those with less have too little. (Frankfurt 2015, pp. 40–41)

In the essay from which these lines are quoted, philosopher Harry Frankfurt makes a strong case against the predominance of the equality principle in contemporary political debate. Instead, he argues, the real problem is poverty, such that too many people in modern societies do not earn enough money to reach a decent living

[2] Note, however, that this rise in inequality took place at a historically low level of societal inequality in the Western world, compared to much more skewed distributions of wealth and well-being in earlier centuries, and in the context of declining inequality on a worldwide scale (Bourguignon and Morrisson 2002; Milanovic 2016; Scheidel 2017).

standard. He argues that economic inequality is unethical if, and only if, it leads to suffering. The challenge of distributive justice is not to give the same to all but to make sure that everyone has enough, which is much more difficult to implement.

> The very concept of having an equal share is itself considerably more transparent and intelligible than the concept of having enough. A theory of equality is much easier to articulate than a theory of sufficiency. The widespread appeal of economic egalitarianism has, unfortunately, masked the importance of systematic inquiry into the analytical and theoretical issues raised by the concept of having enough. (Frankfurt 2015, p. 15)

This is the challenge that we intend to take up and develop further in this volume. Despite the fact that a concern for needs can be traced back to the New Testament (Wood 2014, p. 259) and has been popularized by the slogan used by Karl Marx, "from each according to his abilities, to each according to his needs" (Marx 1975, 24, pp. 86–87), need as a principle of justice has received much less attention both in public and academic debate and in scientific research than equity and equality (Miller 1999; Sen 2009).

As a criterion of fairness in society, the alleviation of poverty, which is taken as an operationalization of the need principle, is almost as popular in modern European societies as is the equity principle. 76% of respondents in the European Social Survey 2018 agreed with the statement, "A society is fair when it takes care of those who are poor and in need regardless of what they give back to society" (Fig. 1.1, lower-right panel). These survey data are in line with findings from experimental studies that suggest that American students prefer distributions that maximize average income subject to a floor constraint (Frohlich and Oppenheimer 1992), a hybrid approach that has aptly been captured by Kenneth Boulding (1962, p. 83): "Society lays a modest table at which all can sup and a high table at which the deserving can feast" (also see Traub et al. 2005).

The basic idea underlying the principle of need-based justice is—again—the humanistic stipulation that every human being should be able to live in dignity (Nussbaum 2011). In practice, however, the identification of need and its transformation into a principle of justice generates multiple and multifaceted problems that are related to the particularities of individual needs.

> [I]n conditions of scarcity, there is no uniquely defensible way of spelling out the principle of distribution according to need. We face conflicting imperatives: to meet as many needs as possible, taking into account how much each costs to satisfy, and to preserve comparative justice by ensuring that people whose needs are similar are treated in the same way. (Brock and Miller 2023)

Most fundamentally, if the specification of needs is particular to an individual, the definition of what constitutes a need also depends on the specific context, which entails the economic conditions and cultural understandings of a specific group or society. Need is ultimately in the eye of the beholder. In order not to enter the fallacy of relativism, a theory of need-based justice has to carefully outline the relationship between the universal claim that a justice principle must make and the particular nature of the problem underlying the claim.

There seems to be agreement over the proviso that a need refers to something that is necessary to fulfill some task or requirement (Brock and Miller 2023; Nullmeier 2020). However, this seemingly simple definition becomes complex as soon as we think about ways to concretize and operationalize the concept and measure its level of implementation. In this book, we focus on four aspects: the identification of needs, the recognition of needs, the sustainability of the need principle, and the scope of need recognition.

1.4 Basic Needs, Capabilities, and Socially Relative Satisfiers

The first problem is to differentiate a need from other justifications for claims on a resource that rest on personal choice (Miller 1999, p. 209), such as desire, interest, or preference (Nullmeier 2020, p. 191). For this reason, several authors have suggested contrasting intrinsic (or basic) needs with instrumental needs (Miller 1999, p. 206). Whereas instrumental needs depend on the desires, interests, or preferences of those who put forward such a claim, intrinsic needs refer to more fundamental biological and social aspects of the human condition that can with some legitimacy be argued to be necessary for "human flourishing" (Doyal and Gough 1991, p. 3) or "eudaimonia" (Aristoteles 350bc, Book 1, p. 3).[3]

When focusing on need as a criterion for a principle of justice, this notion of "flourishing" becomes crucial. Several attempts have been made to concretize this rather elusive concept. Most famously, Maslow (1943) has suggested differentiating between physiological needs, safety, belonging, esteem, and self-actualization, which form the layers in a hierarchical structure of needs, whereby each layer assumes the presence of the lower, more fundamental layers. A further elaboration of this approach has been proposed by Alderfer (1969), who translated Maslow's five hierarchical layers into three categorical dimensions of human need, namely existence, relatedness, and growth.

In the capabilities approach developed by Amartya Sen and Martha Nussbaum, the notion of flourishing has been articulated under the concept of "functionings," which echoes Maslow's and Alderfer's dimensions but goes much further in concretizing the nature of human needs.

> A person's achieved living can be seen as a combination of "functionings" (i.e., doings and beings), and taken together, they can be broadly seen as constituting the quality of life. The functionings on which human flourishing depend include such elementary things as being alive, being well nourished and in good health, moving about freely, and so on. It can also include more complex functionings such as having self-respect and respect of others, and taking part in the life of the community. (Sen 2000, p. 74)

[3] For concise overviews of the normative literature on need-based justice, see Brock and Miller 2023 and Dover 2023.

To further specify the concept of need, the capabilities approach claims that there exist some thresholds for the provision of means below which the conditions and activities constitutive of a dignified life cannot be realized. Put in formal terms, the need principle states that an allocation is just if $A_i \geq T_i$, where T_i is the threshold that satisfies the basic needs of member i (Konow 2001, p. 149). While Sen refused to enumerate the relevant capabilities and to identify thresholds for them, Nussbaum (2011) has extensively elaborated on these problems. Arguing against the meritocratic idea underlying the equity principle, she insists in the spirit of humanism,

> that the political goal for all human beings in a nation ought to be the same: all should get above a certain threshold level of combined capability, in the sense not of coerced functioning but of substantial freedom to choose and act. That is what it means to treat all people with equal respect (Nussbaum 2011, p. 24).

She developed a list of capabilities that includes the following: (1) life, (2) bodily health, (3) bodily integrity, (4) senses, imagination, and thought, (5) emotions, (6) practical reason, (7) affiliation, (8) concern for other species, (9) play, and (10) control over one's environment (Nussbaum 2011, pp. 34–35).

Nevertheless, some argue that any attempt to provide a complete and coherent list of capabilities is bound to fail due to the impossibility of identifying universally relevant capabilities, numerous interdependencies between single needs, and the problem of adjudicating between different needs and the needs of different persons (Nelson 2008).[4] These difficulties fundamentally hamper not only the development of an empirically informed theory of need, but also make the relevance of the need principle difficult to test in real-world contexts.

To develop a more structured approach to a theory of needs that circumvents the relativist fallacy without reverting to a crude universalism, Doyal and Gough (1991) further elaborated the idea of a differentiation between intrinsic and instrumental, or intermediate, needs by claiming (Doyal and Gough 1991, p. 54)

> that since physical survival and personal autonomy are the preconditions for any individual action in any culture, they constitute the most basic human needs—those which must be satisfied to some degree before actors can effectively participate in their form of life to achieve any other valued goal.

While these basic needs are universal, there are different, culturally specific, ways to satisfy these needs. In order to bridge the tension between the universal scope of basic needs and the particular conditions of "socially relative satisfiers," Doyal and Gough introduce, drawing on Sen (1985), "universal satisfier characteristics" that are "those properties of goods, services, activities and relationships which enhance physical health and human autonomy in all cultures" (Doyal and Gough 1991, p. 157). They suggest regarding these as intermediate needs "for which specific satisfiers can act as the means" (Doyal and Gough 1991, p. 157). They suggest that

---

[4] Similar ideas have been developed in political philosophy under the heading of sufficientarianism (Gough 2023).

the basic need of physical survival is satisfied by the following intermediate needs: (1) nutritional food and clean water, (2) protective housing, (3) a non-hazardous work environment, (4), a non-hazardous physical environment, (5) safe birth control and child-bearing, and (6) appropriate health care. They further argue that (1) a secure childhood, (2) significant primary relationships, (3) physical security, (4) economic security, and (5) appropriate education are the intermediate needs that ascertain the basic need of human autonomy. These eleven universal satisfier characteristics can be realized in a variety of culturally specific ways (Doyal and Gough 1991, pp. 157–158).

Without going any further into the details of these deliberations (e.g., Comin and Nussbaum 2014), we learn that both the basic and intermediate needs of human beings can be identified, that some basic needs can be regarded as universal, that they can be satisfied in a variety of ways, and that there is some provision threshold that must be satisfied. This introduces the second problem, which is the determination of the threshold.

1.5 Need Thresholds and the Social Recognition of Needs

What is required for physical survival and personal autonomy of the individual to be satisfied? The problem with any attempt to provide a universal answer to this question is that it depends on the climatic, geographic, historical, cultural, and social circumstances of the situation in which the question is asked, aptly captured in the often-cited remark by Adam Smith (1904 (1776), BK. V, Ch. II, Art. IV, p. 354):

> By necessaries I understand not only the commodities which are indispensably necessary for the support of life, but whatever the custom of the country renders it indecent for creditable people, even the lowest order, to be without. A linen shirt, for example, is, strictly speaking, not a necessary of life. The Greeks and Romans lived, I suppose, very comfortably, though they had no linen. But in present times [...] a creditable day-labourer would be ashamed to appear in public without a linen shirt [...]. Custom [...] has rendered leather shoes a necessary of life in England. The poorest creditable person of either sex would be ashamed to appear in public without them.

It is thus impossible to concretize the abstract notions of physical survival and personal autonomy in terms of a universally applicable set of resources. However, taking the opposite perspective by starting from individual perceptions of a need for specific resources in order to flourish leads to arbitrary need claims based on individual desires and preferences that cannot be aggregated into a universal principle of justice. While individuals may articulate any desire in terms of a need claim, this claim needs to be recognized by others as legitimate in order to become a socially relevant need. A need claim that is disregarded by the community has no chance of being satisfied. On the other hand, once recognized, a need claim is discursively extended to all members of a historically and socially circumscribed community as a right that must be satisfied under particular circumstances. In this sense, needs can be said to be socially and politically constructed (Fraser 1989;

Honneth 2015). The transformation of a particular need claim, which may refer to physical survival or personal autonomy or be based on subjective desire, into a general right through the recognition of the need by others produces a norm that becomes part of the notion of need-based justice in a particular group or society. What may be considered a need in one community may be considered merely a subjective desire in another.

This dependence of the identification of needs on their recognition by others marks the inherently social nature of needs as a principle of justice (Kittel 2020). Although the idea that a just society is one in which needs are satisfied is based on the fundamental premise of human flourishing, which entails a universal claim, the exact content is specific to an individual. This particular element of needs makes an explicit intersubjective legitimization of needs necessary. In this sense, need-based justice constitutes a social relationship and depends on the mutual recognition of each other as human beings who have a right to flourish. In order to make a reasoned judgment about the legitimacy of a need claim, others have to obtain a considerable understanding of the context in which an individual articulates a claim. For this reason, the need principle has been considered adequate for small, tightly knit, solidary communities such as a clan or a family (Liebig and Sauer 2016), where the recognition of needs is often implicit and subject to idiosyncratic reasoning. If need-based justice is to become a relevant principle in larger societies, such mutual insight into particular living conditions cannot be sustained as a mechanism for the recognition of need claims. Instead, societies must develop more general criteria in order to objectify needs.

> [A]ny rational and effective attempt to resolve the potential tension between ostensibly conflicting goals such as these [i.e., needs] must bring to bear both the codified knowledge of experts and the experiential knowledge of those whose basic needs and daily life world are under consideration. [...] It requires a dual strategy of social policy formation which values compromise, provided that it does not extend to the general character of basic human needs and rights. (Doyal and Gough 1991, p. 141)

Societies thus have developed two alternative, though possibly mutually reinforcing mechanisms to solve normative uncertainties such as the definition of needs. One starts from the subjective perspective and evaluation of interested parties who are guided by their individual experiences. The other delegates the judgment to uninterested external parties who are credited with particular expertise regarding the normative question being decided. These two mechanisms mirror the distinction between community and society (Tönnies 1887; Weber 1980 [1921/22]), system and social integration (Lockwood 1964), or system and life world (Habermas 1982). The recognition of needs is thus effectuated by giving a particular conception of needs a universal status within a community. The two modes of transforming a subjective claim into an objective principle can be termed "social" and "factual" objectification.

Social objectification is an informal mechanism by which others recognize a need claim. It rests on the ability of others to understand the specific conditions under which a need claim is being made, hence the importance of transparency of the needs underlying any articulated claim. Claimants have to persuade others of the legitimacy of their claim by proving that their situation does not meet a commonly accepted threshold of need satisfaction in a particular functioning. This approach generalizes case by case from individually perceived needs. The members of the community discursively negotiate the legitimacy of claims and transform these into entitlements that are universally applicable in the community. This flexible approach, which assesses cases in their particularity, is feasible in small, densely connected communities based on a special, reciprocal concern.

For larger communities such as societies, there is a limit to the possibility of such case-specific strategies for the identification and satisfaction of needs (Van Oorschot et al. 2017). The requirement of transparency underlying social objectification is realized in poverty relief programs in many modern welfare states that demand from their clients full disclosure of their living conditions when applying for social assistance (Goodin 2002). However, the assessment of the legitimacy of claims cannot be based on the informal acknowledgment of particular circumstances in the same way as it is done within small communities or families. Instead, societies must formally define thresholds that can be sustained as a reciprocal right accruing to anyone who experiences an undersupply of a particular resource. Societies thus delegate the assessment of individual need claims to agents with special expertise who define standards and compare individual claims to these standards. This mechanism can be described as factual objectification.

From these considerations follows that a theory of need-based justice must systematically include the concepts of transparency and expertise as two conditions for facilitating the recognition of needs as a universal, mutually accepted right in a large, complex society. But even if a society agrees on a specific definition of needs and a certain level of fulfillment that serves as a threshold of need satisfaction, this does not mean that the said definition and threshold are sustainable in the long run. This is the next question that we address.

1.6 The Sustainability of Needs

Until now, we have discussed the problems of identifying and recognizing needs without specifying in more detail what is identified and recognized. While any attempt at concretizing the content would lead back to the various lists of functionings and need satisfiers, for the moment it may suffice to define more precisely the demands on such a list. While individual desires may be unlimited, the real world of human societies is characterized by limited resources and goods. The unconstrained extraction of common resources by some may have disastrous long-term consequences (Hardin 1968). While the opportunity and ability to individually profit from such resources are unequally distributed, many societies have developed institutions that constrain such exploitative behavior (Ostrom 1990).

The sustainability of identified and recognized need thresholds is closely related to this problem. A purely voluntarist approach leads directly into the common pool dilemma because of the unlimited extension of desires that can be expressed in terms of need claims. Hence, the recognized need thresholds need to be sufficiently low to be economically affordable for the society, both for the preservation of resources and for maintaining incentives to invest and work such that the economy produces a sufficient amount of the necessary resources. In fact, the less well-off, who form the majority in the population of current nation states with their right-skewed income distributions, do not use their political power to completely level income inequality through redistribution (Corneo and Gruener 2000). A rational explanation is that with rising redistribution the amount available for redistribution diminishes and thus lowers incentives to further redistribute. That is, society seems to make a trade-off decision between pursuing social goals and the efficiency goal (Barr 1998).

At the same time, the socially recognized definition of needs, represented by thresholds, have to actually satisfy needs, taking into consideration their heterogeneity across individuals and variation across groups. If specific needs are not addressed or need thresholds fail to satisfy needs, at least some people will not flourish, which, in turn, may alienate them from the community and potentially provoke either withdrawal from society and apathy or resistance and social unrest. Both consequences undermine the productive potential of a society. If at all, there is thus a potentially rather narrow band of socially sustainable concepts of need-based distributive justice that can be used as a guiding principle of distributive decisions.

In sum, communities have to balance the recognition of need claims against the long-term economic consequences of satisfying these claims. What remains unresolved is the question of who is entitled to articulate need claims and to participate in the allocation of resources. This leaves the definition of the community as the fourth major problem of the development of a theory of need-based justice.

1.7 Social Scope and Heterogeneity

On top of the heterogeneity of needs within a society, the heterogeneity of needs across societies generates boundaries between those who share the same general worldview and culture and have a compatible conception of need satisfiers, and strangers whose culture entails a different morality generating different ways of satisfying needs. These differences, however, do not necessarily imply that need-based justice is limited by such boundaries: "The idea of common human needs entails the right even of strangers to optimal need-satisfaction" (Doyal and Gough 1991, p. 103). Indeed, it is difficult, in general, to imagine the possibility of drawing boundaries of justice if one postulates that the scope of human dignity is universal. For example, Gosepath (2001, p. 135) claims that "justice is—at least prima facie—immediately universal, and therefore global" and argues that there are no defensible objections against this claim except for political pragmatic reasons. This view involves the thought that

> global justice requires all to be adequately positioned to enjoy the prospects for a decent life, so that they are enabled to meet their basic needs, their basic liberties are protected, and they enjoy fair terms of cooperation in collective endeavours. This requires that we

> ensure social and political arrangements are in place that can underwrite these important goods. (Brock 2009, p. 5)

While building on a weak version of this "moral cosmopolitanism"—which universally mandates taking the consequences of one's actions on others into account and to treat others equally—Miller develops an argument that still draws a line between insiders and outsiders based on the criterion of citizenship in a nation state. The nation state entails a double-layered association between citizens in terms of obligations and identity:

> [E]ach member owes his fellow citizens the duty of maintaining justice between them, so long as she reasonably expects others to perform their duties in turn. [...] With national identity comes a kind of solidarity that is lacking if one looks just at economic and political relationships. People feel emotionally attached to one another because they share this identity. (Miller 2016, p. 27)

What Miller alludes to here is, again, the duality of "system" and "social" integration, according to which political and economic transactions join with social interactions to produce a society and maintain its stability. Being a member of the same political community (Easton 1975) exposes people to the same experiences which generates a feeling of common fate. A common history of collective experiences fosters the development of solidarity among the members of a political system (Gellner 1983). People use ascriptive attributes to socially construct common identities, which foster societal integration and form the fundament of solidarity. This mechanism has consequences for inequality and redistribution. For example, countries that are fragmented with respect to ethnicity, skin color, or religion tend to redistribute less than countries with a more homogeneous population (Alesina and Glaeser 2004; Mijs 2021). A similar observation has been made by social identity theory in the context of small-group research (Tajfel 1982). People exposed to an even minimal identity cue such as being a member of either experimental group A or B develop in-group bias, as they tend to favor people belonging to their own group over outsiders. Numerous replications and extensions in laboratory experiments support and differentiate this basic finding (Lane 2016; Robbins and Krueger 2005). Social proximity thus fosters social values and redistribution within the own group.

But why is the social scope of justice particularly relevant for a theory of need-based justice? A possible answer to this question can be found in the social psychological theory of elementary forms (Fiske 1992). Assuming that people "organize their social life in terms of their relations with other people," this theory "postulates that people in all cultures use just four relational models to generate most kinds of social interaction, evaluation, and affect" (Fiske 1992, p. 689). These four elementary forms are based on the type of comparison between people that are "socially significant" in a particular context, or sphere:

> Communal sharing is like a category or set, all of whose elements are equivalent. [...] Authority ranking is a linear ordering in which everybody's rank can be compared with everyone else's [...]. Equality matching is a relational structure in which people can compare quantities and use the operations of addition and subtraction to assess imbalance [...]. Social relationships organized with reference to market pricing are structured like the rational numbers. (Fiske 1992, p. 690)

According to pluralistic justice theories (Elster 1992; Walzer 1983), different principles of justice apply to different spheres of society. Liebig and Sauer (2016) argue that each of these elementary forms is characterized by reference to a particular principle of justice: Need is relevant in communal sharing contexts, entitlement in authority structures, equality in equality matching, and equity in the market. These elementary forms and the associated justice principles can be mapped onto the four functions that Parsons (1951) considered necessary for the preservation of social structures in his AGIL scheme, that is, latency, goal attainment, integration, and adaptation, respectively (Kittel 2020). Latency refers to society's capacity to maintain the latent patterns and belief systems that facilitate the other three functions. Goal attainment is the capability of society to make collective decisions, which requires some mode of interest aggregation, representation, and intermediation. The notion of integration captures the condition that members of a society are able to interact harmoniously, which requires a common language, but also shared values and norms. Adaptation refers to the ability of a society to interact with its natural and social environment and to produce and distribute the resources necessary for survival.

According to this conceptualization, a theory of need-based justice has to primarily focus on the maintenance and preservation of social relations in situations of communal sharing. Although this elementary form can be thought of as a separate sphere, its fundamental nature implies that it underlies, facilitates, and fosters all other forms. Communal sharing relationships presuppose the existence of a group of people who are considered equivalent and undifferentiated according to some socially constructed criterion, but different from others who do not share this criterion. Thus, due to the categorical definition of relationships, communal sharing marks a boundary between insiders and outsiders, which implies that for a theory of need-based justice, the social scope of the recognition of need claims becomes a particularly relevant challenge.

1.8 Framework for a Theory of Need-Based Justice and Outline of This Volume

In the previous sections, we have outlined core dimensions of the concept of need and the normative theory of need as a principle of justice. The research group "Need-Based Justice and Distribution Procedures" aimed to develop an empirically grounded theory of need-based justice based on the considerations regarding the identification and recognition of need and the sustainability and scope of need-based justice presented in Sects. 1.4 to 1.7 of this chapter. Members of the research group from the five disciplines of philosophy, psychology, sociology, political science, and economics addressed the theoretical aspects and problems of a theory of distributive justice based on need. Most importantly, they collected data mainly through theory-driven controlled laboratory experiments on how subjects actually identify and recognize need, what economic incentive effects need-based redistribution generates, and what scope there is for differentiation of the need principle in the presence of heterogeneity. These theoretical considerations and empirical findings were compiled into "stylized facts" about what are normatively indispensable elements of a theory of need-based justice and how laypeople think about it.

The first edited volume of the research group entitled *Need-Based Distributive Justice. An Interdisciplinary Perspective* (Traub and Kittel 2020) outlines the state of research on need-based justice in the five disciplines when the research group started its work. In his contribution to that volume, Frank Nullmeier (2020) provides a framework for a theory of need-based justice summarized in ten "theses," which have been incorporated into Sects. 1.4 to 1.7 of this chapter, and which we reproduce in condensed form below:

1. The core of the theory of need-based justice is a *conception of need* that defines need as something necessary that goes beyond a preference or desire.
2. A "realistic" theory of need-based justice is based on *normative considerations* and *empirical observations*, which may also contradict each other.
3. The theory of need-based justice is *pluralistic*, in the sense that it combines different principles of justice such as need, equality, and equity.
4. A *strong pluralistic theory* of need-based justice predicts for each situation with which other principles of justice need will be combined.
5. Need must be *socially* or *politically recognized* based on legitimate procedures.
6. To determine what is necessary, methods of *objectification* (which are based on transparent procedures and may involve experts) are required.
7. A theory of need-based justice is about the relationship between available resources and socially or politically recognized needs, the rule being that available resources exceed recognized needs despite (economic) scarcity ("*oversupply*").
8. Meeting recognized needs may require *responsible* behavior on the part of the person in need. Unmet need gaps may be an expression of corrective justice or a combination of need with desert.
9. *Situational*, *social*, and *personal characteristics* determine the extent to which the principle of need is met.
10. Need-based justice is a "strong pluralistic theory of distributive justice with *need as a central and indispensable component*."

In the following chapters, the authors refer to the theses relevant for the respective subject of investigation. In the final chapter (Chap. 11), we then summarize the individual contributions to an "informed" theory of needs-based justice. Our informed theory is based on both the normative consideration and positive evidence obtained through laboratory experiments and points out possible inconsistencies.

Following the subdivision of the core sections of this chapter (Sects. 1.4 to 1.7), this volume is divided into four parts. Part I, "Identification of Needs," provides answers in particular to the question of what constitutes a normatively convincing and quantitatively measurable concept of need that also reflects the perceptions of laypersons. In Chap. 2, Adele Diederich studies whether and how need influences decision-making under risk from a psychological perspective. She shows that the identification of needs is also subject to *framing effects*, and she develops a dual-process model accounting for framing effect and needs. In Chap. 3, philosophers Alexander Max Bauer and Mark Siebel report their findings regarding the measurement of need-based justice. They first take a formal perspective, looking at suitable measures of need and need-based justice. The formal perspective is complemented by empirical research on need as a reference point, personal accountability for need, and the evaluation of different kinds of need.

Part II deals with the "Structures and Processes of the Recognition of Needs." The part has three chapters. In Chap. 4, sociologist Bernhard Kittel provides a detailed overview of his team's research on the social recognition of need. One main focus of this research is on distributional experiments in networks. Kittel also presents a novel experimental design that models need in the laboratory. The political recognition of needs is then addressed in Chap. 5 from a political science perspective by Markus Tepe and Nils Springhorn. In their experiments, the authors make use of two well-known models, the political economic Meltzer–Richard model and the Baron–Ferejohn bargaining model. They examine the influence of need and induced social identities on the subjects' voting behavior and negotiation outcomes. Tanja Pritzlaff-Scheele, Patricia Zauchner, and Frank Nullmeier add the important aspect of deliberation to the political science perspective on need-based justice in Chap. 6. In their group experiments, subjects discuss the application of possible distributional principles. Among other things, the authors investigate which reasons speak for or against the participation of "new" players (i.e., migrants).

The issue of sustainability and thus the "Welfare Consequences of Prioritizing Need-Based Distributions" is examined from an economic perspective in Part III. In his chapter (Chap. 7), Andreas Nicklisch points out the negative incentive effects of redistribution usually assumed in economic theory. However, if people have social preferences, then redistribution in favor of the needy need not necessarily lead to costs in the form of efficiency losses. To test this and other hypotheses, Nicklisch and his team conducted a series of real-effort laboratory experiments, which are reported in this chapter. Chapter 8 by Stefan Traub, Jan Philipp Krügel, and Meike Benker addresses the issue of sustainability of redistribution from a contract-theoretic perspective. The welfare state is modeled in theory and in the experiments conducted as an insurance against lifetime income risks. Traub and his team also compare need-based (= means-tested) redistribution with the unconditional basic income.

Part IV "Differentiation" discusses the conditions of need recognition by examining what role need-based justice plays in the "real world" outside the experimental laboratory, using two important components of the welfare state, viz. social assistance and the health care sector. An essential function of the welfare state is to help those in need in special circumstances to avoid poverty. Chapter 9 turns to the question of whether and how "Street-Level Bureaucrats Understand and Prioritize Need." Kai-Uwe Schnapp uses interviews and survey experiments conducted with employees from German job agencies to examine the extent to which—contrary to the normative impartiality claim of the state—deservingness plays a role in discretionary welfare decisions. Finally, in Chap. 10, Adele Diederich and Marc Wyszynski examine whether need is an important criterion for prioritizing health care services.

Acknowledgments This chapter was written as part of DFG Research Group 2104 "Need-Based Justice and Distributive Procedures," projects B1 "Distributive Preferences and Need-Based Justice in Networks," which was funded by the Austrian Science Fund (references I1888-G11 and I3804-G27) in the DACH framework and D2 "Need-Based Justice as a Social Contract" (reference TR 458/6-2). This funding is gratefully acknowledged. We thank all members of FOR 2104 for making such a project possible.

References

Adams, J. S. (1965): "Inequity in Social Exchange", in L. Berkowitz (ed.): *Advances in Experimental Social Psychology*, vol. 2, 267–299. New York: Academic Press.

Alderfer, C. P. (1969): "An Empirical Test of a New Theory of Human Needs", *Organizational Behavior and Human Performance* 5, 142–175.

Alesina, A., and E. L. Glaeser (2004): *Fighting Poverty in the US and Europe: A World of Difference.* Oxford: Oxford University Press.

Anderson, B. (1991): *Imagined Communities. Reflections on the Origin and Spread of Nationalism.* London: Verso.

Aristoteles. (350bc): *Nicomachean Ethics.* Provided by The Internet Classics Archive. Cambridge: MIT. http://classics.mit.edu/Aristotle/nicomachaen.html

Atkinson, A. B. (2019): *Measuring Poverty Around the World.* Princeton: Princeton University Press.

Barr, N. A. (1998): *The Economics of the Welfare State*. Stanford: Stanford University Press.

Boulding, K. E. (1962): "Social Justice in Social Dynamics", in R. Brandt (ed.): *Social Justice*, 73–92. Englewood Cliffs: Prentice Hall.

Bourguignon, F., and C. Morrisson (2002): "Inequality Among World Citizens: 1820–1992", *American Economic Review* 92 (4), 727–744.

Bremer, B. (2018): "The Missing Left? Economic Crisis and the Programmatic Response of Social Democratic Parties in Europe", *Party Politics* 24 (1), 23–38.

Brock, G. (2009): *Global Justice. A Cosmopolitan Account.* Oxford: Oxford University Press.

Brock, G., and D. Miller (2023): "Needs in Moral and Political Philosophy", in E. N. Zalta, and U. Nodelman (eds.): *The Stanford Encyclopedia of Philosophy.* Stanford University. https://plato.stanford.edu/archives/spr2023/entries/needs

Chaudhuri, A. (2011): "Sustaining Cooperation in Laboratory Public Goods Experiments: A Selective Survey of the Literature", *Experimental Economics* 14, 47–83.

Comin, F., and M. C. Nussbaum (eds.) (2014): *Capabilities, Gender, Equality. Towards Fundamental Entitlements.* Cambridge: Cambridge University Press.

Corneo, G., and H. P. Gruener (2000): "Social Limits to Redistribution", *American Economic Review* 90 (5), 1491–1507.

Dover, M. A. (2023): "Human Needs: Overview", in Franklin, C. (ed.): *Encyclopedia of Social Work* https://doi.org/10.1093/acrefore/9780199975839.013.554

Doyal, L., and I. Gough (1991): *A Theory of Human Need.* New York: Guilford Press.

Dworkin, R. (1981a): "What is Equality? Part 1: Equality of Welfare", *Philosophy and Public Affairs* 10 (3), 185–246.

Dworkin, R. (1981b): "What is Equality? Part 2: Equality of Resources", *Philosophy and Public Affairs* 10 (4), 283–345.

Easton, D. (1975): "A Re-Assessment of the Concept of Political Support", *British Journal of Political Science* 5 (4), 435–457.
Elster, J. (1992): *Local Justice: How Institutions Allocate Scarce Goods and Necessary Burdens.* New York: Russel Sage.
European Social Survey (2018): *ESS Round 9 Source Questionnaire.* London: ESS ERIC Headquarters c/o City, University of London.
Fiske, A. P. (1992): "The Four Elementary Forms of Sociality: Framework for a United Theory of Social Relations", *Psychological Review* 99 (4), 689–723.
Frankfurt, H. G. (2015): *On Inequality*. Princeton: Princeton University Press.
Fraser, N. (1989): "Talking About Needs: Interpretive Contests as Political Conflicts in Welfare-State Societies", *Ethics* 99 (2), 291–313.
Frohlich, N., and J. Oppenheimer (1992): *Choosing Justice: An Experimental Approach to Ethical Theory.* Ewing: University of California Press.
Goodin, R. E. (2002): "Structures of Mutual Obligation", *Journal of Social Policy* 31 (4), 579–596.
Gellner, E. (1983): "*Nations and Nationalism*". Oxford: Blackwell.
Gosepath, S. (2001): "The Global Scope of Justice", *Metaphilosophy* 32 (1/2), 135–159.
Gosepath, S. (2003): "Verteidigung egalitärer Gerechtigkeit", *Deutsche Zeitschrift für Philosophie* 51 (2), 275–297.
Gosepath, S. (2011): "Equality", in E. N. Zalta (ed.): *The Stanford Encyclopedia of Philosophy.* Stanford University. https://plato.stanford.edu/archives/spr2011/entries/equality
Gosepath, S. (2015): "The Principles and the Presumption of Equality", in C. Fourie, F. Schuppert, and I. Wallimann-Helmer (eds.): *Social Equality. On What It Means to Be Equal*, 167–185. Oxford: Oxford University Press.
Gough, I. (2023): "Sufficiency as a Value Standard: From Preferences to Needs", *Ethics, Policy & Environment*, https://doi.org/10.1080/21550085.2023.2269055
Habermas, J. (1982): *Theorie des kommunikativen Handelns*, vols. 1 and 2. Frankfurt/M.: Suhrkamp.
Hardin, G. (1968): "The Tragedy of the Commons", *Science* 162, 1243–1248.
Honneth, A. (2015): *The I in We: Studies in the Theory of Recognition*. Cambridge: Polity Press.
Kittel, B. (2020): "Need-based Justice: A Sociological Perspective", in S. Traub and B. Kittel (eds.): *Need-based Distributive Justice: An Interdisciplinary Perspective* (pp. 91–131). Cham: Springer Nature.
Kittel, B., G. Kanitsar, and S. Traub (2017): "Knowledge, Power, and Self-interest", *Journal of Public Economics* 150, 39–52.
Konow, J. (2001): "Fair and Square: The Four Sides of Distributive Justice", *Journal of Economic Behavior & Organization* 46, 137–164.
Lane, T. (2016): "Discrimination in the Laboratory. A Meta-analysis of Economic Experiments", *European Economic Review* 90, 375–402.
Ledyard, J. O. (1995): "Public Goods: A Survey of Experimental Research", in J. H. Kagel and A. E. Roth (eds.): *The Handbook of Experimental Economics*, 253–348. Princeton: Princeton University Press.
Liebig, S., and C. Sauer (2016): "Sociology of Justice", in C. Sabbagh and M. Schmitt (eds.): *Handbook of Social Justice Theory and Research*, 37–59. Berlin: Springer.
Lockwood, D. (1964): "Social Integration and System Integration", in G. K. Zollschan and W. Hirsch (eds.): *Social Change: Explorations, Diagnosis and Conjectures*, 244–257. London: Routledge and Paul.
Maier, C. S. (1997): *Dissolution, The Crisis of Communism and the End of East Germany.* Princeton: Princeton University Pres.
Marx, K. (1975): "Critique of the Gotha Programme", in K. Marx and F. Engels (eds.): *Collected Works*. New York: International Publishers.
Maslow, A. H. (1943): "A Theory of Human Motivation", *Psychological Review* 50, 370–396.
Mijs, J. J. (2021): "The Paradox of Inequality: Income Inequality and Belief in Meritocracy Go Hand in Hand", *Socio-Economic Review* 19 (1), 7–35.

Milanovic, B. (2016): *Global Inequality. A New Approach for the Age of Globalization.* Cambridge: Belknap.

Miller, D. (1999): *Principles of Social Justice.* Cambridge, Mass.: Harvard University Press.

Miller, D. (2016): *Strangers in Our Midst. The Political Philosophy of Immigration.* Cambridge: Harvard University Press.

Mulligan, T. (2017): *Justice and the Meritocratic State.* New York: Routledge.

Nelson, E. (2008): "From Primary Goods to Capabilities. Distributive Justice and the Problem of Neutrality", *Political Theory* 36 (1), 93–12.

Nullmeier, F. (2020): "Towards a Theory of Need-based Justice", in S. Traub and B. Kittel (eds.): *Need-based Distributive Justice: An Interdisciplinary Perspective*, 191–208. Cham: Springer Nature.

Nussbaum, M. (2011): *Creating Capabilities. The Human Development Approach.* Cambridge: Belknap Press.

Ostrom, E. (1990): *Governing the Commons. The Evolution of Institutions for Collective Action.* Cambridge: Cambridge University Press.

Parsons, T. (1951): *The Social System.* Glencoe, Ill.: Free Press.

Phillips, A. (2004): "Defending Equality of Outcome", *Journal of Political Philosophy* 12 (1), 1–19.

Piketty, T. (2014): *Capital in the Twenty-First Century.* Cambridge: Belknap Press.

Pinggera, M. (2020): "Congruent with Whom? Parties' Issue Emphases and Voter Preferences in Welfare Politics", *Journal of European Public Policy* 28 (12), 1973–1992.

Pomfret, R. (2011): *The Age of Equality. The Twentieth Century in Economic Perspective.* Cambridge: Belknap.

Ravaillon, M. (2016): *The Economics of Poverty. History, Measurement and Policy.* Oxford: Oxford University Press.

Rawls, J. (1971): *A Theory of Justice.* Oxford: Oxford University Press.

Robbins, J. M., and J. I. Krueger (2005): "Social Projection to Ingroups and Outgroups: A Review and Meta-Analysis", *Personality and Social Psychology Review* 9 (1), 32–47.

Rousseau, J.-J. (2013 [1762]): *The Social Contract.* NP: Wordsworth Editions (Everyman's Library, ed. by Ernest Rhys. Philosophy and Theology no. 660).

Saint-Simon, H. D. (1975 [1790]): *Selected Writings on Science, Industry and Social Organization* (ed. and tr. by Keith Taylor). New York: Holmes and Meier.

Scheidel, W. (2017): *The Great Leveler. Violence and the History of Inequality from the Stone Age to the Twenty-first Century.* Princeton: Princeton University Press.

Schutz, A. (1967 [1932]): *The Phenomenology of the Social World.* Evanston: Northwestern University Press.

Sen, A. (1985): *Commodities and Capabilities.* Oxford: Elsevier Science Publishers.

Sen, A. (1990): "Justice: Means versus Freedoms", *Philosophy and Public Affairs* 19 (2), 111–121.

Sen, A. (2000): "Social Justice and the Distribution of Income", in A. B. Atkinson and F. Bourguignon (eds.): *Handbook of Income Distribution*, vol. 1. Amsterdam: Elsevier.

Sen, A. (2009): *The Idea of Justice.* Cambridge, Mass: Belknap Press.

Smith, A. (1790): *The Theory of Moral Sentiments.* London: A. Millar.

Smith, A. (1904 (1776)): *An Inquiry into the Nature and Causes of the Wealth of Nations*, vol. 2. London: Methuen.

Spicker, P. (2006): *Liberty, Equality, Fraternity.* Bristol: Policy Press.

Tajfel, H. (1982): *Social Identity and Intergroup Relations.* Cambridge: Cambridge University Press.

Tavits, M., and J. D. Potter (2015): "The Effect of Inequality and Social Identity on Party Strategies", *American Journal of Political Science* 59 (3), 744–758.

Tönnies, F. (1887): *Gemeinschaft und Gesellschaft. Abhandlung des Communismus und des Socialismus als empirischer Culturformen.* Leipzig: Fues.

Traub, S., and B. Kittel (eds.) (2020): *Need-based Distributive Justice. An Interdisciplinary Perspective.* Cham: Springer Nature.

Traub, S., C. Seidl, U. Schmidt, and M. V. Levati (2005): "Friedman, Harsanyi, Rawls, Boulding– or Somebody Else? An Experimental Investigation of Distributive Justice", *Social Choice and Welfare* 24, 283–309.

Van Oorschot, W., F. Roosma, B. Meuleman, and T. Reeskens (eds.) (2017): *The Social Legitimacy of Targeted Welfare: Attitudes to Welfare Deservingness.* Cheltenham: Edward Elgar.

Walzer, M. (1983): *Spheres of Justice. A Defense of Pluralism and Equality.* New York: Basic Books.

Weber, M. (1980 [1921/22]): *Wirtschaft und Gesellschaft. Grundriß der verstehenden Soziologie* (1922/1980 ed.). Tübingen: Mohr.

Wood, A. W. (2014): *The Free Development of Each. Studies on Freedom, Right, and Ethics in Classical German Philosophy.* Oxford: Oxford University Press.

Part I
Identification of Needs

Chapter 2
Need as One Distribution Principle: Frames and Framing

Adele Diederich

Abstract To make the process of identifying and recognizing needs more transparent and to postulate a theory of need-based justice, we investigated various frames in which decision problems were embedded. External frames in a strict sense, with gain and loss frames in risky choices and need as an additional factor, showed significant differences in choice frequencies. External frames in a loose sense, such as time constraints, different diseases in an Asian Disease paradigm, and the identifiability of a needy person, showed framing effects and mixed results with respect to need. Internal frames measured by personality inventories also showed mixed results. The dual-stage dual-process model includes a normative part and a descriptive part, which both account for framing effects. In one version of the model, the normative part includes the expected utility model modified by the Stone–Geary function.

2.1 Introduction

The transparency hypothesis (Traub and Kittel 2020) guided this research on identifying need from a psychology perspective. In the current context, the transparency hypothesis states that transparency of a decision process contributes to the social objectivity of distribution decisions. To accomplish distributive justice with need as a criterion, it is important to identify determinants that possibly influence the decision-maker's judgments on need. We put a specific focus on determinants that are—in principle—irrelevant to the judgment task and the decision problem. A second objective of our research was to contribute to building a theory of need-based justice based on several theses proposed by Nullmeier (2020). The most relevant theses in this context are Thesis 1, "The core element of the concept of need is the notion of something that is necessary, compelling, imperative, indispensable,

A. Diederich (✉)
Carl von Ossietzky University Oldenburg, Department of Psychology, Oldenburg, Germany
e-mail: adele.diederich@uni-oldenburg.de

B. Kittel, S. Traub (eds.), *Priority of Needs?*,
https://doi.org/10.1007/978-3-031-53051-7_2

essentially required—something that goes beyond mere desires or preferences and takes precedence over desires" (p. 191) and Thesis 2, "A theory of need-based justice should be based on the promotion of both normative and empirical research" (p. 195). Before I report contribution to building a theory of need-based justice, I briefly elaborate on need as used in psychology and on frames in judgment and decision tasks.

In psychology, the concept of *need* or *needs* is used in different contexts and sub-disciplines with different meanings. Needs may refer to an actual state of deprivation or merely a feeling of deficiency, which drives the individual to action to satisfy them. In this sense, needs are motivational forces that activate behavior for the purpose of reaching a goal (for details on need as motive and related concepts see Diederich 2020). Because needs range from physiological or basic survival ones such as breathing, food, sex, and sleep to psychological ones such as cultural, intellectual, and social needs, a natural hierarchy of needs seems to be given (e.g., Alderfer 1969; Maslow 1948, 1987). Whereas, for instance, food and shelter seem to qualify as "necessary, compelling, imperative, indispensable, essential" requirements (Nullmeier 2020, Thesis 1, p. 193) that may be identified by both the person in need and the person judging the need of others, cultural and intellectual needs seem less obviously so, at least from the perspective of the person judging the need of others.

In the context of distributive justice, the term *need* describes one principle for the fair allocation of resources and has a meaning slightly different from that in motivation theories. Needs as actual or felt deficiencies are satisfied by necessities or necessaries, objects that the individual needs to survive or to live satisfactorily. These objects are often called needs as well. Unlike in economics, necessities and necessaries such as goods are not objects of research in psychology. Thus, rather than identifying need by determining quantities, quantities are given, and identification is inferred from the context (see operationalizing need in Sect. 2.2).

Transparency in psychology—or the absence of it—relates to technical details such as obtaining the informed consent of participants, clear instructions for experimental procedures, open access to data (see Klein et al. 2018, for a catalog) but also to experimental design-related topics such as priming, deceiving participants (foremost in social psychology), and frames and framing. In this chapter, I consider the latter.

A decision frame refers to the decision-maker's conception of choice options among which they have to choose, the possible outcomes and conditional probabilities associated with a particular choice (Tversky and Kahneman 1981, p. 453). In other words, a decision frame indicates how the decision-maker perceives, imagines, and interprets the decision situation. Which decision frame a decision-maker adopts may depend, on the one hand, on personal characteristics, on the decision-maker's experiences, and on his/her normative values and habits. This type of framing has also been called *internal* framing (Fischer 1997). Because internal framings may lead to individual differences in the susceptibility to framing manipulations, heterogeneity between people may also be reflected in judgments on need (compare Chap. 1 in this book). On the other hand, the perception and interpretation of a frame may be influenced by how the problem is formulated. This type of framing is called *external* framing. External framings are furthermore used in a "strict" and in a "loose" sense (Kühberger 1998). In their strict form, they refer to the description or formulation of the same fact but from a different perspective, for instance, by using different wordings. In their loose form, they include other manipulations such as presentation formats or different contexts. Both forms are used here and will be elaborated on in Sect. 2.2. *Framing effects* occur when different formulations of the decision problem or irrelevant aspects in the description of the problem lead to different decisions or evaluations. They are based on preference reversals and preference shifts. Framing effects have been explored in numerous experiments across many disciplines with a variety of decision scenarios (for reviews see e.g., Gächter et al. 2009; Gilovich et al. 2002; Kahneman et al. 1982; Kühberger 1998; Levin et al. 1998; Traub 1999), but only a few studies have been conducted in the context of distributive justice, and even fewer with a focus on need. If framings, however, also influence the recognition of need, then it is central to identify the determinants and make them transparent to ensure consistent justice judgments on need.

This chapter is organized as follows. Section 2.2 specifies the general research question, introduces various frames, and explains the relevant experimental paradigms. Section 2.3 states the specific research questions and reports the results of experiments with external frames; Sect. 2.4 refers to those with internal frames. Both sections aim for promoting a theory of need-based justice on empirical grounds (Nullmeier 2020, Thesis 2, p. 195). Section 2.5 briefly describes a dynamic-stochastic framework for dual-process models that account for biases in framing situations; it has been modified to include need. The chapter closes with a brief conclusion (Sect. 2.6).

2.2 Frames and Designs

Description and procedure invariance are core principles of normative models of judgment and decision-making. Accordingly, judgments and choices must be consistent and robust, unaffected by frames, descriptions, or elicitation/measurement techniques.

The transparency hypothesis states that the more transparent the decision process, the higher the acceptance of distribution outcomes. That is, making the assumptions, decision context, or procedures in allocation decisions open and transparent may lead to more consistent justice judgments. This, in turn, may entail that allocation outcomes are recognized as legitimate and enduring. In particular, when policymakers are in the process of recognizing and deciding on needs, they should decide in a way that is consistent and uninfluenced by any irrelevant tasks and problems. Thus, the overarching question for our research is as follows:
How consistent are judgments in the context of need identification?

Before I present specific research questions, let us first describe the frames in more detail, including the research paradigms that were applied here. We used internal and external framing, and, within external framing, frames in both a strict and a loose sense. We also operationalize need in line with a particular paradigm. Specifically, Sect. 2.2.1 describes external frames in a strict sense and introduces experimental paradigms for risky choice framings and attributes framings in the context of need. Section 2.2.2 elaborates on external frames in a loose sense with time constraints, type of disease, the number of affected people, and identifiability of the needy person. Section 2.2.3 lists the personality tests used here to measure individual differences as possible factors for the susceptibility of framings.

2.2.1 *External Frames in a Strict Sense*

The experiments include choice options or statements in which the same critical information is presented in the positive or the negative. The frames in a strict sense include risky choice framing and attribute framing; the frames in a loose sense include time pressure, type of diseases, scope of affected people, and identifiability of the needy person.

2.2.1.1 Risky Choice Framing and Need

The so-called risky choice framing (Levin et al. 1998) is the prototypical framing scenario originally proposed by Tversky and Kahneman (1981). Two choice situations, each with two choice options, are compared. One choice situation is framed as a gain (positive), and the other situation as a loss (negative). Within each choice situation, the decision-maker chooses between a gamble and a sure outcome (or another gamble). The choice situations may be presented as abstract games (lotteries) or as more complex scenarios. Figure 2.1 shows four games in which the gambles in all situations are identical, but the sure option is either framed as a gain (A and C) or a loss (B and D). As elaborated in more detail in the results section, the probabilities for winning/losing the lottery and the points won/lost were varied to create numerous choice options. This allowed us to present gambles multiple times in several rounds to the same participant. Need was induced by obtaining or maintaining a specific need level. Details are reported in Sect. 2.3.1.1. A more complex scenario, but with the same game structure, is the famous Asian Disease paradigm (Tversky and Kahneman 1981). The description of the scenario is typically enriched with details about health programs, specific diseases, and so on. Instead of keeping or losing points, people survive or die. Again, the probabilities for surviving/dying and the number of people were varied to create numerous choice situations. Details are in Sect. 2.3.2. Need here was operationalized in terms of the number of people in need, i.e., those who were to be saved.

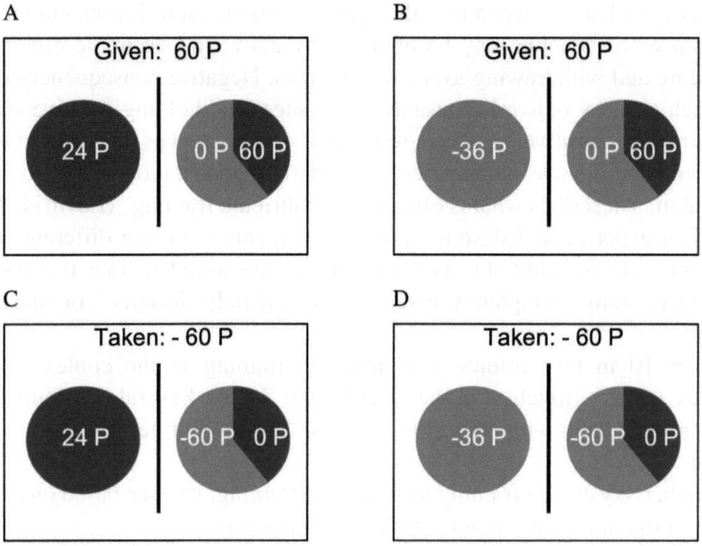

Game examples for a gain frame (A, C) and a loss frame (B, D). (A, B): Before each game, the participant receives points, displayed at the top of the display (Given: 60 Points in this example). (C, D): Before each game, the participant was informed how many points are taken from the initial endowment displayed at the top of the display (Taken: 60 Points in this example). The probabilities of the gambles (right in each panel) are color coded with dark shades referring to keeping the indicated points and light shade with losing them. The sure options (left in each panel) are framed as gain (A, C keep 24 P) or loss (B, D lose 36 P). Source: Own creation based on Diederich et al. (2020).

Fig. 2.1 Game examples

2.2.1.2 Attribute Framing and Need

Presumably the first scholar interested in how distribution problems are presented was Törnblom (1988). He proposed a framework within which the allocation process is explicated in terms of positive and negative outcome allocations, labeled *sign* of outcome allocation. Each of the two outcome allocations includes different forms, which may reflect the intention of the allocator or may be intention neutral. For instance, reward, benefaction, punishment, and revenge may imply certain underlying motives on the part of the distributor, whereas gain, profit, gratification, loss, cost, or burden may not. The forms of allocation outcomes in turn may be achieved in different ways. Törnblom distinguishes three such modes: delivery, withholding, and withdrawal. Delivery means presenting, transferring, handing over, or giving something; withholding means refraining from presenting something; and withdrawal refers to taking away or removing something that the target person possesses (Törnblom 1988, p. 149). Any specific form of outcome allocation may be achieved in any one of the three modes. The consequences, i.e., benefits or harms, depend on the specific combination. For example, positive consequences or benefits may be obtained by delivering desirable outcomes and withholding and withdrawing aversive outcomes. Negative consequences or harms can be achieved by delivering aversive outcomes, withholding positive outcomes, or withdrawing positively valued resources. Consequences may be material or nonmaterial and include status, affect, information, goods, money, and so forth.

Törnblom's describes what is often called "attribute framing" (Levin et al. 1998). The typical experimental design includes statements with two different attributes such as provide or withhold. The participants are asked to rate the statements, for instance, from "completely agree" to "completely disagree" or make yes/no judgments.

Chapter 10 in this volume uses attribute framing in the context of Justice Principles and Prioritization in the Health Care Sector. Several distributive justice principles are judged with respect to fairness. The need principle received specific attention.

For both, risky choice framing and attribute framing, valence based on evaluation typically shifts in the direction of positive descriptions.

2.2.2 *External Frames in a Loose Sense*

Frames in a loose sense go beyond different wordings of the same problem and include, for instance, different contexts. Here we use time constraints, various diseases in the Asian Disease paradigm, the number of people affected by a disease, and the identifiability of the needy person. Need itself may also serve as a frame. In the following, we briefly describe these frames.

2.2.2.1 Time Constraints

Presenting identical choice options while constraining the decision time can produce preference reversal and shifts in preferences or may modify framing effects induced by different wordings (Diederich 2003; Diederich and Busemeyer 2006; Diederich et al. 2018, 2020; Guo et al. 2015, 2017; Igou and Bless 2007; Svenson and Benson 1993). However, the results are mixed and may be related to the exact time constraint used in the specific study. Longer times may foster elaborate processing and thereby weaken the framing effect, while very short ones (especially around 1 second) allow only for intuitive processing, enhancing the framing effect (see Diederich et al. 2018, for a detailed discussion).

2.2.2.2 Type of Disease

Following Mahoney et al. (2011), we varied the disease scenarios to unusual infection, leukemia, and AIDS. The three diseases differ with respect to the populations affected, the public's familiarity with the disease, and the extent to which one views the people affected as responsible for their plight or as lacking control.

2.2.2.3 Number of Affected People

Need was operationalized in terms of the points participants should obtain or keep and in terms of the magnitude of people affected by a disease. For the latter, the decision-maker's choice affects a population that is in need of treatment (medicine or vaccine). We argue that the need increases with the number of affected people (i.e., the population size). Therefore, we included two conditions, a small scope and a large scope, where in the condition large scope the number of affected people was multiplied by one hundred.

2.2.2.4 Identifiability of the Needy Person

In his economic analysis of the value of life, Schelling (1968) distinguished between identified and statistical lives. His hypothesis that people react differently to identified and statistical lives has been supported by several experiments (e.g. Jenni and Loewenstein 1997; Kogut and Ritov 2005a,b; Small and Loewenstein 2003; Small et al. 2007). The effect is nowadays called "Identifiable Others Effect" (Loewenstein et al. 2005) of which the "Identifiable Victim Effect" (e.g., Jenni and Loewenstein 1997) is a special case. It describes the tendency of being more generous to identified victims/persons as compared to unidentified or statistical victims/persons. In this chapter, information about the needy person is varied. Specifically, the same needy person was: (1) described abstractly (simply called a "person"), (2) given a name, a picture, and some more descriptive information, or (3) was present in the same room as the decision-maker.

2.2.3 Internal Framing

Internal framing is influenced by personal characteristics, the decision-maker's experiences, and his/her normative values and habits (see above). The susceptibility of decision-makers to framing manipulations has been attributed to individual differences in risk style, thinking style, and cognitive style (e.g., Kühberger 1998; Mahoney et al. 2011; West et al. 2008).

Several personality traits have been discussed in framing studies. In particular, risk style and thinking style have been utilized to predict individual differences in response to framing problems. For instance, Kühberger (1998) identified risk behavior and thinking styles as important in risky choice situations.

In an Asian Disease setting, Mahoney et al. (2011) measured individual differences in risk styles and thinking styles on various scales (questionnaires). Using the same paradigm with an investment scenario, Mandel and Kapler (2018) included several other scales. Both studies found no relationship between any of the scale values and susceptibility to framing.

With a within-subject design, we probed some of the scales: The Stimulating Instrumental Risk Inventory (SIRI, Zaleskiewicz 2001) measures risk styles based on the reflection/impulsivity approach (e.g., Evans 2008; Kahneman and Frederick 2002). It distinguishes between stimulating and instrumental risk-taking. Stimulating risk is associated with the enjoyment of risk and may lead to faster and less analytical decisions (impulsive). Instrumental risk-taking is motivated by the attainment of a goal. High instrumental risk-takers are expected to carefully analyze the characteristics and values of a risky choice (reflective). The SIRI is composed of two sub-scales, the stimulating risk sub-scale (ST) and the instrumental risk sub-scale (IN).

The Rational-Experiential Inventory (REI; Cacioppo and Petty 1982), with its two sub-scales, rational-analytic (RA) and experiential-intuitive (EX; Pacini and Epstein 1999), is also based on the reflection/impulsivity approach. Experiential-intuitive thinking is characterized by rapid, holistic, and emotional thinking, whereas rational-analytic thinking is slow, analytic, and logical (Epstein 1998).

The actively open-minded thinking (AOT; Baron 1993; Haran et al. 2013) involves a willingness to evaluate evidence that goes against one's beliefs and openness to considering alternative perspectives. AOT values are often associated with less susceptibility to biases (Svedholm-Häkkinen and Lindeman 2018), including framing effects (Sá et al. 1999; West et al. 2008).

For all the aforementioned scales, participants typically rate items on Likert scales.

The next section formulates specific research questions and summarizes the results obtained.

2.3 External Frames: Specific Research Questions and Experimental Results

To build a theory of need-based justice, we relied on various theses. The second thesis states that "A theory of need-based justice should be based on the promotion of both normative and empirical research." (Nullmeier 2020, Thesis 2, p. 195). The empirical results briefly summarized in the following sections contribute to this requirement. I first focus on need in connection with external frames.

Risky choice frame settings have provided ample evidence of framing effects: Participants tend to be risk-averse in a gain frame and risk-seeking in a loss frame (Tversky and Kahneman 1981; Kahneman and Tversky 1984). These results are typically accounted for by Prospect Theory (Kahneman and Tversky 1979) and lately also by dual-process models (Kahneman 2011). In the first series of experiments, we induced need by prompting participants to acquire a minimum number of points (converted into money) during a series of games in order to avoid being excluded from a payoff. This leads to the first specific research question.

2.3.1 *Does Induced Need Influence Risky Choices in a Simple Lottery Game Framed as a Gain or a Loss?*

Induced need may show no additional effect, may affect risky choice behavior per se, regardless of the frame, or may alter the framing effect.

To provide a theoretical (normative) account of when need is involved and to generate specific hypotheses, we consider two approaches: the risk-sensitivity foraging theory and the Stone–Geary utility function.

Risk-sensitivity foraging theories were originally developed to predict risk-taking in animal foraging behavior. One of the most prominent theories is the so-called energy budget rule (Stephens 1981; Stephens and Charnov 1982; Caraco 1980). The model assumes that an animal, e.g., a small bird, has a need (minimum requirement/lack) of food reserves. To ensure its survival, the bird must meet the need at the end of a certain period (e.g., one day). A period is divided into a certain number of foraging intervals. At each foraging interval, the bird has to decide on how much risk to take. The energy budget rule predicts that animals become more risk-seeking when they are unlikely to meet the need through less risky actions. In other words, the more challenging it is to meet the need, the higher is the tendency to take on risk. Moreover, (Stephens 1981) suggests a "sequential component" to risk sensitivity. That is, a forager whose needs are not yet met might engage in riskier actions when there are only a few foraging intervals left as compared to a forager with many intervals left. Mishra and colleagues adopted and modified the energy budget rule to account for human risk behavior in the context of need (Mishra and Fiddick 2012; Mishra et al. 2012; Mishra 2014; Mishra et al. 2017; Mishra and Lalumiere 2010; Pietras et al. 2003; Rode et al. 1999).

Without discussing economic demand theory, which is about the relationship between consumer demand for goods and services and their prices in the market (e.g., in the context of psychology research, Rachlin et al. 1976), need in terms of minimum consumption levels for goods and services can be incorporated by the Stone–Geary utility function (Stone 1954; Geary 1950). It is a functional representation of consumer preferences. For each good, a utility function is defined, comprising the Linear Expenditure System (LES). This system can be split into two components (for details see Deaton and Muellbauer 1980): First, the minimum consumption of each good has to be met. Second, after subtracting the subsistence income that is needed to buy the minimum quantities, the remainder of the consumer's income is spent according to a person's preferences and budget restrictions. Note that the Stone–Geary utility function is defined only for consumption levels exceeding the minimum. Hence, the minimum consumption levels are usually interpreted as indispensable to life. Therefore, participants may become more risk-seeking with increasing induced need, regardless of the frame. This preference shift, however, makes the gain–loss framing effect less likely to occur.

Thus, both frameworks, that is, the risk-sensitivity foraging theory and the Stone–Geary utility function, predict increasing risk-taking behavior with increasing need but are based on different assumptions and mechanisms. For the energy budget rule, decisions are made based on collecting resources, i.e., starting from no or a low resource until an upper limit is reached. In contrast, the Stone–Geary utility framework starts with an endowment of resources, and expenditure decisions are made until a lower limit is reached.[1]

Bringing the sequential component of risk-sensitivity and Stone–Geary utility frameworks together, a forager should take higher risks at the beginning of a period to ensure they meet the minimum consumption level (need) first. Furthermore, risk-taking behavior should decrease as the amount of resources required to meet the need decreases.

2.3.1.1 Experimental Setup and Results

The hypotheses were tested in three experiments (Diederich et al. 2018, 2020). All three experiments used the risky choice framing as described in Sect. 2.2.1.1, with probabilities 0.3, 0.4, 0.6, and 0.7 for winning the gamble. The values given at the beginning of a trial were 25, 50, 75, and 100 for experiment 1, and 20, 40, 60, and 80 for experiment 2 and experiment 3.[2] The need thresholds were set to 0 (control), 2,500, and 3,500 points in experiment 1 and 0, 2,800, and 3,600 in experiment 2. The participant started with 0 points (no endowment) and was expected to reach the given need threshold by playing the game for a preset number of rounds. The third experiment mirrored experiment 2. The participant started with an endowment of 5,600 points and was expected to stay above a need threshold of 3,600, 2,800, or 0 points by playing the game for a preset number of rounds. Note that experiments 2 and 3 include two frames: Within each experiment, need was varied to possibly affect risky decisions; between both experiments, the task was described differently, i.e., gaining versus not losing.

Figure 2.2 shows the choice proportion for the 32 individual games (4 probabilities $\times$ 4 values $\times$ 2 time limits)[3] in the three experiments as a function of frame conditions for the three need conditions for all participants (for details see Diederich et al. 2020). Choice proportions on the diagonal show no framing effects; those in the upper-left and lower-right quadrant indicate preference reversals, i.e., choice probabilities from below 0.5 to above 0.5 or from above 0.5 to below 0.5. Off-diagonal choice proportions in the upper-right and lower-left quadrant indicate preference shifts, i.e., there is a difference in choice behavior, but the tendency to one of the options persists. For all three experiments, we observe preference reversals and preference shifts. For some conditions, participants are more risk-taking in loss frames as compared to gain frames (reversals). For other conditions,

---

[1] This and the next paragraph come from Wyszynski and Diederich (2022, p. 4).

[2] The values of experiment 2 were flanked by plus/minus one point, resulting in the following set: 19, 20, 21, 39, 40, 41, 59, 60, 61, 79, 80, and 81 and collapsed for evaluation. A similar procedure was applied for experiment 3.

[3] Data of the time limit conditions are collated here.

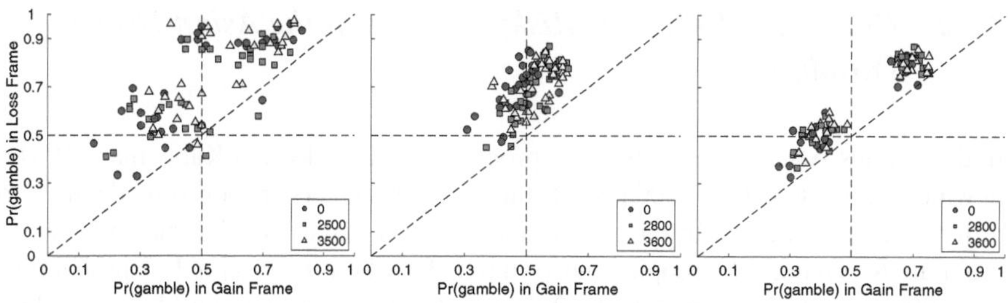

Choice proportions for choosing the gambles as a function of frames for experiments 1 (left), 2 (center), and 3 (right). The symbols and gray shades correspond to the needs conditions with darker shades to lower thresholds. Source: Own creation based on Diederich et al. (2020).

Fig. 2.2 Choice proportions in simple lottery games

the choice frequencies differed significantly but did not cross the 0.5 line (preference shifts). However, it is at first sight difficult to say whether the patterns depend on need. A linear mixed-effect model analysis revealed that the framing effect was indeed statistically significant for all 3 experiments. Furthermore, the proportion of risky choices increased for the highest need threshold as compared to the control (0 points). For experiment 3, this holds for both need thresholds. For experiment 2, we could observe a statistically significant interaction between need and the frame: The framing effect was weaker for both need conditions as compared to the control.

2.3.1.2 Conclusion

With respect to our research question, "Does induced need influence risky choices in a simple lottery game framed as gains or losses?" we conclude the following. Need affects risky choice behavior per se, regardless of the frame. In becoming riskier with high need, the framing effect disappeared. This is exactly what the Stone–Geary framework predicts.

As outlined before, the risk-sensitivity and Stone–Geary utility frameworks make identical predictions with respect to the final outcome but are based on different assumptions. We attempted to disentangle these concepts by studying the sequence of risky decisions within a given number of rounds. However, we could not observe any systematic sequential patterns.

The next experiment uses a slightly different experimental paradigm, frames in a loose sense, as well as a different operationalization of need, to address the second research question.

2.3.2 *Does Need Influence Risky Choices in the Asian Disease Paradigm?*

In the famous Asian Disease problem proposed by Tversky and Kahneman (1981), in which a disease will kill 600 people, the decision-makers are confronted with two different choice frames. In one frame, the decision-maker has the choice between program A, saving 200 people, and program B, where there is a $1/3$ probability that 600 people will be saved and a $2/3$ probability that nobody will be saved. In a second frame, the DM has the choice between program C, where 400 people will die, and program D, where there is a $1/3$ probability that nobody will die and a $2/3$ probability that 600 people will die.[4]

The two scenarios have the same structure as the simple lottery games shown in Fig. 2.1, A, B. Instead of playing for points, a gain frame here is described in terms of saving people, and a loss frame in terms of people dying. However, the paradigms used here differ substantially: The operationalization of need as a threshold to be obtained or maintained is inapplicable in the disease scenario. Therefore, need was defined as the number of people affected by a disease, i.e., people in need. We included two major categories of outcomes, either a small scope of people affected or a Large scope of people affected. This operationalization, however, changed the perspective of the decision-maker. In the lottery game, the decision-maker's choice relates to the coverage of his/her own need, whereas in the disease scenario the decision-maker's choice affects others. That is, the Asian Disease paradigm contains moral decisions about saving (or not saving) lives, and the decision-maker's choice affects a population that is in need of treatment (medicine or vaccine) for a disease. We argue that need increases with the number of people affected (i.e., the population size).

To generate a specific hypothesis, we refer to studies by Harinck et al. (2007) indicating that loss aversion, the underlying factor accounting for risky choice according to Prospect Theory, holds true for choices involving large values, but not for choices involving small ones. Harinck and her associates find that losses loom larger than gains for substantial amounts of money, but the effect disappears or even reverses for small amounts. This pattern has been replicated in another recent study (Mukherjee et al. 2017). Applying this line of reasoning to decisions concerning risky choices in the domain of public health, we hypothesize that when the needy population is large, the willingness to take risks will increase. Notice, however, that this design does not allow for a distinction between the magnitude of need and the magnitude of outcomes.

Similar to (Mahoney et al. 2011), we varied the type of disease: either treatment for an unusual infectious disease, a new agent to treat leukemia, or a new agent to treat AIDS. Beyond adding an element of variability in the design, this feature of

[4] This paragraph comes from Diederich et al. (2018, p. 529).

the experiment allows us to examine the possibility that the effects of framing and need depend on the specific disease. Note that these are frames in a loose sense.

The three diseases differ with respect to the populations affected, the public's familiarity with the disease, and the extent to which one views the people affected as responsible for their plight or as lacking control. Although in all cases the probabilities were explicitly stated, when these probabilities refer to an unusual new disease (or even to AIDS), respondents may take them with a grain of salt. In that case, their choice may reflect the ambiguity (uncertainty) they sense. The effect of ambiguity in the context of framing effects was studied by Osmont et al. (2015), who compared framing effects under risk and ambiguity. In their research, in conditions of ambiguity, participants preferred the sure option over the gamble in both the gain and loss frames. To the extent that an unusual disease evokes ambiguity aversion, we might expect the framing to have a weaker effect in the unusual disease conditions relative to the other diseases. Perceived need, on the other hand, may point to leukemia as the disease most interesting in this context. Among the three diseases, leukemia may evoke the most intense sense of vulnerability and lack of control. Hence, the subjective need for medical intervention may be particularly high.[5]

The effect of vulnerability may affect attitudes toward public policies that would serve the goal of regaining control. For example, physical vulnerability may increase support for providing wider coverage of health insurance, even if the decision-maker remains personally unaffected by such a policy (Bloom 2010; Bazerman et al. 2011). The relevance of the domain as a moderator of the framing effect was highlighted by Krishnamurthy et al. (2001), who found a diminished framing effect in medical treatment decisions among hospital patients, relative to students. They argue that framing might be viewed as a semantic cue in a decision problem, and their findings suggest that the cue becomes less effective when other cues are more salient. To the extent that leukemia is more relevant to our respondents due to perceived need, we would predict that the need may crowd out the effect of framing.

2.3.2.1 Experimental Setup and Results

These hypotheses were tested in experiment 4 (Diederich et al. 2018). At the beginning of a preset number of trials, the DM was introduced to one of the three disease scenarios (unusual infection, leukemia, and AIDS). The "Given" in display Fig. 2.1, A, B was replaced by "X patients" where "X" stands for one of the three diseases. In condition Small, the number of affected people is identical to the endowment in experiment 2 (20, 40, 60, and 80). In condition Large, the numbers were multiplied by one hundred resulting in 2,000, 4,000, 6,000, and 8,000 affected people. The probabilities attached to the risky option were 0.3, 0.4, 06, and 0.7, the same as with the previous studies.

[5] This and the next paragraph come from Diederich et al. (2018, p. 530).

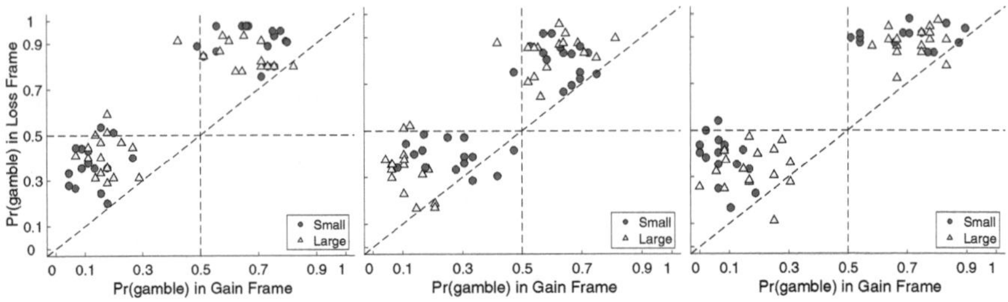

Choice proportions for choosing the risky option as a function of frames for different diseases (left: unusual disease; center: leukemia; right: AIDS). The dark circle corresponds to the Small need condition and the open triangle to the Large need condition. Source: Own creation based on Diederich et al. (2018).

Fig. 2.3 Choice proportions in disease scenarios

Figure 2.3 shows the scatter plots for the three diseases (left: unusual disease; center: leukemia; right: AIDS) and two categories of affected people, i.e., the scope. As before, choice proportions on the diagonal show no framing effects; those in the upper-left and lower-right quadrants indicate preference reversals, and off-diagonal choice proportions in the upper-right and lower-left quadrants indicate preference shifts. For all three disease scenarios, we observe preference shifts, i.e., there is a difference in choice behavior. Nevertheless, the tendency to one of the options persists, meaning there are very few preference reversals.

A linear mixed-effect model analysis reveals a statistically significant framing effect for all three diseases. The risky choice alternative was chosen more often in the loss frame (die) than in the gain frame (save). Need in terms of the scope of affected people had an effect on choice proportions: In condition Small (fewer patients) the risky choice option was chosen more frequently than in condition Large, which contravenes our hypothesis. But we found significant interactions between small variations within a scope (affected people in a scenario) and framing. The participants produced more framing effects when more people were affected in a scenario. This became even more obvious within the Large scope scenario (for details see Diederich et al. 2018). The different disease scenarios showed no main effect, but some interactions indicate that the specific health scenarios differed in some respect. Participants took less risk in loss frame trials for leukemia as compared to the unusual disease condition, which led to a stronger framing effect for the unusual disease than for leukemia, in direct contravention of our hypothesis. With respect to scope (Small, Large), we observed stronger framing effects for AIDS and weaker framing effects for leukemia when more people (Large) were affected by the respective disease as compared to fewer people (Small).

2.3.2.2 Conclusion

With respect to the second research question, we conclude the following. Need, defined here in terms of the overall number of affected people, called scope, affects risky choice behavior, regardless of the frame. When need is high, that is, when the number of people in need is large, the participants tend to be more risk-averse. These results show the opposite effect from the one found in the studies with a simple lottery framing in Sect. 2.3.1.1. Obviously, need is defined differently in both studies, and both use different experimental framings in a loose sense (however, the probabilities and the values are identical in experiments 2 and 4). Another, possibly even more important, difference is the perspective of the decision-maker. In the studies with lottery games, the participant's decision had a direct effect on his/her own need, whereas in the disease scenarios, the participant's decision affected other people's need.

Earlier research on risk-taking in situations that involve choosing for oneself versus choosing for others yielded mixed results, with some finding more risk-taking for others, while other studies find the opposite (e.g., Polman 2012; Garcia-Retamero and Galesic 2012). Stone and Allgaier (2008) and Stone et al. (2013) offer a framework that accounts for the contradictory effects of self-other risk-taking. They propose that the direction of self-other discrepancy in risk preference depends on the social valence of risk-taking (see also Montinari and Rancan 2018). In domains where risk-taking is viewed positively (such as in low-impact relationships), more risky options are selected when choosing for others than when choosing for oneself. By contrast, in domains where risk-taking is viewed negatively (such as health), choices for others are less risky than choices for oneself. These previous findings concur with the current results.

2.3.3 Does the Identifiability of a Needy Person Influence the Decision-Maker's Choice Behavior?

Inspired by common media reports of individual cases (Einzelschicksale) and research on the "Identifiable Others Effect" (e.g., Jenni and Loewenstein 1997; Small and Loewenstein 2003; Kogut and Ritov 2005a,b; Small et al. 2007; Loewenstein et al. 2005), which describes the tendency of being more generous to identified persons as compared to unidentified or statistical persons, we sought to investigate how the identifiability of a needy recipient impacts the effect of need. To fit into the overarching theme, we invented a new game, called the "need game," which allows us to manipulate both needs and frames.

The need game is a modified dictator game, which includes two players, namely, an active donor and a passive recipient. The donor initially owns some endowment, K_D, and the recipient typically has no endowment, $K_R = 0$. In the standard dictator game, the dictator decides how to share the endowment with the recipient, who has no influence on the decision. That is, the dictator alone determines the portion of the endowment shared with the recipient, and the recipient receives that portion. The newly created need game differs in several ways from the standard game. First, the donor does not have a free choice of proportion to share with the recipient but must choose from predetermined amounts: $x_1, \ldots, x_n$. In this chapter, we included three different values: $x_1 = 1$, $x_2 = 10$, and $x_3 = 50$. Second, the selected amount x_i is not simply handed over to the recipient but depends on the outcome of a lottery. That is, x_i is a bet in a lottery with probability p of the donor winning the bet and probability $1-p$ of the donor losing it. Here we included four different probabilities: $p = 0.3, 0.4, 0.6$, and 0.7. The rule of the game is as follows: The recipient receives the amount x_i if the donor loses the bet. In this case, the amount lost is subtracted from the donor's endowment (i.e., $K_D - x_i$) and added to the recipient's account (i.e., $K_R + x_i$). If, however, the donor wins the bet, x_i is added to the donor's endowment (i.e., $K_D + x_i$) and the recipient receives nothing. Third, both players have a minimum threshold (a need) that they must achieve by the end of the game, N_D and N_R, expressed in the same currency as the endowment. They must maintain (the donor) or obtain (the recipient) by playing several rounds of the game. That is, typically at the onset of the game $K_D > N_D$ and $K_R < N_R$ and after t rounds, K_{D_t} must not be $< N_D$ and K_{R_t} should be $\geq NR$. The recipient is paid only when his/her need threshold is obtained; likewise, the donor gets paid only when his/her need threshold is maintained.

The crucial dependent variable in this game is the amount invested by the donor. Obviously, this may depend on various factors such as the probability of winning, the framing of the lottery, the need, and the description of the recipient—the main focus of this chapter. One experiment condition contained no information about the recipient other than that there is another person (no-ID). In a second condition, a person was described in terms of name, age, occupation, and a picture shown (picture-ID). The third condition involved a real person (the one described in condition 2, labeled person-ID) who sat in the same room as the donor during the entire experiment. Furthermore, we included a gain and a loss frame for the lottery and the need condition $N_D = N_R = 2,200$, and $N_D = N_R = 0$, the latter of which served as a baseline control. The need threshold was the same for both players.

Figure 2.4 shows the experimental setup for a gain trial (left) and a loss trial (right). After the probabilities for winning and losing the gamble were displayed, the donor had to invest one of the three amounts by pressing the respective left (L), center (C), or right (R) keys on a device. The need threshold as well as the amounts held by the participants was shown throughout the experiment. The phrase "Other person" referred to the recipient referred to the condition when no additional information of the person was given on the display. For a similar design, see Chap. 8.

2.3.3.1 Results

The variable considered here is the relative frequencies of investing 1, 10, or 50 points. The results of the two experiments are as follows [(see Wyszynski et al.

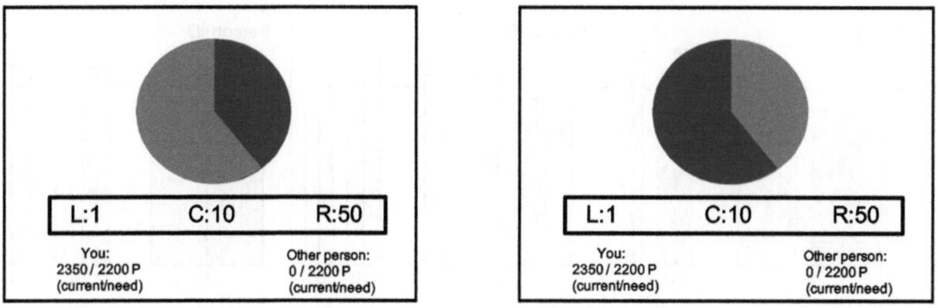

Need game embedded in a lottery frame either as gain (left) or as loss (right). The probability of winning/losing the bet is presented in a pie chart. In a gain trial, the probability of winning is marked in green, and the probability of losing in gray. In a loss trial, the probability of winning is marked in gray and the probability of losing in red. Below the pie charts are the number of points displayed from which the donor can bet on: 1, 10, or 50 points. L, C, and R in front of the bets refer to the keys the participant needs to press to indicate her/his choice. The third row in the display shows the current endowment and need of the donor ("you") and that of the recipient ("Other person"). The last row indicates the remaining time allotted to a given trial. Source: The caption comes from Wyszynski et al. (2020, Fig. 1). The figure has been slightly modified for this chapter.

Fig. 2.4 The need game

2020) for details of the experimental procedure]. We observe no main effect of need but find strong framing effects: The amounts bet on are higher in the gain frame than in the loss frame. As expected, the higher the probability of winning in the gain frame, the higher the amount that was bet; accordingly, the lower the probability of losing in the loss frame, the higher the amount that was bet. Figure 2.5 shows the choice proportions for a gain (dark) and a loss (light gray) for the three different amounts (x-axis) and for the three identity conditions. The upper row shows the results for probabilities of winning that are smaller than 0.5, and the lower row shows the results for the probabilities of winning that are larger than 0.5. The width of a column relates to the number of trials (normalized) with the specified amount chosen; crossing the 0.5 line (dashed) indicates preference reversals. This can be observed for all situations displayed in Fig. 2.5. Furthermore, identity had an effect on the amounts bet on. First, participants placed statistically significantly higher bets on lotteries in the person-ID condition than in the no-ID condition. This can also be inferred from the widths of the bars. Second, person-ID recipients ended up with more points per block of 200 trials than no-ID recipients; and third, the more identifiable the recipient (from no-ID to picture-ID to person-ID), the more often the need threshold was reached at the end of a block.

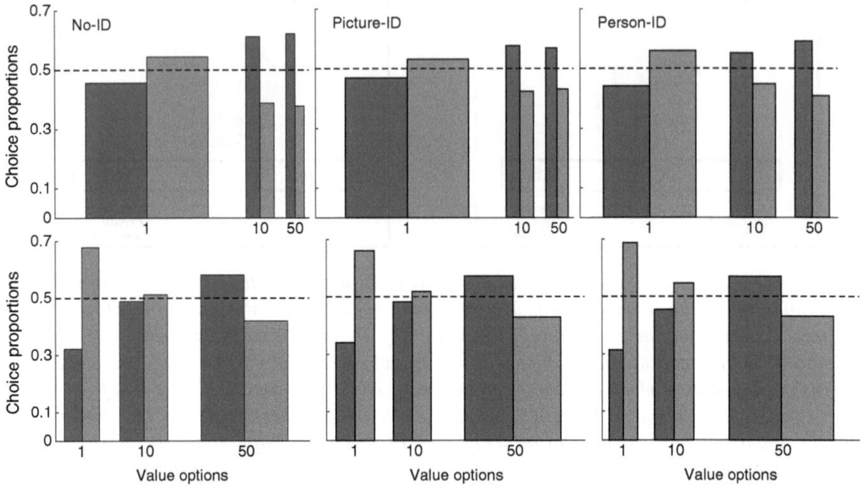

Choice proportions for a gain (dark) and loss (light grey) for the three different amounts 1, 10, and 50 to bet (x-axis) and for the three identity conditions. The upper row shows the results for probabilities to win smaller than .5 and the lower row for probabilities to win larger than .5. The width of a column relates to the number of trials (normalized) with the specified amount chosen; crossing the .5 line (dashed) indicates preference reversals. Error bars are included but too small to be visible. Source: Own creation based on the data of Wyszinski et al. (2020).

Fig. 2.5 Choice proportions in the need game

2.3.4 Conclusion

The results with respect to the identifiable others effect support the findings of Jenii and Lowenstein (1997) and Kogut and Ritov (2005a,b) and provide a clear indication that participants' decisions were motivated not only by the goal of maximizing their own profit but also by consideration of the recipient's welfare. We infer the latter from the effect identifiability of the recipient has on the amount bet.

Furthermore, the donors are not entirely altruistic because they need to keep up their own need level as well. This can best be obtained when betting higher amounts when the probability of winning is also high (lower row in Fig. 2.5). Discussing the possible strategies of individual donors in detail falls outside the scope of this chapter, but based on the data, we can reject the interpretation that the average donor takes risks only for their benefit and—as a side effect—accepts that the recipient receives the lost amount. If this were true, we would expect the proportions for betting 50 points with high probabilities to be much larger. However, since we cannot determine the motivations for betting certain amounts, we avoid speculating about them here.

2.3.5 *Do Time Constraints Matter?*

A frame in a loose sense is the time limit within which a decision-maker has to give a response. Presenting identical choice options but constraining the decision time can produce preference reversals and shifts (e.g., Diederich and Busemeyer 2006; Diederich 2003) or modify wording-induced framing effects (e.g., Guo et al. 2017, 2015). We included time constraints in the five experiments reported earlier to explore the effect of time on choice behavior when need is included. Our data showed a main effect of time limits in experiment 1 (the shorter the time the less risky the choices, Diederich 2020) and interactions with frames in experiments 3 and 4 (framing effects were enhanced under short time constraints, Diederich et al. 2018), but no effect when need was included. Experiment 5 (identity study) showed no time effect at all. Therefore, I will not discuss the results any further here and will instead turn to the next research question.

2.4 Internal Frames

Members of societies are heterogeneous. They differ with respect to attributed characteristics such as gender, age, citizenship but also with respect to acquired characteristics such as personal achievement, merit, and entitlement. Heterogeneity, therefore, became a central determinant for need-based justice during the research endeavor (see the introduction to this volume, Chap. 1). Is identified and eventually recognized need universal or does it depend on group membership? Does it depend on ascribed or acquired characteristics of group members? Is the need principle applicable to all of them in the same fashion or are differentiations allowed and even desirable? Furthermore, does the recognition of a person's or a group's need possibly depend on the characteristics of the judge and decision-maker? To build a theory of need-based justice, we must investigate the possible effects of group heterogeneity and the characteristics of the judges on recognizing needs. While most of the chapters in this volume are concerned with group heterogeneity, this one focuses on individual differences.

As discussed in the previous section, providing more details about the recipient's identity increases the decision-maker's generosity. Whereas this type of heterogeneity is external to the decision-maker as such, heterogeneity naturally exists between different decision-makers as well. Indeed, psychology justice research primarily is concerned with experiences of justice, that is, what a person perceives as just or unjust (see Ellard et al. 2016; Gollwitzer and van Prooijen 2016; Montada and Maes 2016, for history and review) and how this is related to personality traits (see Baumert and Schmitt 2016; Gollwitzer and van Prooijen 2016; Hafer and Bègue 2005; Hafer and Sutton 2016, for summary and review). Besides personality traits such as justice motives and, of course, socioeconomic measures, risk attitudes may influence justice judgments. This brings us to internal framing, which is said to be influenced by personal characteristics and the susceptibility of decision-makers to framing manipulations (see above).

2.4.1 Does the Effect of Need on Gain and Loss Framed Risky Choices Depend on the Individual Characteristics of the Decision-Maker?

The experimental setup was identical to the one described in Sect. 2.3.2. For further details see Wyszynski and Diederich (2023). Note that Mahoney et al. (2011) and Mandel and Kapler (2018) did not find any relation to scale values and framing effects. We, however, investigate individual differences in choice behavior using a within-subject design and psychophysical data collection approach. Comparing our results with those mainly obtained by Mahoney et al. (2011), we found the following: First, in contrast to Mahoney et al. (2011), who observed no impact of SIRI scores on risky choice behavior, our study showed that individuals with high stimulating risk-style scores chose the risky option more often than participants with low scores.

Second, Mahoney et al. (2011) found no relationship between SIRI scores and the strength of the framing effect. Our results, however, show that both sub-scales of the SIRI, i.e., stimulating and instrumental risk, moderated the framing effect: Framing effects were stronger for individuals with high stimulating risk-style scores and high instrumental risk-style scores as compared to low risk-style scores. That is, regardless of whether the tendency to take higher risks is associated with fun (stimulating risk) or motivated by reaching a goal (instrumental risk), it enhanced the framing effect.

Third, Mahoney et al. (2011) did not find any relationship between rational-thinking style and framing effects. Similarly, Shiloh et al. (2002) and Stark et al. (2017), using a between-subject design, observed no moderator effect of rational-thinking style on framing effect. Björklund and Bäckström (2008) found a negative correlation between rational-thinking-style scores and susceptibility to framing effects. Our study has found a moderator effect of rational-thinking style on framing effects for all group memberships, with the strongest effect being on participants with moderate scores. There was no difference between low- and high-scoring members.

Fourth, Mahoney et al. (2011) found that participants with higher experiential-thinking-style scores chose the risky option more often. For one specific decision problem, they found stronger framing effects for individuals with high scores in experiential thinking but not on the composite level (all five problems taken together). In contrast, we have found neither a main effect of experiential thinking on choice behavior nor a significant interaction between experiential thinking and framing. This ambiguous result reflects what has been observed in previous studies (Covey 2014; LeBoeuf and Shafir 2003; Stanovich and West 2008; Stark et al.

2017). There may be various reasons for the contradictory evidence, and we can only speculate about it as systematic research is lacking. For instance, compositions of samples (e. g., undergraduates, graduates, or non-university participants) may lead to different cut-off points for membership categorization. That is, an experiential-thinking score of 70 may have been categorized as high within one sample and low within another sample. Moreover, design-related differences and problem domain variations may influence choice behavior; another possible explanation may be unusual problem descriptions that challenge the participants' reliance on experience (Stark et al. 2017).

Finally, we found a relationship between AOT scores and the strength of framing effects. The effects for participants with moderate AOT scores were weakest among the three groups; the moderator effect of low and high scores on framing was about the same, contrary to previous studies (Sá et al. 1999; West et al. 2008). This finding suggests that further research is needed (for details see Wyszynski and Diederich 2023).

2.5 Dynamic-Stochastic Framework for Dual Processes: The Two-Stage Dual-Process Model

According to the transparency hypothesis, the transparency of a decision process contributes to the social objectivity of distribution decisions, in particular, to forms of distributive justice where need is one major distribution criterion. Therefore, the experiments discussed in the previous sections focused on identifying determinants that possibly influence the decision-maker's judgments on need. The results were mainly descriptive, indicating the absence or presence of an effect and its strength. This final section proposes a dynamic-stochastic framework to account for framing effects and their strength and seeks to extend it to include need as an additional component. Note that this chapter does not test the model on data as this goes beyond the scope of the chapter.

Prospect Theory (Kahneman and Tversky 1979) has been for decades the most common explanation for framing effects in risky choice settings. Several of our results are in accordance with the standard interpretation: Participants are more risk-averse in gain frames and more risk-seeking in loss frames. Although Prospect Theory is a psychological theory, it neither takes into account the dynamics of decision-making, i.e., it is static, nor the fluctuation of preferences, i.e., it is deterministic. As shown in the following, Prospect Theory can be implemented in a dynamic-stochastic framework operating in one of two systems.

Dual-process theories suggest that framing effects may be the result of two different systems of reasoning. One system is often characterized as affective, automatic, rapid, and implicit, whereas another system is often described as rational, controlled, slow, and explicit. For convenience, we will adopt the terminology of Stanovich and West (2000) and Kahneman and Frederick (2002) and describe the two systems as Systems 1 and 2. Note that the popular book *Thinking, Fast and Slow* by Kahneman (2011) points, in particular, to the dynamics of System 1 associated with "thinking fast" and System 2 associated with "thinking slow."

Most dual-process approaches are verbal and do not allow for rigorous, quantitative predictions and testing. Recently, however, Diederich and Trueblood (2018) developed a dynamic-stochastic modeling framework of dual-process theory, which provides an account of the timing and interaction of the two systems. The model builds on research using multistage sequential sampling models (Diederich 1997; Diederich and Oswald 2016) and applies to binary choices. Here we demonstrate the model account for the situation as described in Sect. 2.2.1.1. The section is organized as follows. First, we give a short introduction to the so-called sequential sampling models. Mathematically, they can be described as stochastic processes. Second, we describe the approach for framed risky binary choices with specific preference functions within each system. Third, we show two different ways in which need is implemented in the model and show some testable predictions of the model with respect to choice probabilities and mean choice response times.

2.5.1 Preliminaries

The basic ideas of the model are based on Decision Field Theory (Busemeyer and Townsend 1993) and Multiattribute Decision Field Theory (Diederich 1997) and are as follows. We assume that decisions are based on a preference state, denoted $P(t)$, presenting the relative preference strength for choosing one option (here the gamble, G) over another (here, the sure option, S) at time t. Assume that a positive value of $P(t)$ represents a momentary preference for option G, whereas a negative value of $P(t)$ represents a momentary preference for option S. Preference strength is updated from one moment, t, to the next, $t + h$, by an input valence, $V(t)$, which reflects the momentary comparison of the consequences of options G and S with $V(t) = V^G(t) - V^S(t)$, where $V^G(t)$ is the momentary valence for the gamble and $V^S(t)$ for the sure option. The valence fluctuates because the decision-maker's attention switches back and forth between anticipated consequences. Technically, this process can be described as a stochastic process (e.g., Cox and Miller 1977). Here we focus on the mean valence, $E[V(t)] = \mu_t$, that is, the valence that drives the preference process, on average, to a decision criterion, θ_G, for choosing the gamble G or to a decision criterion, θ, for choosing the sure option S. Thus, the parameter μ, called *drift rate* of the stochastic process, indicates the direction and strength of preference for choosing option G or S.

Without loss of generality, assume that for $\mu > 0$ preference is for choosing option G, whereas for $\mu < 0$ the preference is for choosing S. "The larger the absolute value of μ [δ in the original text], the stronger the preference for the given choice option. For $\mu = 0$ the decision maker is indifferent between the two choice options. The preference process stops, and a final decision is made as soon as the preference state exceeds a decision threshold or boundary: If $P(t) > \theta_G$, the DM [decision maker] chooses the gamble G, and if $P(t) < -\theta_S$, the DM chooses the sure option S. The decision threshold is assumed to be set prior to the decision task by the DM and depends, among other things, on the time available for a decision. Under short time limits, the boundaries are assumed to be smaller than under no time limits. Thus, the probability of choosing option G over S is determined by $P(t)$ reaching the positive threshold before reaching the negative threshold." (Diederich and Trueblood 2018, p. 272).

2.5.2 Two-Stage Dual-Process Model for Framed Risky Choices

For the dual-process framework, we assume that the input valence not only depends on the comparison value but also on the system in which the decision-maker is operating. Let us consider System 1 first. As outlined in Sect. 2.2, individuals were given an initial amount of money. They were then offered the sure option of retaining a portion of the initial amount or the gamble to keep all of the initial amount with the risk of losing all of it. In the gain frame, the sure option was framed as "keeping" a subset of the initial amount. In the loss frame, the sure option was framed as "losing" a subset of the initial amount. The gamble options in the gain and loss frames are identical. Therefore, under a gain frame (g), preference evolves in System 1 by comparing the consequences when choosing the gamble and the sure option, producing valence values $V^G(t)$ and $V^{S_g}(t)$ at any moment in time with $E[V^G(t) - V^{S_g}(t)] = \mu_{gt}$. Similarly, under a loss frame (l), the preference process starts in System 1 by comparing the consequences when choosing the gamble and the sure option, producing valence values $V^G(t)$ and $V^{S_l}(t)$ at any moment in time with $E[V^G(t) - V^{S_l}(t)] = \mu_{lt}$. To align the model with the experimental conditions and to allow for quantitative predictions, we assume that preferences are constructed[6] and related to parametric functions. Prospect Theory is therefore a suitable candidate (Kahneman and Tversky 1979; Tversky and Kahneman 1992). Examples of other functions are found in Diederich and Trueblood (2018).

According to Prospect Theory, the value $\mathscr{V}$ of a simple prospect that pays x with probability p (and nothing otherwise) is given by

$$\mathscr{V}(x, p) = w(p)v(x), \tag{2.1}$$

[6] This is a typical assumption from a psychology viewpoint. Preferences vary because of personal and situational circumstances. In addition, dynamic-stochastic models assume that preferences fluctuate because the anticipated consequences may vary even during one trial. Note that this is quite different from most decision models in economics in which fixed preferences are elicited and they vary only due to environmental circumstances, which are not identical from one situation to another.

where the decision weight w measures the impact of probability p on the attractiveness of the prospect and v the subjective value of the consequence x. With

$$w(p) = \frac{p^\gamma}{(p^\gamma + (1-p)^\gamma)^{1/\gamma}} \tag{2.2}$$

the probability weighting function $w(p)$ produces an inverse S-shaped function for $\gamma < 1$, accounting for overweighting low probabilities and underweighting moderate to high probabilities (for an overview of other functional forms of $w(p)$ see, e.g., Fox and Poldrack 2009). With

$$v(x) = \begin{cases} x^\alpha & \text{if } x \geq 0 \\ -\lambda|x|^\beta & \text{if } x < 0 \end{cases} \tag{2.3}$$

the value function $v(x)$ is concave for gains, convex for losses, and steeper for losses than for gains, accounting for risk-averse behavior in the gain domain and risk-seeking behavior in the loss domain. Thus, the mean difference in valence (drift rate) in System 1 for a gain frame is

$$\mu_{1_g} = \mathcal{V}_G - \mathcal{V}_{S_g} \tag{2.4}$$

and for a loss frame

$$\mu_{1_l} = \mathcal{V}_G - \mathcal{V}_{S_l}. \tag{2.5}$$

System 2, the deliberate or rational system, should not be affected by frames, that is, $V(t) = V^G(t) - V^S(t)$, where $V^G(t)$ is the momentary valence for the gamble and $V^S(t)$ for the sure option. A proper candidate for constructing preferences, therefore, is, for instance, expected utility theory (von Neumann and Morgenstern 1953).

According to expected utility theory, EU, the expected utility of an option is the utility of the outcome $u(x)$, times the probability of its occurrence.

$$EU(x, p) = p \cdot u(x). \tag{2.6}$$

The mean difference in valence when operating in System 2 is therefore

$$\mu_2 = EU(G) - EU(S). \tag{2.7}$$

The model makes predictions about the size of the framing effect (bias). In particular, 1) the bias is a function of the time the decision-maker operates in System 1, and 2) the bias is a function of the time (limit) the decision-maker has for making a choice. It also makes predictions about the patterns of choice probabilities and mean choice response times. Note that risk attitudes of the decision-maker, reflected in the shape of the utility function, do not affect any of the qualitative predictions. For details see Diederich and Trueblood (2018) and Diederich (2023).

2.5.3 *Two-Stage Dual-Process Model for Risky Choices with Need Threshold*

There are at least two possible ways to incorporate need into this framework. Need may affect the initial preference state toward choosing the gamble or toward choosing the sure option or need may affect the rate of accumulation, that is, the drift rate. We briefly discuss both possibilities. For ease of communication, Figs. 2.6 and 2.8 refer to the different versions.

2.5.3.1 Need Influence on Initial Preference State

Given a need level, the decision-maker might be particularly risk-averse for accumulating at least some points toward the threshold (or avoid losing too many points). In this case, the decision-maker may have a priori bias for choosing the sure option. It is also possible that for a high need level, the decision-maker is particularly risk-seeking. In this case, the decision-maker is a priori biased toward choosing the gamble. This can be implemented in the model by moving the starting point closer to one of the decision criteria. In accordance with the previous agreement for $P(0) > 0$, the initial preference state (the starting point of the process) is moved closer to the decision criterion θ_G for choosing the gamble; for $P(0) < 0$ the initial preference state is moved closer to the decision criterion θ_S for choosing the sure option.

Figure 2.6 shows these situations for a gain frame. The mean valence in System 1 is directed toward choosing the sure option ($\mu_1 < 0$ toward criterion θ_S). For System 2, $\mu_2 = 0$, i.e., the decision-maker is indifferent between choosing the sure option or

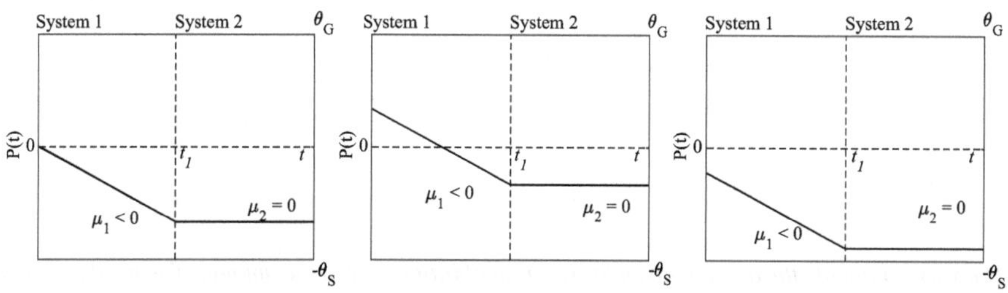

Source: Own creation based on the model by Diederich (2023).

Fig. 2.6 Schematic presentation of a dynamic dual-process framework with different a priori biases

the gamble. This occurs when the expected values of the gamble and the sure option are identical and the decision-maker is risk neutral. In the left panel, no a priori bias for choosing the sure option over the gamble is assumed, thus $P(0) = 0$. The middle panel shows an a priori bias toward choosing the gamble. Thus, the starting point of the process is $P(0) > 0$, closer to the θ_G criterion. The right panel shows an a priori bias toward choosing the sure option, reflected in $P(0) < 0$. Note that an a priori bias for choosing one option more often over the other is independent of the values and probabilities of a specific game and may also be linked to the decision-maker's personality: Some of us are more risk-seeking than others (see Sect. 2.4).

Note that the predicted choice probabilities and mean choice response times depend not only on the size of the a priori bias, i.e., how close it is to the criteria for choosing the gamble θ_G or the sure option θ_S, but also on whether the bias points in the same direction for gain and loss frames. Due to space limitations, Fig. 2.7 shows only the predicted choice probabilities for the gamble. The filled symbols indicate the predictions for a gain frame, and the open symbols for a loss frame. Panel (A) presents the predictions when assuming no bias. The predictions of choice probabilities in (B) and (C) assume that the a priori bias is the same for both the gain and loss frames. In particular, panel (B) refers to the situation where $P(0) > 0$, that is, favoring gambles a priori. Panel (C) assumes a priori biases toward the sure

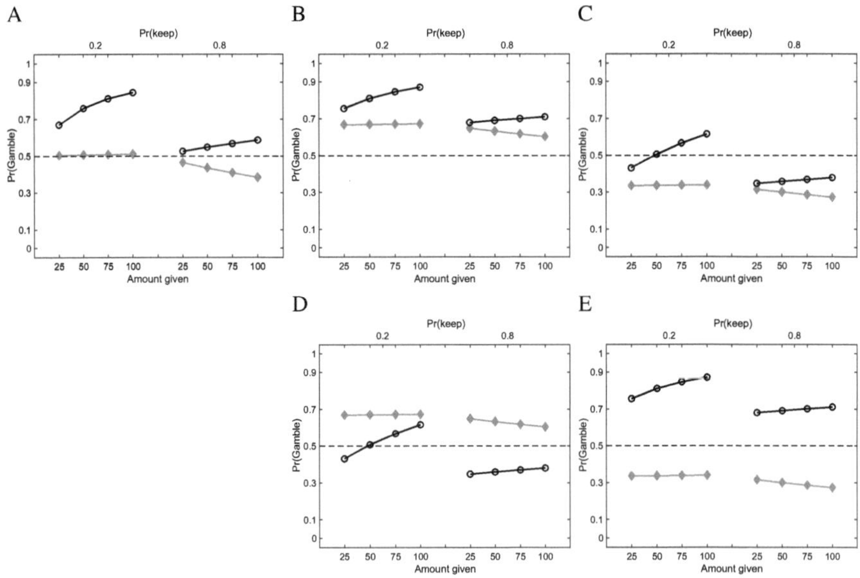

The x-axes indicate the amount given for two probabilities to keep the amount. The filled symbols indicate the predictions for a gain frame, the open symbols for a loss frame. For details see text. Source: Own creation based on the model by Diederich (2023).

Fig. 2.7 Predicted choice probabilities assuming various a priori biases

option, i.e., $P(0) < 0$. Panel (D) and (E) refer to conditions in which the assumption is that the biases depend on the frames. In particular, in panel (D), $P(0) > 0$ in a gain frame and $P(0) < 0$ in a loss frame. The reverse is true for the situation presented in panel (E), i.e., $P(0) < 0$ in a gain frame and $P(0) > 0$ in a loss frame.

2.5.3.2 Need Influence on Preference Accumulation

Another way to incorporate need into the framework is to assume that the preference for choosing the gamble or the sure option is directly affected by it. For instance, in Sect. 2.3.2, we briefly mentioned that the Stone–Geary utility function, U, may account for the need threshold situation, that is,

$$U = \prod_i (q_i - \gamma_i)^{\beta_i}, \tag{2.8}$$

where q_i is the consumption of good i, and β and γ are parameters and $q_i = \gamma_i + \beta_i / p_i (y - \sum_j \gamma_j p_j)$, where y is total expenditure, and p_i is the price of good i (Stone 1954). That is, instead of assuming an expected utility or expected value function for System 2, a more sophisticated function may be mapped onto the drift rate. Note that this extension is still a normative (rational) function and, therefore, suitable for System 2.

To adjust this to our experimental design and proceed pragmatically, we may set $p_i = 1$, for all i, and interpret y as the difference between the initial amount given to the decision-maker and the need threshold. Obviously, this is fixed for a given situation. Because the game is played for several rounds (Diederich et al. 2020), q_i may be interpreted as the amount lost in each round i, which can be zero or negative. This is not the place to derive complicated functions and solutions. For demonstration, we simply assume here that the values offered in the gambles are reduced by some amount (a parameter to be estimated from the data). Figure 2.8 shows the predicted choice probabilities of choosing the gamble (left panels), the mean choice response times for choosing the gamble (middle panels), and the mean choice response time for choosing the sure option (right panels) as a function of the amounts given and the probabilities of keeping the amount given (see Sect. 2.2.1.1 for the experimental paradigm). The upper row refers to a no-need situation; the lower row is when need is included. The filled symbols indicate the predictions for a gain frame, and the open symbols show the predictions for a loss frame. As predicted by the Stone–Geary assumption, the choice probabilities for choosing the gamble (the risky option) increase when need is involved (left panels). The mean choice response times are shorter when there is a need than when no need is given. Furthermore, the mean choice response times for risky decisions (open symbols) are shorter than for the sure ones when choosing the gamble (middle panels). The opposite patterns hold when a sure choice is made (right panels).

The dynamic dual-process model appears to be very flexible. However, it imposes strong, testable restrictions on the choice probability/mean choice response time pat-

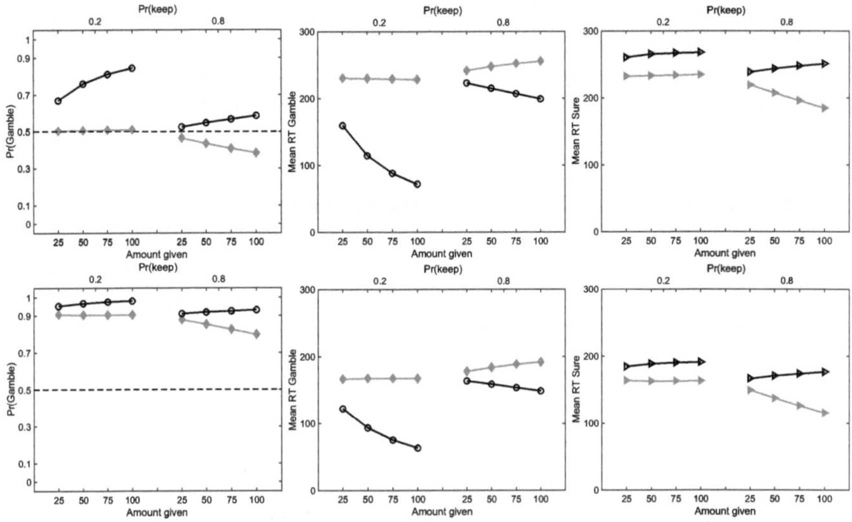

The x-axes indicate the amount given for two probabilities to keep the amount. The filled symbols indicate the predictions for a gain frame, the open symbols for a loss frame. See text for further details. Source: Own creation based on the model by Diederich (2023).

Fig. 2.8 Predicted choice probabilities and mean choice response times for a no-need condition (upper panels) and a need condition (lower panels)

terns (e.g., Diederich and Oswald 2014; Diederich and Trueblood 2018; Diederich 2023). A (quasi) psychophysical approach has been shown to be promising as a rigorous test. That is, instead of including many participants in very few trials, we offered many trials to a few participants (e.g., Diederich 2003; Guo et al. 2017; Diederich et al. 2020; Wyszynski and Diederich 2022).

2.6 General Conclusion

The overarching goal of this research was to build an informed theory of need-based justice. While need has many facets in psychology, originally defined as a motive to prompt an individual to act, but also as one justice principle in the triad with equity and equality, the current contribution is to determine possible factors that influence the identification and recognition of need. Need in this context is given as an external object (quantity) rather than a psychological concept, but it could be considered as an ideal that is important to the decision-maker. That is, we addressed the first thesis of Nullmeier (2020) for building the theory: "[. . .] something that is necessary, compelling, imperative, indispensable, essentially required [. . .]."

We showed in several experiments that the wording, that is, the frame in which a decision problem is presented, influenced the decision-maker's judgments when need was involved.

That is, a theory of need-based justice must not only include normative concepts of what is a fair and just distribution but also of what people think it is and how their judgments are influenced by various (irrelevant) criteria. By that, we met the second thesis: "A theory of need-based justice should be based on the promotion of both normative and empirical research." The dual-process model presented in the final chapter also refers to these two requirements by promoting a normative (rational) part and a descriptive (observed behavior) part, both acting in concert.

Finally, we addressed the impact of different personality scores on decision-making situations that involve need. That is, heterogeneity is considered here between decision-makers rather than between needy recipients or even entire groups. This is often neglected when investigating variability between groups. However, variability in the personality of decision-makers may be one factor that partly accounts for observed outcomes.

Acknowledgments The chapter presents results from the project "Framing in need determination," funded by the German Research Foundation (DFG) (DI506 13–1,13–2). It was part of the DFG research group FOR 2104 "Need-based Justice and Distributive Procedures."

References

Alderfer, C. P. (1969): "An Empirical Test of a New Theory of Human Needs", *Organizational Behavior and Human Performance* 5, 212–240.

Baron, J. (1993): "Why Teach Thinking? An Essay", *Applied Psychology* 42, 191–214.

Baumert, A., and M. Schmitt (2016): "Justice Sensitivity", in C. Sabbagh, and M. Schmitt (eds.): *Handbook of Social Justice Theory and Research*, 161–180. New York: Springer.

Bazerman, M. H., F. Gino, L. L. Shu, and C. J. Tsay (2011): "Joint Evaluation as a Real-World Tool for Managing Emotional Assessments of Morality", *Emotion Review* 3 (3), 290–292.

Björklund, F., and M. Bäckström (2008): "Individual Differences in Processing Styles: Validity of the Rational–Experiential Inventory", *Scandinavian Journal of Psychology* 49 (5), 439–446.

Bloom, P. (2010): "How Do Morals Change?", *Nature* 464 (7288), 490.

Busemeyer, J. R., and J. T. Townsend (1993): "Decision Field Theory: A Dynamic Cognition Approach to Decision Making", *Psychological Review* 100, 432–459.

Cacioppo, J. T., and R. E. Petty (1982): "Risk Taking Propensity of Entrepreneurs", *Academy of Management Journal* 23, 509–520.

Caraco, T. (1980): "On Foraging Time Allocation in a Stochastic Environment", *Ecology* 61 (1), 119–128.

Covey, J. (2014): "The Role of Dispositional Factors in Moderating Message Framing Effects", *Health Psychology* 33 (1), 52–65.

Cox, D. R., and H. B. Miller (1977): *The Theory of Stochastic Processes*. London: Chapman & Hall.

Deaton, A., and J. Muellbauer (1980): *Economics and Consumer Behavior*. Cambridge: Cambridge University Press.

Diederich, A. (1997): "Dynamic Stochastic Models for Decision Making under Time Constraints", *Journal of Mathematical Psychology* 41 (3), 260–274.

Diederich, A. (2003): “Decision Making under Conflict: Decision Time as a Measure of Conflict Strength”, *Psychonomic Bulletin and Review* 10 (1), 167–176.
Diederich, A. (2020): “Identifying needs: The Psychological Perspective”, in S. Traub, and B. Kittel (eds.): *Need-Based Distributive Justice: An Interdisciplinary Perspective*, 59–89. Cham: Springer Nature.
Diederich, A. (2023): “A Dynamic Dual Process Model for Binary Choices: Serial versus Parallel Architecture”, forthcoming in *Computational Brain and Behavior*.
Diederich, A., and J. R. Busemeyer (2006): “Modeling the Effects of Payoff on Response Bias in a Perceptual Discrimination Task: Bound-Change, Drift-Rate-Change, or Two-Stage-Processing Hypothesis”, *Perception and Psychophysics* 68 (2), 194–207.
Diederich, A., and P. Oswald (2014): “Sequential Sampling Model for Multiattribute Choice Alternatives with Random Attention Time and Processing Order”, *Frontiers in Human Neuroscience* 8 (697).
Diederich, A., and P. Oswald (2016): “Multi-Stage Sequential Sampling Models with Finite or Infinite Time Horizon and Variable Boundaries”, *Journal of Mathematical Psychology* 74, 128–145.
Diederich, A., and J. S. Trueblood (2018): “A Dynamic Dual Process Model of Risky Decision Making”, *Psychological Review* 125 (2), 270–292.
Diederich, A., M. Wyszynski, and I. Ritov (2018): “Moderators of Framing Effect in Variations of the Asian Disease Problem: Time Constraint, Need, and Disease Type”, *Judgment and Decision Making* 13 (6), 529–546.
Diederich, A., M. Wyszynski, and S. Traub (2020): “Need, Frame, and Time Constraints in Risky Decision Making”, *Theory and Decision* 89, 1–37
Ellard, J. H., A. Harvey, and M. J. Callan (2016): “The Justice Motive: History, Theory, and Research”, in C. Sabbagh, and M. Schmitt (eds.): *Handbook of Social Justice Theory and Research*, 127–143. New York: Springer.
Epstein, S. (1998): “Cognitive-Experiential Self-Theory”, in D. F. Barone, M. Hersen, and V. B. Van Hasselt (eds.): *Advanced Personality*, 211–238. Boston: Springer.
Evans, J. S. B. (2008): “Dual-Processing Accounts of Reasoning, Judgment, and Social Cognition”, *Annual Review of Psychology* 59, 255–278.
Fischer, K. (1997): *Tun oder lassen? Die Rolle von Framing-Prozessen für die Wahl von Handlungen oder Unterlassung in Entscheidungssituationen*. Frankfurt/Main: Peter Lang.
Fox, C. R., and R. A. Poldrack (2009): “Prospect Theory and the Brain”, in P. W. Glimcher, E. Fehr, C. Camerer, and R. A. Poldrack (eds.): *Neuroeconomics: Decision Making and the Brain*, 145–173. London: Academic Press.
Gächter, S., H. Orzen, E. Renner, and C. Starmer (2009): “Are Experimental Economists Prone to Framing Effects? A Natural Field Experiment”, *Journal of Economic Behavior & Organization* 70, 443–446.
Garcia-Retamero, R., and M. Galesic (2012): “Doc, What Would You Do If You Were Me? On Self-Other Discrepancies in Medical Decision Making”, *Journal of Experimental Psychology: Applied* 18 (1),38–51.
Geary, R. C. (1950): “A Note on ‘A Constant-Utility Index of the Cost of Living”’, *The Review of Economic Studies* 18 (1), 65–66.
Gilovich, T., D. Griffin, and D. Kahneman (2002). *Heuristics and Biases. The Psychology of Intuitive Judgment*. Cambridge: Cambridge University Press.
Gollwitzer, M., and J. W. van Prooijen (2016): “Psychology of Justice”, in C. Sabbagh, and M. Schmitt (eds.): *Handbook of Social Justice Theory and Research*, 61–82. New York: Springer.
Guo, L., J. S. Trueblood, and A. Diederich (2015): “A Dual-Process Model of Framing Effects in Risky Choice”, in Cognitive Science Society (ed.): *Proceedings of the 37th Annual Conference of the Cognitive Science Society*. Austin, TX.
Guo, L., J. S. Trueblood, and A. Diederich (2017): “Thinking Fast Increases Framing Effects in Risky Decision Making”, *Psychological Science* 28 (4), 530–543.

Hafer, C. L., and L. Bègue (2005): "Experimental Research on Just-World Theory: Problems, Development, and Future Challenges", *Psychological Bulletin* 131 (1), 128–167.
Hafer, C. L., and R. Sutton (2016): "Belief in Just World", in C. Sabbagh, and M. Schmitt (eds.): *Handbook of Social Justice Theory and Research*, 145–160. New York: Springer.
Haran, U., I. Ritov, and B. A. Mellers (2013): "The Role of Actively Open-Minded Thinking in Information Acquisition, Accuracy, and Calibration", *Judgment and Decision Making* 8, 188–201.
Harinck, F., E. Van Dijk, I. Van Beest, and P. Mersmann (2007): "When Gains Loom Larger than Losses: Reversed Loss Aversion for Small Amounts of Money", *Psychological Science* 18 (12), 1099–1105.
Igou, E. R., and H. Bless (2007): "On Undesirable Consequences of Thinking: Framing Effects as a Function of Substantive Processing", *Journal of Behavioral Decision Making* 20 (2), 125–42.
Jenni K., and G. Loewenstein (1997): "Explaining the Identifiable Victim Effect", *Journal of Risk and Uncertainty* 14 (3), 235–257.
Kahneman, D. (2011): *Thinking, Fast and Slow*. New York: Farrar, Straus and Giroux.
Kahneman, D., and S. Frederick (2002): "Representativeness Revisited: Attribute Substitution in Intuitive Judgment", in T. Gilovich, D. Griffin, and D. Kahneman (eds.): *Heuristics and Biases: The Psychology of Intuitive Judgment*, 49–81. Cambridge: Cambridge University Press.
Kahneman, D., P. Slovic, and A. Tversky (1982): *Judgment under Uncertainty: Heuristics and Biases*. Cambridge: Cambridge University Press.
Kahneman, D., and A. Tversky (1979): "Prospect Theory: An Analysis of Decision under Risk", *Econometrica* 47, 263–291.
Kahneman, D., and A. Tversky (1984): "Choices, Values and Frames", *American Psychologist* 39 (4), 341–350.
Klein, O., et al. (2018): "A Practical Guide for Transparency in Psychological Science", *Collabra: Psychology* 4 (1), 20.
Kogut T., and I. Ritov (2005a): "The 'Identified Victim' Effect: An Identified Group, or just a Single Individual?", *Journal of Behavioral Decision Making* 18 (3), 157–167.
Kogut T., and I. Ritov (2005b): "The Singularity Effect of Identified Victims in Separate and Joint Evaluations", *Organizational Behavior and Human Decision Processes* 97 (2), 106–116.
Krishnamurthy, P., P. Carter, and E. Blair (2001): "Attribute Framing and Goal Framing Effects in Health Decisions", *Organizational Behavior and Human Decision Processes* 85 (2), 382–399.
Kühberger, A. (1998): "The Influence of Framing on Risky Decisions: A Meta-Analysis", *Organizational Behavior and Human Decision Processes* 75 (1), 23–55.
LeBoeuf, R. A., and E. Shafir (2003): "Deep Thoughts and Shallow Frames: On the Susceptibility to Framing Effects", *Journal of Behavioral Decision Making* 16 (2), 77–92.
Levin, I. P., S. L. Schneider, and G. J. Gaeth, (1998): "All Frames Are not Created Equal: A Typology and Critical Analysis of Framing Effects", *Organizational Behavior and Human Decision Processes* 76 (2), 149–188.
Loewenstein, G., D. Small, and J. Strnad (2005): "Statistical, Identifiable and Iconic Victims and Perpetrators", *SSRN Working Paper* 678281.
Mahoney, K. T., W. Buboltz, I. P. Levin, D. Doverspike, and D. J. Svyantek (2011): "Individual Differences in a Within-Subjects Risky-Choice Framing Study", *Personality and Individual Differences* 51 (3), 248–257.
Mandel, D. R., and I. V. Kapler (2018): "Cognitive Style and Frame Susceptibility in Decision-Making", *Frontiers in Psychology* 9, 1461.
Maslow, A. H. (1948): "'Higher' and 'Lower' Needs", *Journal of Psychology* 25, 433–436.
Maslow, A. H. (1987): *Motivation and Personality*, 3rd ed. New York: Addison-Wesley.
Mishra, S. (2014): "Decision-Making under Risk: Integrating Perspectives from Biology, Economics, and Psychology", *Personality and Social Psychology Review* 18 (3), 280–307.
Mishra, S., P. Barclay, and A. Sparks (2017): "The Relative State Model: Integrating Need-Based and Ability-Based Pathways to Risk-Taking", *Personality and Social Psychology Review* 21 (2), 176–198.

Mishra, S., and L. Fiddick (2012): "Beyond Gains and Losses: The Effect of Need on Risky Choice in Framed Decisions", *Journal of Personality and Social Psychology* 102 (6), 1136–1147.

Mishra, S., M. Gregson, and M. L. Lalumiere (2012): "Framing Effects and Risk-Sensitive Decision Making", *British Journal of Psychology* 103 (1), 83–97.

Mishra, S., and M. L. Lalumiere (2010): "You Can't Always Get What You Want: The Motivational Effect of Need on Risk-Sensitive Decision-Making", *Journal of Experimental Social Psychology* 46 (4), 605–611.

Montada, L., and J. Maes (2016): "Justice and Self-Interest", in C. Sabbagh, and M. Schmitt (eds.): *Handbook of Social Justice Theory and Research*, 109–125. New York: Springer.

Montinari, N., and M. Rancan (2018): "Risk Taking on Behalf of Others: The Role of Social Distance", *Journal of Risk and Uncertainty* 57 (1), 81–109.

Mukherjee, S., A. Sahay, V. C. Pammi, and N. Srinivasan (2017): "Is Loss-Aversion Magnitude-Dependent? Measuring Prospective Affective Judgments Regarding Gains and Losses", *Judgment and Decision Making* 12 (1), 81–89.

Nullmeier, F. (2020): "Towards a Theory of Need-Based Justice", in S. Traub, and B. Kittel (eds.): *Need-Based Distributive Justice: An Interdisciplinary Perspective*, 191–208. Cham: Springer Nature.

Osmont, A., M. Cassotti, M. Agogué, O. Houdé, and S. Moutier (2015): "Does Ambiguity Aversion Influence the Framing Effect During Decision Making?", *Psychonomic Bulletin & Review* 22 (2), 572–577.

Pacini, R., and S. Epstein (1999): "The Relation of Rational and Experiential Information Processing Styles to Personality, Basic Beliefs, and the Ratio-Bias Phenomenon", *Journal of Personality and Social Psychology* 76, 972–987.

Pietras, C. J., M. L. Locey, and T. D. Hackenberg (2003): "Human Risky Choice under Temporal Constraints: Tests of an Energy-Budget Model", *Journal of the Experimental Analysis of Behavior* 80 (1), 59–75.

Polman, E. (2012): "Self-Other Decision Making and Loss Aversion", *Organizational Behavior and Human Decision Processes* 119 (2) 141–150.

Rachlin, H., L. Green, J. H. Kagel, and R. C. Battalio (1976): "Economic Demand Theory and Psychological Studies of Choice", in G. H. Bower (eds.): *Psychology of Learning and Motivation*, vol. 10, 129–154. New York: Academic Press.

Rode, C., L. Cosmides, W. Hell, and J. Tooby (1999): "When and Why Do People Avoid Unknown Probabilities in Decisions under Uncertainty? Testing some Predictions from Optimal Foraging Theory", *Cognition* 72 (3), 269–304.

Sá, W., R. West, and K. Stanovich (1999): "The Domain Specificity and Generality of Belief Bias: Searching for a Generalizable Critical Thinking Skill", *Journal of Educational Psychology* 91, 497–510.

Schelling, T. C. (1968): "Game Theory and the Study of Ethical Systems", *Journal of Conflict Resolution* 12 (1), 34–44.

Shiloh, S., E. Salton, and D. Sharabi (2002): "Individual Differences in Rational and Intuitive Thinking Styles as Predictors of Heuristic Responses and Framing Effects", *Personality and Individual Differences* 32 (3), 415–429.

Small, D. A., and G. Loewenstein (2003): "Helping a Victim or Helping the Victim: Altruism and Identifiability", *Journal of Risk and Uncertainty* 26 (1), 5–16.

Small, D. A., G. Loewenstein, and P. Slovic (2007): "Sympathy and Callousness: The Impact of Deliberative Thought on Donations to Identifiable and Statistical Victims", *Organizational Behavior and Human Decision Processes* 102 (2), 143–153.

Stanovich, K. E., and R. F. West (2000): "Individual Differences in Reasoning: Implications for the Rationality Debate?", *Behavioral and Brain Sciences* 23 (5), 645–665.

Stanovich, K. E., and R. F. West (2008): "On the Relative Independence of Thinking Biases and Cognitive Ability", *Journal of Personality and Social Psychology* 94 (4), 672–695.

Stark, E., A. S. Baldwin, A. W. Hertel, and A. Rothman (2017): "The Role of Rational and Experiential Processing in Influencing the Framing Effect", *Journal of Social Psychology* 157 (3), 308–321.

Stephens, D. W. (1981): "The Logic of Risk-Sensitive Foraging Preferences", *Animal Behaviour* 29 (2), 628–629.

Stephens, D. W., and E. L. Charnov (1982): "Optimal Foraging: Some Simple Stochastic Models", *Behavioral Ecology and Sociobiology* 10 (4), 251–263.

Stone, R. (1954): "Linear Expenditure Systems and Demand Analysis: An Application to the Pattern of British demand", *Economic Journal* 64 (255), 511–527.

Stone, E. R., and L. Allgaier (2008): "A Social Values Analysis of Self-Other Differences in Decision Making Involving Risk", *Basic and Applied Social Psychology* 30 (2), 114–129.

Stone, E. R., Y. S. Choi, W. B. de Bruin, and D. R. Mandel (2013): "I Can Take the Risk, but You Should Be Safe: Self-Other Differences in Situations Involving Physical Safety", *Judgment and Decision Making* 8 (3), 250–267.

Svedholm-Häkkinen, A. M., and M. Lindeman (2018): "Actively Open-Minded Thinking: Development of a Shortened Scale and Disentangling Attitudes towards Knowledge and People", *Thinking and Reasoning* 24 (1), 21–40.

Svenson, O., and L. Benson III (1993): "Framing and Time Pressure in Decision Making", in O. Svenson, and A. J. Maule (eds.): *Time Pressure and Stress in Human Judgment and Decision Making*, 133—144. New York: Springer.

Törnblom, K. Y. (1988): "Positive and Negative Allocations: A Typology and a Model for Conflicting Justice Principles", in E. J. Lawler, and B. Markovsky (eds.): *Advances in Group Processes*, vol. 5, 141–168. London: JAI Press.

Traub, S. (1999): *Framing Effects in Taxation. An Empirical Study Using the German Income Tax Schedule*. Heidelberg: Physica, Contributions to Economics.

Traub, S., and B. Kittel (eds.) (2020): *Need-Based Distributional Justice: An Interdisciplinary Perspective*. Cham: Springer Nature.

Tversky, A., and D. Kahneman (1981): "The Framing of Decisions and the Psychology of Choice", *Science* 211 (4481), 453–458.

Tversky, A., and D. Kahneman (1992): "Advances in Prospect Theory: Cumulative Representation of Uncertainty", *Journal of Risk and Uncertainty* 5 (4), 297–323

von Neumann, J., and O. Morgenstern (1953): *Theory of Games and Economic Behavior*, 3rd ed. Princeton, NJ: Princeton University Press.

West, R. F., M. E. Toplak, and K. E. Stanovich (2008): "Heuristics and Biases as Measures of Critical Thinking: Associations with Cognitive Ability and Thinking Dispositions", *Journal of Educational Psychology* 100, 930–941.

Wyszynski, M., A. Diederich, and I. Ritov (2020): "Gamble for the Needy! Does Identifiability Enhance Donation?", *PLOS ONE* 15, e0234336

Wyszynski, M, and A. Diederich (2022): "Keep Your Budget Together! Investigating Determinants on Risky Decision-Making about Losses", *PLOS ONE* 17, e0265822

Wyszynski, M., and A. Diederich (2023): "Individual Differences Moderate Effects in an Unusual Disease Paradigm: A Psychophysical Data Collection Lab Approach and an Online Experiment", *Frontiers in Psychology* 14, 1086699.

Zaleskiewicz, T. (2001): "Beyond Risk Seeking and Risk Aversion: Personality and the Dual Nature of Economic Risk Taking", *European Journal of Personality* 15, S105–S122.

Chapter 3
Measuring Need-Based Justice: Empirically and Formally

Alexander Max Bauer and Mark Siebel

Abstract The formal part of this chapter is concerned with measures of need-based justice. According to the measures we propose, a distribution is unjust (i) the more it deviates from absolute need satisfaction and equal degrees of need satisfaction, (ii) the more the given undersupply could have been mitigated by transfers, or (iii) the more resources are used for oversupply instead of need satisfaction. These measures are compared, i.e., as to the satisfaction of need-oriented relatives of axioms prominent in poverty measurement; and we have a critical eye on the proposals of Jasso and Miller. The empirical part reports on three vignette studies conducted to find out how people evaluate the justice of given distributions and how they distribute goods when aiming at justice. The main goal was to measure the significance ascribed to need. This significance was compared with the significance ascribed to effort or equality; and it was shown that a need's influence decreases when the corresponding person is accountable for having a higher amount of it. In the third study, we found out that needs that are not directed at bare survival, such as the need for participation in social life, are attributed lower degrees of importance. The chapter concludes with some implications of our research for a theory of need-based justice.

3.1 Introduction

Nullmeier (2020, p. 193) has suggested that a "theory of need-based justice should be based on the promotion of both normative and empirical research." In this chapter, the formal part (Sects. 3.2.1–3.2.3) introduces measures of need-based justice. Such measures are meant to compute how just distributions of a specific good are based on how well they satisfy the corresponding needs. Their input is, therefore, the individuals' endowments and needs, and their output is a number

A. M. Bauer · M. Siebel (✉)
Carl von Ossietzky University Oldenburg, Institute of Philosophy, Oldenburg, Germany
e-mail: alexander.max.bauer@uni-oldenburg.de; mark.siebel@uni-oldenburg.de

B. Kittel, S. Traub (eds.), *Priority of Needs?*,
https://doi.org/10.1007/978-3-031-53051-7_3

representing the distribution's degree of need-based justice. Given that need-based justice plays a central role in many theories of justice and given the enormous number of inequality measures, it is quite surprising that almost no measure of need-based justice has been proposed so far. To close this gap, we suggested three measures resting on varying notions of need-based justice. According to these measures, a distribution is unjust (i) the more it deviates from absolute need satisfaction and equal degrees of need satisfaction, (ii) the more the given undersupply could have been mitigated by transfers, and (iii) the more resources are used for oversupply instead of need satisfaction. Before introducing and comparing our measures in Sect. 3.2.2, we have a critical eye on two proposals from the literature in Sect. 3.2.1. The comparison of our measures reveals, among other things, that only two of them satisfy need-oriented relatives of axioms that are prominent in poverty measurement.

The empirical part (Sects. 3.3.1–3.3.4) reports on vignette studies that were conducted to find out how people evaluate the justice of given distributions and how they distribute goods when aiming at justice. The main goal was to measure the significance ascribed to need. Among other things, this significance was compared with the significance ascribed to effort or equality. In line with Nullmeier (2020, pp. 193–197, 206f.), need-based justice is considered a central ingredient in a pluralistic theory of justice. Furthermore, we examined whether need's influence on the outcome changes when the person with the need is accountable for their higher amount. The results underscore Nullmeier's (2020, p. 204) thesis that corrective justice may interfere with distributive justice: "Self-inflicted need gaps usually lead to punishment in the form of (partial) denial of the meeting of these needs." Finally, we measured the changing influence of different kinds of needs. Nullmeier (2020, p. 201) states that "survival cannot be the only criterion for deciding what is necessary." However, even if there are additional needs that are not directed at bare survival, it remains to be seen whether they are attributed differing degrees of importance. We were able to show, inter alia, that it makes a significant difference whether a person needs something for bare survival or for participation in social life. The chapter concludes with some implications of our research for a theory of need-based justice (Sect. 3.4).

3.2 The Formal Perspective: Measures of Need-Based Justice

Perhaps the most famous attempt to measure needs is the Human Development Index (HDI) developed in the context of the United Nations Development Programme. This measure is based on operationalizations of the capability approach (Sen 1999; Nussbaum 2011). The HDI incorporates three dimensions: health (indicator: life expectancy), education (indicators: expected and mean years of schooling), and standard of living (indicator: gross national income per capita). However, the HDI at best provides the extent to which these needs are *on average* fulfilled in a country. It disregards inequalities in need satisfaction within countries and therefore neglects the *comparative* aspect of need-based justice (see Sect. 3.2.2). Moreover, since the purpose of the HDI is to capture gross human development, its focus is quite different from ours. We are not seeking an indicator of *overall* need satisfaction but would like to determine how just distributions of a *specific* good, such as housing space, are with respect to the satisfaction of the corresponding need. The task is to compare, in a mathematical way, the parties' need for and endowments of a particular good in order to arrive at a number that represents the degree of need-based justice of the good's distribution.

For the same reason, although need is an important ingredient in social welfare orderings (Ebert 1984), equivalence scales (Ebert and Moyes 2003), the sequential Lorenz dominance criterion (Atkinson and Bourguignon 1987), and its descendants (Moyes 2012), these models can hardly be compared to the ones proposed in this chapter. The former try to cope with the fact that the well-being of a household does not only depend on its income but also on its needs, which are determined, among other things, by the household's size. Accordingly, these accounts do not consider an income distribution as equally just because every household has the same earnings, and they do not consider a household poor just because its earnings undercut a certain threshold. The measures, or orderings, of inequality and poverty attached to these accounts rather make use of "household types" as a further input that reflects a household's needs. Hence, inequality in this sense can be understood as inequality in the satisfaction of needs and thus as representing the comparative aspect of need-based justice. Again, however, these accounts are supposed to give blanket information about the satisfaction of *all* of the households' needs. By contrast, we aimed at information about the satisfaction of needs for a *specific* good.

To be as precise as possible, some notation and terminology are needed. Let there be a set $\mathbb{I}$ of n individuals. These individuals could be persons, but we may equally think of households, companies, and so forth. Each individual $i \in \mathbb{I}$ is endowed with a particular amount ω_i of a good and exhibits a certain need ν_i of that good. An individual i is undersupplied if their need is not satisfied, viz., $\omega_i < \nu_i$; they are oversupplied if $\omega_i > \nu_i$; and they receive an exact supply if $\omega_i = \nu_i$. A measure of need-based justice may then be characterized as a function whose arguments are the individual endowments ω_1 to ω_n, as well as the individual needs ν_1 to ν_n, and whose values are numbers representing a degree of need-based justice (cf. Traub et al. 2017, p. 6).

The quantitative information given by a measure is chiefly called for in situations of scarcity. When the total amount of a good does not suffice to satisfy all needs, the question arises of which distribution would be the least unjust. This question cannot be answered without doing some mathematics. For even if the answer is simply that we should see to it that as many needs as possible are satisfied, the operation of addition is in play. Or consider the answer that the amount of unmet need should be minimized. This answer remains vague until it is clarified how unmet need is to be calculated. Moreover, mathematics is a helpful impetus for stating more precisely what need-based justice is, or to distinguish different kinds of need-based justice that are often conflated, thus achieving a more nuanced understanding of this topic (cf. the arguments for using graphs in Kagan 2012, p. 46).

In Sect. 3.2.1, we introduce two measures of need-based justice known from the existing literature. They have already been discussed in Siebel and Schramme (2020, pp. 42–45). In Sect. 3.2.2, we present and compare three new measures from our project that further develop the idea of need-based justice.

3.2.1 The Measures of Miller and Jasso

Need-based justice could be measured by simply counting the individuals whose needs are unsatisfied. The higher this number, the more unjust the distribution. However, this index is way too simple because it does not take into account the *extent* to which needs are unsatisfied and the *proportion* of unsatisfied needs. A distribution across ten individuals all of whose needs are almost met would be as unfair as a distribution across ten individuals who are severely undersupplied. Still more, it would make no difference if the undersupplied were joined by people who receive much more than they need. The latter shows that Sen's (1981, p. 186) focus axiom for the measurement of poverty must not be transferred to need-based justice.[1] The focus axiom states that the degree of poverty ought to be sensitive merely to changes in the poor. By contrast, need-based justice also depends on the rich, meaning the people whose needs are satisfied.

To solve this problem, a more sophisticated index may help to calculate the ratio of individuals with unsatisfied needs to the entire population of individuals. This index bears an analogy to the so-called headcount ratio, which measures poverty by the fraction of people who are below the poverty line. Frankfurt (1987, p. 31) seems to advocate it when recommending that scarce resources be distributed "in such a way that as many people as possible have enough or, in other words, to maximize the incidence of sufficiency." Just like the simple measure, however, the more sophisticated one ignores the *extent* of undersupply (cf. Casal 2007, p. 298). A distribution in which 40% lack half of what they need will be regarded just as unfair as a distribution in which 40% lack only a tiny amount. To avoid such an oversimplification, we need an account of the degree to which people are (under)supplied.

Siebel and Schramme (2020, pp. 42–45) introduced and critiqued two measures that account for degrees of need satisfaction. The first one was proposed by Miller (1999, pp. 217f.). His measure is based on the idea that the more inequality there is in unmet need, the more unjust the distribution. To mathematize unmet need, Miller suggests taking the *difference* between an individual's endowment and their need.[2] Likewise, the divergence between two unsatisfied needs is given by the difference between the corresponding need gaps, measured in absolute values. The

[1] Cf. Springhorn (2022, pp. 493f.). For an overview of poverty measures, cf. Seidl (1988).

[2] Cf. Miller (1999, p. 320, fn. 27). Surprisingly, Miller (1999, p. 221) later reformulates the underlying principle in terms of the ratio: "if my needs are half-satisfied, so should yours be."

overall injustice of a distribution is then calculated by adding up all of the need gaps. For example, if there are three households needing 90 m^2 each, and the first household receives 90 m^2 (need gap 0 m^2), the second household 60 m^2 (need gap -30 m^2), and the third household 30 m^2 (need gap -60 m^2), then the injustice is $|0\ m^2 - (-30\ m^2)| + |0\ m^2 - (-60\ m^2)| + |(-30\ m^2) - (-60\ m^2|$ and thus 120 m^2.[3]

Miller (1999, p. 219) is well aware that his measure is not without shortcomings. Firstly, it is subject to the levelling-down objection: it allows for one absurd solution in which justice can be met by decreasing endowments for all because this may equalize unmet need.[4] Moreover, oversupplied people do not enter into Miller's calculation, with the result that his index satisfies the focus axiom: the degree of need-based justice is sensitive merely to changes in the undersupplied. Finally, since Miller measures unmet need by the *difference* between what the person has and what they need, his index provides values in the unit by which the corresponding good is measured. If the good is, say, vitamin C measured in milligrams, then justice will also be measured in milligrams. This is odd in itself because milligrams do not seem to be meaningful justice units (cf. Jasso 1978, p. 1403). In addition, it has the unwelcome consequence that Miller's index is neither unit-invariant nor scale-invariant (cf. Springhorn 2022, p. 488), two axioms that are prominent in measuring poverty. That is, the values for the previous example do not stay the same if housing space is measured in square inches instead of square meters, and they change if both endowments and needs are doubled or multiplied by another number.

This does not hold for the index that can be extracted from Jasso's theory of justice.[5] According to Jasso, the degree of justice of an endowment is given by the natural logarithm of the ratio between actual endowment and just endowment. To obtain a measure of need-based justice, it immediately suggests itself to equate the just endowment with the need of the individual at hand, thereby arriving at $\ln(\omega_i/\nu_i)$. This measure emits the value 0, representing perfect justice, when endowment and need are identical; it provides negative numbers in cases of undersupply and positive numbers in cases of oversupply.

Since the logarithmic function merely provides justice values for single individuals, the question arises of how to aggregate these numbers in order to arrive at a value for a whole distribution. Jasso (1999, p. 144) discusses two candidates, the arithmetic mean of the individual degrees of justice and the arithmetic mean of their absolute values. Both accounts are problematic. The mean of the individual degrees of justice merges positive values for oversupply and negative values for

[3] In Hassoun's (2009, p. 262) view, Miller does not simply equate need-based injustice with inequality in need gaps but "adds the total amount of remaining need to this inequality to give a score for need improvement." Although Hassoun's interpretation conflicts with how Miller describes his own measure, surprisingly, Hassoun is still able to explain the injustice values assigned by Miller (1999, p. 218) when he discusses a concrete example (cf. Siebel 2017, p. 7; Siebel and Schramme 2020, pp. 43f.).

[4] Cf. the levelling-down objection to egalitarianism discussed by Nozick (1974, p. 229) and Temkin (1993, pp. 247f.).

[5] Cf., inter alia, Jasso (1978, 1980, 1990, 1999, 2007) and Jasso and Wegener (1997).

undersupply and thereby allows for unfortunate compensation. For example, a distribution exactly satisfying the needs of two persons would be as just as a distribution in which one of them gets half of what they need and the other twice as much. The mean will be the same, namely, 0, but the latter distribution is obviously not as just as the former. Although the mean of the absolute values is superior in this respect, there may be identical values regardless of whether there is only undersupply or only oversupply. For example, the injustice emerging from two individuals endowed with half of what they need is identical to the injustice of two individuals possessing twice as much (cf. Springhorn 2022, p. 477).

A further disadvantage of Jasso's measure is that it does not only treat *under*supply as unjust but also *over*supply. Thereby, it implements one of the four basic principles of need-based justice distinguished by Siebel and Schramme (2020, pp. 38–42). Two of these principles can be traced back to Plato's *Republic*, where we find a forerunner of the phrase "To each their own" (cf. Plato 1973, 433e–434a, 433a). An application of this idea to distributions suggests that everyone should receive what is due to them. To obtain a conception of *need*-based justice, we may again equate these legitimate endowments with the *needs* of the recipients. Following this idea, everyone receives their own if everyone receives what they need.

However, the slogan "To each what they need" is still ambiguous. It could mean that neither more nor less is allowed such that all deviations from exact satisfaction of needs, i.e., both undersupply and oversupply, are unjust. On the other hand, the slogan could be understood as saying that only undersupply is unfair because the crucial point is that no one receives *less* than they need. Anyway, under both interpretations the slogan is purely qualitative in merely stating under which conditions a distribution is just or not. But we can sift out relative principles at least, viz., principles establishing which of two distributions is more unjust. In the notation introduced beforehand, the two variants of the Platonic conception read as follows:

- (PC1) A distribution among the individuals in a set $\mathbb{I}$ is just with respect to needs if and only if $\omega_i = \nu_i$ for all $i \in \mathbb{I}$; and it is increasingly unjust the more the ω_i lie below or above the corresponding ν_i.
- (PC2) A distribution among the individuals in a set $\mathbb{I}$ is just with respect to needs if and only if $\omega_i \geq \nu_i$ for all $i \in \mathbb{I}$; and it is increasingly unjust the more the ω_i lie below the corresponding ν_i.

These principles are *noncomparative* in the sense of Feinberg's (1974, p. 300) "Noncomparative Justice": "When our task is to do noncomparative justice to each of a large number of individuals, we do not compare them with each other, but rather we compare each in turn with an objective standard and judge each (as we say) 'on his merits.'" Laying aside the question of whether needs are *objective* standards, this is exactly what we do when we apply (PC1) or (PC2). For each individual, we make an isolated comparison of its endowment with its need, and we declare the whole distribution just if these individual comparisons turn out all right.

The measure derived from Jasso's theory of justice conforms to (PC1) because it condemns both undersupply and oversupply as unjust.[6] Pointing in the same direction, Kagan (2012, pp. 82f.) argues in *The Geometry of Desert* that there is a level of well-being beyond which people do not deserve more because no one deserves unlimited well-being. But Kagan is concerned with desert, and it seems that need is different in this respect. Needs are not marks for precision landing but minimal requirements. Exceeding them leads to injustice if there remain undersupplied parties. It may also lead to injustice if the oversupply of some parties is greater than the oversupply of others. But this does not imply that universal oversupply necessarily generates injustice.[7] Otherwise, the land of milk and honey would be unfair just because everyone has more than they need.

Analogous difficulties affect Robeyns' (2017, p. 2) limitarianism, according to which "it is not morally permissible to have more resources than are needed to fully flourishing [sic] in life." Fully flourishing in life might be a more ambitious goal than satisfaction of needs. But exceeding this ambitious goal also appears to be unjust only if there are some people who are not able to fully flourish in life and possibly if the surplus is unequally distributed. Excess by itself does not seem to generate injustice. All in all, (PC2) appears to be more appropriate than (PC1), at least when we remain with noncomparative justice.

3.2.2 *The Measures of Siebel, Springhorn, and Traub and Colleagues*

The main impetus of Siebel's account is that a measure of need-based justice ought not to be based solely on a Platonic principle precisely because these principles merely capture the *noncomparative* element of need-based justice.[8] Consider two households, both needing 120 m^2 of living space. In the first distribution one household receives 360 m^2, while the other receives 60 m^2; in the second distribution the first household receives 120 m^2, while the latter household again receives 60 m^2. Then (PC2) correctly stigmatizes both distributions as unjust because household 2 has only half of what it needs. However, there is a further injustice concerning needs not registered by (PC2). Household 1 is massively oversupplied in the first scenario and supplied exactly in accordance with its needs in the second. Hence, in the first scenario, household 1 would suffer no serious harm if it passed 60 m^2 to household 2 in order to satisfy the latter's need. In the second scenario, by contrast, even a small transfer would result in household 1 being undersupplied. The first distribution, therefore, seems to be more unjust than the second one. The Platonic conception is not able to reproduce this line of reasoning because exact supply is

[6] Another example is to be found in Bauer (2022).

[7] Cf. Feinberg (1974, p. 306), Kagan (2012, pp. 179f.), Nullmeier (2020, p. 203).

[8] An initial version of Siebel's measure is to be found in the working paper Siebel (2017).

attributed the same influence on justice as extreme oversupply, and this holds even when there are undersupplied individuals.

For this reason, Siebel adds a *comparative* element, which can be found in Aristotle. In book V of the *Nicomachean Ethics*, Aristotle (2009, pp. 84f.) presents his famous proportionality conception of justice:

> The just, then, is a species of the proportionate [...]. For proportion is equality of ratios, and involves four terms at least [...]; and the just, too, involves at least four terms, and the ratio between one pair is the same as that between the other pair; for there is a similar distinction between the persons and between the things. As the term A, then, is to B, so will C be to D, and therefore, alternando, as A is to C, B will be to D.

The "things" are the actual endowments of the persons. Aristotle is thus saying that a distribution is just if the ratio between these endowments is identical to the ratio between the "persons." But what does the latter mean? Let us assume that Aristotle is talking here about what the persons *should* receive. Then a distribution among two persons is just if the ratio between what one person receives and what she should receive is identical to the ratio between what the other person receives and what she should receive. In other words, we are to ensure equal ratios between actual and legitimate endowments in order that no one has an advantage over the other.[9]

Again, we obtain a conception of *need*-based justice if we equate the legitimate endowments with the *needs* of the recipients. This specification results in the following principle:

- (AC1) A distribution among the individuals in a set $\mathbb{I}$ is just with respect to needs if and only if the ratio ω_i / ν_i is the same for all $i \in \mathbb{I}$; and it is increasingly unjust the more the ratios ω_i / ν_i diverge.

If there are two families, one of them requiring 120 m^2 of housing space and the other one 90 m^2, then endowing both with 60 m^2 is unfair according to (AC1). For the first family has to make do with half of what it needs, whereas the second family gets at least two-thirds and thus has a relative advantage. According to Feinberg (1974, p. 299), "[a]ll comparative justice involves, in one way or another, equality in the treatment accorded all the members of a class." The Aristotelian conception is comparative in this sense because it requires equality of need satisfaction, the latter being attained if all ratios between endowments and needs are identical.

According to Nullmeier (2020, pp. 202f.), such principles exceed a "monistic theory of need-based justice" because "the principle of need is combined with a second principle," which is in this case "proportionality." But this would mean that a theory stating that a distribution is more just the more needs are satisfied is not monistic either because it includes a second criterion of justice, namely, headcount. We rather propose taking proportionality as the *mathematical* part of (AC1), while the *name-giving* part is (AC1)'s focus on needs. A theory stating that goods should

[9] Aristotle's conception of distributive justice was applied by sociologists as early as the 1950s (cf. Sayles 1958, Homans 1961, Patchen 1961, Adams 1965, Walster et al. 1976).

be distributed in proportion to effort contains the same mathematical formula but will be called "effort-based" because it focuses on effort.

(AC1) determines that goods should be distributed in proportion to needs not only under but also above the threshold. By analogy with the Platonic conception (PC2), however, one could argue as follows. If all needs are met, then other principles, such as desert or equality, might see to it that a distribution is unjust, but there is nothing to complain about from the perspective of need-based justice (cf. Woozley 1973, p. 34). The corresponding variant of the Aristotelian conception states:

- (AC2) A distribution among the individuals in a set $\mathbb{I}$ is just with respect to needs if and only if either $\omega_i \geq \nu_i$ for all $i \in \mathbb{I}$ or the ratio ω_i / ν_i is the same for all $i \in \mathbb{I}$; and it is increasingly unjust in the second case the more the ratios ω_i / ν_i diverge.

Whereas it seems quite clear that the Platonic variant (PC2) is to be preferred over (PC1), there is no obvious choice among the Aristotelian variants. Strong sufficientarians, such as Frankfurt (1987, p. 21), will endorse (AC2) because they do not only hold the positive thesis that people must have enough to live a decent life but also the negative thesis that "if everyone had enough, it would be of no moral consequence whether some had more than others" (cf. Casal 2007, for a critique). In contrast, Feinberg (1974, p. 315) points out that comparative considerations may still play a role if all parties are well provided for. He suggests that noncomparative justice is *more serious* because not getting what one needs is worse than being oversupplied to a smaller degree than others (cf. Feinberg 1974, p. 317). But this does not entail that different levels of oversupply have *no* influence on need-based justice. Among other things, they seem unfair if they result in different increases in well-being. Let there be a single household needing 60 m^2 and a family needing 120 m^2, as well as space of more than 180 m^2 to be distributed. Presumably, a fifty-fifty divide of the surplus would give undue preference to the single person insofar as the per-person increase in comfort is higher. It therefore appears fairer to follow (AC1) by dividing the surplus in proportion to the households' needs.

The Aristotelian principles (AC1) and (AC2) are both able to discriminate between the cases that were problematic for the Platonic conceptions. Nonetheless, taken by themselves they are insufficient because they only take into account how much the ratios of endowments to needs resemble each other and thereby ignore the noncomparative issue of whether needs are satisfied in the first place. Hence, even if the households in question have to live in flats all too small, a distribution is just according to both variants of Aristotle's conception if all of them have only half of what they require.[10] If there is no more housing space available, such a distribution may be called "as fair as possible given the circumstances." But this should be understood as saying that the distribution is the least unjust.

Siebel's "Plaristonic" approach thus consists in merging a Platonic with an Aristotelian principle. To keep the first attempt short and simple, he suggests combining

[10] Cf. Feinberg (1974, p. 300), Jasso (1978, p. 1402), and Miller (2007, p. 9).

(PC2) with (AC1). The underlying idea is that need-based *justice* consists in need *satisfaction* complying with the ideals prescribed by these principles. The Platonic part states that needs are to be met. But need-based justice does not exhaust itself with need satisfaction because, in line with Aristotelian principles, it also includes equal levels of need satisfaction. That is, Siebel is not only interested in whether all parties have their needs met but whether what they receive is able to fulfil their needs to the same extent.

To convert this qualitative account into a measure, Siebel suggests implementing the simple idea that a distribution is increasingly unjust the more the actual levels of need satisfaction diverge from the ideal levels. To be more precise, a distribution is increasingly unjust the more divergence there is from satisfied needs (the Platonic ideal) and from equal degrees of need satisfaction (the Aristotelian ideal). The general recipe for such a measure reads as follows:

1. We need a function S_i for measuring to what extent an individual i's need is satisfied. The arguments of this function are i's endowment ω_i and its need ν_i.
2. Given the measure of need satisfaction, we have to determine to what extent the needs of the individuals should be satisfied according to the Platonic and the Aristotelian ideals.
3. The next step is to find functions PD_i and AD_i to measure how much an individual's actual degree of need satisfaction diverges from the degrees advocated by the given ideals. The arguments of these functions are the values of S_i and the ideal degrees from (2).
4. The numbers obtained in step (3) tell us how much *individual* degrees of need satisfaction diverge from the ideals. Since we are concerned with distributions among at least two individuals, we have to specify the divergence within the whole group. In other words, we need aggregation functions PD and AD for the *overall* divergence from the Aristotelian and the Platonic ideals. The arguments are the values of PD_i and AD_i, i.e., the individual divergences.
5. Finally, to combine both kinds of deviation, a function is needed to bring together the values of PD and AD. Since its output is the overall deviation from both ideals, this function constitutes the Plaristonic measure of need-based justice.

Having completed our introduction of Siebel's index, we will next present Springhorn's approach.[11] His index differs from the others developed in our project insofar as it is located at the individual level. This does not mean that, like Jasso's measure, it assigns an individual a justice value merely on the basis of *their* endowment and need. Rather, it assigns justice values to individuals on the basis of the endowments and needs of *all* parties involved.

The core thesis behind Springhorn's index is that undersupply is increasingly unjust the more it could have been mitigated by transfers. That is, while receiving more than needed is never unjust, receiving less than needed is unfair if there is

[11] An initial version of this index was presented in the working paper Springhorn (2017) and the final version in Springhorn (2022).

an opportunity to increase the endowment by taking something from other parties. Note that this idea has two remarkable consequences. First of all, if an individual is undersupplied but the others have nothing to donate, the undersupply will not be unjust because it cannot be mitigated (cf. Springhorn 2022, pp. 482, 484f.). This is clearly at odds with the Platonic principles mentioned in the previous section. For these principles the rule that having less than needed is invariably unjust, no matter whether others can help or not. Furthermore, undersupply is unjust on Springhorn's account even if the other parties are worse off than the individual in question. Hence, Springhorn leaves out whether mitigation of undersupply occurs at the cost of a worse off individual.

Another consequence of Springhorn's core thesis is that, in contrast to the Aristotelian principles, identical degrees of need satisfaction do not necessarily lead to justice. Consider two households possessing only half of the income they need. If there are no other households with income, it is, of course, not possible to simultaneously improve the situation of both households. However, since the situation for each individual household can be improved by transferring money from the other household, the conditions of both would be considered unjust according to Springhorn's measure.

Springhorn (2022, pp. 490f.) presents his index as emerging in five steps. We describe it in four steps of a slightly different order because this seems easier to relate to. Firstly, like Siebel, Springhorn takes the ratio of endowment and need, ω_i/ν_i, to represent individual degrees of need satisfaction. Secondly, he prefixes Jasso's logarithm in order to guarantee a certain type of sensitivity that will be explained when we come to differences between the measures. Thirdly, he multiplies the logarithm by the ratio of the total endowment to the total need of the other individuals involved in the distribution. In this way, undersupply is weighted by the opportunity to mitigate it, where the latter is given by the percentage to which the needs of the other parties are satisfiable on average. For example, if there is a surplus, then the injustice assigned to the undersupply of the individual in question is greater the higher the surplus. If there is scarcity, then the injustice decreases with increasing scarcity. Fourthly, since Springhorn wants all cases of oversupply to be judged in the same way as exact supply, namely, as being just, he makes use of the minimum of the value described and 0.

Although Springhorn's formula measures the injustice of individual endowments, there is an outlook on the justice of whole distributions (cf. Springhorn 2022, pp. 492f.). To aggregate single values, one could simply use their arithmetic mean. In contrast to Jasso's account, this does not lead to the unfortunate compensation of undersupply by oversupply because a single individual that has less than they need generates injustice. However, Springhorn also points to an effect he views as a disadvantage. When the endowment of an undersupplied party rises, the injustice of the whole distribution is not automatically reduced. The reason is that, while the injustice for this individual will be smaller, the injustice for all other undersupplied parties will be greater because the possibility of upgrading them increases.

Finally, we come to Traub et al.'s index. Their considerations are similar to Springhorn's proposition that undersupply is increasingly unjust the more it could have been mitigated by transfers. The measure by Traub et al. assumes that a distribution is increasingly unjust the more resources are used for oversupply instead of need satisfaction, or in short, the more it is inefficient (cf. Traub et al. 2017, pp. 8–10).

The starting point of Traub et al. is the same as for the other indices, namely, a measure of need satisfaction. However, there are two deviations from the former accounts. Firstly, corresponding to poverty measurement, which assumes a common poverty line, Traub states that the individuals have identical needs ν. If there are differences between them resulting in differing needs, these are to be factored in by an equivalence scale that adjusts endowments. Secondly, Traub and colleagues do not use the ratio ω_i/ν_i, but the minimum of this ratio and 1. The reason is that they want to avoid varying degrees of oversupply. If an individual's endowment ω_i is greater than the common need ν, the minimum sees to it that need satisfaction does not exceed 1. Accordingly, no matter whether an individual's endowment is equal to their need, slightly greater, or significantly greater, the degree of need satisfaction is always 1 (cf. Traub et al. 2017, p. 5).

The next step consists of defining the "allocation efficiency" of a distribution, which depends on two factors. One of them is the aggregate surplus L, i.e., the sum of the differences between the endowments and needs of the oversupplied parties. The other one is the overall endowment Ω, i.e., the sum of all endowments. Roughly, the allocation efficiency is given by $1 - L/\Omega$. The more surplus there is in relation to the overall endowment, the less efficient the distribution is because a higher percentage of the resources is not used for meeting needs. The maximum efficiency 1 is reached when there is no oversupply, meaning that L is 0 (cf. Traub et al. 2017, pp. 5f.).

The index Traub et al. favor characterizes injustice as depending on three factors. The degree of injustice is greater (i) the smaller the efficiency, (ii) the fewer supplied parties there are, and (iii) the smaller the need satisfaction of the undersupplied parties. Traub et al. conclude with proofs showing that this index satisfies certain axioms, as well as numerical examples illustrating the characteristics of the index (cf. Traub et al. 2017, pp. 10–14).

Having introduced the three measures developed in our project, we draw a brief comparison between them starting with some similarities.

Similarity 1: In the background of all of the measures, there is a clear distinction between need-based *justice* and need *satisfaction*. That is, our measures do not equate these quantities by simply taking a distribution to be increasingly unjust when fewer needs are met. Rather, they avoid such an oversimplification by regarding need-based justice as somewhat dependent on need satisfaction, but not identical to it (cf. Springhorn 2022, pp. 477–480).

Similarity 2: A further common feature is that measurement of need satisfaction is based on Aristotle's ratio of endowment to need.[12] Of course, while Siebel and

[12] In the preliminary version, Siebel (2017, pp. 11f.) makes use of Jasso's logarithm (cf. Springhorn 2022, p. 474, fn. 3). This choice is critiqued by Miller (2020, p. 289).

Springhorn just take ω_i/ν_i, Traub et al. use the minimum of this ratio and 1 in order to avoid differing degrees of oversupply. But this difference is less significant than the ones we find when comparing the ratio with the other proposals on the table, namely, Jasso's logarithm of this ratio, $\ln(\omega_i/\nu_i)$, and Miller's difference of endowment and need, $\omega_i - \nu_i$.[13]

A key advantage of Aristotle's and Jasso's accounts is that, unlike Miller's, they are unit-invariant and scale-invariant. However, in contrast to Aristotle's ratio, Jasso's logarithm of this ratio is subject to at least three difficulties. First of all, it introduces an evaluation that could be seen as inappropriate in this context. Since the logarithm is a nonlinear function, undersupply automatically carries greater weight than oversupply of equal absolute value. For example, giving a family 20 m^2 less than its need of 100 m^2 results in a higher deviation from the value for exact need satisfaction than giving 20 m^2 more. It might make sense to say that the undersupply is more unjust than the oversupply, but it is odd to say that the undersupply itself, i.e., its extent, is greater than the oversupply. Moreover, the logarithm is not defined for 0. Hence, endowments of 0 are either not allowed or must be captured by the limit $\ln(\omega_i/\nu_i)$ strives towards when ω_i is getting smaller, i.e., $-\infty$. But then zero endowments gain an overwhelming influence. Finally, in contrast to the logarithm of the ratio, the pure ratio allows for an intuitively accessible interpretation because it provides a percentage to express the extent to which the given need is satisfied. For example, 0.8 means that 80% of the need is satisfied and 1.2 means that 120% of the need is satisfied.

Kagan (2012) warns against using the ratio within a theory of desert. His belief is that comparative desert is achieved when the ratios of well-being to virtue are identical. However, two of his arguments are based on *negative* numbers for levels of well-being and virtue.[14] They are thus not applicable to need-based justice because there exist neither negative endowments nor negative needs. But Kagan (2012, p. 356) also points to difficulties arising from *zero* levels of virtue, and these difficulties *are* transferable. The ratio between endowment and need is inappropriate if an individual has no need for the given good because division by 0 is not allowed. Hence, the following considerations are restricted to scenarios in which every party needs at least a small amount of the good in question. This is an innocent constraint because individuals without need do not matter when we are interested in need-based justice.

Similarity 3: In Sect. 2.1, we already pointed out that an index of need-based justice differs from a poverty index by not being subject to the focus axiom. That is, changes in the income of the rich, as far as they do not result in poverty, should not have an influence on how poor a society is. In contrast, changes in the endowments of people whose needs are satisfied can have an influence on need-based justice even

[13] While we are concerned here with need *satisfaction*, Eriksson (2012) examines which of these measures better fits experimental data on *justice* evaluations.

[14] Cf. Kagan (2012, pp. 355, 357), and Walster et al. (1976, pp. 3f.). The latter have also pointed out that equality of ratios can lead to absurd results when negative quantities are allowed.

when they do not result in undersupply. The indices developed in our project have this insight in common. As we will see below, however, they differ with respect to other axioms from poverty measurements.

Similarity 4: The final commonality is that the indices in question have a maximum representing justice, while smaller numbers represent degrees of injustice. The maximum of Siebel's and Springhorn's measure is 0, the measure by Traub et al. has a maximum of 1. Feinberg (1974, p. 297) wrote the following in a footnote of "Noncomparative Justice":

> As many writers have observed, it is much more convenient, when doing moral philosophy, to speak of injustice than to keep to the positive term, justice. That greater convenience is an undeniable fact, but I shall not speculate here whether it has any theoretical significance.

We think it has theoretical significance. There are clearly different degrees of *injustice*, and we refer to them by saying, e.g., that a distribution is "more," "less," "only slightly," or "highly unjust." But such gradations, taken literally, hardly make sense in the case of *justice* because a distribution cannot be more just than just. Of course, we use formulations such as "This is more just" or "This is less just." A closer look reveals, though, that "more just" means *less unjust* and "less just" means *more unjust*. The negative term "injustice" is thus more convenient than the positive term "justice" because it allows for gradations to be taken literally. We will now turn to the important differences.

Difference 1: Above all, the measures are grounded in different conceptions of need-based justice. To put these conceptions in a nutshell:

- *Siebel:* A distribution is increasingly unjust the more it deviates from absolute need satisfaction and equal degrees of need satisfaction.
- *Springhorn:* A distribution is increasingly unjust the more the given undersupply could have been mitigated by transfers.
- *Traub and colleagues:* A distribution is increasingly unjust the more resources are used for oversupply instead of need satisfaction.

Since the underlying conceptions are different, it is no surprise that the corresponding measures display differences in their specific properties.

Difference 2: For a quite essential difference, Siebel's account differs from those of Springhorn as well as Traub et al. in not satisfying further analogues to poverty axioms besides the focus axiom. For example, Springhorn (2022, pp. 487f., 500) and Traub et al. (2017, pp. 7f., 10f.) prove that their measures show *monotonicity* in endowments. Roughly, if an undersupplied individual receives a larger amount of the good, then injustice decreases; if the endowment decreases, injustice increases. There is also *sensitivity* in endowments. Among other things, when the endowment of an undersupplied individual is increased by a fixed amount, then the decrease in injustice is greater the larger the initial undersupply of the individual.[15] Consider two households, both needing 120 m^2 of living space. While one of them owns 90 m^2, the other one owns only 60 m^2. If the living space of both households is raised by 15 m^2, injustice diminishes more drastically in the case of the second household because 15 m^2 is a larger proportion of 60 m^2 than of 90 m^2.

The Platonic part of Siebel's measure is monotonic. When the endowment of an undersupplied individual grows, then this part registers less injustice because there is a larger amount of need satisfaction. However, since the Aristotelian part requires identical degrees of need satisfaction, it can happen that overall injustice increases when an undersupplied individual receives more. Although the distribution converges to the Platonic ideal of full need satisfaction, it might have reached a point at which it diverges too much from the Aristotelian ideal of equal need satisfaction (cf. Springhorn 2022, p. 489). For the same reason, sensitivity does not generally hold. Raising the endowment of a worse-off individual can result in a smaller decrease in injustice than raising the endowment of an individual who is better off because the resulting disparity in need satisfaction becomes larger.

Difference 3: A less essential variation is that, whereas Siebel's and Springhorn's indices have no minimum, the index by Traub et al. has one, namely, 0, representing the highest degree of injustice (cf. Traub et al. 2017, p. 6). The minimum is reached when all parties involved receive nothing (cf. Traub et al. 2017, p. 10). Springhorn's measure does not provide a value in this case because the logarithm $\ln(\omega_i/\nu_i)$ is not defined if ω_i is 0. It remains to be discussed whether a minimum makes sense. After all, one could argue that injustice further increases when one party receives nothing while the other one's oversupply increases. The Aristotelian principle (AC1) supports this concern.

Difference 4: The previous variation is connected with a more serious one concerning the treatment of all-embracing oversupply. When everyone has what they need, the measures of Springhorn (2022, p. 492) and Traub et al. (2017, p. 6) provide the maximum value independently of how much each endowment exceeds the need threshold. In other words, the *comparative* dimension of need-based justice does not matter in situations of overall abundance. The argument is that there may still be a reason to complain of injustice when all needs are met, but such a reason is not grounded in need but in a different principle of justice, such as effort or equality. Thus considered, need-based justice is one of the ingredients in a *pluralistic* theory of justice. For example, a pluralistic theory might combine need and effort by ruling that a distribution is just when all needs are satisfied and the surplus, if there is one, is distributed in proportion to effort (cf. Boulding 1962, p. 83).

In connection with the Aristotelian principles (AC1) and (AC2), however, we have seen that there is also reason for thinking that different degrees of oversupply may generate injustice. For when a surplus is redistributed, the well-being of the

[15] The sensitivity axiom shows some resemblance to the "Priority View" supported by Parfit (1997, p. 213) and Crisp (2003, p. 751). Regarding axioms of monotonicity and sensitivity for need-based justice, see Bauer (2019).

involved parties may increase in proportion to their need threshold. For example, if there is a single person and a family, it seems unfair to equally distribute excess living space among them because the comfort of the single person will be boosted to a higher degree. Rather, the one-person household should get less than the family. But this would mean that comparative considerations on need, e.g., equal degrees of need satisfaction, still play a role in situations of abundance (cf. Feinberg 1974, pp. 315–317), which is captured by Siebel's measure.

3.2.3 Summary

Although need-based justice is an important kind of distributive justice, there exist hardly any measures of how just distributions of a specific good are with respect to satisfaction of the corresponding needs. To fill this gap, we proposed three indices of need-based justice that implement diverse ideas and therefore have different features. After considering and critiquing two further measures proposed in the literature, we compared these indices in Sect. 3.2.2.

Future research could merge the formal perspective and the empirical perspective we are about to present in the following sections by testing the empirical adequacy of measures of need-based justice, that is, by comparing them with empirically found evaluations of need-based justice. To take a single example, Springhorn's measure significantly differs from the ones by Siebel and Traub et al. in letting an individual's undersupply be just if it cannot be mitigated by transfers because the other parties do not possess any amount of the good in question. Hence, one could think about studies in which vignettes of such scenarios are introduced in order to examine whether subjects deem undersupply just in these cases. Furthermore, different measures may compete with each other in terms of how well they mirror the justice evaluations and distributive decisions of participants in empirical studies. To this end, we need scenarios in which the competing measures give clearly different verdicts.

Whatever the result of such research may be, it will be in line with Nullmeier's (2020, p. 193) proposition that, "[p]rogress in the field of need-based justice can only fruitfully take place in the mode of an empirically enlightened normative theory and a normatively informed positive theory."

3.3 The Empirical Perspective: Studies on Need-Based Justice

In the following, we introduce three empirical studies. The first one (Sect. 3.3.1) examines how laypeople's evaluations of distributive situations are influenced by information about need and especially a need threshold. The second study

(Sect. 3.3.2) reviews third-party distributive decisions and how they are affected by information about need, effort, and accountability. The final study (Sect. 3.3.3) investigates how participants evaluate different kinds of needs and how these influence third-party distributive decisions.

3.3.1 Needs as Reference Points

If people consider need as an important distributive principle, then there should be a connection between the extent of need satisfaction following a distribution and how just that distribution is perceived to be. With the study presented in this section, we took a first step to find out more about this connection.[16]

We assume that people do not think of a distribution in purely binary terms, i.e., as just or unjust, but also make more fine-grained differentiations concerning the distribution's *degree* of justice. The corresponding justice evaluation function may be assumed to be monotonically increasing with respect to a person's endowment: the more a person receives, the more need-based justice there is (contrast Sect. 3.2.2). But how about the function's other properties? For example, what influence does a need threshold—the point of perfectly met need—exert on it? How does the function behave below, above, and at such a need threshold? Different theories of distributive justice, such as prioritarianism, sufficientarianism, and utilitarianism, would make different predictions. We investigated laypeople's justice evaluations to shed some light on their justice evaluation functions and how they are influenced by such a threshold.

For that purpose, we designed a vignette study with two between-subjects treatments, one of which referenced need while the other did not. The aim was to compare subjects' justice evaluations regarding a set of hypothetical distributive situations presented to them. In the *Need Treatment*, subjects were asked to imagine that it would be the state's obligation to meet people's need for housing. The need we introduced was an amount of living space (1000 fictive units per household) that people of the region in question consider necessary for a decent life. In conformity with Nullmeier's (2020, pp. 191–193) first thesis, we thus presented need as an intersubjectively acknowledged amount of some good that is required to live in decency. To free the evaluations from comparative considerations, we further told participants that households are basically identical and will receive the same amount of living space. In the *No-Need Treatment*, everything was exactly the same aside from the fact that we left out all information concerning need.

One hundred nine people participated in this study, mostly students of various disciplines with a median age of 25 years and roughly an equal distribution of

[16] This study was first published as a working paper (Weiss et al. 2017). A strongly revised version can be found in the working paper Bauer et al. (2023b). Parts of the data have also been analyzed in a working paper by Bauer (2018), which was later published as Bauer (2019).

gender. They were shown a total of 11 scenarios in which different amounts of living space are provided, ranging from nothing up to 2000 units, and increased in increments of 200 units. In between-subjects treatments, our participants saw either the vignette of the Need or the No-Need Treatment. They were then presented with two different tasks, a *Global Rating Task* and a *Relative Rating Task*. In the former, subjects were shown all 11 scenarios below each other on a single screen. Next to every scenario, a slider was available to rate the scenario's justice on a scale from 0% ("not at all just") to 100% ("perfectly just"). This is akin to methods from psychometrics, welfare economics, and sociological justice research. In the Relative Rating Task, participants were presented with pairs of scenarios that are adjacent in terms of living space (i.e., 0 and 200 units, 200 and 400 units, and so forth). In this task, they rated the difference in justice between the two scenarios on an 11-point scale, i.e., how much more just one scenario is than the other, ranging from 1 ("equally (un)just") to 11 ("much more just").

Figure 3.1 depicts the mean justice evaluations, as well as their 95% confidence intervals, for the Global Rating Task and both treatments on a [0, 1] scale in dependence of units of living space (0, 200, 400, and so forth). In the No-Need Treatment, justice evaluations seem to rise nearly linearly with increasing units of space. In the Need Treatment, however, there is a clearly visible jump in the evaluations at the need threshold of 1000 units. Moreover, evaluations of endowments below the threshold are (except for the case of 0 units) significantly lower in the Need Treatment compared to the No-Need Treatment. At and above the threshold, they are (except for the cases of 1600 units or more) significantly higher.

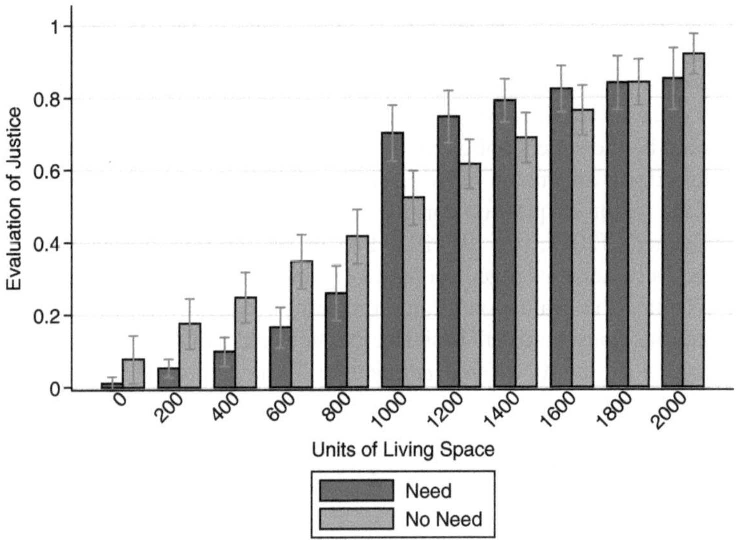

Data source: Weiss et al. (2017).

Fig. 3.1 Mean justice evaluations in the Global Rating Task by treatment

These features are further supported by the Relative Rating Task. Pairwise justice comparisons on the 11-point scale meander around 3 and 4 points in the No-Need Treatment. In the Need Treatment, comparisons below the threshold result in relatively low increases of justice ratings, namely, about 1 or 2 points, which are also significantly lower than in the No-Need Treatment (except for the comparison of 600 and 800 units). Ratings increase steeply, viz., by 7 points, when the need threshold is met. Ratings in the Need Treatment are also significantly higher than in the No-Need Treatment. Above the threshold, the pairwise comparisons result in ratings of about 3 to 5 points with no notable difference between treatments.

Hence, information about a need threshold leads to a *sigmoid* justice evaluation function: below the need threshold it is convex; above the threshold it is concave. Note that the convexity of the function below the threshold raises an ethical problem, for it would mean that injustice can be reduced to a greater amount by helping those who have only slightly less than they need than by helping those who have the least. The corresponding precept would violate the "Priority View": "benefiting people matters more the worse off these people are" (Crisp 2003, p. 751). We are thus confronted with a clash between normative and positive theory (cf. Nullmeier 2020, p. 193).

A result that does not violate normative theory is that introducing a need threshold, besides changing the shape of the justice evaluation function, also leads to *converging* evaluations. After all, the panel-level standard deviation is significantly lower in the Need Treatment compared to the No-Need Treatment. This points to the possibility that need as a criterion for distributive justice might be helpful in reaching a normative consensus because it generates more coherence among evaluations.

A closer look at the individual justice ratings reveals that our participants show quite diverse patterns. Apparently, there is no universal tendency in judging the different scenarios but five distinct types. In the Need Treatment, the evaluation function of eight subjects is hump-shaped, reaching a maximum at or somewhat above the need threshold before starting to decline again, indicating that they consider oversupply to be unfair. We call this *strict sufficientarianism*. Another four subjects show binary evaluations, i.e., evaluations that are (close to) 0 for scenarios with undersupply and 1 for scenarios with supply or oversupply. Hence, those participants seem to consider distributive justice not as a gradual matter; undersupply is equally unjust, no matter the degree. This way of distinguishing between insufficient and sufficient endowments we call *qualitative sufficientarianism*. The evaluations of seven further participants increase with units of living space below the need threshold, reaching a maximum of 1 when arriving at the threshold, and then remaining at 1 for scenarios of oversupply. Since there is a differentiation between degrees of unjust insufficiency, this is called *quantitative sufficientarianism* by us. Contrary to this, 16 subjects evaluate scenarios with undersupply as equally unjust, while their evaluations increase at and above the threshold. We dub this evaluation of undersupply *strict prioritarianism*. Finally, the ratings of another 17 subjects rise with increasing units of living space, which we term *utilitarianism*.

In the No-Need Treatment, the picture is less heterogeneous. A clear majority shows an increasing justice evaluation function: more living space is perceived as more just. Hence, utilitarian concerns appear to dominate this treatment. Interestingly enough, however, we can observe some instances of the other types as well. It seems that, even without information on need, 1000 units of living space served as a reference point in some cases, perhaps simply because it was exactly half of the maximum amount.

To sum up, information about need is highly relevant to evaluating distributive justice. However, in our study, we found quite different patterns of evaluations. The analysis of individual justice ratings showed that a large proportion of the subjects can be assigned to one of three justice types: sufficientarianism, prioritarianism, or utilitarianism. Whether using need thresholds as reference points is desirable from a normative point of view is up for discussion. Focusing on those who are already close to a certain threshold might lead to the neglect of those who are farthest away and therefore are the more needy.

3.3.2 Need and Accountability

Our first study has shown that information on need clearly influences justice evaluations. In the next study, we turn to subjects as impartial decision-makers.[17] They were shown a vignette in which we asked them to imagine two hypothetical persons. The persons' homes are heated with firewood, and each has enough to survive the coming winter. Additional wood is needed, however, to avoid feeling cold. To ensure this, the community they live in permits them to cut wood in the community forest. Since the persons are short of money, this is their only means of getting the needed firewood. Our subjects' task was to distribute the chopped wood among the two persons in a way they think is most just.

While, without any further information, an equal allocation of resources might be the logical default, we introduced factors that differentiate person A from B and could thus justify unequal distributions of firewood. They were presented as heterogeneous regarding (i) their *need*, i.e., the quantity of firewood necessary to avoid feeling cold; (ii) their *productivity*, i.e., the quantity of firewood chopped; and (iii) their *accountability*, i.e., whether they are responsible for their greater need or having chopped less than the other.

The variations in need and productivity were implemented on the within-subjects level. The cases were split into two scenarios presented to each subject in a randomized order. In the *Need Scenario*, both persons have chopped an equal amount of wood across all cases but experience different quantities of need. In the *Productivity Scenario*, they have the same need but have chopped different amounts

[17] This study was first introduced as a working paper (Bauer et al. 2020) and was later published as Bauer et al. (2022).

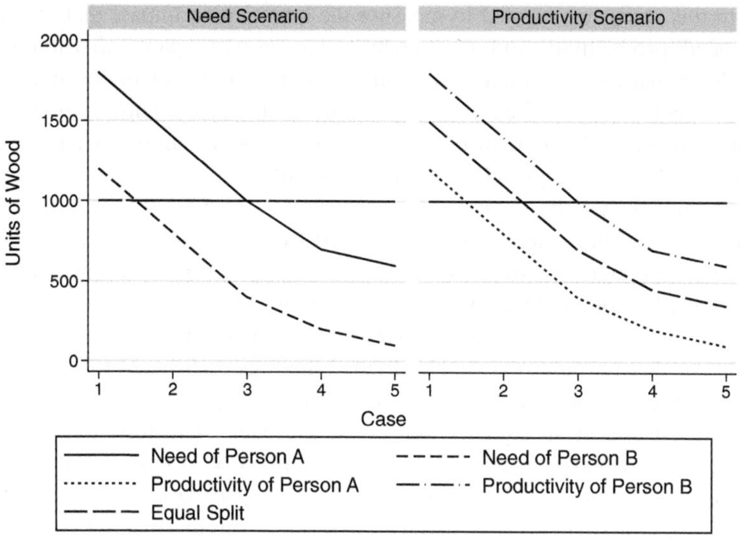

Source: Based on Bauer et al. (2020).

Fig. 3.2 Parametrization by scenario and case

Table 3.1 Parametrization by scenario and case

	Need scenario					Productivity scenario				
Case	1	2	3	4	5	1	2	3	4	5
Need A	1800	1400	1000	700	600	1000	1000	1000	1000	1000
Need B	1200	800	400	200	100	1000	1000	1000	1000	1000
Productivity A	1000	1000	1000	1000	1000	1200	800	400	200	100
Productivity B	1000	1000	1000	1000	1000	1800	1400	1000	700	600
Equal split	1000	1000	1000	1000	1000	1500	1100	700	450	350
Productivity share A	0.50	0.50	0.50	0.50	0.50	0.40	0.36	0.29	0.22	0.14
Need share A	0.60	0.64	0.71	0.78	0.86	0.5	0.5	0.5	0.5	0.5

Source: Based on Bauer et al. (2020)

of wood. The persons can be categorized with respect to their supply situation, namely, as having chopped less wood than they need, as having chopped exactly as much wood as they need, or as having chopped more wood than they need. Each participant made five distributive decisions per scenario. The ten cases are displayed in Fig. 3.2 and Table 3.1.

Regarding the variation in accountability, our study was composed of two between-subjects treatments. In the *High Accountability Treatment*, participants were informed that person A has kept on smoking heavily despite warnings from their doctor. This gave rise to a metabolic disease, which is why A needs a warmer room or has cut less wood than B. In the *Low Accountability Treatment*, the metabolic disease of A is not evoked by their actions but is congenital.

With this study, we wanted to measure the quantitative impact that information about need, productivity, and accountability has on participants' distributive decisions. Note that the systematic variation of accountability for higher neediness or lower productivity is not the only novel feature. Contrary to many other studies, we let our participants freely distribute the available amount among A and B, that is, without offering them a preselected set of distributions.

We assumed that the decisions reveal how far need is acknowledged by the subjects and to what extent this is influenced by the factors we vary. To analyze this, we constructed two outcome measures. Firstly, since the number of logs to be distributed among the two persons varies across certain cases, we had a look at the normalized *share of logs distributed to person A*, where A is always worse off than B. For that purpose, we simply divided the logs distributed to A by the total number of logs available. Secondly, because an equal split can be seen as a logical default, departures from equality hint at the presence of factors that are deemed relevant for distributive justice. Hence, we additionally examined the normalized *deviation from an equal split in favor of person A*. For the sake of normalization, we first determined the *need share* of A, which is given by dividing the need of A by the combined need of A and B, as well as A's *productivity share*, which is given by dividing that person's productivity by the total productivity. As can be seen in Table 3.1, the need share of person A increases in the Need Scenario, while the productivity share decreases in the Productivity Scenario.

Among the hypotheses we wanted to test was, first, that person A, who is always worse off than B, receives more on average than she has produced but less than she needs because participants will try to at least partially compensate A for her disadvantage. Secondly, we assumed that this willingness to compensate the worse-off person would be reduced if she is accountable for needing more wood or having chopped less wood. For example, in the Accountability Treatment, we should see a lower share distributed to A. Thirdly, the Need Scenario and the Productivity Scenario are mirror images of each other. For example, when A has a need share of 0.6 in the Need Scenario, they have a productivity share of 0.4 in the Productivity Scenario. We assumed that the share our participants allocate to A is oriented towards such relative values instead of the absolute numbers we presented to them. Therefore, the shares we observe in the scenarios should be symmetrical insofar as the deviation from an equal split should be the same between scenarios.

Figure 3.3 displays the average choices of our participants, a random sample of 200 people from an online access panel, stratified by the three characteristics gender, age, and equivalent household net income. The left panel contains bar charts of A's share by treatment and scenario; the right panel contains range plots of the deviation by treatment and scenario. The short-dashed lines on the left represent the need share of A and the dashed lines A's productivity share. As becomes apparent, the mean share of logs A receives is significantly higher than their productivity share and lower than their need share across all treatments, scenarios and cases, supporting our hypothesis on *partial compensation*. Our hypothesis regarding *accountability* is also supported by the data because the treatment effect on the share is clearly visible and significant (except for the first case of the Need Scenario). This also

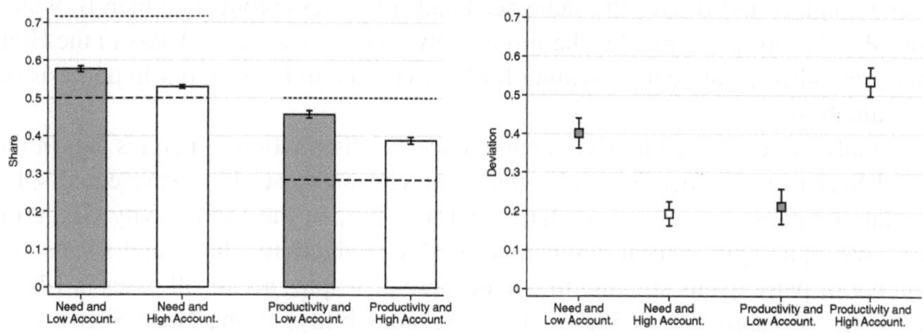

Source: Bauer et al. (2022), Fig. 3, upper panels.

Fig. 3.3 Share and deviation by scenario and treatment

holds for the deviation displayed on the right side. Both in the Need Scenario and the Productivity Scenario, all five cases show significant effects that are negative in the Need Scenario and positive in the Productivity Scenario. The hypothesis of symmetry, however, has to be rejected. Our participants tended to deviate more from an equal split when person A's worse situation was due to her lower productivity than when it was due to her greater need.

Just as in our first study, we also investigated subjects' *individual* distributions. We first sorted the choices they made into several mutually exclusive groups. For the Need Scenario, we obtained the choices "A gets less than the equal split," "A gets the equal split," "A is partially compensated," "A gets her need share," and "A gets more than her need share." For the Productivity Scenario, we obtained "A gets less than her productivity share," "A gets her productivity share," "A is partially compensated," "A gets the equal split," and "A gets more than the equal split." In a second step, we examined whether participants consistently made the same choices in all cases of a scenario.

For the Need Scenario, equal split, partial compensation, and need share account for most of the choices, namely, 89% in the Low Accountability Treatment and 92% in the High Accountability Treatment. When person A is responsible for their situation, choices significantly shift towards an equal split, increasing from 44% to 66%. A portion of choices could additionally be explained by what we call "net split." Here, A and B receive the number of logs they need plus or minus half of the oversupply or the undersupply, respectively. A total of 8% of the choices in the Low Accountability Treatment and 5% in the High Accountability Treatment are in line with this principle; in case 2 it is even 23% and 12%.

In the Productivity Scenario, 85% of the choices in the Low Accountability Treatment and 94% of the choices in the High Accountability Treatment allot person A's productivity share to her, compensate her partially, or split the logs equally among A and B. The equal-split choices decrease significantly in the High Accountability Treatment, from 35% to 19%. There is a notable percentage of choices, 14% and 5%, in which participants gave more than 50% of the logs to A even though A and B have the same need and A was less productive than B, which we call a "swap" principle. Furthermore, individual choices favor A less in the High Accountability Treatment, providing further evidence in favor of our hypothesis on accountability.

Finally, we examined how coherent choices of distribution principles are. In the Need Scenario, the four principles that were chosen most often were equal split, partial compensation, A's need share, and net split. In the Productivity Scenario, we have equal split, partial compensation, A's productivity share, and swap. The number of participants sticking to one of these principles across all cases is 17.6% (Low Accountability) and 38.5% (High Accountability) in the Need Scenario as well as 24.2% (Low Accountability) and 29.4% (High Accountability) in the Productivity Scenario. Net split was never used consistently. Hence, the coherence of choices is relatively poor.

3.3.3 Kinds of Needs

For our third study, we built upon the vignette presented in the previous section.[18] A random sample of 100 participants from an online access panel, stratified by the three characteristics gender, age, and equivalent household net income, was introduced to hypothetical persons in need of firewood. This time, however, we altered *what* they need the wood for. As Nullmeier (2020, p. 201) put it, "survival cannot be the only criterion for deciding what is necessary." There are further needs, but they may be of varying importance. Four different kinds of needs were presented to our subjects. In the first experiment, they had to rate the importance of each kind. In the second experiment, they had to make allocation decisions between two hypothetical persons experiencing the same or different kinds of needs.

The participants in the first experiment were asked to imagine four different people in need of firewood for different reasons. One of the persons needs the wood for *Survival*, which means that they rely on it to not get life-threateningly ill during the coming winter. Another one needs the wood for *Decency*, which means that the wood is required to ensure that it does not get inhumanly cold in their home. The third person needs wood for *Belonging*, meaning that it is common practice to meet up in the community center, with everyone bringing some wood to heat the center. Finally, the wood can be needed for a certain type of *Autonomy*. In this case, the person has a studio in which they spend their free time to create art. To be able to do so, they need to heat the studio with firewood. To ease comprehension and make the different kinds of needs as salient as possible, each vignette was accompanied by an illustration, as depicted in Fig. 3.4.

After having learned about the four kinds of needs, each kind was presented to subjects on a single screen in randomized order. A full-sized version of the

[18] The third study has been published as Bauer et al. (2023a).

Source: Bauer et al. (2023), Fig.1, drawn by Douwe Dijkstra.

Fig. 3.4 Illustrations of the four kinds of needs: Survival (upper left), Decency (upper right), Belonging (lower left), and Autonomy (lower right)

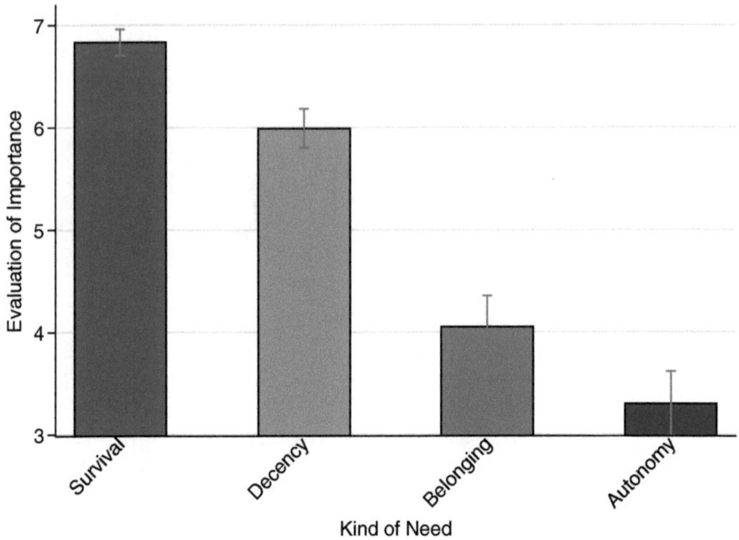

Source: Based on Bauer et al. (2023), Fig. 2.

Fig. 3.5 Means of ascribed importance to the four kinds of needs

illustration was shown, while a single sentence summed up what the wood was needed for in the given situation. Subjects were then asked to indicate, on a scale from 1 ("doesn't need the wood at all") to 7 ("absolutely needs the wood"), how much they think the person needs the wood in this situation.

Given the normative literature from philosophy, we expected that the importance of the kinds of needs that are more basic in theory is evaluated higher on average than the importance of those kinds of needs that are less basic in theory. Looking at the means of our participants' evaluations, we supposed that they are highest for Survival, followed, in this order, by Decency, Belonging, and Autonomy. As can be seen in Fig. 3.5, this is exactly what we found. Additionally, a one-way analysis of variance reveals that pairwise comparisons of all kinds of needs show significant differences. We can thus conclude that our participants' hierarchy of the needs' importance is aligned with the one we predicted from normative theory.

In our second experiment, a random sample of 200 participants from an online access panel, stratified by the three characteristics gender, age, and equivalent household net income, was again introduced to our four kinds of needs. Here the description was closer to the original vignette presented in Sect. 3.3.2 by describing two persons who experience one of the four kinds of needs each in different constellations. Afterwards, participants were shown a number of cases in which persons A and B had either the same kind of need (*Paired Cases*) or different kinds (*Mixed Cases*). In each case, there was a fixed amount of wood both had chopped. Participants' task was to distribute this wood among A and B in the way they thought to be most just. The amount available (1000 logs), however, was just enough to

Table 3.2 Cases presented to participants in the Equal Productivity Scenario and the Unequal Productivity Scenario

Person	Case					
	1	2	3	4	5	6
A	Survival	Survival	Survival	Decency	Decency	Belonging
B	Decency	Belonging	Autonomy	Belonging	Autonomy	Autonomy

Source: Bauer et al. (2023a), Tab. 3.

meet the need of *one* person. Each case was presented with illustrations and a short caption indicating the kinds of needs A and B experienced.

As a within-subjects variation, those cases were presented in two scenarios, an *Equal Productivity Scenario*, where each person has chopped 500 logs, and an *Unequal Productivity Scenario*, where A has chopped 200 logs and B 800 logs. Each scenario consisted of seven cases, with six of them being Mixed Cases, as depicted in Table 3.2. Additionally, each subject saw one randomly chosen Paired Case. The order of the scenarios as well as the order of cases and the positions of persons A and B on the screen was randomized.

In light of the theoretical literature and the findings from the first experiment, we hypothesized that the kinds of needs are perceived as varyingly important. If a party experiences a kind of need that is more basic in theory, subjects grant this party more firewood than the other one. More exactly, we expected the differences to reflect the hierarchy already known: Survival > Decency > Belonging > Autonomy. Additionally, we assumed that our subjects make coherent decisions in the sense of being additive. Additivity obtains if the difference between two kinds of needs that are not next to each other in the hierarchy equals the sum of the differences between the covered needs. For example, the difference between Survival and Belonging should be equal to the difference between Survival and Decency plus the difference between Decency and Belonging. Our final hypothesis was that the two scenarios affect distributive decisions. In the Unequal Productivity Scenario, where person A has chopped notably less wood than B, we expected A to receive significantly less wood than in the Equal Productivity Scenario.

To test our hypotheses, we looked at the *mean differences* between the endowments to A and B. Figure 3.6 shows these differences for the four Paired Cases, viz., the cases with identical kind of need, by the two scenarios. In the Equal Productivity Scenario, participants distribute nearly equally between A and B. In the Unequal Productivity Scenario, however, where A has cut way fewer logs than B, A gets fewer logs. The quantity seems to depend on the kinds of needs A and B experience. If the wood is needed for Survival, the low productivity of A is only slightly reflected in distribution decisions: a appears to be compensated with a nearly equal amount. For Decency, the mean difference grows, and it is largest for Belonging and Autonomy. However, even in those cases, A gets more wood than he has cut.

Furthermore, we examined the Mixed Cases, viz., cases with differing kinds of needs. Figure 3.7 shows the mean differences for the six possible combinations

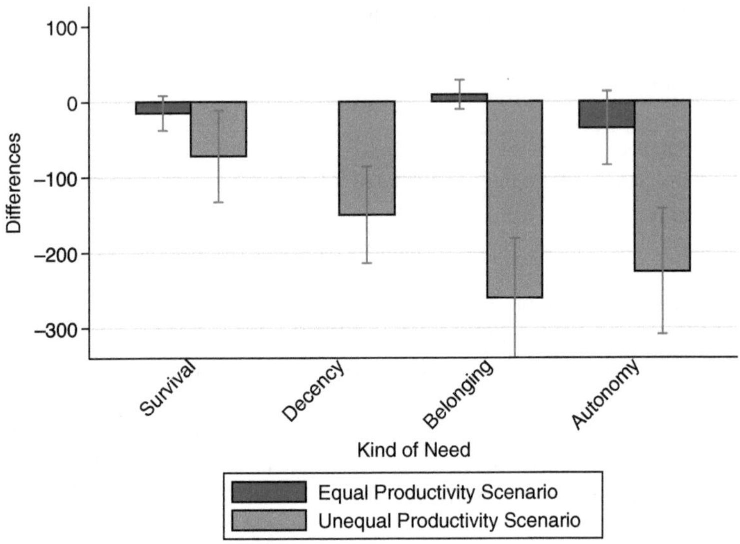

Source: Bauer et al. (2023), Fig. 4.

Fig. 3.6 Mean differences for the Paired Cases by scenario

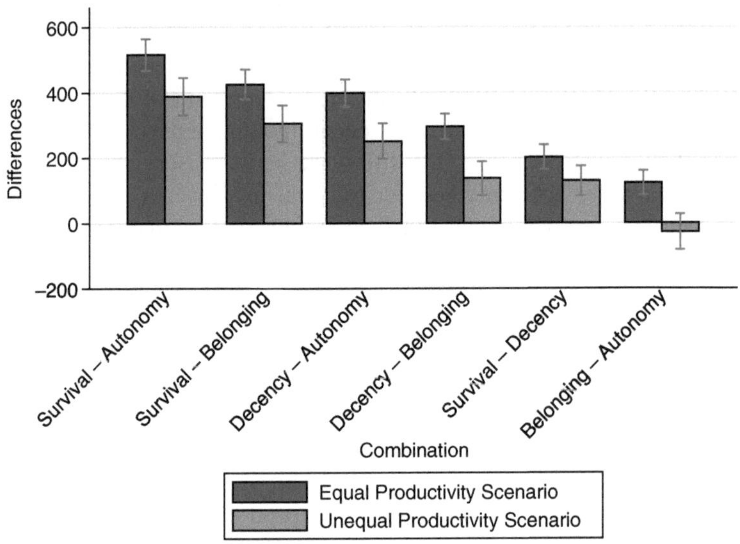

Source: Bauer et al. (2023), Fig. 5.

Fig. 3.7 Mean differences for the Mixed Cases by scenario

arising from our four kinds of needs (see Table 3.2), both for the Equal Productivity Scenario and the Unequal Productivity Scenario. For all combinations, mean differences are smaller in the Unequal Productivity Scenario. This means that participants gave less wood to the person with the more basic need when he contributed less to the amount available for distribution. Since we have specified that 1000 logs are just enough to satisfy one person's need, this hints at a lower willingness to compensate a more basic need if the person experiencing it has contributed less to the amount available. However, even in the Unequal Productivity Scenario, the less productive person gets partially compensated in nearly all combinations.

We also see that the mean differences are larger for combinations of kinds of needs that are not next to each other in the hierarchy. The difference is largest for the combination Survival–Autonomy, just as in the theory, as it covers all four kinds of needs. Combinations embracing three kinds of needs, i.e., Survival–Belonging and Decency–Autonomy, exhibit a smaller difference. The smallest differences can be observed for combinations that are made up of kinds of needs directly next to each other in the hierarchy. Still more, Fig. 3.7 hints at additivity. We tested this with two one-way ANOVAs (one for every Productivity Scenario) with Bonferroni correction. The result was that the additions have total values that do not differ significantly from the benchmark combinations. Therefore, we concluded that our subjects' distribution decisions were coherent.

3.3.4 Summary

The first study (Sect. 3.3.1) focused on laypeople's evaluations of given distributions. Those evaluations, we saw, are influenced by information about need. The introduced need threshold served as a reference point relative to which distributive justice was assessed. Besides, we found a lower standard deviation when information about need was present, indicating that the available information led to more coherent justice evaluations.

The second study (Sect. 3.3.2) investigated third-party distributive decisions. One of the main results was that subjects tend to partially compensate people who experience higher need. However, when a person is accountable for their higher need, willingness to compensate decreases. As Nullmeier (2020, p. 204) stipulated: "Socially and politically recognized needs are often not met or only met to a limited extent if the origins of the need gap can be attributed to the person in need and his or her intentional behavior."

Our last study (Sect. 3.3.3) dealt with different kinds of needs. The first experiment showed that participants evaluate kinds of needs as variably important, thereby following a particular hierarchy. The second experiment revealed that participants also differentiate between those kinds of needs when making third-party distributive decisions. More basic kinds of needs are deemed more worthy of compensation than less basic ones. Furthermore, participants' decisions are influenced by information about productivity, and they are coherent over the different kinds of needs.

3.4 Conclusion

In closing, we want to offer some suggestions for, and perhaps also constraints on, a theory of need-based justice that our findings imply. These implications are mainly oriented towards the theses Nullmeier (2020) presented in *Towards a Theory of Need-Based Justice*. They emerge from individual considerations of the formal part and the empirical part, as well as from an overall view.

Firstly, poverty is undoubtedly a main impediment to need satisfaction. It is therefore tempting to assume that an index of need-based justice can be modeled on a poverty index. Our theoretical reflections have shown that this is problematic. For example, whereas the focus axiom is a plausible constraint on a poverty index, its need-oriented relative has to be rejected. More precisely, while the conditions of the rich do not influence how poor a society is, the endowments of oversupplied people influence need-based justice. It remains to be seen, however, which further poverty axioms are relevant to the measurement of need-based justice.

Secondly, need-based justice could be a non-monolithic affair. The three measures developed in the project lean on diverse concepts, none of which appears to be in a position to claim primacy. The injustice of a distribution may be generated by (i) the deviation from absolute need satisfaction and equal degrees of need satisfaction, (ii) the chance to mitigate undersupply by transfers, and (iii) the resources used for oversupply instead of need satisfaction. The fact that the resulting measures differ in essential properties, e.g., in the satisfaction of certain axioms, does not mean that some of them have to be dismissed. Instead, "need-based justice" could be a polysemous term whose different uses fit a variety of situations. It would be no surprise, then, that different authors advocate different axioms.

Thirdly, in line with Nullmeier's (2020, p. 193) dictum that a "theory of need-based justice should be based on the promotion of both normative and empirical research,"[19] we must examine the *empirical* adequacy of measures of need-based justice. Even if there is polysemy, there could be a measure that comes closest to empirically found justice evaluations and distributive decisions.[20] Such a measure has the advantage that it best captures "what the people think," to use Miller's (1999, p. 61) vivid phrase.

Fourthly, one of our studies showed that theory and empirical evidence may clash. On average, our participants evaluated undersupply in a *convex* manner: the more an endowment approaches the need threshold, the greater the decrease in injustice. For example, if the threshold is 1000 units of living space, receiving 800 instead of 600 units results in a greater decrease of injustice than receiving 400 instead of 200 units. A policy following convexity states that less undersupplied

[19] For further perspectives on the interdependences of normative theories and empirical research, see Bauer and Meyerhuber (2020).

[20] Cf. Koscholke and Jekel's (2015) study on the empirical adequacy of probabilistic measures of coherence. They found that one of the measures being discussed is able to strongly approximate subjects' judgments.

people should be prioritized when a surplus is to be distributed. Such a policy can be justified by *sufficientarianism*: if the general aim is to furnish as many people as possible with what they need, a surplus should be given to those people whose needs can be satisfied more easily because their need gap is relatively small. But *prioritarianism*, which states that we have to prioritize the worst off, is a serious competitor to sufficientarianism. Nullmeier (2020, p. 193) stated that "normative considerations should not be [. . .] instrumentalized for the affirmation of the given as a normative ideal." We need to take this caveat seriously. Our empirical result appears to support sufficientarianism. It remains to be seen, though, how participants react when they realize that their judgments promote neglect of the worst off. For the result of such a study could confirm prioritarianism.

Fifthly, we come to a terminological matter. Nullmeier (2020, p. 203) suggests that "the principle of need is combined with a second principle" when it is claimed that, e.g., a surplus should be distributed in proportion to need. The second principle here would be "proportionality." We do not see the benefit in restricting the use of "need-based justice" in such a way. Rather, we would consider a principle of need-based justice to be a principle focusing on the satisfaction of *needs* instead of, say, recognition of *effort*. Understood in this way, the rule that a surplus should be distributed in proportion to need is a principle of need-based justice, while the rule that it should be distributed in proportion to effort is a principle of effort-based justice. Taking into account proportions or, say, differences, is much more a *modus* rather than a *principle*.

Sixthly, this does not undermine Nullmeier's (2020, pp. 193–197, 206f.) thesis that need-based justice is a central part of a *pluralistic* theory of justice. It might very well be the case that the principle of need has to be supplemented by further principles in order to obtain a full theory of justice. A candidate suggested by our empirical research is effort. From a normative perspective, one may argue that a distribution is just if all needs are satisfied and a possible surplus is split in proportion to effort. This means that the criterion of need gains priority in the sense of Nullmeier's (2020, p. 207) "lexineed" principle: "before any other criterion comes into play, the complete satisfaction of all needs must take place."

Seventhly, in contrast to the aforementioned normative principle, we found empirical evidence that, although need is a strong principle, it is moderated by effort even in situations of scarcity. Information on need significantly changes people's judgments on distributive justice, leading away from equal distributions, which would be the default mode when no other normatively relevant information is present. It does not only change the shape of the justice evaluation function but also leads to converging evaluations. Need could thus be seen as a principle that allows for more consent because it generates more coherence among evaluations. However, if there is also information on effort, the influence of need is diminished. To be sure, a person who needs more than others is always partially compensated for her disadvantage, no matter how productive she was. Hence, the principle of need is still influential. But the compensation is smaller if the person is less productive.

Eighthly, *accountability* is a further moderator. Nullmeier (2020, p. 204) points out that distributive justice may come into conflict with corrective justice. In one of our studies, the willingness to compensate the worse off person decreases when this person is accountable for needing more or producing less than another person. When a higher need or lower productivity is self-inflicted, corrective justice appears to come into play insofar as people are punished. Whether or not this is justified from a normative point of view, it has to be taken into consideration by any theory of need-based justice that aims at political implementation.

Finally, a theory of need-based justice has to account for the fact that there is a hierarchy of different kinds of needs (cf. Nullmeier 2020, p. 201). Here we found a match between theory and empirical results. In the normative literature, needs are differentiated by how basic they are. For example, bare survival is more basic than living in decent circumstances, e.g., having a warm home. Moreover, the latter is more basic than participating in social life, which is in turn more basic than self-actualization, e.g., by producing art. The subjects in our experiments followed this hierarchy. Among other things, the more basic a need, the more resources they allocated to the person with this need. Again, however, this effect is moderated by effort. There is a lower willingness to compensate a more basic need if the person experiencing it has contributed less to the available resources. This is additional support for a *pluralistic* theory of distributive justice that may center need but also has to make allowances for further principles, such as effort or equality.

Acknowledgments This chapter presents results from the project "Measures of Need-based Justice, Expertise and Coherence," which has been part of the DFG research group FOR 2104 "Need-based Justice and Distributive Procedures" (DFG Grants SI 1731/2–1 and SI 1731/2–2). We would like to thank the whole research group for many years of stimulating interdisciplinary cooperation in a remarkably friendly atmosphere. Special thanks go to Bernhard Kittel and Stefan Traub for looking after this atmosphere and to Stefan, our co-opted project member, for stimulating a philosopher's project with economic ideas.

References

Adams, J. S. (1965): "Inequity in Social Exchange", in L. Berkowitz (ed.): *Advances in Experimental Social Psychology*, vol. 2, 267–299. New York: Academic Press.

Aristotle (2009): *Nicomachean Ethics*. Transl. by W. D. Ross. New York: Oxford University Press.

Atkinson, A., and F. Bourguignon (1987): "Income Distributions and Differences in Needs", in G. Feiwel (ed.): *Arrow and the Foundations of the Theory of Economic Policy*, 350–370, New York: MacMillan.

Bauer, A. M. (2018): "Monotonie und Monotoniesensitivität als Desiderata für Maße der Bedarfsgerechtigkeit. Zu zwei Aspekten der Grundlegung empirisch informierter Maße der Bedarfsgerechtigkeit zwischen normativer Theorie, formaler Modellierung und empirischer Sozialforschung", *FOR 2104 Working Paper* 2018–01.

Bauer, A. M. (2019): "Zur Grundlegung empirisch informierter Maße der Bedarfsgerechtigkeit. Zwei Desiderata zwischen normativer Theorie, formaler Modellierung und empirischer Sozialforschung", in A. M. Bauer and M. I. Meyerhuber (eds.): *Philosophie zwischen Sein und Sollen. Normative Theorie und empirische Forschung im Spannungsfeld*, 179–220. Berlin and Boston: Walter de Gruyter.

Bauer, A. M. (2022): "Sated but Thirsty. A Prolegomenon to Multidimensional Measures of Need-Based Justice", *Axiomathes* 32, 529–538.

Bauer, A. M., and M. I. Meyerhuber (eds.) (2020): *Empirical Research and Normative Theory. Transdisciplinary Perspectives on Two Methodical Traditions between Separation and Interdependence*. Berlin and Boston: Walter de Gruyter.

Bauer, A. M., F. Meyer, J. Romann, M. Siebel, and S. Traub (2020): "Need, Equity, and Accountability. Evidence on Third-Party Distributive Decisions from an Online Experiment", *FOR 2104 Working Paper* 2020–01.

Bauer, A. M., F. Meyer, J. Romann, M. Siebel, and S. Traub (2022): "Need, Equity, and Accountability, Evidence on Third-Party Distribution Decisions from a Vignette Study", *Social Choice and Welfare* 59, 769–814.

Bauer, A. M., J. Romann, M. Siebel, and S. Traub (2023a): "Winter is Coming. How Laypeople Think About Different Kinds of Needs", *PLoS ONE* 18 (11), e0294572.

Bauer, A. M., A. Diederich, S. Traub, and A. R. Weiss (2023b): "When the Poorest Are Neglected. A Vignette Experiment on Need-Based Distributive Justice", *SSRN Working Paper* 4503209.

Boulding, K. E. (1962): "Social Justice in Social Dynamics", in R. Brandt (ed.): *Social Justice*, 73–92. Englewood Cliffs: Prentice Hall.

Casal, P. (2007): "Why Sufficiency Is Not Enough", *Ethics* 117, 296–326.

Crisp, R. (2003): "Equality, Priority, and Compassion", *Ethics* 113, 745–763.

Ebert, U. (1984): "Social Welfare, Inequality, and Poverty When Needs Differ", *Social Choice and Welfare* 23, 415–448.

Ebert, U., and P. Moyes (2003): "Equivalence Scales Reconsidered", *Econometrica* 71, 319–343.

Eriksson, K. (2012): "The Accuracy of Mathematical Models of Justice Evaluations", *Journal of Mathematical Sociology* 36, 125–135.

Feinberg, J. (1974): "Noncomparative Justice", *Philosophical Review* 83, 297–338.

Frankfurt, H. (1987): "Equality as a Moral Ideal", *Ethics* 98, 21–43.

Hassoun, N. (2009): "Meeting Need", *Utilitas* 21, 250–275.

Homans, G. C. (1961): *Social Behavior. Its Elementary Forms*. London: Routledge & Kegan Paul.

Jasso, G. (1978): "On the Justice of Earnings. A New Specification of the Justice Evaluation Function", *American Journal of Sociology* 83, 1398–1419.

Jasso, G. (1980): "A New Theory of Distributive Justice", *American Sociological Review* 45, 3–32.

Jasso, G. (1990): "Methods for the Theoretical and Empirical Analysis of Comparison Processes", *Sociological Methodology* 20, 369–419.

Jasso, G. (1999): "How Much Injustice Is there in the World? Two New Justice Indexes", *American Sociological Review* 64, 133–168.

Jasso, G. (2007): "Studying Justice. Measurement, Estimation, and Analysis of the Actual Reward and the Just Reward", in K. Törnblom and R. Vermunt (eds.): *Distributive and Procedural Justice*, 225–254. London: Routledge.

Jasso, G., and B. Wegener (1997): "Methods for Empirical Justice Analysis, Part I. Framework, Models, and Quantities", *Social Justice Research* 10, 393–430.

Kagan, S. (2012): *The Geometry of Desert*. New York: Oxford University Press.

Koscholke, J., and M. Jekel (2015): "Probabilistic Coherence Measures. A Psychological Study of Coherence Assessment", *Synthese* 194, 1303–1322.

Miller, D. (1999): *Principles of Social Justice*. Cambridge, MA: Harvard University Press.

Miller, D. (2007): "Human Rights, Basic Needs, and Scarcity", *Working Paper Series* SJ007. Centre for the Study of Social Justice and Department of Politics and International Relations.

Miller, D. (2020): "Needs-Based Justice. Theory and Evidence", in A. M. Bauer and M. I. Meyerhuber (eds.): *Empirical Research and Normative Theory. Transdisciplinary Perspectives on Two Methodical Traditions Between Separation and Interdependence*, 273–294. Berlin and Boston: Walter de Gruyter.

Moyes, P. (2012): "Comparisons of Heterogeneous Distributions and Dominance Criteria", *Journal of Economic Theory* 147, 1351–1383.

Nozick, R. (1974): *Anarchy, State, and Utopia*. New York: Basic Books.

Nullmeier, F. (2020): "Towards a Theory of Need-Based Justice", in S. Traub and B. Kittel (eds.): *Need-Based Distributive Justice. An Interdisciplinary Perspective*, 191–208. Cham: Springer.

Nussbaum, M. (2011): *Creating Capabilities: The Human Development Approach*. Cambridge: Harvard University Press.

Parfit, D. (1997): "Equality and Priority", *Ratio* 10, 202–221.

Patchen, M. (1961): *The Choice of Wage Comparisons*. Englewood Cliffs, NJ: Prentice Hall.

Plato (1973): *The Republic and Other Works*. Transl. by B. Jowett. New York: Anchor Books.

Robeyns, I. (2017): "Having too Much", in J. Knight and M. Schwartzberg (eds.): *Wealth: NOMOS LVI*, 1–44. New York: New York University Press.

Sayles, L. R. (1958): *Behavior of Industrial Work Groups. Prediction and Control*. New York: Wiley.

Seidl, C. (1988): "Poverty Measurement. A Survey", in D. Bös, M. Rose and C. Seidl (eds.): *Welfare and Efficiency in Public Economics*, 71–147. Heidelberg: Springer.

Sen, A. (1999): *Development as Freedom*. Oxford: Oxford University Press.

Sen, A. (1981): Poverty and Famines. An Essay on Entitlement and Deprivation. Oxford: Clarendon.

Siebel, M. (2017): "To Each According to His Needs. Measuring Need-Based Justice", *FOR 2104 Working Paper* 2017–14.

Siebel, M., and T. Schramme (2020): "Need-Based Justice from the Perspective of Philosophy", in S. Traub and B. Kittel (eds.): *Need-Based Distributive Justice. An Interdisciplinary Perspective*, 21–58. Cham: Springer.

Springhorn, N. (2017): "Comparative and Noncomparative Measurement of Need-Based Justice", *FOR 2104 Working Paper* 2017–15.

Springhorn, N. (2022): "On the Measurement of Need-Based Justice", *Economics & Philosophy* 38, 466–500.

Temkin, L. (1993): *Inequality*. Oxford: Oxford University Press.

Traub, S., A. M. Bauer, M. Siebel, N. Springhorn, and A. R. Weiss (2017): "On the Measurement of Need-Based Justice", *FOR 2104 Working Paper* 2017–12.

Walster, E., E. Berscheid, and G. W. Walster (1976): "New Directions in Equity Research", in L. Berkowitz and E. Walster (eds.): *Advances in Experimental Social Psychology*, vol. 9, 1–42. New York: Academic Press.

Weiss, A. R., A. M. Bauer, and S. Traub (2017): "Needs as Reference Points. When Marginal Gains to the Poor Do Not Matter", *FOR 2104 Working Paper* 2017–13.

Woozley, A. D. (1973): "Injustice", in R. C. Roberts (ed.): *Injustice and Rectification*, 31–42. New York: Peter Lang.

Part II
Structures and Processes of the Recognition of Needs

Chapter 4
The Social Recognition of Needs

Bernhard Kittel

Abstract The satisfaction of needs depends on the willingness of others to forgo own payoffs to the benefit of the claimant. Given the heterogeneity and subjectivity of individual needs, it is difficult to assess whether a need claim is based on a true lack of resources or whether the claimant misrepresents the need. Hence, the recognition of a need claim by others depends on some mechanism of social objectivation. Under what conditions are distributive claims recognized as legitimate needs by a social group instead of being dismissed as subjective desires? The chapter addresses three conditions of the social recognition of needs. First, inequality aversion theory suggests that needs are likely to be satisfied as long as the transfer does not produce a rank reversal between the donor and the recipient. Second, information is crucial. If donors can verify the veracity of a need claim, the willingness to satisfy a claim rises. Third, need is particularly salient as a principle of justice in solidary groups. Hence, the satisfaction of needs depends on social proximity.

4.1 Introduction

Under what conditions are distributive claims recognized as legitimate needs by a social group instead of merely as subjective desires? As a principle of justice, need is considered salient in solidary communities (Liebig and Sauer 2016). People must perceive and experience social bonds with others in order to make these others' fates a precept of their behavior towards them. The concreteness, subjectivity, and heterogeneity of needs separate the principle of need-based justice from other justice principles, which rely on more abstract, objectified, and homogeneous concepts. Equity refers to allocations to an individual in proportion to their contributions,

B. Kittel (✉)
University of Vienna, Department of Economic Sociology, Wien, Austria
e-mail: bernhard.kittel@univie.ac.at

B. Kittel, S. Traub (eds.), *Priority of Needs?*,
https://doi.org/10.1007/978-3-031-53051-7_4

equality to the idea that everyone should get the same, and entitlement to the proposition that people with higher status should get more.

Need as a criterion of justice has an ambivalent relationship with society. On the one hand, as the European Social Survey (ESS) data reported in Chap. 1 reveal, there is a broad consensus in the European population that the mutual satisfaction of needs is an important moral principle underlying and fostering social order and cohesion in a society. On the other hand, public discourse is characterized by a general suspicion that individual need claims may be excessive and not justified by an objective shortfall of resources. The mechanism mediating between need satisfaction as a principle of justice and the containment of excessive claims is the social recognition of needs. Based on the fundamental principle of reciprocity, this mechanism mutually guarantees the provision to individuals of resources that satisfy a societally agreed threshold of capabilities and functionings (Sen 1985; Nussbaum 2011). This chapter contributes to the search for "a process by which needs are determined as socially or politically recognized" (Nullmeier 2020, p. 198) and explores some conditions that may be conducive to the establishment of a need-based social order. In the process, it offers some experimental tests of the hypothesis that "[s]ituational, social and personal individual characteristics together determine the extent to which the principle of need is met" (Nullmeier 2020, p. 205).

To assess the social recognition of needs in distributive decisions, I will first elaborate in Sect. 4.2 on the implicit assumptions undergirding the concept of "social recognition of needs." In Sect. 4.3, I will abstract from needs and focus on the tension between self-interest and social values. In Sect. 4.4, I motivate and explain the operationalization of needs and social recognition used in all the experiments discussed in this chapter. Section 4.5 focuses on evidence supporting the hypothesis that others' needs are relevant in distributive decisions. Section 4.6 discusses individual factors that raise the likelihood of distributions that satisfy the needs of others. In Sect. 4.7, the focus shifts to contextual factors that may affect the recognition of needs by others, such as the size of the claim, information about the truth of the claim, and group membership. Section 4.8 concludes this chapter.

4.2 The Social Recognition of Needs

The term "social recognition of needs" requires some explanation. In this chapter, to recognize something means "to acknowledge [its] existence, validity, or legality."[1] The recognition of a claim thus goes beyond the mere acceptance of the existence or truth of a claim such as "A has a particular need." To recognize that claim implies that it is considered salient and consequential: that is, "A's need must be satisfied." To recognize a claim is thus to assert that claim's moral value. The term "social" refers, in the spirit of Max Weber (1978 [1921/22], p. 22), to the fact that recognition

[1] https://www.lexico.com/definition/recognize, accessed July 21, 2021.

involves some form of interaction with other people and that it is other people who recognize an individual's need. This specification also implies that it is a peer group that does the recognizing. In larger, structured social groups, recognition may be delegated to a representative entity or an authority. In that case we speak of "political recognition" (see Chap. 5).

The social recognition of needs thus refers to the acknowledgment of the existence, validity, or legality of an individual need claim by other people who are related to the claimant and form some sort of community. For a claim to be recognizable, the three elements of recognition must be present: the claim must be perceived by others (Fraser 1989), it must be identified as a real individual shortage (Sen 2000), and there must be a consensus in the community that transfers from other people to the claimant are legitimated by some general rule, which may be an explicit legal or an implicit social norm (Bowles and Gintis 2000; Goodin 2002; Mau 2004).

Among peers, these criteria appear at the level of moral judgment and imply a sense of priority (Brock and Miller 2019). In other words, "[c]laims based upon what a person needs frequently have a distinctive poignancy. They are likely to arouse a more compelling sense of obligation, and to be treated with greater urgency, than claims based merely upon what someone wants" (Frankfurt 1984, p. 1). From this perspective, volitional needs, which satisfy a desire, are to be distinguished from constrained volitional needs, which satisfy self-inflicted dependencies such as an addiction, and from non-volitional needs, which are entirely out of the control of the person in need. Only the latter two qualify as needs that have a chance of being socially recognized, but it seems evident that non-volitional needs generate a stronger sense of urgency than constrained volitional needs. The recognition of needs thus mandates that "a person's need for a certain object is 'true' or 'authentic' only if the person needs the object regardless of whether or not she wants it. A need is 'false' or 'inauthentic,' on the other hand, if the person needs the object only because he desires it" (Frankfurt 1984, p. 12). In a similar way, other scholars separate basic from instrumental needs (Baybrooke 1987; Miller 1999), whereby "basic" refers to fundamental, nonnegotiable, social roles or dimensions of life, such as physical health and personal autonomy (Doyal and Gough 1991), while instrumental needs can be roughly identified with the satisfaction of desires, which are negotiable.

The social recognition of needs not only means that others make those needs a precondition for their actions, but that the satisfaction of that particular need also makes it an entitlement for all other members of the community. Others are expected to contribute to the satisfaction of an individual's need, while they can themselves expect to legitimately claim the same entitlement whenever they are in the same situation (Kittel 2020, pp. 101–105). These expectations are generalized, in the sense of not addressing a specific other, and constitute a "structure of reciprocity" (Molm et al. 2007; Molm 2010). In this structure, the principle of need-based justice becomes a social norm that mandates the satisfaction of a specific need in a particular case based on generally accepted standards (Homans 1961, Opp 2015). The social recognition of need as a principle of justice is thus an emergent phenomenon at the social level. Recognizing a need as a mutual entitlement is thus not merely an act of humanitarianism; rather, it makes that need claim a part of the normative order that defines reciprocal obligations and is institutionalized in the welfare regime (Bowles and Gintis 2000; Goodin 2002; Mau 2004).

In a world of limited resources, the satisfaction of needs by others implies that these others sacrifice their own endowments, entitlements, or opportunities to the benefit of the needy. They may do this by, for example, satisfying the need out of their own pocket or using common resources to which they have contributed. Although the satisfaction of others' needs is an individual act, it may be socially embedded in two ways. In an implicit way, an actor may be influenced by the normative order prevailing in their social environment. Explicitly, the satisfaction of others' needs may be negotiated in a social exchange setting.

4.3 Self-Interest and Beyond

In the broader field of social exchange theory, in which network exchange theory has developed out of elementary theory (Emanuelson 2013; Willer et al. 2014) scholars emphasized the structural conditions that determine behavior in exchange settings. In a long series of experiments starting with Cook and Emerson (1978),[2] much evidence has been collected on the effect of the structure of the network on relative power, which has been shown to depend on the availability of alternative exchange partners (Molm 2014, p. 204). Set within the rational choice framework, work in this field has almost uniformly assumed—although this is not a logical consequence of this framework (Opp 1999; Diekmann 2022)—that agents' decisions are self-regarding, that is, based on the maximization of their own payoffs. This assumption implies the corollary, namely, that it is inconceivable for agents to take any context into account other than those elements that constrain their opportunities for maximizing their payoffs.

Induced value theory (Smith 1976), which has become the basic premise of experimental economics (Weimann and Brosig-Koch 2019, p. 15–16), assumes that monetary payoffs override any alternative motivations in the laboratory. Sociologists working in the social exchange tradition have critiqued this assumption. In their work, two provisions have been typically used to ensure that subjects do actually maximize their payoffs. First, subjects are often explicitly primed to "assume a proself orientation" (Willer et al. 2014, p. 204) and are instructed to "earn as many points as they can" (Willer and Emanuelson 2008, p. 182). These scholars thus rely on explicit experimenter demand effects to ensure that subjects behave according to the assumptions underlying their theories. Second, an even more radical approach

[2] In an earlier contribution, Emerson (1964) explored the possibilities of experimental tests. But from Cook and Emerson (1978) onwards we can speak of a systematic and continuous research program (Molm 2014).

is to preclude allocations beyond those agents in the network whose cooperation is necessary for a decision to be made, such that social values and other-regarding preferences, for example, altruism, are ruled out by experimental design (Molm 2014).

In experiments that are based on network exchange theory, the typical procedure is to let subjects negotiate the distribution of a joint endowment in dyads, which form part of a larger network. Dyadic interaction has been the focus of early social exchange theory (Homans 1961; Blau 1964a; Emerson 1976) and experimental economics, where it is mostly discussed in terms of the dictator game (Kahneman et al. 1986; Engel 2011) and the ultimatum game (Güth et al. 1982; Güth and Kocher 2014). Whereas these economic experiments typically focus on individual decisions, sociological studies in the social exchange tradition analyze the outcomes of negotiations that are structured by the network (Molm 2014). In most studies on exchanges in networks consisting of more than two connected nodes, subjects are "negatively connected" (Cook and Emerson 1978), which means that each subject can agree with no more than one other subject on the distribution of the joint endowment (Molm 2014, p. 203). In social exchange theory, justice has been traditionally conceptualized in terms of the Aristotelian proportionality principle (Adams 1965), which states that individual returns must be proportional to individual investments. "The rule of justice is a social norm, which stipulates that people ought to receive a fair return for their investments in exchange transactions, and which functions to promote those social investments that are necessary for furnishing services that are in demand and valued by the members of the community" (Blau 1964b, p. 196). Conceptualizing justice as a social norm implies a wider social context in which the dyadic interaction takes place because norms necessarily presuppose the existence of a social group in which they are valid and respected. Justice as equity has remained the dominant conception in subsequent sociological and social psychological studies on social exchange (Cook and Hegtvedt 1983; Hegtvedt and Markovsky 1995; Hegtvedt 2006).

Whereas attention to needs has mostly been discussed in the context of dyadic interaction constellations, the emergence of social phenomena—social facts (Durkheim 1982 [1895])—requires at least a third actor (Simmel 1964 [1908]; Lindemann 2010; Lindenberg 2015). The reason is that social phenomena—for example, social embedding, norms, group-level motivation, and status hierarchies (Lindenberg 2015)—transcend individual volition only when the group consists of at least three members. A similar argument can be made for the social recognition of something, such as a need, as a mutual obligation. In dyads, the recognition of someone else's needs as a relevant criterion for distribution is purely individual. Each negotiation partner can change her mind at any time and retract an earlier agreement. If at least three subjects are present when a deal between two is made, the retraction of an agreement may risk the result that a new agreement between the other group members worsens the outcome of the defecting individual. An agreement gains normative weight because a distribution among more than two subjects requires the invocation of a general rule to legitimize a distributive proposal. The normative foundation of such a general rule must necessarily refer to

Fig. 4.1 Two network structures

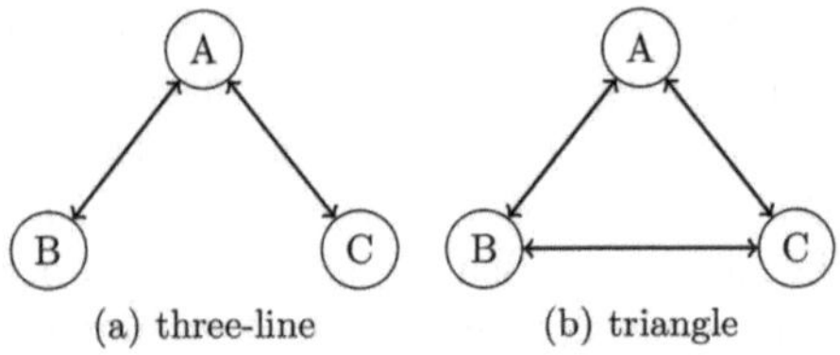

Source: Kittel, Neuhofer and Schwaninger (2017, p. 5).

some principle of justice that is acceptable to others (Cook and Hegtvedt 1983). The unilateral retraction of an agreement becomes ineffective when the other subjects, assuming equal power, insist on the validity of the rule underlying the earlier agreement.

More generally, while summarizing work on justice with a specific emphasis on the network exchange literature, Hegtvedt (2005) observes that groups determine the standard of comparison for the evaluation of individual allocations. She also finds that group structure—characterized, for example, by power and status differences, group identity, and interaction processes within the group—also affects justice evaluations. Although justice has not been a major focus of network exchange theory, it has been a latent topic in this research tradition because it deals with the conditions of relative allocations in distributive processes.

In the following, I study two versions of the three-node network, the 3-line and the triangle. In the simplest extension to the dyad, in which one node is added to the dyad by means of one edge forming the 3-line network A-B-C, B has two potential negotiation partners, while A and C can only negotiate with B (Fig. 4.1, left panel). Hence, the endowment is shared by either B and A or B and C by design. Given that B has two options, a self-regarding payoff maximizer in this position is expected to use that position's structural power to play A and C off against each other. Several solution concepts have been developed to predict the distribution of outcomes (Willer and Emanuelson 2008). For example, the network control bargaining model (Braun and Gautschi 2006) predicts that B obtains 83% and either A or C receives 17%, leaving nothing for the third agent (Schwaninger et al. 2019, 262).[3] A further extension is the triangle, in which network power is equally distributed (Fig. 4.1, right panel). In this case, the prediction is that two of the three players each obtain 50% of the endowment and the third nothing.

However, while this approach may be useful for exploring power structures in networks, the imposition of payoff-maximizing behavior by the experimenter produces confirmatory bias regarding the self-interest assumption (Zizzo 2010; De Quidt et al. 2018) and also constitutes a severe behavioral restriction that is rare to find in real social settings and therefore undermines the relevance of the laboratory results for field observations. It is a stylized fact from research on social

[3] These shares are calculated by using the formulae and weights given in Braun and Gautschi (2006, 10–12).

values and social preferences that the vast majority of people fall into one of two types (Murphy and Ackermann 2014; Kerschbamer 2015): one type indeed holds purely self-regarding preferences and maximizes their own profits by disregarding others; the second type, which is more common in the population, also takes others' outcomes into account when making decisions (Traub et al. 2023).

Such other-regarding preferences may take various forms: inequality aversion and concern for need satisfaction are the ones of interest in this chapter. Consequently, both social value theory (Messick and McClintock 1968; Bogaert et al. 2008; Murphy and Ackermann 2014) and modern behavioral economics (Fehr and Schmidt 1999; Bolton and Ockenfels 2000; Charness and Rabin 2002) have developed models of behavior that assume a wider spectrum of motivations and, in particular, include a concern for the other's payoffs. Other models focus on guilt aversion (Cartwright 2019) and social norms as drivers of behavior (Krupka and Weber 2013). In particular, the latter model is the context dependency of individual behavior (Levitt and List 2007) when they assume that "individuals care about behaving in a manner consistent with social norms" (Krupka and Weber 2013, 496).

These considerations have also been taken up in the network exchange literature. The evaluation of distributive outcomes thus necessarily involves issues of fairness and justice (Hegtvedt 2005). Most notably, Willer et al. (2013, p. 126) have argued that "prosocials are seen as concerned with equity, not just dyadically, but for all others in the group" and they have elaborated ways in which this idea can be incorporated into social exchange models. However, an experiment directly testing this hypothesis in the network-exchange framework has not found evidence that the behavior of prosocials differs from proselfs (Lewis and Willer 2017).

In a further study, Schwaninger et al. (2019) conduct network exchange experiments to test the effect of restricting allocations to members of the dyad. In this experiment, which we report on later in this chapter, they explore what happens when members of the dyad have the opportunity to behave prosocially in the triangle and the 3-line network. They compare the traditional setup in which the endowment can only be shared between the two members of a dyad (exclusive treatment) with a setup in which the members of the dyad can also allocate a share to the third player (inclusive treatment). It turns out that in the inclusive treatment, on average, the members of the dyad allocate 10% of the endowment to the third player. A breakdown of this average reveals that two distributions are focal: the self-regarding solution, which entails no transfer to the third player (65%), and the solidary solution, which produces a three-way even split (24%). A second result is that the amount transferred to the third player slightly declines over consecutive rounds of the game, without, however, reaching zero within the 10 rounds administered in the experiment.

Two remarks are important with respect to these observations. First, contrary to the assumption in traditional network exchange literature, many people do not maximize their own payoffs when they have the opportunity to include others. Second, according to a meta study of dictator game experiments (Engel 2011), the share of people in dyads that give at least a small amount to the third player (35%) is substantially smaller than the 64% of people who transfer at least some amount to the third player when they can decide individually on the allocations. The setup chosen by Schwaninger et al. (2019) involves two stages: the three players first have to agree on who will form the dyad, and then the two players in the dyad bargain over the distribution of the endowment. One or both of the players may switch to an alternative dyad if the third player offers a better deal.[4] The large share of dyads that do not transfer any resources to the third player may be explained by the fact that groups tend to make more self-interested decisions than individuals (Charness and Sutter 2012).

Neuhofer et al. (2022) study the transferability of the findings from Schwaninger et al. (2019) to similar settings in different cultural environments. They compare the results obtained in Vienna, Austria, with results of the same experiment conducted at universities in Tianjin, China, and Kyoto, Japan. They find that the results for the exclusive treatment are robust across cultures and those for the inclusive treatment point in the same direction, although they reveal some variation in the effect of social values and the average size of transfers to the third player.

To explore these results in more detail, Schwaninger (2021) studied dyadic bargaining between subjects scoring differently on the social value orientation scale in the presence of a third subject. He found that the size of the third subject's share is less important to the decision maker than the fact that players in the dyad equally share the cost of the transfer to the third subject. When the two members of the dyad differ in their social values, the more self-serving decision maker is more likely to impose her preferences. The reason for this is that prosocial decision makers more often refrain from giving more to the third subject when the other member of the dyad refuses. Schwaninger (2021, p. 21) concludes that "[t]he bargaining problem involves two conflicting fairness aspects, and the more self-serving aspect has to be respected first. If there is a conflict between the distributional preferences of the bargainers, the outcome depends on the subject who has stronger preferences."

These analyses show that both self-regarding and other-regarding preferences—or social values—influence distributive decisions in small groups that are internally structured as a network. While self-regarding behavior is observed in only about one-third of cases in experiments on dyads, there is a substantive increase of self-regarding decisions to two-thirds when the number of subjects increases from two to three. This marks an important qualitative change. In dyadic distributive decisions embedded in a three-node network, inequality-averse people are confronted with a dilemma: on the one hand, they are in a situation of disadvantageous inequality if their bargaining partner exhibits self-regarding preferences; on the other hand, they experience advantageous inequality vis-à-vis the third player. According to Fehr and Schmidt (1999), inequality-averse people dislike disadvantageous inequality more than advantageous inequality. When faced with conflicting interests, decision

[4] This two-step procedure captures Max Weber's idea of market exchange: "On the one hand, there is a 'struggle of competition' between all those who are potentially interested in an exchange; and on the other hand (sic) there is an 'interest struggle' between the two parties who end up by engaging in an exchange" (Swedberg 2005, p. 243).

makers will, according to this perspective, prefer their own over others' benefits. The finding that such people reduce their transfer to the third player when their more self-regarding bargaining partner refuses to give an equally sized share to the third player is in line with this proposition. This observation also explains the more self-regarding outcomes in the three-player situation.

In sum, it would be misleading to infer from the small share of collective decisions shown in these experiments that the majority of people are self-regarding. Preferences are more complex and depend on the specific structural and social context. But we can conclude from the previous discussion that the observed collective outcomes are the result of individual strategies of inequality avoidance, that is, strategies in which the dislike of disadvantageous inequality counts more than the dislike of advantageous inequality.

4.4 Measuring the Social Recognition of Needs

Need-based justice transcends the common understanding of equality by shifting emphasis from the equal distribution of a resource, which is the simple form of equality, to the idea of equality in human dignity. The equal distribution of a resource is not necessarily just because some put less effort into improving the outcome, have less resources at the beginning, or are confronted with more dire circumstances. Whereas the invested effort may give reason for using the equity principle, the latter two conditions may motivate to shift towards the need principle. Kittel (2020, p. 102) defines the social recognition of needs as a social norm if it generates the mutual expectation that others will satisfy a stated need in a solidary community. The challenge is to show that the satisfaction of thresholds is due to need-based justice rather than some other motivation.

To measure the need level, we first require a method of translating needs from natural settings to the laboratory. Researchers have explored various approaches to generating needs in the laboratory. One approach is to produce "real" needs. For example, Kause et al. (2018) let subjects ride a stationary bicycle for 25 minutes and then observed the sharing of water between subjects. However, approaches in this vein are limited by ethical concerns, because depriving human beings from basic physical needs is a serious attack on the well-being of participants in the experiment.

When the satisfaction of others' needs is an isolated decision, with no expectation of future direct or indirect interaction, it can be seen as an act of altruism. The source of such humanitarian action may be a sense of moral duty, which suggests that there is a normative basis for individual action. Experimental studies that test conditions for altruism are typically framed as dictator games in which one player, the dictator, is endowed with a sum of money and is then asked, under full anonymity, whether she wants to transfer a share of this sum to another player who is passive in the interaction (Kahneman et al. 1986; Forsythe et al. 1994). Typically, about one-third of players maximize their own income, whereas the remaining two-thirds give about 42% on average (Engel 2011). However, in a setting, in which any possibility of being identified is meticulously ruled out, Dana et al. (2007) show that subjects do actually exploit the moral wiggle room to their own benefit. Various sociodemographic and situational factors affect these outcomes, which we do not further elaborate on here. We instead highlight studies that focus on the impact of need.

Brañas-Garza (2006) implemented two variants of the dictator game. In one treatment, he informed dictators that recipients are poor, and in another, he replaced monetary transfers with medicine. He then compared the outcomes of these two treatments to a baseline treatment, a pure dictator game with no information. He found that the percentage of subjects maximizing their own profits dropped from 71.4 in the no-information treatment to 22.4 in the poverty treatment to 2.7 in the medicine treatment. The percentage of those who transferred the full endowment increased from 0 to 40.8 and to 74.6, respectively. Average transfers amounted to 9.5% of the endowment in the no-information treatment, 65% in the poverty treatment, and 90% in the medicine treatment. Thus, the information that the recipient is poor raised both the share of subjects behaving altruistically and the amount transferred to the recipient. Specifying the exact nature of the need raised transfers even more.

Cappelen et al. (2013) devised a dictator game in which, to generate a sense of entitlement, the players earned their initial endowment through effort. Dictators were matched with recipients located in one of two rich or two poor countries. The location also affected the value of the earned endowment. They found that both high-income and low-income dictators gave more to low-income than to high-income recipients and that high-income dictators gave a larger share than low-income dictators. However, a more detailed analysis revealed that the overwhelming majority of dictators weighed entitlement to the earned endowment more strongly than the needs of the other, while only a small fraction of dictators was responsive to poverty. Cappelen et al. (2013, p. 591) interpreted this observation as suggesting that "the participants seem to have traded off one fairness view with another in a self-serving fashion."

Kause et al. (2018) distinguished between primary and secondary goods when comparing sharing behavior in a dictator game after players exercised on a stationary bike in the laboratory. They found that altruistic behavior is more widespread and transfers are more generous in the sharing of water, a primary good, than money, a secondary good. They also found that earned endowments reduce money transfers compared to the windfall condition but not water transfers. These results provide evidence that people do indeed differentiate between basic and instrumental needs.

Combining the dictator game with a risky choice framework, Wyszynski et al. (2020) explored the effect of a required minimum number of points on the amount donated by the dictator to the recipient. They compared different levels of identifiability of the recipient. Being shown a picture of the recipient raised donations, and the presence of the recipient in the room raised donations even more. However, overall, the authors conclude, "there was no main effect of need but we found that a preset need level gets donors to satisfy the need of identified recipients more often" (Wyszynski et al. 2020, p. 16).

A more direct measure of needs is to provide individual information about subjects' actual life circumstances. Traub et al. (2023) compared treatments in which participants obtain objective information about other players' circumstances—income, public transfers, time investment to reach the laboratory—with treatments in which the other players themselves make need claims and legitimize their claims by what they intend to buy with the payoff from the experiment. The main finding is that objective information alone is not sufficient to increase the amount of transfers, but that participants do indeed increase allocations in response to direct need claims by others when they are supported by objective information. This observation suggests that the recognition of needs as a principle of justice, rather than just a humanitarian act, requires that subjects actively articulate their needs and justify their claims with information that can be independently evaluated. This result points to the salience of trust in distributive decision processes.

In all five designs described above, transfers to the recipient are made by an individual dictator who has sole control over the available resource. Needs are introduced as part of the description of the recipient or as an exogenous condition. These experiments thus focus on individual social values or preferences and the willingness to engage in humanitarian acts but do not capture needs as a socially recognized principle of justice.

In the papers discussed below, the research group takes a different approach. Needs are introduced as an exogenous condition that operationalizes a crucial idea developed in the capability approach: for a dignified life the satisfaction of basic needs has to exceed a certain minimum threshold below which survival in human dignity is impossible (Sen 1985; Nussbaum 2011; Comin and Nussbaum 2014). Basic needs are those resources that are required to lead a dignified life. For example, humans need a certain daily intake of calories, which varies individually with individual dispositions and activities. When the threshold for their daily intake is not met, human beings suffer and may eventually die.

For the principle of need-based justice, the proviso that some set of basic needs must be covered is derived from outcome equality. For the simple equality principle, it suffices to equalize outcomes. Equality of opportunity is concerned with the equalization of initial endowments and does not address outcomes. Both principles do not say anything about the consequences of distributions. Concerns about need are, as Frankfurt (1984) has pointed out, more fundamental in the sense that they address issues of survival, which is a more fundamental concept of equality because it is rooted in the idea of equality in human dignity. Thus, distributions are need-satisfying if they equalize outcomes not in terms of final payoffs but in terms of the possibility to remain "in the game (of life)."

The transfer of these ideas to a laboratory experiment requires a need that conforms to ethical standards and thus must involve a less dramatic condition in which social interactions take place. At the risk of being charged of trivializing human needs, I assume that the social mechanisms at work in fundamental need situations underlying the capability approach are of the same type as the social mechanisms that guide interactions in the laboratory. This assumption does not address the nature of the needs involved but only behavior in response to the need.

Nevertheless, it requires some explanation. Whatever sort of survival is at stake, it depends on access to sufficient resources to satisfy the needs involved in the situation. In the laboratory, a need can be generated by differentiating between a condition in which participants are engaged in some activity that is meaningful to them, in the present case by generating payoff, and a condition in which that activity is not meaningful, because it does not generate a payoff. To the extent that participants experience a laboratory session in which they produce payoff as meaningful, the notion of survival can be operationalized as the continuation of active participation in a laboratory session.

This analogy suggests to generate needs in the laboratory by means of a two-stage experiment. In the first stage, subjects decide on the division of an endowment among the members of a group and thus reveal their distributive preferences. In the second stage, each subject has the opportunity to individually and in private earn additional money. Needs are induced by the stipulation that subjects can only move on to the second stage if they meet an exogenously set individual threshold in the first stage.

Manipulating need levels under such conditions is straightforward: systematically varying the thresholds assigned to the subjects generates various constellations. Kittel et al. (2020) set the size of the resource to 24 points and assign individual thresholds between 0 and 12 points. With three subjects per group, a distribution rule based on the equality principle thus mandates that each subject obtains 8 points. Equal distribution provides a reference point and is often observed as a default in laboratory experiments with student participants (Selten 1987; Diermeier and Morton 2005). Realized distributions may deviate from this default equal distribution according to the preferences of decision makers, which may reflect self-interest or a social norm such as one of the principles of justice.

When there is an undersupply of needed resources in a society, some needs cannot be satisfied, which raises the question of how one can "evaluate the degree or fulfillment of the principle of need-based justice" (Nullmeier 2020, p. 204). In this situation, need satisfaction becomes a zero-sum game. To avoid situations in which not all needs can be satisfied by design and participants would be restricted in their distributive choices, the sum of thresholds in the reported experiments does not exceed the available resource. When there is an oversupply of the resource, all needs can be satisfied and the remainder distributed according to some other criterion. The recognition of needs is then measured by the fraction of needs that are satisfied in a realized distribution.

4.5 Need Satisfaction in Networks

Are needs a factor considered by decision makers in laboratory experiments? This question has a normative and a behavioral aspect. An indirect measure of the normative aspect is to ask players to rank distributions representing different principles of distributive justice and to aggregate these individual rankings into a group ranking for the three players who formed a group in the experiment (Kittel et al. 2017). Assume that the decision maker (x) has threshold 5, the first other player (y) 9, and the second other player (z) 1. Then a distribution of tokens (x, y, z) represents a distributive principle. For example, (24, 0, 0) indicates a purely self-regarding (individualistic) preference.

However, as argued above, the satisfaction of need claims does not necessarily result from the application of the need principle; the same distribution may correspond with alternative principles of justice. For example, the equal distribution (8, 8, 8) also satisfies need thresholds below 8 points and thus covers all need-based distributions with need thresholds equal to or lower than 8. The need principle can also be combined with self-regarding preferences. For example, two of the three players may agree on the bare satisfaction of the third player's need threshold. If this threshold is below the equal share, the two players can distribute the remainder between them according to some other principle.

For instance, a distribution of (14, 9, 1) for thresholds (5, 9, 1) suggests a concern for needs, because all thresholds are satisfied. However, it is combined with self-regarding preferences of the first player, because all tokens that are not required to satisfy the others' needs are allocated to herself. Similarly, (8, 8, 8) represents equality and (8, 9, 7) is the closest approximation to equality that also satisfies all need thresholds (5, 9, 1) while at the same time giving slight preference to one's own over others' payoffs ($x > z$), in line with Fehr and Schmidt (1999). An unequal distribution would be, for example, (12, 12, 0) and a need-satisfying unequal distribution approximating equality within the deciding dyad x, y would be (12, 11, 1).

Table 4.1 reports the distribution of preferences at the individual level and at the aggregate level of groups that were formed randomly. The rankings are summarized by means of a Borda count. According to this measure, the combinations that satisfy needs are chosen in 39% of cases at the individual level and in 62% of cases at the group level. A separate analysis of the different combinations with need included as a variable shows a slight advantage of individualism over equality (19% vs. 17%) at the individual level, but a clear domination of individualism over equality at the

Table 4.1 Individual and collective distributive preferences

Distributive principle	Individual level		Group level	
Need	0.39		0.62	
(Need + individualism)		*0.19*		*0.35*
(Need + equality)		*0.17*		*0.24*
(Need + unequal)		*0.03*		*0.03*
Individualism	0.32		0.14	
Equality	0.17		0.12	
Unequal	0.12		0.12	
Sum	1.00		1.00	

Borda counts of individual and aggregated rankings. The three combinations of need with other principles sum to the percentage for need. Source: Kittel et al. (2017, p. 15)

group level. This observation is in line with the result reported above that the more self-regarding preference prevails in dyadic decisions in the group context. The importance of self-interest is also evidenced by the 32% of individuals who prefer an individualistic distribution. However, at the group level this share drops to 14%, to the benefit of those who combine need and individualism. Hence, in groups, the presence of other-regarding individuals can moderate individualism and establish a group preference that combines individualism with need satisfaction. Overall, this analysis suggests that the combination of individualism with the satisfaction of needs appears to be a rather popular principle. This observation echoes both the preferences observed in European populations (see Chap. 1) and the popularity of efficiency with a floor constraint observed in laboratory experiments (Frohlich and Oppenheimer 1992; Traub et al. 2005).

Do these preferences translate into actual choices? Kittel et al. (2020) examine whether heterogeneous needs affect the distribution of outcomes in negatively connected exchange networks. Following the approach outlined above, they operationalize players' need as a threshold of tokens required to gain access to the next stage in which they can earn additional income. In line with Schwaninger et al. (2019), an offer is not restricted to the negotiating dyad but can be made to all network members.

Figure 4.2 summarizes the main findings of this experiment for the example of the threshold distribution (5, 9, 1). The two upper panels refer to the triangle network. Points represent distributions, which are defined by the percentage allocated to each of the players. The left panel shows the clear dominance of four focal points: one equal distribution in the middle of the triangle formed by the shares allocated to the three subjects and the three midpoints of the edges, which represent equal shares among the three possible dyads. The right panel shows that introducing the thresholds, which are represented by the three lines cutting the surface of the triangle, leads to the majority of allocations shifting towards points located within or at the edges of the triangle formed by the three thresholds. This indicates that all three thresholds are satisfied in these situations. Nevertheless, some dyads disregard the third player in their decisions and remain on the edges between the nodes of the network.

The two lower panels refer to the three-line network. The left panel shows three more densely populated focal points: the three-way equal distribution and the two midpoints of the edges that include player A, who holds the powerful node. Notably, few observations are located in the two ranges on the edges, which represent an allocation of more than 50% to A. This suggests that hardly any subjects A make use of their power to enforce a share that comes close to the predictions made in traditional network exchange theories (Braun and Gautschi 2006; Willer and Emanuelson 2008). The right panel presents the introduction of thresholds into this network. As in the upper right panel, this change leads to a shift of points to the area enclosed by the three thresholds, with a higher density near the highest threshold. This suggests that many groups approximate the equal distribution conditional on the threshold levels. Again, however, some dyads disregard the third player's threshold.

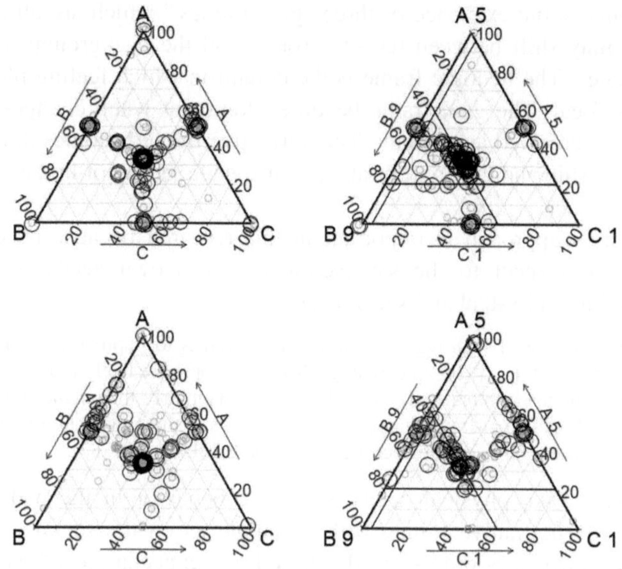

The figure shows accepted offers in the triangle (top) and three-line (bottom) network. Players are denoted with the letters A, B, C and the axes are labeled correspondingly. The three lines drawn in the right graphs mark the need threshold for each subject, which is also noted numerically next to the letter of the player (i.e. B9 has a threshold of nine tokens). Point indicators are slightly jittered. Source: Kittel, Neuhofer and Schwaninger (2017, p. 18).

Fig. 4.2 Accepted offers

To summarize, these results suggest that need is an important criterion for distributive decisions. Both in stated normative preferences and in observed behavior, many subjects negotiating in dyads use exogenously imposed thresholds as a yardstick for allocations in distributive decisions. In the next sections, I will discuss some factors that help explain the observed variation in the recognition of needs. I will proceed in two steps. First, I will elaborate on the impact of individual frames and perceptions on people's willingness to recognize others' needs. Second, I will discuss the effects of social factors and structural conditions on need recognition.

4.6 Frames, Perceptions, and the Recognition of Needs

The importance of frames and subjective perceptions for behavior is acknowledged across several disciplines in the social and behavioral sciences (Goffman 1974; Kahneman and Tversky 1979; Mercer 2005). People identify their contextual conditions as being of a particular type, which, in turn, induces them to perceive particular actions as more or less feasible or appropriate. In this vein, Lindenberg

(2013) postulates the existence of three "goal frames," which are all continuously present but may shift between the foreground and the background depending on contextual cues. The hedonic frame is the default in which feeling pleasant in the condition is focal. The gain frame becomes dominant when changes in personal resources are perceived as relevant. The normative frame becomes dominant when group membership and the appropriateness of specific behavior in that group set the scene.

Lindenberg's approach is important in this research because he develops his argument with respect to the satisfaction of one's own needs, which can be differentiated into physical and social needs.

> [T]he overarching goal with regard to need satisfaction is to improve [...] the way one feels at the moment. [...] [I]n a hedonic goal-frame, people are likely to react much more strongly to being made to feel bad, say, by being treated unfairly, than in the other two goal-frames. [...] A gain goal-frame flanks need satisfaction in the sense that it focuses on the resources necessary for need satisfaction. (Lindenberg 2013, pp. 82–83)

While one's own physical needs determine behavior in the hedonic and the gain frame, the normative frame, with its emphasis on the social need of group membership, introduces others' needs and others' expectations of their own need satisfaction into the definition of the situation. It is thus in the normative frame that others' needs may become focal and their satisfaction may become a goal for decision makers, which potentially competes with the satisfaction of the decision maker's needs. In the normative frame, however, needs compete with other principles of justice, which become more relevant depending on the type of social relationship in question (Liebig and Sauer 2013, 2016). Hence, in a social situation characterized by solidary community others will expect the satisfaction of needs to guide behavior (Liebig and Sauer 2013, 2016). Likewise, one can observe the dominance of equality in peer groups, equity in market exchanges, and entitlement in hierarchies. Building on goal frame theory, Liebig and Sauer (2013) hypothesize that people will orientate their behavior towards the principle of justice appropriate for a particular relationship if they expect reputation gains from this choice. More generally, this proposition implies that the normative goal frame is activated when people aim at satisfying social needs.

Esser and Kroneberg (2015) have further developed this approach to integrate the concept of frames into a theory of action. They distinguish three sequential mechanisms that guide the choice of behavior: people first select a frame out of a set of available alternative interpretations of the situation; they then activate scripts, that is, certain programs of action that are known to be appropriate for that frame; and finally, they choose between alternative scripts. Hagauer et al. (2019) build on this conceptualization to explore the problem of frame selection in the context of distributive decision problems. To assess the subjects' perception of the game, they categorized subjects by using their responses to open-ended questions in posttreatment questionnaires. Particularly, 25% of responses referred to profit, competition, power, or bargaining and were classified as proself. Further, 24% could be associated with fairness and cooperation and were classified as prosocial. The remaining 51% described their perception in neutral terms which do not allow for a classification with regard to social values. Hagauer et al. (2019, 21) find that subjects' perceptions of the game did not respond to small variations in the design of the experiment or the treatment. Instead, sociodemographic variables—such as gender, the cultural background measured by the mother tongue, and the length of study—appeared to have a substantial impact.

Hagauer et al. (2019, , pp. 21–24) also studied the effect of frames on goals. Subjects were asked to rank factors that might influence their decision. Those who ranked payoff maximization first were classified as having a proself goal. The authors find that the frame correlates with the subjects' goal in the distributive decision. Finally, they also find that the frame has a stable and statistically significant effect on the distributive outcome, which is conceptualized as inequality of payoffs and measured by the range between the highest and the lowest payoffs. At the same time, neither treatments nor sociodemographic variables were statistically related to the inequality of payoffs. In addition, subjects with more experience in experiments tended to behave less selfishly.

Hence, this study yields evidence supporting the view that people perceive situations in terms of earlier experiences and that these perceptions affect the way in which they behave in that situation. Put in Lindenberg's terms, those who have activated the gain frame tend to behave more selfishly and those who have activated the normative frame are more willing to share resources with others.

4.7 Contextual Determinants of Need Satisfaction in Networks

Having established the relevance of needs in distributive decisions and the importance of the individual's perception of the situation in which need claims are made, the next step is to study how the satisfaction of others' needs responds to changes in the contextual conditions framing the decision. In the following, I discuss the findings regarding the effect of threshold levels, availability of information about the threshold level, and group identity on the satisfaction of needs. Before, however, it is necessary to elaborate on the baseline expectations for individual decisions.

In Sect. 4.3, I have referred to the robust finding that many people are inequality averse. The simplest form of inequality aversion concerns the relative shares of a given resource allocated to oneself and others as envisaged by Fehr and Schmidt (1999). Combining the theory of inequality aversion with Lindenberg's goal frame theory, we can further develop our reasoning with respect to the conditions of need-based justice. The proposition that harm to oneself weighs heavier than harm to others (Fehr and Schmidt 1999) suggests that people who have activated the normative frame and thus care about others' needs may have to cope with a conflict between the norms that they seek to fulfil and the gain frame that remains active in the background.

> Often the goal frame and background goals will be in conflict. For example, if being cooperative is quite expensive, the normative goal-frame and the gain goal in the background are incompatible. This may not change the goal-frame from a normative one to a gain goal-frame—that is, the background motive may not affect the orientation (the ordering of alternatives is still in terms of appropriateness, not in terms of price), but it may lead to the choice of a less appropriate (but cheaper) alternative. (Lindenberg 2013, p. 84)

This dilemma can be described as some sort of a "reservation clause" that becomes effective once allocations to others imperil allocations to oneself, up to the extreme of one's own survival. A likely candidate criterion for this clause is the differentiation between basic and instrumental needs. The reservation clause, we may argue, thus introduces a limit to altruistic behavior when the allocation to another person conflicts with the satisfaction of one's own basic needs. Note that, other than in the case of the equality principle, one cannot interpret self-regarding preferences as envy or greed.

Based on these considerations, we can derive expectations about subjects' responses to others' needs. The first type, self-interested people—or, in the terminology of Lindenberg (2013), people whose gain frame is activated—are expected to be unresponsive to variation in the level of others' needs and to always choose the strategy that maximizes their own earnings. For the analysis of need-based justice, the only interesting characteristics of self-interested people are their share in the population and the effects of their presence on the behavior of the second group, that is, other-regarding people. To the extent that interactions are characterized by reciprocity, self-regarding behavior may ignite a self-reinforcing dynamic that undermines other-regarding concerns in the whole population, such as the breakdown of cooperation regularly observed in experiments on the provision of public goods (Marwell and Ames 1979; Fehr and Gächter 2000; Diekmann and Lindenberg 2015).

A second type includes inequality-averse people who are concerned with equal allocations and disregard any other conditions of the distributive problem. These strict, but myopic egalitarians will consistently choose an equal allocation of an endowment, that is, (8, 8, 8) for a group of three distributing 24 tokens, irrespective of, for example, the satisfaction of individual needs, which may exceed the share legitimized by the equality principle.

The third type strives for some combination of their own and others' payoffs. Unlike the first and second type, they are concerned with needs, albeit in different ways. On the one hand, they may combine a concern for needs with self-regarding or efficiency preferences. These people care about the satisfaction of others' needs, but, once all needs are satisfied, will maximize their own earnings using the surplus resources. Such a combination is frequently observed in laboratory experiments (Frohlich and Oppenheimer 1992; Engelmann and Strobel 2004; Traub et al. 2005). However, the choice set implemented in these experiments usually involves a floor constraint providing some uniform minimum for all, which, strictly speaking, cannot be interpreted in terms of need-based justice because this minimum payment is unresponsive to individual needs. On the other hand, for inequality-averse people, the equal distribution is a natural attractor, a focal point chosen as a default when there is no sufficient reason to deviate from it. Those who also take the more fundamental level of equality into account, that is, equality of capabilities, will take another person's needs as a sufficient reason to deviate from equality but will otherwise distribute the surplus as equally as possible. As long as the joint resource that is to be distributed is sufficiently large to cover all needs and no needs are larger than the allocation of $1/n$, with n representing the number of involved persons, the equal distribution will cover the distribution according to needs. As a result, in situations like this, one cannot discern whether equality or need determined the outcome.

However, the problem can be even more intricate than this. Assuming an allocation problem involving two players (who may be a collective agent, such as a dyad), we can distinguish four combinations of the player's own and others' needs when the dyad acts as a collective agent. This depends on whether need thresholds are below or above the allocation that would result from an equal distribution of the endowment, that is, (16, 8). First, when the other player's threshold is below the equal share, provided that one's own threshold is also satisfied by the equal distribution, advantageous inequality aversion pushes allocations towards equality and the other's threshold is automatically covered by the equal distribution. However, when one's own needs rise above the equal share, aversion against disadvantageous inequality becomes relevant. When one's own needs are compromised, the other's needs become secondary. Thus, in this case the satisfaction of one's own threshold has priority over equality, meaning the decision makers will first satisfy their own needs and then the other's needs and finally allocate the remainder in a way that approximates equality.

The third combination is a situation where the other player's needs are above the amount allocated by an equal distribution and the decision maker must choose between the need principle, on the one hand, and either the equality principle or self-interest, on the other hand. When satisfying the other's need requires an allocation that exceeds the allocation to self, which is necessarily the case when the other needs more than the equal share, the decision maker must allocate less than the equal share to herself in order to satisfy the other's need. Thus, disadvantageous inequality aversion conflicts with the satisfaction of the other's needs. Moreover, efficiency concerns and self-regarding preferences pull in the same direction as inequality aversion. A concern for others' needs thus has to overcome substantial counterforces in this case, and since, in line with inequality aversion theory, such generosity is unlikely to occur in practice, satisfaction of the other's needs is expected to decline as the amount the other requires increases.

This problem of rank reversal has been further elaborated by Zauchner (2023). In a laboratory experiment, she shows that uninvolved "social planners" are more likely to equalize the payoffs of subjects when the necessary transfer does not reverse the relative size of those subjects' initial endowments. However, she also showed that the satisfaction of needs raises the willingness to deviate from this principle of rejecting re-rankings.

The conflict between one's own and others' needs is exacerbated in the fourth combination in which both one's own and the other's needs are larger than the equal share of a resource. This situation occurs when the resource is insufficient to cover all needs and the satisfaction of needs turns into a zero-sum game in which only one of the two players will complete the game with their needs met. In this case, one's own survival tops the other's survival for all empirically observable types of decision makers (Murphy and Ackermann 2014). Given that this combination is ruled out by the design of the experiments reported here, I do not consider it further.

This reasoning can be tested empirically by evaluating the effect of different thresholds on the satisfaction of needs. Using the three-line network, Kittel et al. (2020) compare the need satisfaction rates, that is, the percentage of players whose need thresholds are satisfied, for central players in the 3-line network, their partners in the dyad, and third players at thresholds of 1, 5, 9, and 12 tokens.

They show that the thresholds of those who form a dyad are almost always satisfied, irrespective of the threshold level (note that central players were never assigned a threshold of 12). In contrast, the third player's satisfaction of needs decreases substantially as the threshold increases. While more than two-thirds of thresholds of 1 token are satisfied, this share drops to slightly over 50% for thresholds of 5. Above the equal share, that is, 8 tokens, about 25% of the third players' thresholds are satisfied. These observations support the argument developed above that the goal of satisfying the needs of others loses its normative appeal as soon as it implies that the resulting inequality in the distribution is disadvantageous to oneself.

Any need claim must be comprehensible to others, but greater needs require particular evidence of their veracity in order to overcome the self-serving bias in allocative decisions. Kittel et al. (2021) thus compare allocations to third players in a treatment where the threshold is public information (transparency) with a treatment where the information about individual thresholds is private (opacity).

Figure 4.3 presents their results. The share of satisfied need thresholds declines when threshold levels increase. But while there is no difference between transparent and opaque needs below the equal distribution (8 tokens per player), the need satisfaction of third players with thresholds above the equal distribution drops to almost zero when their claims cannot be independently verified. In contrast, the share of satisfied transparent need thresholds that exceed equality is about one-quarter. These differences between transparent and opaque needs are statistically significant.

Kittel et al. (2021) also report a seemingly paradoxical observation: although third players' needs are satisfied less often when they are opaque, the payoffs that third players receive are larger in the opaque than in the transparent condition. The reason is that decision makers use their knowledge of others' thresholds as anchor points for allocations but more often opt for equal allocations when they do not know others' thresholds. Transparency, therefore, substantially lowers allocations to third players with low thresholds. This result points to an important social mechanism that influences distributive decisions: when there is insufficient information about the other person's life conditions, people opt for the equality principle. But as soon

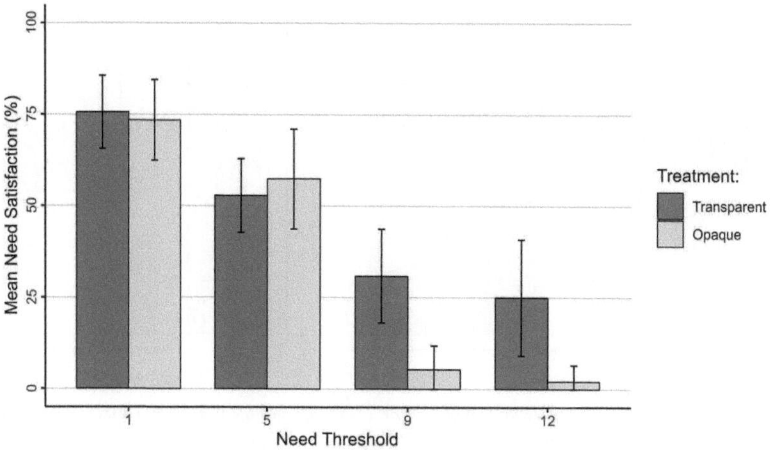

Source: Kittel, Neuhofer and Schwaninger (2021, p. 14).

Fig. 4.3 Outsider's need satisfaction rates for transparent and opaque needs

as they are offered such information, they make use of it to adjust their allocations. The need threshold is such a condition, and self-serving bias causes the downward pull of others' low needs to be stronger than the upward pull of others' high needs.

The willingness to recognize and satisfy others' needs has been associated with social proximity (Liebig and Sauer 2016; Kittel 2020). People who feel closer to each other are expected to better understand each other's needs, and their more intense awareness of others' living conditions raises the probability that they will satisfy these needs. An important condition of the development of social proximity is communication. People who speak to each other develop some common understanding of their situation and a sense of community. Hence, distributive outcomes may depend on the communication mode. Comparing free-form communication, in which players can state anything they like in a chat facility, with a restricted communication mode where distributive preferences can only be stated by means of numbers, Neuhofer (2021, p. 22) finds that "[t]he frequency of entitlement or equity-based distributions decreases notably, whereas equality-based distributions increase slightly and need-based distributions increase substantially when communication is free-form." Moreover, based on a qualitative content analysis of chat protocols, she observes that, "[w]hereas references to the norm of equality increase the frequency of equal outcomes and decrease the frequency of need-based and entitlement/equity-based outcomes, references to immediate interaction partners increase entitlement/equity-based distributions and decrease equality and need-based distributions" (Neuhofer 2021, p. 22).

According to minimal group theory, small cues such as being assigned the same color may generate solidarity in randomly formed groups (Tajfel 1982). Kittel et al. (2022) use a group task conducted in an initial stage of a laboratory experiment to induce differences in solidary feelings among participants. They then compare the

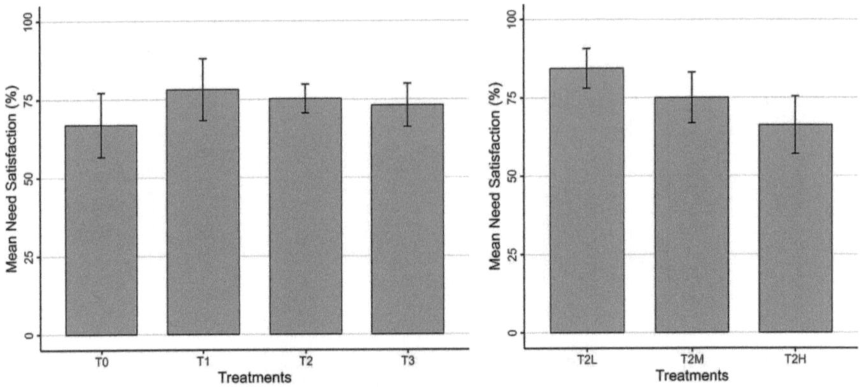

Left panel: Group compositions; right panel: Group composition & outsider threshold. Source: Kittel, Schwaninger and Szendrő (2022, pp. 9 & 11).

Fig. 4.4 Group solidarity and need satisfaction rates

satisfaction of needs within groups of three in the second stage. The groups vary with regard to the number of subjects who have worked together in the previous stage. They expect that solidarity will be highest when all three group members share the experience of previous cooperation and lowest when people perform the tasks individually or all come from different groups. They also expect to find an insider-outsider effect when two group members share a previous group experience while the third member completed the task in a different group. Further, they systematically vary the thresholds assigned to the three group members, resulting in three scenarios in which the outsider either has a low, medium, or high threshold.

The results presented in Fig. 4.4 suggest that the story is somewhat more complex. The left panel shows the need satisfaction rates for the four group compositions. The individual task condition (T0) indeed results in the lowest average need satisfaction rate, but the common condition (T3) does not induce the highest rate. Also, the second-highest need satisfaction rate for the insider-outsider treatment (T2) is not in line with expectations. Groups in which all members do the group task but all come from different groups (T1) have the highest need satisfaction rates. However, none of the differences are statistically significant. The right panel disaggregates T2 into the three possible scenarios regarding the outsider's need threshold. The authors find that the need satisfaction rate declines with the rising thresholds of the outsider and that the difference between the lowest and the highest thresholds is statistically significant. These observations suggest that group tasks do indeed induce solidarity within the group, but that this solidarity is conditional on the individuals' status within the group and on their need levels. People seem to be willing to cover the small needs of outsiders, but rarely satisfy outsider needs that exceed their own allocation. No such discriminatory effect is observed when the player with the highest needs is one of the two group members who were in the same group task in the previous stage of the experiment. These results suggest that the preceding joint task raises solidarity and that mixed groups respond to the level of the outsider's need threshold. While the insiders are very much willing to satisfy the low needs of the third player, they are extremely reluctant to cover an outsider's high-need thresholds.

4.8 Conclusion

The results reported in this chapter suggest that the social recognition of needs depends on the interplay of situational, social, and personal conditions. In distributive decisions people consider different justice principles and respond to the frames defined by the decision situation. To a large extent, the effect of contextual conditions depends on the way in which subjects perceive the situation. Moreover, while self-interest consistently plays a role, a decontextualized conception of equality, which restricts attention to the division of the resource at hand, appears as a strong focal point with normative appeal for many decisions as long as the decision situation does not provide a reason to deviate from this approach. Need thresholds provide such a reason, but their impact on distributive decisions depends on the implications of applying them. In particular, the equal distribution appears to be a critical threshold above which few need claims are recognized by others. This result can be explained by the stronger effect of disadvantageous than of advantageous inequality, but is also congruent with the general assumption of self-interested utility maximization. The latent presence of self-interest also explains the observation that transparent low thresholds have a stronger pull effect on allocations than transparent high thresholds.

While needs are subjective, the satisfaction of needs rests on their social recognition (Nullmeier 2020, p. 200). Hence, knowledge of others' needs is a critical condition for the willingness of—collective—decision makers to accept allocations to the needy, most notably when they are larger than allocations to themselves. However, this condition is not sufficient to raise the need satisfaction rate for high-need thresholds beyond about 25%. Low-need thresholds are more frequently satisfied, with rates up to 75%. However, the downside of the transparency of low-need thresholds from the perspective of claimants is that it leads to smaller allocations than when the thresholds are opaque. In the latter case, lack of information pushes the equality principle to the foreground. Thus, we observe a transparency dilemma: when there is proof of the veracity of need claims, more claims are satisfied, but the claim becomes an anchor for allocations and small needs are covered by small transfers; when need claims cannot be verified, transfers tend to be geared towards the equal distribution, therefore leading to allocations above the threshold if this is low, but these claims are more rarely recognized. This observation is congruent with the stylized fact derived from many previous studies that people choose the equal distribution when there is no reason to deviate from it.

So far, we have observed that self-interest is constantly present as a motive, which activates as soon as one's own allocations become lower than allocations to others or even risk falling below one's own need threshold. We have also established that both the threshold level and the transparency of needs are exogenous attributes of the decision situation that affect the satisfaction of others' needs. Another factor affecting need satisfaction rates is the social structure of the group. Decision makers tend to take group membership into account to avoid disadvantageous inequality for themselves: people allocate less to outsiders when their need thresholds are high. Thus, the size of the threshold and group membership interact.

The experiments conducted in the reported studies frame the decision situation as one of oversupply (Nullmeier 2020, p. 202): in principle, all needs can be satisfied and there remains a surplus that can be distributed according to additional criteria, such as equality, equity, or self-interest. Thus, the plurality of justice principles applied in distributive decisions is created by design. However, the fact that decision makers take needs into account when they have the opportunity to choose other principles to guide the distribution of the total resource is not self-evident. Note that in the case of undersupply, the urgency of the satisfaction of one's own needs transforms any distributive problem into a zero-sum decision dominated by self-interest.

"Need-based justice can only be developed meaningfully as an element of a pluralistic theory of justice" (Nullmeier 2020, p. 196). The presented results underscore this proposition. Moreover, the findings also support the proposition that need takes precedence over other principles of distributive justice when the decision maker's own interests are not strongly compromised (Nullmeier 2020, p. 191). People seem to have a bundle of justice conceptions in their mind when confronted with the task of distributing a resource in a group. From this bundle, they select the principle or principles that they perceive to be the most appropriate in the given situation.

Acknowledgments This chapter reports, summarizes, and discusses results from the project "Distributive Preferences and Need-Based Justice in Networks," which formed part of the research group FOR 2104 "Need-Based Justice and Distribution Procedures." The research was funded in whole by the Austrian Science Fund (FWF), grants I1888-G11 and I3804-G27. With much gratitude I acknowledge the contributions of the members of the project team, most notably Sabine Neuhofer and Manuel Schwaninger, as well as, in alphabetic order, Helena Hagauer, Hermann Helke, Georg Kanitsar, Réka Szendrő, Lilla Tolnai, and Marvin Waibel. Their input, ideas, and work constitute an invaluable asset without which it would not have been possible to write this chapter. The responsibility for its contents is solely mine, however.

References

Adams, J. S. (1965): "Inequity in Social Exchange", in L. Berkowitz (ed.): *Advances in Experimental Social Psychology*, Vol. 2, New York: Academic Press, 267–299.
Baybrooke, D. (1987): *Meeting Needs*. Princeton: Princeton University Press.
Blau, P. M. (1964a): *Exchange and Power in Social Life*. New Brunswick: Transaction Publishers.
Blau, P. M. (1964b): "Justice in Social Exchange", *Sociological Inquiry* 34 (2), 193–206.

Bogaert, S., C. Boone, and D. Carolyn (2008): "Social Value Orientation and Cooperation in Social Dilemmas: A Review and Conceptual Model", *British Journal of Social Psychology* 27 (3), 453–480.
Bolton, G. E., and A. Ockenfels (2000): "ERC: A Theory of Equity, Reciprocity, and Competition", *American Economic Review* 90 (1), 166–193.
Bowles, S., and H. Gintis (2000): "Reciprocity, Self-Interest, and the Welfare State", *Nordic Journal of Political Economy* 26 (4), 33–53.
Brañas-Garza, P. (2006): "Poverty in Dictator Games: Awakening Solidarity", *Journal of Economic Behavior & Organization* 60 (3), 306–320.
Braun, N., and T. Gautschi (2006): "A Nash Bargaining Model for Simple Exchange Networks", *Social Networks* 28 (1), 1–23.
Brock, G., and D. Miller (2019): "Needs in Moral and Political Philosophy", in E. N. Zalta (ed.): *The Stanford Encyclopedia of Philosophy, Stanford: Metaphysics Research Lab, Stanford University*. https://plato.stanford.edu/archives/sum2019/entries/needs/.
Cappelen, A. W., K. O. Moene, E. O. Sørensen, and B. Tungodden (2013): "Needs versus Entitlements. An International Fairness Experiment", *Journal of the European Economic Association* 11 (3), 574–598.
Cartwright, E. (2019): "A Survey of Belief-Based Guilt Aversion in Trust and Dictator Games", *Journal of Economic Behavior & Organization* 167, 430–444.
Charness, G., and M. Rabin (2002): "Understanding Social Preferences with Simple Tests", *Quarterly Journal of Economics* 117 (3), 817–869.
Charness, G., and M. Sutter (2012): "Groups Make Better Self-Interested Decisions", *Journal of Economic Perspectives* 26 (3), 157–176.
Comin, F., and M. C. Nussbaum, (ed.) (2014): *Capabilities, Gender, Equality. Towards Fundamental Entitlements*. Cambridge: Cambridge University Press.
Cook, K. S., and R. M. Emerson (1978): "Power, Equity and Commitment in Exchange Networks", *American Sociological Review* 43 (5), 721–739.
Cook, K. S., and K. A. Hegtvedt (1983): "Distributive Justice, Equity, and Equality", *Annual Review of Sociology* 9, 217–241.
Dana, J., R. A. Weber, and J. Xi Kuang (2007): "Exploiting Moral Wiggle Room: Experiments Demonstrating an Illusory Preference for Fairness", *Economic Theory* 33 (1), 67–80.
De Quidt, J., J. Haushofer, and C. Roth (2018): "Measuring and Bounding Experimenter Demand", *American Economic Review* 108 (11), 3303–3338.
Diekmann, A. (2022): "Rational Choice Sociology: Heuristic Potential, Applications and Limitation", in K. Gërxhani, N. D. de Graaf and W. Raub (eds.): *Handbook of Sociological Science. Contributions to Rigorous Sociology*, 100–119. Cheltenham: Edward Elgar.
Diekmann, A., and S. Lindenberg (2015): "Cooperation: Sociological Aspects", in J. D. Wright (ed.): *International Encyclopedia of the Social & Behavioral Sciences*, Vol. 4, http://dx.doi.org/10.1016/B978-0-08-097086-8.32031-1
Diermeier, D., and R. B. Morton (2005): "Experiments in Majoritarian Bargaining", in D. Austen-Smith and J. Duggan (eds.): *Social Choice and Strategic Decisions. Essays in Honor of Jeffrey S. Banks*, 201–226. Berlin: Springer.
Doyal, L., and I. Gough (1991): *A Theory of Human Need*. New York: Guilford Press.
Durkheim, E. (1982 [1895]): *The Rules of Sociological Method*. New York: The Free Press.
Emanuelson, P. (2013): "An Elementary Theory of Social Structure", *International Review of Social Research* 3 (3), 13–20.
Emerson, R. M. (1964): "Power-Dependence Relations: Two Experiments", *Sociometry* 27 (3), 282–298.
Emerson, R. M. (1976): "Social Exchange Theory", *Annual Review of Sociology* 2, 335–362.
Engel, C. (2011): "Dictator Games: A Meta Study", *Experimental Economics* 14, 583–610.
Engelmann, D., and M. Strobel (2004): "Inequality Aversion, Efficiency, and Maximin Preferences in Simple Distribution Games", *American Economic Review* 94 (4), 857–869.

Esser, H., and C. Kroneberg (2015): “An Integrative Theory of Action. The Model of Frame Selection”, in E. J. Lawler, S. R. Thye and J. Yoon (eds.): *Order on the Edge of Chaos: Social Psychology and the Problem of Social Order*, 63–85. New York: Cambridge University Press.

Fehr, E., and K. M. Schmidt (1999): “A Theory of Fairness, Competition, and Cooperation”, *Quarterly Journal of Economics* 114 (3), 817–868.

Fehr, E., and S. Gächter (2000): “Cooperation and Punishment in Public Goods Experiments”, *American Economic Review* 90 (4), 980–994.

Forsythe, R., J. L. Horowitz, N. E. Savin, and M. Sefton (1994): “Fairness in Simple Bargaining Experiments”, *Games and Economic Behavior* 6 (3), 347–369.

Frankfurt, H. G. (1984): “Necessity and Desire”, *Philosophy and Phenomenological Research* 45 (1), 1–13.

Fraser, N. (1989): “Talking About Needs: Interpretive Contests as Political Conflicts in Welfare-State Societies”, *Ethics* 99 (2), 291–313.

Frohlich, N., and J. Oppenheimer (1992): *Choosing Justice: An Experimental Approach to Ethical Theory*. Ewing: University of California Press.

Goffman, E. (1974): *Frame Analysis*. New York: Harper and Row.

Goodin, R. E. (2002): “Structures of Mutual Obligation”, *Journal of Social Policy* 31 (4), 579–596.

Güth, W., R. Schmittberger, and B. Schwarze (1982): “An Experimental Analysis of Ultimatum Bargaining”, *Journal of Economic Behavior & Organization* 3 (4), 367–388.

Güth, W., and M. G. Kocher (2014): “More than Thirty Years of Ultimatum Bargaining Experiments: Motives, Variations, and a Survey of the Recent Literature”, *Journal of Economic Behavior & Organization*, 108, 396–409.

Hagauer, H., B. Kittel, and M. Schwaninger (2019): “Fairness in Bargaining: How Self-selected Frames Affect the Fairness of Negotiated Outcomes”, in M. Debus, M. Tepe and J. Sauermann (eds.): *Jahrbuch für Handlungs- und Entscheidungstheorie, Band* 11, 3–31. Wiesbaden: Springer VS.

Hegtvedt, K. A. (2005): “Doing Justice to the Group”, *Annual Review of Sociology* 31, 25–45.

Hegtvedt, K. A. (2006): “Justice Frameworks”, in P. J. Burke (ed.): *Contemporary Social Psychological Theories*, 46–69. Stanford: Stanford University Press.

Hegtvedt, K. A. and B. N. Markovsky (1995): “Justice and Injustice”, in K. S. Cook, G. A. Fine and J. House (eds.): *Sociological Perspectives on Social Psychology*, 257–280. Needham Heights, MA: Allyn & Bacon.

Homans, G. C. (1961): *Social Behavior: Its Elementary Forms*. London: Routledge & Kegal Paul.

Kahneman, D., and A. Tversky (1979): “Prospect Theory: An Analysis of Decision under Risk”, *Econometrica* 47 (2), 263–292.

Kahneman, D., J. L. Knetsch, and R. Thaler (1986): “Fairness and the Assumptions of Economics”, *Journal of Business* 59 (4), S285–S300.

Kause, A., O. Vitouch, and J. Glück (2018): “How Selfish Is a Thirsty Man? A Pilot Study on Comparing Sharing Behavior with Primary and Secondary Rewards”, *PLoS ONE* 13 (8), e0201358.

Kerschbamer, R. (2015): “The Geometry of Distributional Preferences and a Non-Parametric Identification Approach: The Equality Equivalence Test”, *European Economic Review* 76, 85–103.

Kittel, B. (2020): “Need-based Justice: A Sociological Perspective”, in S. Traub and B. Kittel (eds.): *Need-based Distributive Justice: An Interdisciplinary Perspective*, 91–131. Cham: Springer Nature.

Kittel, B., S. Neuhofer, and M. Schwaninger (2017): “Need-Based Justice in Social Exchange Networks”, *FOR 2104 Working Paper* 2017–04.

Kittel, B., S. Neuhofer, and M. Schwaninger (2020): “The Impact of Need on Distributive Decisions: Experimental Evidence on Anchor Effects of Exogenous Thresholds in the Laboratory”, *PLoS ONE* 15 (4), 0228753.

Kittel, B., S. Neuhofer, and M. Schwaninger (2021): “The Dark Side of Transparent Needs. An Experiment on Information and Need-Based Justice”, *FOR 2104 Working Paper* 2021–04.

Kittel, B., M. Schwaninger, and R. Szendrő (2022): "Need-Based Justice Beyond Social Ties: Experimental Evidence on the Scope of the Need Principle", *FOR 2104 Working Paper* 2022–03.

Krupka, E., and R. A. Weber (2013): "Identifying Social Norms Using Coordination Games: Why Does Dictator Game Sharing Vary?", *Journal of the European Economic Association* 11 (3), 495–524.

Levitt, S. D., and J. A. List (2007): "What Do Laboratory Experiments Measuring Social Preferences Reveal About the Real World", *Journal of Economic Perspectives* 21 (2), 153–174.

Lewis, P. D., and D. Willer (2017): "Does Social Value Orientation Theory Apply to Social Relations?", *Sociological Science* 3, 249–262.

Liebig, S., and C. Sauer (2013): "Soziologische Gerechtigkeitsanalyse: Überlegungen zur theoretischen Fundierung eines Forschungsfeldes", *Analyse & Kritik* 35 (2), 371–394.

Liebig, S., and C. Sauer (2016): "Sociology of Justice", in C. Sabbagh and M. Schmitt (eds.): *Handbook of Social Justice Theory and Research*, 37–59. Berlin: Springer.

Lindemann, G. (2010): "Die Emergenzfunktion des Dritten–ihre Bedeutung für die Analyse der Ordnung einer funktional differenzierten Gesellschaft", *Zeitschrift für Soziologie* 39 (6), 493–511.

Lindenberg, S. (2013): "Social Rationality, Self-Regulation, and Well-Being: The Regulatory Significance of Needs, Goals, and the Self", in V. Nee, R. Wittek and T. A. B. Snijders (eds.): *The Handbook of Rational Choice Social Research*, 72–112. Stanford: Stanford University Press.

Lindenberg, S. (2015): "The Sociology of Groups", in J. D. Wright (ed.): *International Encyclopedia of the Social & Behavioral Sciences*, Vol. 10, 434–440. Elsevier.

Marwell, G., and R. A. Ames (1979): "Experiments on the Provision of Public Goods. I. Resources, Interest, Group Size, and the Free-Rider Problem", *American Journal of Sociology* 84 (6), 1335–1360.

Mau, S. (2004): "Welfare Regimes and the Norms of Social Exchange", *Current Sociology* 52 (1), 53–74.

Mercer, J. (2005): "Prospect Theory and Political Science", *Annual Review of Political Science* 8, 1–21.

Messick, D., and C. G. McClintock (1968): "Motivational Bases of Choice in Experimental Games", *Journal of Experimental Social Psychology* 4 (1), 1–25.

Miller, D. (1999): *Principles of Social Justice*. Cambridge, Mass.: Harvard University Press.

Molm, L. D. (2014): "Experiments on Exchange Relations and Exchange Networks in Sociology", in M. Webster Jr. and J. Sell (eds.): *Laboratory Experiments in the Social Sciences (2nd ed.)*, 199–224. Amsterdam: Elsevier.

Molm, L. D., J. L. Collett, and D. R. Schaefer (2007): "Building Solidarity Through Generalized Exchange: A Theory of Reciprocity", *American Journal of Sociology* 113 (1), 205–242.

Molm, L. D. (2010): "The Structure of Reciprocity", *Social Psychology Quarterly* 73 (2), 119–131.

Murphy, R. O., and K. A. Ackermann (2014): "Social Value Orientation: Theoretical and Measurement Issues in the Study of Social Preferences", *Personality and Social Psychology Review* 18 (1), 13–41.

Neuhofer, S. (2021): "Let's Chat About Justice in a Fair Distribution Experiment", *FOR 2104 Working Paper* 2021–03.

Neuhofer, S., M. Schwaninger, B. Kittel, and G. Yang (2022): "Solidarity with Third Players in Exchange Networks: A Replication Study", in J. Sauermann, M. Tepe and M. Debus (eds.): *Jahrbuch für Handlungs- und Entscheidungstheorie, Band* 12, 109–136. Wiesbaden: Springer VS.

Nullmeier, F. (2020): "Towards a Theory of Need-based Justice", in S. Traub and B. Kittel (eds.): *Need-based Distributive Justice: An Interdisciplinary Perspective*, 191–208. Cham: Springer Nature.

Nussbaum, M. (2011): *Creating Capabilities. The Human Development Approach*. Cambridge: Belknap Press.

Opp, K.-D. (1999): “Contending Conceptions of the Theory of Rational Action”, *Journal of Theoretical Politics* 11 (2), 171–202.

Schwaninger, M. (2021): *Sharing with the Powerless Third: Other-Regarding Preferences in Dynamic Bargaining. FOR 2104 Working Paper* 2021–02.

Schwaninger, M., S. Neuhofer, and B. Kittel (2019): “Offers Beyond the Negotiating Dyad: Including the Excluded in a Network Exchange Experiment”, *Social Science Research* 79 (March), 258–271.

Selten, R. (1987): “Equity and Coalition Bargaining in Experimental Three-Person Games”, in A. E. Roth (ed.): *Laboratory Experimentation in Economics. Six Points of Views*, 42–98. Cambridge: Cambridge University Press.

Sen, A. (1985): *Commodities and Capabilities*. Oxford: Elsevier.

Sen, A. (2000): “Social Justice and the Distribution of Income”, in A. B. Atkinson and F. Bourguignon (eds.): *Handbook of Income Distribution*, Vol. 1, 59–85. Amsterdam: Elsevier.

Simmel, G. (1964 [1908]): *The Sociology of Georg Simmel*. Glencoe: The Free Press.

Smith, V. (1976): “Experimental Economics: Induced Value Theory”, *American Economic Review* 66 (2), 274–279.

Swedberg, R. (2005): “Markets in Society”, in N. J. Smelser, and R. Swedberg (eds.): *The Handbook of Economic Sociology*. Princeton: Princeton University Press.

Tajfel, H. (1982): *Social Identity and Intergroup Relations*. Cambridge: Cambridge University Press.

Traub, S., C. Seidl, U. Schmidt, and M. V. Levati (2005): “Friedman, Harsanyi, Rawls, Boulding–or Somebody Else? An Experimental Investigation of Distributive Justice”, *Social Choice and Welfare* 24, 283–309.

Traub, S., M. Schwaninger, F. Paetzel, and S. Neuhofer (2023): “Evidence on Need-Sensitive Giving Behavior: An Experimental Approach to the Acknowledgment of Needs”, *Journal of Behavioral and Experimental Economics* 105, 102028.

Weber, M. (1978 [1921/22]): *Economy and Society. An Outline of Interpretive Sociology*. Berkeley: University of California Press.

Weimann, J., and J. Brosig-Koch (2019): *Methods in Experimental Economics*. Berlin: Springer.

Willer, D., and P. Emanuelson (2008): “Testing Ten Theories”, *Journal of Mathematical Sociology* 32, 165–203.

Willer, D., E. Gladstone, and N. Berigan (2013): “Social Values and Social Structure”, *Journal of Mathematical Sociology* 37 (2), 113–130.

Willer, D., P. Emanuelson, M. J. Lovaglia, B. Simpson, S. R. Thye, H. Walker, M. Corra, S. Gilham, D. Lewis, T. Patton, Y. Chacon, and R. Chacon (2014): “Elementary Theory: 25 Years of Expanding Scope and Increasing Precision”, in S. R. Thye and E. J. Lawler (eds.): *Advances in Group Processes*, Vol. 31, 175–217. Bingley, U.K.: Emerald.

Wyszynski, M., A. Diederich, and I. Ritov (2020): “Gamble for the Needy! Does Identifiability Enhances Donation?”, *PLoS ONE* 15 (6), e0234336.

Zauchner, P. (2023): *Needs versus Ranks. Can Needs Considerations Reduce the Negative Effect of Rank Reversals on the Acceptance of Redistribution?* Bremen: Doctoral Thesis, Universität Bremen.

Zizzo, D. J. (2010): “Experimenter Demand Effects in Economic Experiments”, *Experimental Economics* 13 (1), 75–98.

Chapter 5
The Political Recognition of Needs

Markus Tepe and Nils Springhorn

Abstract This chapter discusses the political recognition of needs and the role of expertise in allocation decisions. It reviews three aspects of the political recognition of needs: First, it presents two alternative politico-economic decision frameworks for studying the behavioral consequences of need-based justice. Second, it discusses the scope and differentiation of the principle of need-based justice. Specifically, it explores the conditions under which voters' social identity may lead to an exclusive or inclusive application of the need principle. Third, this chapter will elaborate on the role of expertise in the political recognition and collective satisfaction of needs. Expertise can either help with problem-solving by objectifying needs or provide some moral authority that increases the chances of a collectively agreed allocation satisfying needs. The final section summarizes the main findings and discusses their implications for developing a concise theory of need-based justice.

5.1 Introduction

Democratic societies are often confronted with situations in which they have to agree on the distribution or allocation of a pooled resource or a windfall profit. In such instances, the three most common ethical references for collectively determining a just distribution or allocation are the principles of equity, equality, and need (Miller 1999; Sen 2009). Need, as a principle of distributive justice, can determine the allocation of shares of a joint resource. Needs differ from the two alternative principles of justice, equality and equity. Equality means that all players receive the same share, whereas equity links the individual share to some criterion,

M. Tepe (✉)
Universität Bremen, SOCIUM Research Center on Inequality and Social Policy, Bremen, Germany
e-mail: markus.tepe@uni-bremen.de

N. Springhorn
Carl von Ossietzky Universität Oldenburg, Department of Social Sciences, Oldenburg, Germany
e-mail: n.springhorn@uni-oldenburg.de

B. Kittel, S. Traub (eds.), *Priority of Needs?*,
https://doi.org/10.1007/978-3-031-53051-7_5

such as prior performance, to justify deviations from equal distribution (Miller 1999; Sen 2009; Konow 2003). Equity links individual payoffs to an individual input, such as contributions, efforts, or merit. Differences in individual inputs are commonly accepted as a legitimate reason for unequal distributions and allocations. Both principles, however, focus on the universal application of justice and thus ignore any heterogeneity in the subjects' needs. Equality and equity, thus, cannot be relevant to all distributive decisions (Frohlich and Oppenheimer 1992). Need-based justice emphasizes satisfying the needs of the most vulnerable members of a given society. However, this presupposes a social process of recognizing individual needs for a "minimally decent life" (Miller 1999, p. 210).

Nullmeier (2020) suggests a set of ten propositions to develop a concise theory of need-based justice. This chapter will address the fourth proposition, which states that "need is one of several criteria for determining a just order" (Nullmeier 2020, 196) and the fifth proposition, according to which "there can be no theory of need-based justice without reference to a process by which needs are determined as socially or politically recognized" (Nullmeier 2020, p. 198). This chapter is concerned with how democratic societies organize the collective recognition of individual needs and how they vote on distributions or allocations.

This chapter reviews three aspects of the political recognition of needs: First, it presents two alternative politico-economic voting models for studying the behavioral consequences of need-based justice. These include a simplified version of the Meltzer and Richard (1981, henceforth MR) model and the Baron and Ferejohn (1989, henceforth BF), model. Second, it discusses the social scope and differentiation of the principle of need-based justice. It explores the conditions under which voters' social identity may lead to an exclusive or inclusive application of the need-based justice principle. Third, this chapter will discuss the role of expertise in the political recognition of need as a means of ensuring need-satisfying allocations. Expertise can help with problem-solving by objectifying needs or providing some moral authority that increases the chances of a collectively agreed allocation satisfying needs. Decisions about need-based allocations can also be entirely delegated to professional experts. In the following, we offer a conceptualization of needs and need-based justice in economic voting.

5.2 The Political Recognition of Needs

Before examining the political process of need recognition in democratic societies, this section will briefly lay out the theoretical foundation of need-based justice. As a concept, need refers to something necessary or indispensable that goes "beyond mere desires or preferences" (Nullmeier 2020, p. 191). Maslow's (1943) theory of human motivation probably remains the most prominent approach to classifying needs. The theory suggests a hierarchy of needs, with physiological needs at the bottom, followed by safety, love/belonging, and esteem, and with self-actualization at the top (Diederich 2020). The lower the need is in the hierarchy, the more important it is. Other concepts, such as absolute poverty (Streeten et al. 1981), rely on expert knowledge regarding the minimum-cost diet that secures the physical survival of an individual (Seidl 1988). Restricting needs purely to physical survival, however, ignores the fact that the satisfaction of both physiological and psychological needs contributes to mental health and well-being (Deci and Ryan 2000; Ryan and Deci 2000). The subjectivity of needs is emphasized in relative deprivation theories (Runciman 1966; Townsend 1974).

Sen (1983) proposed the concept of absolute neediness. A person is absolutely needy if she/he does not have the capability, e.g., in terms of income, to partake in the commonly accepted activities of the community. This conceptualization of needs is key to the capabilities approach (Sen 2009; Nussbaum 2000, 2011). The idea of understanding needs in terms of capabilities can also be found in other contributions. For example, Braybrooke (1987) argues for a model based on a normal course of life, Daniels (1979) for a normal range of opportunities, Schuppert (2013) for agency, and Sher (2014) for leverage, meaning the capacity to acquire additional goods.

For Rawls, "need" plays a vital role in providing fundamental goods, meaning goods required for citizens to express their interests and use their freedoms (Rawls 2005; Maffettone 2010). Rawls' difference principle permits divergence from strict equality as long as the inequalities in question would make the least advantaged in society materially better off than they would be under strict equality (Rawls 2001). Thus, according to Rawls (2001, p. 199–203), citizens cannot see themselves as complete members of society if their basic requirements are not met. This idea has been further elaborated in the "capabilities" approach developed by Sen (1973, 2000). Nussbaum (2011, p. 24) builds on this approach by introducing the idea of "thresholds" for a set of "human functionings" that are required for a dignified life: "[A]ll should get above a certain threshold level of combined capability, in the sense not of coerced functioning but of substantial freedom to choose and act."

Experimental studies that have tested Rawls' theory against other theories of justice find a surprising regularity: Subjects maximize the average income under the restriction that each obtains some minimum (Frohlich and Oppenheimer 1992; Lissowski et al. 2016; Bond and Park 2016; Cruz-Doña and Martina 2016; Michelbach et al. 2003; Traub et al. 2005, 2009). This empirical regularity represents a combination of different justice principles, namely, Harsanyi's (1955) utilitarianism, which means maximizing expected utility, and Rawls' difference principle (Konow 2001). As Boulding (2013, p. 83) put in more flowery terms, "Society lays a modest table at which all can sup and a high table at which the deserving can feast."

Needs vary across individuals, but no plausible universal principle for determining allocations has yet been elaborated (Brock 2013; Miller 2013a). Perhaps the closest to a universal principle is the notion of a "minimally decent life" (Miller 1999, p. 210) and of "thresholds" for a set of human "functionings" (Nussbaum 2011). Both approaches assume survival in a specific social context is only possible if some minimum requirement is fulfilled. This may be a particular amount of calories per day or, as in the famous quote from Smith (1776, p. 869–870), at least one pair of leather shoes in England. These needs vary across societies and depend on the agreement of the members of a society (Miller 1999, p. 225).

Miller (1999, p. 203–229) offers a general discussion of need satisfaction and the goals it can fulfill. Miller (1999, p. 210) points to the existence of "instrumental" needs for which neither an objective standard of legitimacy can be identified nor individual claims can be accepted as such by a community. The commodities needed to make a "minimally decent life" in a specific society are subject to processes of social recognition (Miller 1999, p. 210). The substance of what is required to make a "minimally decent life" varies with the natural and social environment of the society, implying that the only foundation of collective recognition of instrumental need claims is that "members of the society have agreed that it should count" (Miller 1999, p. 225).

Having set out the conceptual basis of need-based justice, the chapter will review the political recognition of needs in democratic societies using two different politico-economic decision frameworks: simplified versions of the MR and BF models. Both models can be solved analytically, which provides a prediction of how rational self-interested actors should decide. Both models can also be turned into an experimental vehicle to study the behavioral consequences of justice principles. Although in both models political recognition is established by majority voting, they differ significantly concerning the decision situation they capture. In the MR model, members of a society vote on a redistributive tax rate. Thus, the MR model is used to study the role of need-based justice in the context of redistribution. In the BF model, members of a society vote on the allocation of a scarce resource (e.g., windfall gains). Welfare politics is often understood as a matter of redistribution; thus, many studies using the MR model investigate the willingness to redistribute from one societal group to another. There are many other instances in welfare politics, however, where a society may have to decide on the allocation of a resource or income from a resource, for example, revenues from natural resources such as oil and gas, rights of way, or public licenses (e.g., UMTS, 5G). The decision on how to allocate the benefits from windfall gains can be studied with the help of the BF model, where democratic societies vote on the allocation of a resource.

The following subsections will review simplified versions of the MR and BF models and discuss how they have been used to study need-based justice. In presenting these two politico-economic frameworks and their contribution to the study of need-based justice, this chapter focuses on causal study designs, specifically laboratory experiments. In laboratory experiments, the experimental setting is usually explained to subjects in neutral terms that have a minimum of moral or emotional connotations (Dickson 2011, p. 59). Subjects receive a fixed contribution for participating in the study (show-up fee) and a variable payoff that depends on their own decisions. In game-theoretic experiments, their payoff depends on the decisions of their fellow players (Dickson 2011, p. 61). Monetary incentives are systematically used in laboratory experiments to induce self-interested preferences and to reveal social preferences (Dickson 2011, p. 63). The principle of using monetary incentives derives from Smith's (1776; 1982) induced value theory.

Ample survey evidence shows that individual needs are considered an essential criterion for determining allocations (Gaertner and Schokkaert 2012; Hülle et al. 2017) and that they are most popular among the less affluent strata of society (Reeskens and van Oorschot 2013). In contrast to these observational findings on need-based justice, laboratory experiments allow a high degree of control over exogenous and endogenous variables (Iyengar 2011). Rather than reporting stated moral preferences, laboratory evidence provides a means of making the workings of moral principles in human decision-making more visible. In addition, laboratory experiments provide an opportunity to test the predictive power of solutions derived from the assumption of rational egoism against real moral agents. These attributes make them particularly valuable in identifying the behavioral consequences of need-based justice.

5.3 Needs in Voting on Redistribution

5.3.1 Simplified Meltzer Richard Model

The simplified version of the MR model is the workhorse for studying votes on redistribution. The original model seeks to identify equilibrium tax rates and income redistribution (Meltzer and Richard 1981). The critical parameter of interest in these applications is citizens' labor-leisure choice, in which voters anticipate the disincentive effects of taxation on labor supply. The simplified version of the MR model abstracts away from efficiency considerations. It focuses on self-interest versus fairness (Agranov and Palfrey 2015, p. 47).

In the simplified MR model, the collective recognition of needs is modeled as follows. Assume N individuals have an ordered gross income of $x_1, \ldots, x_N \in \mathbb{R}_+$, such that $x_1 \leq \ldots \leq x_N$. A redistributive mechanism is used to generate net incomes $y_1, \ldots, y_N \in \mathbb{R}_+$. For this purpose, two vectors are determined $x = (x_1, \ldots, x_N)$ and $y = (y_1, \ldots, y_N)$ and the average gross income $\bar{x} = 1/N \sum_{i=1}^{N} x_j$. The linear tax rate is $r \in [0, 1]$ and is determined by majority voting. The sum of taxes is $d = (r, x) = r \sum_{i=1}^{N} x_i$. From this, a lump sum is paid to each individual with $z = (r, x) = \frac{d(r,x)}{N} = \frac{r \sum_{i=1}^{N} x_i}{N} = r\bar{x}$. Thus, the net income for individual i is $y_i = z(r, x) + (1 - r)x_i$. In this framework, a rational and egoistic voter chooses $r = 0$ if her/his gross income is above the average gross income and $r = 1$ if her/his gross income is below the average gross income and remains indifferent if her/his gross income is equal to the average gross income. In the following, we discuss how this generic model and its baseline hypothesis have been applied to the study of need-based justice.

5.3.2 *Studying Need-Based Justice Using the Meltzer-Richard Model*

The MR model has been used in various ways to uncover the behavioral implications of need-based justice. Lorenz et al. (2017) show that the MR model can induce preferences for need-based justice through equivalence framing. Equivalence framing is characterized by presenting the same decision situation using two or more different formulations. The "Asian Disease" experiment by Kahneman and Tversky (1981) is a prominent example. Lorenz et al. (2017) show that equivalence framing techniques can manipulate the recognition of needs in the MR framework. The linear tax rate in the MR model can be determined by the group choosing a minimum net income $y_m in$ rather than the tax rate directly. Based on the collectively accepted minimum net income $y_m in$, r is determined by $r = \frac{y_m in - x_1}{\bar{x} - x_1}$. This simple reformulation of the redistribution mechanism and the choice decision is used as an equivalence framing. Lorenz et al. (2017) test the effect of the equivalence framing described above on the linear tax rate $r \in [0, 1]$. The laboratory evidence shows that when asking a group to agree on a minimum income, compared to voting on the tax rate, the individually preferred and collectively agreed proportional tax rate increases. It is noteworthy that this framing effect is robust, regardless of numerical communication among voters (Lorenz et al. 2017, Figs. 1 and 2).

In a follow-up study, Paetzel et al. (2018) investigate whether the equivalence framing effect can be minimized by providing an information tool that objectifies the basis for the group members' decisions. The question is whether transparency diminishes the effect of equivalence framing on need recognition in the context of votes on redistribution (Kittel et al. 2021). The experimental findings show that the equivalence framing effect on the individually preferred and collectively agreed tax rate is more substantial when information to objectify the choice decision is unavailable (low transparency). Once information is available to group members (high transparency), the effect of equivalence framing on the individually preferred tax rate decreases. After group communication, the equivalence framing effect has almost completely disappeared and cannot be detected in the collective decision (Paetzel et al. 2018, Fig. 2). These findings suggest that using equivalence framing to highlight social need is an effective instrument for increasing the willingness to redistribute. The framing effect, however, can be mitigated and fully absorbed through the provision of information to voters.

The MR model has also been used to study how different causes of income inequality affect the willingness to recognize needs (Tepe et al. 2021a). It is a stylized fact that people who believe that income inequality results from bad luck rather than lack of effort are more willing to redistribute. This pattern is consistent with cumulative evidence from voting experiments on redistribution (Agranov and Palfrey 2015; Krawczyk 2010; Durante and Putterman 2014; Lefgren et al. 2016; Esarey et al. 2012a). Survey evidence also indicates that subjective beliefs about responsibility, merit, and luck are important determinants of popular support for state redistribution (e.g., Fong 2001; Esarey et al. 2012b; van Oorschot 2006, 2000).

Extending this line of research, Tepe et al. (2021b) investigate how deserved and undeserved differences in productivity affect the willingness to redistribute to the needy. They design a real-effort laboratory experiment in which they manipulate the assignment of pay rates (societal "reward rules") that translate performance on a real-effort counting task into pre-tax earnings. The study distinguishes between three treatment conditions: the same pay rate for all group members ("equal" reward rule), differential (low, medium, and high) but random pay rates ("luck" rule), and differential pay rates based on subjects' performance in a quiz with voluntary preparation opportunity ("merit" rule). The laboratory findings show that redistribution is significantly higher with the "luck" rule than with the "merit" rule. This finding suggests that subjects consider the causes of income inequality when recognizing individual needs in the MR framework.

Although robust experimental evidence based on the MR framework exists on how need-based justice affects votes on redistribution, there are also viable restrictions. Efficiency concerns represent one restriction to applying need-based justice in votes on redistribution. Tepe et al. (2021a) investigate the effect of inefficiency on the individually preferred and collectively agreed linear tax rate in the MR framework. For this purpose, the simplified MR model is related to the leaky-bucket argument of Okun (1975), which assumes an inevitable trade-off between equality and efficiency. The laboratory experimental findings show that an inefficient redistribution regime significantly lowers the willingness to redistribute, regardless of whether or not the group member would benefit from redistribution. Moreover, the negative effect of inefficiency on the tax rate is not proportional to the size of the inefficiency, which means that even a low level of inefficiency leads to a comparatively significant reduction in the tax rate.

The experimental literature on the MR model reviewed above offers strong evidence of the behavioral consequences of need-based justice in redistributive decisions. However, a particularly relevant feature of allocation regimes is their ability to target a resource only to needy people. This type of need-based targeting is not possible in the MR model. The advantage of the MR framework is that the redistribution is determined by choosing a single parameter, the linear tax rate $r \in [0, 1]$. This feature, however, limits the form of redistribution. Specifically, it does not allow for differential or discriminatory treatment of group members. In what follows, this chapter will draw on a simplified version of the BF model to study the role of need-based justice in the political recognition of needs.

5.4 Needs in Bargaining Over Allocations

5.4.1 Simplified Baron Ferejohn Model

The original BF model represents an extension of the Rubinstein (1982) bargaining model, which is useful for studying legislative bargaining with more than two parties. The original model focuses on comparing legislative amendment rules (Diermeier and Morton 2005; Fréchette et al. 2005). However, the generic decision situation in the BF model can also be used to study how democratic societies vote on the allocation of a windfall gain. Thus, the simplified version of the BF model, outlined below, provides an alternative decision framework for studying the collective recognition of needs in allocation choices.

The simplified bargaining procedure consists of the following steps: Group members must allocate an exogenous resource among themselves. First, each group member makes an allocation proposal $S = s_1^i, \ldots, s_M^i$, where s_j^i is the share of the resource that the group member i's proposal provides for group member j. Second, one group member is randomly selected, and that group member's allocation proposal is presented to the other group members for a vote (*proposal on the floor*). All group members have the same probability that their allocation proposal will be selected for voting ($p_i = 1/M$). The voting group members cannot change the allocation proposal (S_i). They can agree or disagree with the allocation proposal (*closed rule*). Analogous to the voting mechanism in the MR model, decisions are made by majority voting, i.e., for the simple case of a group with three members, a majority already exists if one of the voting group members agrees with the allocation proposal (S_i) ($2 : 1$). Third, if the condition for a majority is met, the allocation proposal (S_i) is implemented. If the majority condition is not met, the proposals from the first round are deleted, and all group members make a new allocation proposal (S_i). From these proposals, one is again randomly chosen and presented to the other group members for voting. This process is repeated for a finite number of rounds. In contrast to the original BF model, there is no discount factor that diminishes the size of the resource in the next round when no agreement is reached.

In the BF model, the rational prediction for the 3-player case in this setup is the following: The proposer offers one respondent one-third of the resource and keeps the rest of the resource for herself/himself. The other group member is left empty-handed, i.e., she/he receives an offer of zero. The respondent that gets the offer of one-third of the resource agrees because this is her/his expected value. Thus, egoistic and risk-neutral agents are predicted to utilize their proposer power to offer one group member the expected value and leave the other empty-handed. The existing experimental results obtained in the original BF model, however, suggest that there is a consistent reluctance to propose allocations in which the coalition partner gets a payoff as low as predicted (McKelvey 1991) and that there is a more equal distribution under the closed rule than predicted by the rational solution that assumes egoistic agents (Fréchette et al. 2003; Agranov and Tergiman 2014).

5.4.2 *Incorporating Needs into the Simplified Baron Ferejohn Model*

The simplified version of the BF model has been used to incorporate individual need thresholds (Springhorn 2021). The original and simplified BF model does not consider that players may differ in their individual needs. Springhorn (2021) extends the simplified BF model by assuming that a player must be offered at least the expected value and enough to cover her/his individual need. Analogous to the simplified BF model, a risk-neutral agent wants to get at least her/his expected value and to get her/his individual needs met. Players with smaller needs seem to have an advantage over players with larger needs. This is because, from the proposer's point of view, approval of their allocation proposal is cheaper to obtain from players with smaller needs than those with larger needs. Therefore, the proposer should favor those with smaller needs. Springhorn (2021) refers to this as low-need power, which is analogous to proposer power.

An astonishing result is that the low-need advantage can become a strategic disadvantage: By assuming that low-need players are preferred by the proposer, their expected value grows. The expected value of these players can grow so much that their agreement is more expensive than that of higher-need players. For those players, the need is large, but the expected value is small. Springhorn (2021) adds a second extension to the BF model to avoid this disadvantage, which leaves the low-need players empty-handed. Players are assumed to "underbid" competing players. In other words, they have to accept an offer that is below the offer that can be accepted by a player with a larger need. Due to mutual undercutting, the corresponding limit is the demand of the competing responder.

A successful allocation proposal must provide the player with the smallest demand i an offer at least as large as the maximum of i's demand and i's expected value. In addition, in cases where i's expected value is larger than the demand of the player with the next-largest demand j, the proposal must be at least as large as the maximum of i's demand and the smallest possible value below j's demand. However, there are also several notable cases where the solution must be further differentiated (Springhorn 2021). For example, it must be considered that unlike in the simplified BF model, there are cases in which no analytical solution is available. This is when the resource is insufficient to cover both the proposer's demand and the player's smallest demand.

Similar considerations can be made for the proposer. The proposer's need is met as long as the conditions for a solution are fulfilled. Similar to the low-need player, the amount that the proposer receives depends on the size of the resource, the size of other players' needs, and the size of the proposer's own needs. Allocation to the proposer can be significantly smaller than the rationally expected allocation if needs are not considered. What is particularly interesting is that in the 3-player case considered by Springhorn (2021), proposer power has a smaller effect on allocations than predicted by the BF model. This might explain why in virtually all empirical studies, we observe smaller proposer payoffs than predicted by the BF model (Baranski and Morton 2022). We test the empirical validity of this solution for the 3-player case with individual needs. What follows is a discussion of the results of this test.

5.4.3 Studying Need-Based Justice Using the Baron Ferejohn Model

We experimentally test the predictive power of the BF model with and without individual need thresholds. In line with the model proposed by Springhorn (2021), we vary the need thresholds between group members. Taking advantage of the improvement in the technical and organizational requirements for online experiments, we implemented the experiment in SMARTRIQS and conducted a heterogenous population sample rather than sampling students (Cappelen et al. 2015; Henrich et al. 2010). SMARTRIQS is an open-source solution that allows researchers to design and implement interactive online experiments using the popular survey platform Qualtrics (Molnar 2019). Both treatment conditions were conducted in Germany on an online access panel provided by Bildendi, a commercial survey company.

Following the simplified BF model, the respondents had to decide in groups of three how to allocate 60 points between them, some with and some without need thresholds. Negotiation to allocate the 60 points proceeds in three steps: First, each group member makes a distribution proposal. Second, a distribution proposal is randomly selected, and the other two group members vote on the chosen proposal. The group member whose allocation proposal is put to the vote does not vote herself/himself since her/his agreement with the allocation proposal is implicit. Third, the procedure starts again if both voting members reject the proposal. Otherwise, the 60 points are distributed according to the allocation proposal that receives a majority. In total, 765 subjects completed the web-based online experiment, of which 420 subjects played the simplified BF model without need (control) and 345 subjects played the simplified BF model with individual need thresholds (treatment).

Figure 5.1 summarizes the main result from the two experiments. The three facets show three quantities of theoretical interest, namely, the number of points the proposer demands herself/himself ("demand"), the number of points the proposer offers on average to the other two players ("offer"), and finally, the percentage of coalitions in which one of the other two players gets no points ("propose coalition"). The game's theoretical solution for the BF model without an individual need threshold (bars in dark grey) is to keep 40 points for herself/himself as a proposer and to offer one co-player 20 points. Figure 5.1 shows that, on average, proposers make proposals that are more beneficial for themselves. However, the proposals deviate strongly from the game's theoretical solution. The average offer to the other two players is slightly below 20 points, and the number of coalitions excluding one

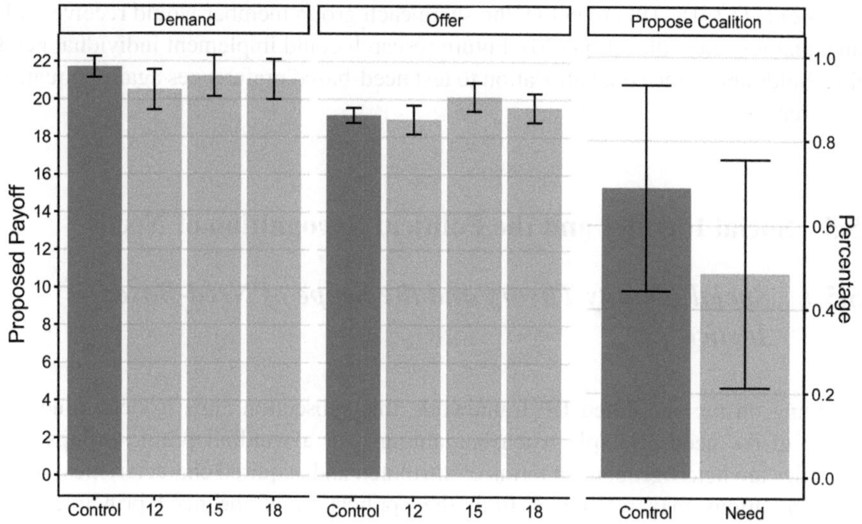

Fig. 5.1 BF model without (control) and with (treatment) individual needs (12, 15, 18)

co-player is close to zero. Hence, in most cases, the proposer makes offers in which the windfall profit is divided equally among group members (20 points for each player), which is consistent with prior experimental results regarding the original BF model (McKelvey 1991; Fréchette et al. 2003).

In the BF model with individual need thresholds, a respondent's need threshold must be met to receive a payoff. We set respondents' needs to $A = 12$, $B = 15$, and $C = 18$ points. Payoffs are given at the end of the game only to players for whom the negotiated payoff meets their need thresholds. Players for whom the negotiated payoff provides fewer points than their need receive zero points. In this example, player A needs at least 12 points, player B needs 15 points, and player C needs 18 points. The rational solution for this specific parametrization is as follows (Springhorn 2021): A proposes 17 points to B (that means A offers B one point less than she/he would have to offer C) and 0 to C to keep 43 for herself/himself, B proposes 17 to A (that means B offers A one point less than she/he would have to offer C) and 0 to C and keeps the 43 for herself/himself, and C is predicted to propose 14 to A (that means C offers A one point less than she/he would have to offer B)and 0 to B and keeps 46 for herself/himself.

The experimental findings summarized in Fig. 5.1 (lighter grey bars) show that subjects' behavior in the experiment does not correspond with the game-theoretic solution. Rather than considering varying levels of individual need, subjects again offered equal allocations of the shared resource and the windfall gain. As in the case of the simplified BF model without need, a formal extension that considers individual needs cannot adequately predict human behavior. Instead, it becomes clear in both experiments that an equal distribution of the resource dominates. The findings are limited by the fact that, in this experiment, all individual need thresholds (12, 15, 18) are below the share each group member would receive with an equal resource allocation (20). Future research could implement individual need thresholds above the equal allocation to test need-based preferences against equality preferences.

5.5 Social Identity and the Political Recognition of Needs

5.5.1 Social Identity Theory and the Scope of Need-Based Justice

Building on the simplified BF framework, this subsection aims to determine the scope of the need principle when bargaining over a windfall profit. Groups and societies are heterogeneous in terms of attributed and acquired characteristics. Such differentiations may restrict or limit the application of the need principle (see Chap. 1). This section reviews studies on how social group membership affects the collective recognition of need and allocation of a resource. The goal is to answer the following research questions: How does social categorization affect the collective recognition and legitimacy of an individual's need?

The effect of group membership on public spending and redistributive preferences has been studied primarily from the perspective of religious-ethnic and national groups (see Stichnoth and Straeten 2013 and Costa-Font and Cowell 2015 for literature reviews). Previous studies suggest that more heterogeneous societies have lower levels of redistribution (Alesina and Glaeser 2004; Alesina and Ferrara 2005; Luttmer 2001; Dahlberg et al. 2012). Lee and Roemer (2006), drawing on the MR model, show that racism among American voters leads to a reduction in the level of redistribution because redistribution that benefits not only one's own ethnic group but also other ethnic groups is rejected by racist voters. Other studies document a negative relationship between national pride and willingness to redistribute (Shayo 2009; Miller and Ali 2013b). While emphasizing the exclusionary effect of religious-ethnic and national group membership on redistributive preferences, Hall (2017) sees national group identity as the basis for welfare redistribution. Here, group identity becomes a necessary condition for the acceptance and legitimacy of state redistribution.

The effect of group identity on individual decision behavior has been systematically described in Tajfel and Turner's (1979) social identity theory (SIT) (Akerlof and Kranton 2000, 2005). Social identity is understood here as the part of a person's self-concept that she/he derives from his or her actual or perceived membership to a social group. SIT has three main components: first, the classification of self and others into basic categories (social categorization); second, identification with in-group members; and third, the comparison of the in-group with the out-group. Tajfel and Turner (1979) show that an individual who identifies with a group acts in a way that improves the status of his or her group, even when this action does not increase the individual's own utility (see also Brewer 1979, Bourhis and Gagnon 2001). This in-group bias ensures that people tend to treat others who belong to their own social group (in-group) better than those who belong to a different group (out-group).

The effect of group identity on individual decision behavior in classical game-theoretic problems has been investigated in several laboratory experimental studies (see Lane 2016 for a literature review). Regardless of the experimental vehicle used (including Charness et al. 2007 for the Battle of the Sexes; Bernard et al. 2016 for the Public-Good Game; or Goette et al. 2006 for the Dictator Game), the findings are usually mixed. A meta-analysis of economic experiments concludes that there is only weak evidence for in-group bias or out-group discrimination (Lane 2016). Concerning the effect of group membership on redistributive preferences, only three studies using laboratory experiments exist that explicitly refer to the MR model. Klor and Shayo (2010) show that membership in an artificially created group systematically affects redistribution preferences, even when controlling for subjects' selfish, altruistic, and risk-averse preferences. Chen and Li (2009) also find that redistribution preferences are affected by group membership. Belardinelli and Stanig (2017) use the laboratory design developed by Agranov and Palfrey (2015) and find no evidence that social categorization affects redistributive preferences. The above literature review shows that there is no research on the effect of social categorization on voting for allocation of a windfall gain.

5.5.2 *Studying the Scope of Need-Based Justice Using the Baron Ferejohn Model*

Tepe and Paetzel (2022) use the simplified version of the BF model to examine the effect of social group membership on need-based justice. Based on the minimal group paradigm (Tajfel and Turner 1979), the study tests whether social categorization leads to a more exclusionary or inclusive application of the need principle. The minimal group paradigm shows that even allegedly meaningless social groups, such as groups favoring the painting of Klee versus groups that favor paintings by Kandinsky, have behavioral implications. In the experiment by Paetzel and Tepe (2022), subjects had to rate paintings by Klee and Kandinsky first. The rating was used to create two groups: Klee fans and Kandinsky fans. An additional tournament was conducted between the Klee and Kandinsky fans to strengthen the group's identity. The experiment distinguishes three treatment conditions: homogeneous social groups, heterogeneous social groups, and a control treatment without social categorization. In the homogeneous social group treatment, all five members belong to the same social group (Klee fans or Kandinsky fans). In the heterogeneous social group treatment, three members belong to the same social categorization and two members to the other social categorization. Next, subjects played the simplified version of the BF model in which they allocated a resource of 150 points. The rational solution is that the proposer keeps 90 tokens for herself/himself and offers 30 tokens to a second person and another 30 tokens to a third, and two group members get an offer of 0 points. The experiment was programmed in ztree (Fischbacher 2007) and conducted on a student sample (hroot, Bock et al. 2014). In total, about 180 subjects played the BF model over 20 periods (Akerlof and Kranton 2000).

The authors expected that social group identity would affect three quantities of interest, namely, what proposers keep for themselves (proposer's demand), what proposers offer to others (offer to others), and the coalition size, as the rational solution expects the exclusion of two members of the group. The experimental evidence shows that, similar to the previous BF experiments, the amount the proposer keeps for herself/himself is too low compared to the rational solution. In the control treatment without social categorization, the proposer offers an equal resource allocation. The experimental evidence suggested five key findings. The rational solution has very limited capacity to predict voting behavior in allocating a windfall gain. However, even a meaningless social identity affects the acceptance of allocations. The effect of social identity on the allocation of a windfall gain depends on the composition of voter groups. Homogeneous groups tend towards a "universal" application of the equality principle. On the other hand, heterogeneous groups show a pattern of in-group favoritism; hence, a "restricted" application of the equality principle. Social identities thus play an essential role in determining whether equal distributions are applied exclusively or inclusively.

A particularly challenging question that arises from these results is what the implications might be for policymakers. In particular, which policy measures could promote a more inclusive application of need-based justice? Two options suggest themselves here. First, deliberative decision-making procedures could mitigate the negative effect of social identities. However, this requires that all members are willing to deliberate according to the rules of democratic discourse (Goldberg and Bächtiger 2022). Second, a solution to the problem of exclusive need-based justice may be found in institutional design (Sunstein and Thaler 2003). In particular, policymakers could design democratic allocation regimes in which ascribed features and social identity remain unknown to decision-makers. Whether there are institutions that can fulfill this requirement remains a question. Social identities often function on subtle cues perceived and understood only by people with the same identity.

5.6 Expertise and the Political Recognition of Needs

5.6.1 Expertise in Public Policymaking

This subsection addresses whether groups are more likely to choose distributions that are need-satisfying when they can rely on the recommendation of a neutral expert in the decision-making process. It reviews research on how expertise affects the political recognition of needs. Expertise is defined as the ability to solve allocation problems based on impartiality and comprehensive information about the problem at hand. To operationalize impartiality, we design the experiment such that the expert is not affected by the consequences of her/his advice.

Policy research provides several examples of society shifting political debates to advisory bodies (e.g., Mayntz et al. 2008; Landwehr 2009; Harms et al. 2021). The use of experts in these cases serves to objectify political decisions by providing a scientific basis (Diederich 2001a,b). Huckfeldt and others (Ahn et al. 2013; Huckfeldt et al. 2014) investigate the ability of citizens to recognize and acknowledge political expertise because they see this as a central prerequisite for deliberative democracy. In a series of group experiments, they show that the attribution of political expertise is based on ascriptive characteristics and citizens' political attitudes (Ahn et al. 2013). Cooper and Neuhaus (2000), Swol and Sniezek (2005), and Norton and Isaac (2012) examine the effect of the ascriptive characteristics of experts on the recognition of expert recommendations. These studies, however, are not concerned with justice principles. Previous studies on the effect of expertise in the context of justice judgments consider the independence of expertise (Bosmans and Schokkaert 2004; Traub et al. 2005; Amiel et al. 1999). Nevertheless, none of these studies has explored how expert advice influences the political process that transfers personal needs into collectively accepted needs and redistributes them accordingly.

Expertise, as defined earlier, can influence the political recognition of needs in at least three distinct ways. First, the expert may function as a neutral broker. Their neutral position and knowledge can help to validate need claims. Second, experts may possess some moral authority. Third, apart from evaluating need claims and providing moral expertise, societies can pass on certain administrative tasks to experts acting as uninvolved social planners (Mayntz et al. 2008; Fischer 2003, 2009).

5.6.2 Expertise as a Validation Device

Tepe et al. (2017) investigate the effect of experts on the validation of need claims and whether they help increase the chances of need-satisfying allocations. They argue that whereas equity and equality only require a procedural consensus among the group members to determine allocations of a shared resource, the acceptance of a need claim depends on an additional consensus about the substantive content of the allocation. This requirement constitutes a much more challenging demand for the group's decision-making because individual claims are difficult to operationalize and evaluate. In real-world societies, two mechanisms are frequently used to evaluate need claims and facilitate the recognition of such claims. First, societies require transparency as a condition for awarding benefits. In order to obtain social security benefits, many countries require applicants to reveal their financial assets, relationship status, and other means of survival. Second, the social welfare calculation is based on an expert committee's evaluation of the elements necessary for a "minimally decent life." Thus, transparency and expertise are used as checks on individual claims.

When individual needs are private knowledge and individual claims are difficult to verify, experts can often probe the plausibility of claims. Experts may also serve as an instrument to objectivize political disputes through scientific knowledge. Several studies have explored respondents' justice perceptions of various income distributions, with respondents adopting the role of either an external observer or an involved dictator looking from behind the veil of ignorance (Bernasconi 2002; Bosmans and Schokkaert 2004; Traub 2002; Traub et al. 2005, 2009; Amiel et al. 1999) The influence of expertise in the sense of specialist knowledge has not been analyzed broadly, however. Hurley et al. (2011) studied which redistributive principles are preferred when the participants are only informed of the principles, the resulting redistribution, or both. Konow (2003) supplied some subjects with additional quantitative information on their initial position and supported the hypothesis that better-informed observers reach a stronger consensus on distributive justice.

In the experimental study by Tepe et al. (2017), the task of the group members is to decide on the distribution of an exogenous resource under the restriction that each member must reach a demand threshold to receive a payoff. The study also builds on the BF framework and introduces a need threshold (Nussbaum 2011). It sets a common threshold for all players but randomly allocates heterogeneous initial endowments. Need is operationalized as the difference between an individual's initial endowment and the threshold that they must reach to survive or, put in terms of a laboratory experiment, to obtain payoffs beyond the show-up fee. The expert is a neutral group advisor who knows the group's gross income distribution and whose payoff is independent of the group's decision. The expert's task is to make an allocation proposal for the group, which is shown to the group members before negotiations begin.

Empirical results from the above laboratory experiment show that most groups autonomously choose the need-based distribution when resources are abundant. When the resource to be allocated is the same size as the sum of individual needs, 47.3% of all groups agree on a distribution that satisfies all needs; when the resource is larger than the sum of needs, this share increases to 81.7%. Expert involvement in the groups' decision processes does not further increase this rate. The results differ when information about levels of need is public knowledge. The expert's role is either insignificant or is even associated with a lower incidence of need satisfaction. The findings suggest that need-satisfying allocations dominate even in the absence of an expert.

5.6.3 *Expertise as a Moral Authority*

Another way to think about the effect of expertise on allocations of a windfall profit is to consider the moral authority of experts. The source of advice can influence the way people think about allocation choices. Hemesath et al. (2023) combined the simple version of the three-person BF model with a framing experiment that provides different information cues. The simplest case of a framing experiment is to randomly give participants one of two variants of the same survey question, where the two variants differ solely in the order of the questions. Framing experiments are often implemented in surveys (Druckman 2001) as they test changes in attitude or behavior in response to political communication. There is already extensive literature on how the characteristics and attributes of an expert affect whether his or her statements and recommendations are believed (Cooper and Neuhaus 2000). More recently, scholars in behavioral economics have begun to study how people deal with the advice of systems that make their inferences based on artificial intelligence (Chugunova and Luhan 2022; Klockmann et al. 2022; Krügel et al. 2023). Drawing on this literature, Hemesath et al. (2023) test the effect of moral advice in the BF framework that either comes from a human or a machine. In the experiment, subjects are confronted with four types of expert advice. The expert advice gives either the rational solution to the game (proposer should keep 2/3 for herself/himself and offer 1/3 of the resource to one of the two group members) or gives moral advice saying that the just solution is to offer each group member 1/3 of the resource. Second, we vary the type of expert that gives advice. The expert is either presented as a human with expertise in bargaining or as an artificial intelligence that studies human bargaining. The 2 × 2 factorial design was implemented in the simplified BF model and has been programmed in SMARTRIQS. The web-based online experiment was conducted on a population sample provided by Bilendi. In total, 1669 subjects completed the web-based online experiment. Moreover, 420 were in the control group playing the simplified BF model, 314 respondents received moral advice from a machine, 323 subjects received moral advice from a human expert, 303 respondents received rational advice from a machine, and 309 subjects received rational advice from a human expert.

Findings from the framing experiment can be summarized in two points: First, regardless of the type of expert—a human expert on bargaining or artificial intelligence—the advice presenting the game-theoretical solution leads to increases in egoistic proposals. This effect is stronger for the advice given by artificial intelligence compared to a human expert. Second, moral advice increases the share of equal offers. This effect is not affected by the type of expertise. This finding is very much in line with and contributes to previous findings on task-dependent algorithm aversion (Castelo et al. 2019). Citizens' trust in algorithmic decision-making depends on the type and nature of the task that is automated. According to this research, algorithms are less trusted and relied upon for tasks that are subjective compared to those that are objective.

5.6.4 *Need-Based Justice Among Experts and Lay Citizens*

While we have so far dealt with the question of how expertise can contribute to the realization of need-satisfying allocations in the BF model, we will now discuss whether expertise also matters in questions of need-based prioritization. The question is whether there are people who have expertise in need-based justice due to their professional activity. Against this background, Dietrich et al. (2023) investigate whether the prioritization decisions of experienced bureaucrats differ from those of the ordinary population in the context of administrative discretion.

Administrative discretion in social welfare requires balanced normative judgments that safeguard impartiality and differentiation between claimants. In order to maintain societal legitimacy, discretionary decisions must be, to some degree, consistent with citizens' sense of justice. Dietrich et al. (2023) transfer the idea of representative bureaucracy to the domain of moral judgment in administrative dilemma situations. They explore the moral principles applied in administrative decision-making in the context of social needs. The impact of discretionary decisions in the context of social welfare makes it a purposeful environment to study the role of moral judgment among state employees and lay citizens. Specifically, Dietrich et al. (2023) compare state employees and future civil servants with lay citizens to determine which moral principles they use to prioritize particular needs in social welfare. Do state employees follow the principle of "justice as impartiality" (Mendus 2008, p. 427) and treat everyone as Max Weber would have it, "sine ira et studio," without anger and prejudice, or do they favor certain groups and discriminate against others? This study argues that it is crucial to gain a deeper understanding of the moral principles that guide state employees' and citizens' discretionary decision-making in moral dilemmas since a certain degree of congruence between the moral judgments of administrators and those being administrated is key to administrative legitimacy and co-production.

Dietrich et al. (2023) compare the discretionary behavior of state employees and future civil servants with those of citizens in the context of moral dilemmas. Respondents were tasked with prioritizing one of two equally eligible welfare claimants for the payment of a household commodity. They conducted an experiment in which they varied welfare claimants' profiles along the following lines: earned deservingness (e.g., welfare dependency due to no fault of their own), need (e.g., dependent children), and attributes that may lead to discrimination (e.g., age, gender, ethnic background). While there are some signs of discrimination, need is the single most important factor shaping respondents' prioritization choices. More importantly, they find no substantial differences in prioritization choices between state employees and citizens, indicating a congruence in their moral choices.

5.7 Conclusions

How do the reported findings contribute towards developing an empirically informed, concise theory of need-based justice? According to the fifth proposition (Nullmeier 2020, p. 198), need-based justice requires a process of recognizing individual needs in society. A central theme of this chapter has been how democratic societies organize the collective recognition of individual needs and how they vote on distributions. We presented experimental evidence from two alternative politico-economic models used to study the collective recognition of needs under laboratory conditions: a simplified version of the Meltzer and Richard (1981, MR) model and the Baron and Ferejohn (1989, BF) model. In the MR model, members of society vote on a redistributive tax rate. In the BF model, members of a society vote on the allocation of a scarce resource (e.g., windfall gains). Findings for both models, MR and BF, show that equality preferences matter. In both cases, there is robust evidence that the rational solution assuming self-interested agents fails to predict respondents' behavior in the MR and BF model.

In the BF model, equivalence framing can be an effective tool for shifting voters' attention to the poorest members of the group and thereby increasing support for redistribution. However, this effect can be mitigated by making the distributive consequences of voters' tax choices transparent. Another feature restricting the application of need-based justice in the MR model is the redistribution mechanism's efficiency. Regardless of whether the voters are net payers or beneficiaries of redistribution, at a certain level of loss through redistribution, inefficiency preferences set in and restrict voters' willingness to redistribute. Deservingness is another powerful restriction on redistribution to the poorest group members in the MR model. Thus, need appears to affect voters' tax choices, but the above factors must be considered in any policy of need-based justice.

Experimental results for the BF model point in a similar direction. Respondents' proposals and bargaining behavior are guided by equality preferences. However, there are mixed findings on the effect of individual need thresholds on need satisfaction. In the refined BF model that accounts for differences in individual need thresholds, respondents continue to make and accept equal allocations regardless of individual differences in needs. Notwithstanding, we also find that transparency about individual needs can foster agreement on need-satisfying allocations. Similar to the MR model, there is robust evidence that the application of need-based justice in votes on common resource allocation is subject to some restrictions. Social group identity is an influential factor shaping who is included and who is excluded from the allocation. Social group identity creates in-group favoritism in that respondents propose equal allocation only to their fellow social group members. These observations support the proposition that "need is one of several criteria for determining a just order" (Nullmeier 2020, p. 196).

Findings on the objectivation of needs through expertise in the BF model are sobering. First, we find that expertise, understood as having more decision-relevant information than others, does not necessarily prompt respondents to pay more attention to individual needs in the allocation of a joint resource. Instead, respondents use this information to their personal advantage. Second, when expertise is framed as a moral authority, we find that algorithmic advice has a slightly stronger impact on respondents proposing egoistic allocations of a joint resource than when the same advice comes from a human expert. In the moral advice condition, the focal point of equal allocations was so strong that expertise had no effect at all.

The political recognition of need is a central challenge of social policy. Based on the findings compiled here, it cannot be concluded that expertise, whether grounded in knowledge or authority, will likely lead to allocations more in line with needs. The conclusion that there is no shortcut to the political recognition of needs via expertise is sobering. Neither citizens nor politicians can escape the responsibility of engaging in political dialogue about the validity of need claims and the mutual recognition of needs. More worrying in this context seems to be that the societal conditions for such a discourse are increasingly deteriorating due to political polarization and scarcity of resources (e.g., Busemeyer et al. 2022), posing new challenges for implementing need-based justice in welfare policies.

Acknowledgments This chapter reviews and discusses results from the project "Need-Based Justice, Group Membership, and Expertise," which formed part of the research group FOR 2104 "Need-Based Justice and Distribution Procedures" (TE1022/2-2). Our special thanks go to Sebastian Hemesath who prepared the experimental data and analysis for Fig. 5.1.

References

Agranov, M., and C. Tergiman (2014): "Communication in Multilateral Bargaining", *Journal of Public Economics* 118, 75–85.

Agranov, M., and T. R. Palfrey (2015): "Equilibrium Tax Rates and Income Redistribution: A Laboratory Study", *Journal of Public Economics* 130, 45–58.

Ahn, T.-K., R. Huckfeldt, A. K. Mayer, and J. B. Ryan (2013): "Expertise and Bias in Political Communication Networks", *American Journal of Political Science* 57, 357–373.

Akerlof, G. A., and R. E. Kranton (2000): "Economics and Identity", *Quarterly Journal of Economics* 115, 715–753.

Akerlof, G. A., and R. E. Kranton (2005): "Identity and the Economics of Organizations", *Journal of Economic Perspectives* 19, 9–32.

Alesina, A., and E. La Ferrara (2005): "Preferences for Redistribution in the Land of Opportunities", *Journal of Public Economics* 89(5–6), 897–931.

Alesina, A., and E. L. Glaeser (2004): *Fighting Poverty in the US and Europe: A World of Difference*. Oxford: Oxford University Press.

Amiel, Y., J. Creedy, and S- Hurn (1999): "Measuring Attitudes Towards Inequality", *Scandinavian Journal of Economics* 101, 83–96.

Baranski, A., and R. Morton (2022): "The Determinants of Multilateral Bargaining: A Comprehensive Analysis of Baron and Ferejohn Majoritarian Bargaining Experiments", *Experimental Economics* 25, 1079–1108.

Baron, D. P., and J. A. Ferejohn, (1989): "Bargaining in Legislatures", *The American Political Science Review* 83 (4), 1181–1206.

Belardinelli, P., and P. Stanig (2017): "Group Membership, Structural Inequality, and Preferences for Redistribution", *EPSA 2017 Conference Paper*.

Bernard, M., F. Hett, and M. Mechtel (2016): "Social Identity and Social Free-Riding", *European Economic Review* 90, 4–17.

Bernasconi, M. (2002): "How Should Income Be Divided? Questionnaire Evidence From the Theory of 'Impartial Preferences"', in P. Moyes, C. Seidl, and A. Shorrocks (eds.): *Inequalities: Theory, Experiments and Applications*, 163–195. Vienna: Springer. (*Journal of Economics/Zeitschrift für Nationalökonomie*, Supplement 9.)

Bock, O., I. Baetge, and A. Nicklisch (2014): "hroot: Hamburg Registration and Organization Online Tool", *European Economic Review* 71, 117–120.

Bond, D., and J.-C. Park (2016): "An Empirical Test of Rawls's Theory of Justice: A Second Approach, in Korea and the United States", *Simulation and Gaming* 22, 443–462.

Bosmans, K., and E. Schokkaert (2004): "Social Welfare, the Veil of Ignorance and Purely Individual Risk: An Empirical Examination", *Research on Inequality* 11, 85–114.
Boulding, K. E. (2013): "Social Justice in Social Dynamics", in R. Brandt (ed.): *Social Justice*, vol. 56, 73–92. Englewood Cliffs, NJ: Prentice Hall.
Bourhis, R. Y., and A. Gagnon (2001): "Social Orientations in the Minimal Group Paradigm", in: R. Brown, and S. L. Gaertner (eds.): *Intergroup Processes, Blackwell Handbook in Social Psychology*, vol. 4., 89–111. Oxford: Blackwell.
Braybrooke, D. (1987): *Meeting Needs*. Princeton: Princeton University Press.
Brewer, M. B. (1979): "In-Group Bias in the Minimal Group Situation: A Cognitive-Motivational Analysis", *Psychological Bulletin* 86, 307–324.
Brock, G. (2013): "Needs and Distributive Justice", in J. Gaus, and F. D'Agostino (eds.): *The Routledge Companion to Social and Political Philosophy*, 444–455. London: Routledge.
Busemeyer, M., P. Rathgeb, and A. Sahm (2022): "Authoritarian Values and the Welfare State: The Social Policy Preferences of Radical Right Voters", *West European Politics* 45 (1), 77–101.
Cappelen, A. W., K. Nygaard, E. Ø. Sørensen, and B. Tungodden (2015): "Social Preferences in the Lab: A Comparison of Students and a Representative Population", *The Scandinavian Journal of Economics* 117 (4), 1306–1326.
Castelo, N., M. W. Bos, and D. R. Lehmann (2019): "Task-Dependent Algorithm Aversion", *Journal of Marketing Research* 56 (5), 809–825.
Charness, G., L. Rigotti, and A. Rustichini (2007): "Individual Behavior and Group Membership", *American Economic Review* 97 (4), 1340–1352.
Chen, Y., and S. Xin Li (2009): "Group Identity and Social Preferences", *American Economic Review* 99 (1), 431–457.
Chugunova, M., and W. J. Luhan (2022): "Ruled by Robots: Preference for Algorithmic Decision Makers and Perceptions of Their Choices", *Max Planck Institute for Innovation and Competition Research Paper* No. 22–04.
Cooper, J., and I. Neuhaus (2000): "The "Hired Gun" Effect: Assessing the Effect of Pay, Frequency of Testifying, and Credentials on the Perception of Expert Testimony", *Law and Human Behavior* 24, 149–171.
Costa-Font, J., and F. Cowell (2015): "Social Identity and Redistributive Preferences: A Survey", *Journal of Economic Surveys* 29 (2), 357–374.
Dahlberg, M., K. Edmark, and H. Lundqvist (2012): "Ethnic Diversity and Preferences for Redistribution", *Journal of Political Economy* 120 (1), 41–76.
Daniels, N. (1979): "Wide Reflective Equilibrium and Theory Acceptance in Ethics", *The Journal of Philosophy* 76 (5), 256–82.
Deci, E. L., and R. M. Ryan (2000): "The 'What' and 'Why' of Goal Pursuits: Human Needs and the Self-Determination of Behavior", *Psychological Inquiry* 11 (4), 227–68.
Dickson, E. S. (2011): "Economics vs. Psychology Experiments: Stylization, Incentives, and Deception", in J. N. Druckman, D. P. Green, J. H. Kuklinski, and A. Lupia (eds.): *Advances in Experimental Political Science*, 58–70. Cambridge: Cambridge University Press.
Diederich, A. (2001a): "A Rational Reconstruction of Expert Judgements in Organ Allocation. A Conjoint Measurement Approach", *Analyse und Kritik* 23, 245–261.
Diederich, A. (2001b): "Expertenurteile zur Organallokation", *Transplantationsmedizin* 13, 101–107.
Diederich, A. (2020): "Identifying Needs: The Psychological Perspective", in S. Traub, and B. Kittel (eds.): *Need-Based Distributive Justice. An Interdisciplinary Perspective*, 59–89. Cham: Springer Nature.
Diermeier, D., and R. Morton (2005): "Experiments in Majoritarian Bargaining", in D. Austen-Smith and J. Duggan (eds.): *Social Choice and Strategic Decisions. Essays in Honor of Jeffrey S. Banks*, 201–226. Berlin: Springer.
Dietrich, B., M. Jankowski, K.-U. Schnapp, and M. Tepe (2023): "Prioritizing Exceptional Social Needs. The Role of Discrimination And Client Deservingness in State Employees' and Citizens' Discretionary Behavior", *FOR 2104 Working Paper* 2023–01.

Druckman, J. N. (2001): "The Implications of Framing Effects for Citizen Competence", *Political Behavior* 23 (3), 225–256.

Durante, R., and L. Putterman (2014): "Preferences for Redistribution and Perception of Fairness: An Experimental Study", *Journal of the European Economic Association* 12 (4), 1059–1086.

Esarey, J., T. Salmon, and C. Barrilleaux (2012a): "Social Insurance and Income Redistribution in a Laboratory Experiment", *Political Research Quarterly* 65 (3), 685–698.

Esarey, J., T. Salmon, and C. Barrilleaux (2012b): "What Motivates Political Preferences? Self-interest, Ideology, and Fairness in Laboratory Democracy", *Economic Inquiry* 50 (3), 604–624.

Fischbacher, U. (2007): "ZTree: Zurich Toolbox for Readymade Economic Experiments", *Experimental Economics* 10 (2), 171–178.

Fischer, F. (2003): *Reframing Public Policy. Discursive Politics and Deliberative Practice*. Oxford: Oxford University Press.

Fischer, F. (2009): *Democracy and Expertise*. Oxford: Oxford University Press.

Fong, C. (2001): "Social Preferences, Self-Interest, and the Demand for Redistribution", *Journal of Public Economics* 822, 225–246.

Fréchette, G. R., J. H. Kagel, and S. F. Lehrer (2003): "Bargaining in Legislatures: An Experimental Investigation of Open versus Closed Amendment Rules", *American Political Science Review* 97 (2), 221–232.

Fréchette, G. R., J. H. Kagel, and M. Morelli (2005): "Gamson's Law versus Noncooperative Bargaining Theory", *Games and Economic Behavior* 51, 365–390.

Frohlich, N., and J. A. Oppenheimer (1992): *Choosing Justice: An Experimental Approach to Ethical Theory*. Berkely: University of California Press.

Gaertner, W., and E. Schokkaert (2012): *Empirical Social Choice. Questionnaire-Experimental Studies on Distributive Justice*. Cambridge: Cambridge University Press.

Goette, L., D. Huffman, and S. Meier (2006): "The Impact of Group Membership on Cooperation and Norm Enforcement: Evidence Using Random Assignment to Real Social Groups", *American Economic Review* 96, 212–216.

Goldberg, S., and A. Bächtiger (2022): "Catching the 'Deliberative Wave'? How (Disaffected) Citizens Assess Deliberative Citizen Forums", *British Journal of Political Science* 53 (1), 1–9.

Hall, P. (2017): "The Political Sources of Social Solidarity", in K. Banting, and W. Kymlicka (eds.): *The Strains of Commitment. Solidarity in Diverse Societies*, 210–232. Oxford: Oxford University Press.

Harms, P., C. Landwehr, M. Lutz, and M. Tepe (2021): "Deciding How to Decide on Public Goods Provision: The Role of Instrumental versus Intrinsic Motives", *Research and Politics* 8 (2).

Harsanyi, J. C. (1955): "Cardinal Welfare, Individualistic Ethics, and Interpersonal Comparisons of Utility", *Journal of Political Economy* 63, 309–321.

Henrich, J., S. Heine, and A. Norenzayan (2010): "Most People Are Not WEIRD", *Nature* 466, 29.

Hemesath, S., M. Tepe, and N. Springhorn (2023): *The Behavioral Implications of Moral Advice from Artificial Intelligence*, unpublished manuscript.

Huckfeldt, R., M. T. Pietryka, and J. Reilly (2014): "Noise, Bias, and Expertise in Political Communication Networks", *Social Networks* 36, 110–121.

Hülle, S., S. Liebig, and M. J. May (2017): "Measuring Attitudes Toward Distributive Justice: The Basic Social Justice Orientations Scale", *Social Indicators Research* 136, 663–692.

Hurley, J., N. Buckley, K. Cuff, M. Giacomini, and D. Cameron (2011): "Judgments regarding the fair division of goods: The impact of verbal versus quantitative descriptions of alternative principles", *Social Choice and Welfare* 37(2), 341–372.

Iyengar, S. (2011): "Laboratory Experiments in Political Science", in J. N. Druckman, D. P. Green, and J. H. Kuklinski (eds.): *Advances in Experimental Political Science*, 73–88. Cambridge: Cambridge University Press.

Kahneman, D., and A. Tversky (1981): "The Framing of Decisions and the Psychology of Choice", *Science* 211 (1981), 453–458.

Kittel, B., S. Neuhofer, and M. Schwaninger (2021): "The Dark Side of Transparent Needs. An Experiment on Information and Need-based Justice", *FOR 2104 Working Paper* 2021–04.

Klor, E., and M. Shayo (2010): "Social Identity and Preferences Over Redistribution", *Journal of Public Economics* 94 (3), 269–278.

Klockmann, V., A. von Schenk, and M. C. Villeval (2022): "Artificial Intelligence, Ethics, and Intergenerational Responsibility", *Journal of Economic Behavior and Organization* 203, 284–317.

Konow, J. (2001): "Fair and Square: The Four Sides of Distributive Justice", *Journal of Economic Behavior & Organization* 46, 137–164.

Konow, J. (2003): "Which Is the Fairest One of All? A Positive Analysis of Justice Theories", *Journal of Economic Literature* 41, 1188–1239.

Krawczyk, M. (2010): "A Glimpse Through the Veil of Ignorance: Equality of Opportunity and Support for Redistribution", *Journal of Public Economics* 94 (1–2), 131–141.

Krügel, S., A. Ostermaier,and M. Uhl (2023): "Algorithms as Partners in Crime: A Lesson in Ethics by Design", *Computers in Human Behavior* 138, 107483.

La Cruz-Doña, R. de, and A. Martina (2016): "Diverse Groups Agreeing on a System of Justice in Distribution: Evidence from the Philippines", *Journal of Interdisciplinary Economics* 11, 35–76.

Landwehr, C. (2009): *Political Conflict and Political Preferences: Communicative Interaction between Facts, Norms and Interests*. Colchester: ECPR Press.

Lane, T. (2016): "Discrimination in the Laboratory: A Meta-Analysis of Economics Experiments", *European Economic Review 90* 375–402.

Lee, W., and J. E. Roemer (2006): "Racism and Redistribution in the United States: A Solution to the Problem of American Exceptionalism", *Journal of Public Economics* 90 (6), 1027–1052.

Lefgren, L. J., D. P. Sims, and O. B. Stoddard (2016): "Effort, Luck, and Voting for Redistribution", *Journal of Public Economics* 143, 89–97.

Lissowski, G., T. Tyszka, and W. Okrasa (2016): "Principles of Distributive Justice", *Journal of Conflict Resolution* 35, 98–119.

Lorenz, J., F. Paetzel, and M. Tepe (2017): "Just Don't Call It Tax! Framing in an Experiment on Voting and Redistribution", *Journal of Experimental Political Science* 4 (3), 183–194.

Luttmer, E. F. P. (2001): "Group Loyalty and the Taste for Redistribution", *Journal of Political Economy* 109 (3), 500–528.

Maffettone, S. (2010): *Rawls: An Introduction*. Cambridge: Polity Press.

Maslow, A. H. (1943): "A Theory of Human Motivation", *Psychological Review* 50 (4), 370–96.

Mayntz, R., F. Neidhardt, P. Weingart, and U. Wengenroth (eds.) (2008): *Wissensproduktion und Wissenstransfer–Wissen im Spannungsfeld von Wissenschaft. Politik und Öffentlichkeit*. Bielefeld: Transcript Verlag.

McKelvey, R. D. (1991): "An Experimental Test of a Stochastic Game Model of Committee Bargaining", in T. Palfrey (ed.): *Laboratory Research in Political Economy*, 139–68. Ann Arbor: Univ. Mich. Press.

Meltzer, A. H., and S. F. Richard (1981): "A Rational Theory of the Size of Government", *Journal of Political Economy* 89, 914–927.

Mendus, S. (2008): "Impartiality", in B. Honig, J. S. Dryzek, and A. Phillips (eds.): *The Oxford Handbook of Political Theory*, 423–435. Oxford: Oxford Univ. Press.

Michelbach, P. A., J. T. Scott, R. E. Matland, and B. H. Bornstein (2003): "Doing Rawls Justice: An Experimental Study of Income Distribution Norms", *American Journal of Political Science* 47, 523.

Miller, D. (1999): *Principles of Social Justice*. Cambridge, Mass.: Harvard University Press.

Miller, D. (2013): *Justice for Earthlings. Essays in Political Philosophy*. Cambridge: Cambridge University Press.

Miller, D., and S. Ali (2013): "Testing the National Identity Argument", *European Political Science Review* 6 (2), 237–59.

Molnar, A. (2019): "SMARTRIQS: A Simple Method Allowing Real-Time Respondent Interaction in Qualtrics Surveys", *Journal of Behavioral and Experimental Finance* 22, 161–169.

Norton, D. A., and R. M. Isaac (2012): "Experts with a Conflict of Interest: A Source of Ambiguity?", *Experimental Economics* 15, 260–277.

Nullmeier, F. (2020): "Towards a Theory of Need-Based Justice", in S. Traub, and B. Kittel (eds.): *Need-Based Distributive Justice. An Interdisciplinary Perspective*. Cham: Springer Nature.

Nussbaum, M. C. (2000): *Women and Human Development: The Capabilities Approach*. Cambridge: Cambridge University Press.

Nussbaum, M. C. (2011): *Creating Capabilities: The Human Development Approach*. Cambridge, Mass: Belknap Press of Harvard University Press.

Okun, A. M. (1975): *Equality and Efficiency: The Big Trade-Off.* Washington, DC: Brookings Institution.

Paetzel, F., and M. Tepe (2022): Social Identity in Coalition Bargaining. An Experimental Analysis, EPSA Conference Paper.

Paetzel, F., J. Lorenz, and M. Tepe (2018): "Transparency Diminishes Framing-Effects in Voting on Redistribution: Some Experimental Evidence", *European Journal of Political Economy* 55, 169–184.

Rawls, J. (2001): *Justice as Fairness: A Restatement*. Cambridge, Mass.: Harvard University Press.

Rawls, J. (2005): *Political Liberalism*. Columbia Classics in Philosophy (Expanded Ed.). New York: Columbia University Press.

Reeskens, T., and W. van Oorschot (2013): "Equity, Equality, or Need? A Study of Popular Preferences for Welfare Redistribution Principles Across 24 European Countries", *Journal of European Public Policy* 20, 1174–1195.

Rubinstein, A. (1982): "Perfect Equilibrium in a Bargaining Model", *Econometrica* 50 (1), 97–109.

Runciman, W. G. (1966): *Relative Deprivation and Social Justice: A Study of Attitudes to Social Inequality in Twentieth-Century England*. London: Rontledge and Kegan Paul.

Ryan, R. M., and E. L. Deci (2000): "Self-Determination Theory and the Facilitation of Intrinsic Motivation, Social Development, and Well-Being", *American Psychologist* 55 (1), 68–78.

Schuppert, F. (2013): "Distinguishing Basic Needs and Fundamental Interests", *Critical Review of International Social and Political Philosophy* 16 (1), 24–44.

Seidl, C. (1988): "Poverty Measurement: A Survey", in D. Bös, M. Rose, and C. Seidl (eds.): *Welfare and Efficiency in Public Economics*, 71–147. Berlin, Heidelberg: Springer.

Sen, A. (1973): *On Economic Inequality*. Oxford: Clarendon Press.

Sen, A. (2000): "Social Justice and the Distribution of Income", in A. B. Atkinson, and F. Bourguignon (eds.): *Handbook of Income Distribution*, vol. 1, 59–85. Amsterdam: Elsevier.

Sen, A. (2009): *The Idea of Justice*. London: Allen Lane.

Sen, A. (1983): "Poor, Relatively Speaking", *Oxford Economic Papers* 35 (2), 153–69.

Shayo, M. (2009): "A Model of Social Identity with an Application to Political Economy, Nation, Class and Redistribution", *American Political Science Review* 103, 147–74.

Sher, G. (2014): *Equality for Inegalitarians*. Cambridge: Cambridge University Press.

Smith, A. (1776): *An Inquiry into the Nature and Causes of the Wealth of Nations*. London: W. Strahan and T. Cadell.

Smith, V. L. (1976): "Experimental Economics: Induced Value Theory", *The American Economic Review* 66 (2), 274–279.

Smith, V. L. (1982): "Microeconomic Systems as an Experimental Science", *The American Economic Review* 72 (5), 923–955.

Springhorn, N. (2021): "Bargaining According to the Baron-Ferejohn Model, Taking into Account Need", *FOR2104 Working Paper* 2021–06.

Stichnoth, H., and K. van der Straeten (2013): "Ethnic Diversity, Public Spending, and Individual Support for the Welfare State: A Review of the Empirical Literature", *Journal of Economic Surveys* 27 (2), 364–389.

Streeten, P., S. Burki, M. Ul-Haq, N. Hicks, and F. Stewart (1981): *First Things First: Meeting Basic Human Needs in Developing Countries*. New York: Oxford University Press.

Sunstein, C. R., and R. H. Thaler (2003): "Libertarian Paternalism Is Not an Oxymoron", *The University of Chicago Law Review* 70 (4), 1159–1202.

Tajfel, H., and J. C. Turner (1979): "An Integrative Theory of Intergroup Conflict", in W. G. Austing, and S. Worchel (eds.): *The Social Psychology of Intergroup Relations*, 33–48. Monterey, CA: Brooks/Cole.

Tepe, M., and F. Paetzel (2022): *Social Identity in Coalition Bargaining. An Experimental Analysis*, unpublished manuscript.
Tepe, M., B. Kittel, and M. Lutz (2017): "Expert Advice in Need-Based Allocations", *FOR2104 Working Paper* 2017–24.
Tepe, M., F. Paetzel, J. Lorenz, and M. Lutz (2021): "Efficiency Loss and Support for Income Redistribution. Evidence from a Laboratory Experiment", *Rationality and Society* 33 (3), 313–340.
Tepe, M., P. Vanhuysse, and M. Lutz (2021): "Merit, Luck and Taxes. Societal Reward Rules, Self-Interest and Ideology in a Real-Effort Voting Experiment", *Political Research Quarterly* 74 (4), 1052–1066.
Townsend, P. (1974): "Poverty as Relative Deprivation: Resources and Style of Living", in D. Wedderburn (ed.): *Poverty, Inequality and Class Structure*, 15–41. Cambridge: Cambridge University Press.
Traub, S. (2002): "The Framing of Tax Reliefs", *Public Finance* 53, 243–261.
Traub, S., C. Seidl, and U. Schmidt (2009): "An Experimental Study on Individual Choice, Social Welfare, and Social Preferences", *European Economic Review* 53, 385–400.
Traub, S., C. Seidl, U. Schmidt, and M. V. Levati (2005): "Friedman, Harsanyi, Rawls, Boulding–Or Somebody Else? An Experimental Investigation of Distributive Justice", *Social Choice and Welfare* 24, 283–309.
van Oorschot, W. (2000): "Who Should Get What, and Why? On Deservingness Criteria and the Conditionality of Solidarity Among the Public", *Policy and Politics* 28 (1), 33–48.
van Oorschot, W. (2006): "Making the Difference in Social Europe: Deservingness Perceptions Among Citizens of European Welfare States", *Journal of European Social Policy* 16 (1), 23–42.
Van Swol, L. M., and J. A. Sniezek (2005): "Factors Affecting the Acceptance of Expert Advice", *British Journal of Social Psychology* 44, 443–461.

[illegible]

Chapter 6
Deliberation and Need-Based Distribution

Tanja Pritzlaff-Scheele, Patricia F. Zauchner, and Frank Nullmeier

Abstract Justifications are important for the satisfaction of need claims by a group or society. Participants in a group can make their reasons for a need-based distribution transparent through deliberative processes. Furthermore, deliberative procedures allow people in need to have their say on how resources should be distributed. In this chapter, we analyze the relationship between the transparency of reasons and the acceptance of need-based distributions. While strict equality in resource distribution is often intuitively perceived as fair, the acceptance of a distribution according to need requires justification. Reasons have to be given for the prioritization of needs, and these reasons have to be made explicit during a process of deliberation. Based on a mixed-methods design using quantitative and qualitative data from two series of experiments, we find that, in addition to transparency in the sense of information disclosure, the explicit expression of reasons for need claims has an effect on decisions about how to distribute resources. Moreover, the actual participation of people in need has an effect on the acceptance of a need-based distribution. Thus, deliberative processes based on reason-giving and the participation of individuals in need lead to a higher acceptance of need-based distributions. We refer to this effect as the deliberation effect.

6.1 Introduction

When it comes to the acceptance of (re)distributive policies by a group or society, need is one among "several criteria for determining a just order" (Nullmeier 2020, p. 196). According to Nullmeier, the "core element of the concept of need is

---

T. Pritzlaff-Scheele (✉)
University of Bremen, Center for Decision Research, Bremen, Germany
e-mail: tanja.pritzlaff@uni-bremen.de

P. F. Zauchner · F. Nullmeier
University of Bremen, SOCIUM Research Center on Inequality and Social Policy, Bremen, Germany
e-mail: Patricia.zauchner@uni-bremen.de; frank.nullmeier@uni-bremen.de

B. Kittel, S. Traub (eds.), *Priority of Needs?*,
https://doi.org/10.1007/978-3-031-53051-7_6

the notion of something that is necessary, compelling, imperative, indispensable, essentially required—something that goes beyond mere desires or preferences and takes precedence over desires" (Nullmeier 2020, p. 191). However, complex and sometimes contradictory considerations collide on individual and societal levels when people deliberate and decide on what is necessary in this sense. What counts as a need and what level of need satisfaction society has to provide are questions that cannot be objectively answered. The recognition of needs "requires specific procedures in which what is recognized as need is also argumentatively identified as what is necessary" (Nullmeier 2020, p. 198). What counts as a need is a controversial and highly debated issue within societies.

This chapter rests on three overarching hypotheses regarding justifications for a need-based distribution: Firstly, we postulate that explicit reasons are required for the acceptance of a need-based distribution because, when public resources are distributed according to need, different—and often complex—criteria of fairness come into play (Michelbach et al. 2003). The more implicit assumptions about fairness remain, the more difficult it is to implement a need-based distribution. Explicit reasons are important in need-based distributions because the latter often constitute a form of unequal distribution (Gosepath 2015, pp. 177–179) that deviates from the more intuitive equal distribution. Rainer Forst, for example, characterizes the egalitarian perspective on justice in the following way: "Egalitarians argue for the primacy of the equal distribution of goods, according to which other arguments for legitimate unequal distributions—for instance, ones based on need, merit or prior claims—then have to be treated as special reasons" (Forst 2014, p. 23). When a need-based distribution is interpreted as an unequal (re)distribution of resources, it requires some sort of justification that does not seem to be necessary in cases of equal distribution.

Secondly, we assert that *deliberation* is the most appropriate procedure for making justifications for need-based distribution transparent.[1] According to Myers and Mendelberg (2013, p. 700), there are "multiple definitions" of the concept of deliberation. One distinction is whether deliberation includes actual decision-making or whether it is a form of "pre-vote communication" (Brandts et al. 2022, p. 680). While Myers and Mendelberg include decision-making in their definition of deliberation,[2] Habermas separates deliberation and decision-making into two different stages and even separates them institutionally between the public sphere and the political system (Habermas 1997, pp. 287ff.). In his understanding, "the communication structures of the public *sphere* relieve the public *of the burden of decision making*, the postponed decisions are reserved for the institutional-

[1] The impact of transparency and information disclosure on deliberation and decision-making has been studied in various fields, ranging from democratic theory (Baume 2021; Elster 2015; Fung 2013; Naurin and Reh 2018) and theories of justice (Lim 2019; Kelly 2021) to experimental economics (Paetzel et al. 2018; Fehrler and Hughes 2018).

[2] Myers and Mendelberg "define deliberation as small-group discussion intended to make a decision or to change the content or basis of public opinion that is either prompted by or speaks to a governmental unit or political actor" (Myers and Mendelberg 2013, p. 700).

ized political process" (Habermas 1997, p. 362). Many empirical applications of deliberative formats follow this understanding and limit deliberation to pure consultation without binding decision-making (for overviews, see Bächtiger et al. 2018; Curato et al. 2021). While we do not follow the Habermasian conception of a deliberating public sphere and a separate political system "specialized for collectively binding decisions" (Habermas 1997, p. 300), we consider deliberation and decision-making, in our case voting, as two different stages of a procedure that leads to a binding determination on how to distribute resources. When it comes to the experimental operationalization of deliberation, Brandts et al. (2022, p. 682) refer to any form of pre-vote communication as deliberation. In contrast, we follow the Habermasian understanding that deliberation is a specific form of communication that requires explicit reason-giving. We will thus study the hypothesis that pre-vote communication in the sense of reason-based deliberation has an effect on the decision to distribute resources according to need (deliberation effect).

Finally, we hold that to make a case for need-based distribution, the people in need have to be included in the deliberative process. Following a Habermasian understanding of the practice of argumentation, we highlight not only the importance of reason-giving, but also the importance of participation in the sense of "public debate and complete inclusion of all those affected" (Habermas 2003, p. 37). While it is possible that participants in a deliberative process who are not in need act according to other-regarding preferences (Cooper and Kagel 2015) and therefore support need-based distribution, we assume that there is nevertheless a stronger effect in favor of a need-based distribution when the people in need are able to participate in the deliberative process and articulate reasons for a distribution that meets their needs.

Based on quantitative and qualitative data from two series of laboratory group experiments, we study the impact of explicit reasons in deliberation on decisions about need-based (re)distribution (quantitative data), as well as the specific criteria and reasons brought forward by group members in order to justify a need-based distribution (qualitative data). To study the impact of deliberation (reason-giving and participation) on the acceptance of need as a principle of distribution, we developed an experimental design that includes several stages of "reason-giving" by the participants. Groups of five had to deliberate and decide on the (re)distribution of a common fund.

In the following, we present the theoretical background behind the overarching hypothesis that reason-giving is of vital importance to a need-based (re)distribution (Sect. 6.2) followed by a closer look at the design features of our group experiments (Sect. 6.3). In Sect. 6.4, we present quantitative results from our first series of experiments that hint at a "deliberation effect" when it comes to the acceptance of a need-based (re)distribution—and to a lower acceptance of a strictly egalitarian (re)distribution after deliberation. In Sect. 6.5, we present findings from a second series of experiments. Through an analysis of qualitative data, we highlight the different kinds of justifications participants give for a need-based distribution. We also show that the participation of people in need in deliberative processes is very important. We conclude the chapter with a brief summary of our main findings and some remarks on the operationalization of need in group experiments and its effect on our results.

6.2 Need-Based (Re)Distribution and Deliberation

The argument that need-based distribution requires justification is based on the understanding that need-based distribution is a form of unequal distribution. Following an analysis of Nydegger and Owen's (1974) study of a two-person bargaining experiment that ended in an agreement to split the resource evenly, Selten (1987, p. 47) highlights the importance of justifications for unequal distributions: "Why did they apply the egalitarian standard of comparison? One may say that in this case the reason was the lack of any justification for an uneven split. Neither ethical nor power-related considerations give rise to another system of weights." According to Cheryl L. Eavey, Selten's discussion translates into the following maxim: "egalitarian norms apply unless justifications exist for unequal divisions of rewards" (Eavey 1991, p. 457). Therefore, individuals must provide reasons if their peers are to accept an unequal distribution of resources.

In a study on the effects of achievement, luck, and efficiency considerations on adults' distributive behavior, Almås et al. (2010) notice that unless these factors come into play, "there is no apparent fairness argument justifying an unequal division of the money" (Almås et al. 2010, p. 1177). Similarly, David Miller finds that whereas "appeals to desert or to need to justify a distribution must imply that these considerations carry positive moral weight, equality may be invoked on grounds of simplicity or convenience rather than because an equal distribution of resources is regarded as substantively just" (Miller 1999, p. 63). This line of argument suggests that a distribution based only on need requires a justification, but a distribution based only on the principle of equality does not seem to require a justification. Things get more complicated when reasons for distributions are based on more than one principle of justice.

As Michelbach et al. outline, "distributive justice judgments involve several distinct allocation principles" (Michelbach et al. 2003, p. 523; see also Scott et al. 2001). Experimental findings suggest that "people make trade-offs when judging societal fairness and preference" (Ordóñez and Mellers 1993, p. 139). Moreover, many studies across time and academic disciplines suggest that the individual fairness views that determine preferences for or against need-based distributions are highly context-dependent: These fairness views reflect, among other things, beliefs about the "perceived cause of the need state" (Lamm and Schwinger 1980, p. 426). For example, welfare recipients are deemed less deserving of help when they are attributed a "responsibility for being in need" (Michoń 2021, p. 209) than when the cause of the need is out of their control (Michoń 2021, p. 209–210; Appelbaum 2001). These considerations are discussed in more depth in studies referring to the concept of "deservingness" (van Oorschot et al. 2017; Fischbacher et al. 2021; Almås et al. 2010).

Findings from various studies also show that the overall acceptance rate for an unequal distribution depends, at least in part, on the source of initial inequality (Valero 2022; Fischbacher et al. 2021) Differences in the willingness to redistribute—and in the perceived legitimacy of redistribution—depend on whether the initial unequal distribution of income is based on luck or effort (Valero 2022; p. 880; see also Clark and D'Ambrosio 2015; Mollerstrom et al. 2015; Becker 2013; Durante et al. 2014; Lefgren et al. 2016). However, there is little research on the actual reasons people give for their complex, context-dependent—and even contradictory—preferences regarding distributive fairness (Starmans et al. 2017; Giacomini et al. 2014; Asada et al. 2020).

If explicit reasons are necessary for the acceptance of a distribution of resources according to need, it is of vital importance that adequate contexts are created in which these reasons can be presented to others. According to deliberative democratic theory, deliberative arenas, like, for example, forms of citizen deliberation, provide the framework in which advocates of a need-based distribution can make their reasons transparent and explicit. Mendelberg and Karpowitz (2007) study how "people deliberate about distributive justice, and in particular, about a guaranteed minimum income to the poor" (Mendelberg and Karpowitz 2007, p. 101). Using data and discussion transcripts from an experiment by Frohlich et al. (1987; see also Frohlich and Oppenheimer 1990), Karpowitz and Mendelberg interpret the experimental findings from a deliberative perspective. Their findings show that deliberation can enhance distributive justice and the degree to which people "consider the needs of the least fortunate" (Mendelberg and Karpowitz 2007, p. 123), but that these effects depend on the structure of the specific deliberative setting, especially on decision rules and the gender composition of the deliberating group. The argument that deliberation may enhance distributive justice is also brought forward in empirical deliberative research to promote deliberative forms of citizen participation (Zimmermann et al. 2018).

Deliberative approaches to justice suggest that not only any type of communication, but reason-based *deliberation*, is necessary for ensuring the recognition of needs. According to Mendelberg and Karpowitz (2007, p. 102), deliberation, "ideally, is a process of communication in which people must address needs and perspectives quite different from their own. Those needs and perspectives are conveyed through reasoned arguments that are universal and generalizable, drawing on basic understandings with which other participants can agree." In deliberative settings, communication is ideally based on reason-giving and the exchange of arguments. Reason-giving is "fundamentally about making arguments that are mutually understandable to others who do not share the speaker's opinions and worldviews" (Adams 2014, p. 3).

As Gutmann and Thompson (1996, p. 271) point out, abstract principles are not sufficient for determining the "goods and services that are necessary for living a good life and making use of other opportunities, such as the opportunity to compete for a skilled job" and which society therefore has to provide. According to them, what goods and services count as "basic opportunities" in this sense and which level of support is necessary should not be decided solely based on the principle of need, since needs are, as they put it, "omnivorous" (Gutmann and Thompson 1996, p. 274). It takes a rational and argument-based process of democratic deliberation to identify the goods and services that can be accepted as needs, which society has to provide to those who claim to be in need, and to determine the level at which these goods should be provided: "What counts as a basic opportunity—both the scope and the level at which it is funded—is to be determined through democratic deliberation. A standard for basic opportunities must be publicly defended on moral grounds, consistent with the requirements of reciprocity among citizens. Through public deliberation among accountable agents, a democratic government should aim at finding a level and a scope of basic opportunities that are mutually acceptable to morally motivated citizens, regardless of their differences in income and wealth, race or ethnicity, health or disability" (Gutmann and Thompson 1996, pp. 217, 219).

Therefore, need as an abstract principle cannot and should not be considered the sole basis for a distribution of resources. However, the application of the need principle can be specified and justified through a reason-based deliberative process. Through the "weighing of different arguments, which is the central idea of democratic deliberation," people are more likely to understand "the arguments used by those who have an opposing view on the issue" (Setälä and Herne 2014, p. 60–61). As has been shown in empirical applications of deliberative principles (see Deliberative Polls® by Fishkin 2009), deliberation not only builds participants' knowledge about the issues discussed but can cause significant opinion changes (Setälä and Herne 2014, p. 61). In deliberative settings, opinion change is "at least partly driven by learning, in the broadest of senses—by the assimilation of new perspectives and interpretations, as well as the acquisition of more or less factual information" (Luskin et al. 2002, p. 4809). Moreover, at the individual level, being part of a deliberating group that has to decide on a joint issue may lead to a kind of "we-mode reasoning" (Schwenkenbecher 2019, 2021). Deliberation, therefore, is not only important as a sphere of reason-giving, but also as a sphere of inclusive participation.

These considerations lead to the following hypotheses: (1) A deliberative process raises the acceptance of needs as a distributive principle by the group. (2) When justifications for a need-based distribution are made transparent to all members of a deciding group, the acceptance of strict equality diminishes. (3) When people in need are included in the deliberative process and are therefore able to present reasons for a distribution that meets their needs, the acceptance of need-based distribution increases.

6.3 Deliberation and Reason-Giving in Group Experiments

To study the effect of deliberation (reason-giving) and participation on the acceptance of need-based distribution, we developed an experimental design that includes several stages of "reason-giving" by the participants. The basic design was as follows. Groups of five had to deliberate and decide on the (re)distribution of a common fund. The group members could either choose to accept a proposed distribution of the common fund or reject the proposed distribution and choose an alternative distribution.

Before the group decision, participants were able to deliberate on their choice of distribution. In addition to "everyday language" communication via chat, participants were asked to state reasons for their individual choices and suggestions on how to distribute resources at three different stages during the experiment. Participants were, for example, asked to complete a sentence that started with "I am in favor of this proposal/I am against this proposal because ..." to make them formulate explicit reasons for their choices. With these "reason-giving" stages, we implemented a design feature in our experiments that explicitly highlights the role of deliberation in the sense of reason-giving in decisions on (re)distribution. We conducted two series of experiments with this basic design. In one series of experiments, we manipulated the level of communication and in the other we manipulated the level of participation of the participants.

In the following two sections, we present quantitative and qualitative findings from these two series of experiments[3] that show the importance of explicit reasons and participation of the people in need for the acceptance of need-based (re)distribution. In addition to analyzing the quantitative data produced by the decision on (re)distribution, we conducted a qualitative content analysis of the text data produced during the "reason-giving" stages. The reasons given by the individual participants were visible to all other group members and therefore affected the others by presenting them with different perspectives on the decision. During the experiment, participants came to understand themselves as part of a group tasked with making a joint decision. Participants transitioned from thinking of themselves as individual decision-makers to thinking of themselves as contributors to a joint decision—a contributor who also takes into account options that are "only collectively available" (Schwenkenbecher 2021, p. 12). Moreover, the second series of experiments in which we manipulated the level of participation of the participants shows that, for those in need, being a member of the deliberating group is of vital importance to ensure that one's needs are met.

[3] The first series of experiments was programmed with z-Tree (Fischbacher 2007). The experiments were conducted at the Wiso Experimental Lab at the University of Hamburg (total participants: 635) and were organized and administrated with the software hroot (Bock et al. 2014). The second series of experiments was programmed with oTree (Chen et al. 2016). The experiments were conducted at the Vienna Center for Experimental Economics (total participants: 180). Participants were recruited with ORSEE (Greiner 2015).

6.4 Deliberation Effects

In the first series of our experiments (Zauchner and Pritzlaff-Scheele 2017),[4] we expected that it would make a difference for the acceptance of a need-based distribution whether the initial endowments were randomly assigned (a lottery) or whether they were the result of a preceding test (effort). We believed this would be especially true for cases where the resource was a common fund created from proportional deposits—i.e., cases in which the "high performers" in a test (real effort task) have to contribute the highest amounts to a fund that is redistributed afterwards—as opposed to a windfall. We assumed that in contexts of effort-dependent unequal distribution and/or redistribution, the number of resources distributed according to need would decrease while the number of resources distributed according to effort would increase. Moreover, we expected that the extent to which need is accepted as a distribution criterion depends on (1) the level of information people have about existing needs and (2) the acknowledgment of reasons presented in favor of a need-based distribution. Therefore, we studied the effects of group deliberation on the acceptance of need as a distribution principle.

In all treatment variations of the experiment, the five group members (players 1 to 5) had unequally distributed initial endowments and were asked to distribute or redistribute a common fund of 20 tokens. The situation before (re)distribution was the following: Player 1 had 9 tokens, player 2 had 14 tokens, player 3 had 17 tokens, player 4 had 23 tokens, and player 5 had 37 tokens.[5] All five members had to cover minimum consumption costs (15.5 tokens) during five consecutive rounds of the experiment. In all treatment variations, the unequally distributed initial endowments led to a situation in which two of the five group members needed a share of the common fund to meet the consumption costs (players 1 + 2), and one of these two players (player 1) needed more than an equal share of 4 tokens of the common fund; otherwise, player 1 would run into debt.

Depending on the treatment variation, the initial suggestion presented to the group was either an equal split of the common fund (4/4/4/4/4), a "weaker first" distribution that assigned more than the minimum consumption costs to the participants with the lowest initial endowments (11/6/3/0/0), or a "mixed" distribution (6.5/1.5/1/4/7) that covered only the minimum consumption of the two participants in need while distributing the rest of the common fund in proportion to effort.[6]

[4] The experiments were conducted in July and November 2016 and in May, June, July, and August 2018 at the Wiso Experimental Lab at the University of Hamburg. We would like to thank Olaf Bock and his team.

[5] In the distribution treatments, the starting position 9/14/17/23/37 resulted directly from a lottery or an effort task. In the redistribution condition, the initial numbers were higher (player 1, 10.8 token; player 2, 16.8; player 3, 20.4; player 4, 27.6; player 5, 44.4). At the beginning of the redistribution treatments, every member had to contribute to the common fund of 20 tokens an amount that was in proportion to their initial endowment (player 1, 1.8; player 2, 2.8; player 3, 3.4; player 4, 4.6; player 5, 7.4). This contribution led to a starting position of 9/14/17/23/37, which was the same as in the distribution treatments.

If the group rejected the proposed distribution, the members had to suggest an alternative distribution of the common fund.

In the treatment groups, participants were able to communicate via chat and take part in the reason-giving stages (deliberation treatment). This treatment is our operationalization of deliberation in the Habermasian sense. It not only consists of communicative exchange via chat but includes actual reason-giving by the participants. During the experiment, the reasons for the individual choices were made transparent to the other group members (transparency of reasons). To test the effects of deliberation (chat and reason-giving) on people's willingness to accept a need-based distribution, we ran two types of control treatments. In one version of the control treatment, participants were able to communicate via chat (transparency of communication), but they were not asked to present reasons for their decisions in a separate reason-giving stage ("chat only" treatment). In the other version of the control treatment, communication was not possible at all ("no communication" treatment), yet the preferences[7] of the participants were made transparent to all group members (transparency of information).[8]

Overall, our data shows that acceptance of the "weaker first" (re)distribution (11/6/3/0/0) is very high before the group chat and only increases after the group chat under all conditions of the deliberation treatment (distribution/lottery, distribution/effort, redistribution/lottery, redistribution/effort). Conversely, acceptance of the strictly equal (re)distribution (4/4/4/4/4) and the mixed distribution (6.5/1.5/1/4/7) diminishes across all treatment variations from before to after the group chat (see Table 6.1).

Table 6.2 extends the content of Table 6.1 for two of the conditions (distribution/lottery and redistribution/effort) and additionally shows the acceptance rates of the proposed distributions in the "no communication" control treatment as well as the "chat only" control treatment. The first two groups of rows show the numbers for the proposed equal distribution. Acceptance of an equal distribution decreases in the "chat only" and the deliberation treatments. In the distribution/lottery condition, the decrease is more substantial in the deliberation groups than in the "chat only" groups, while for the redistribution/effort condition the decrease is more substantial in the "chat only" groups than in the deliberation groups. For the redistribution/effort condition, we additionally ran the "no communication" treatment. Without communication, the acceptance of an equal distribution increases.

The next two groups of rows show the numbers for the weaker first principle. While acceptance of the weaker first principle increases in both conditions of the deliberation treatment, the results for the "no communication" and the "chat only"

[6] The "mixed" principle combines a floor constraint with the maximization of income (similar to the "Boulding" principle discussed by Traub et al. 2005; see also Boulding 1962).

[7] Preferences in the sense of yes/no during voting or numerical values in alternative distributions.

[8] The total number of groups was 128, i.e., 84 deliberation ($N = 420$), 29 chat only ($N = 145$), and 15 no communication ($N = 75$). Due to technical difficulties, we were not able to use the data of one of the 84 deliberation groups, so the actual number of deliberation groups was 83 ($N = 415$).

Table 6.1 Attitude change deliberation treatment, chat and reason-giving (83 groups, $N = 415$)

	Distribution lottery	Distribution effort	Redistribution lottery	Redistribution effort	Total
Equal distribution					
Acceptance before	45.0%	63.3%	51.4%	57.5%	53.8%
Acceptance after	7.5%	60.0%	34.3%	47.5%	35.9%
Attitude change	−37.5pp	−3.3pp	−17.1pp	−10.0pp	−17.9pp
N	40	30	35	40	145
Weaker first					
Acceptance before	82.5%	76.0%	94.3%	68.6%	80.7%
Acceptance after	100.0%	96.0%	100.0%	74.3%	92.6%
Attitude change	17.5pp	20.0pp	5.7pp	5.7pp	11.9pp
N	40	25	35	35	135
Mixed					
Acceptance before	40.0%	53.3%	50.0%	77.1%	54.8%
Acceptance after	32.5%	30.0%	10.0%	68.6%	36.3%
Attitude change	−7.5pp	−23.3pp	−40.0pp	−8.6pp	−18.5pp
N	40	30	30	35	135

This table summarizes the relative acceptance rates of the proposed distribution procedures before (personal statements) and after (votes for acceptance) the group chat for the various distribution/redistribution and lottery/effort treatment combinations of each proposed distribution. The third row of each proposed distribution shows the percentage points change between acceptance rates before and after the distribution. Positive values indicate that acceptance rates increased. Negative values indicate that acceptance rates decreased

groups are mixed. In the condition distribution/lottery, acceptance of the weaker first principle increases in the "no communication" groups, while it stays the same in the "chat only" groups. In the condition redistribution/effort, acceptance of the weaker first principle decreases in the "chat only" groups.

The last two groups of rows show the numbers for the mixed principle. Acceptance of the mixed principle, which ensures that the minimum consumption costs of players 1 and 2 are covered with no surplus, decreases in both the "chat only" and the deliberation treatments under the condition distribution/lottery. In the redistribution/effort condition, acceptance of the mixed principle decreases in the deliberation treatment but stays the same in the "chat only" treatment.

While the quantitative results show a deliberation effect in the sense of an increase in acceptance of the "weaker first" principle and a decrease in the acceptance of an equal distribution, there are several aspects of the findings that seem to be inconclusive when it comes to the acceptance of need as a principle of distribution. Therefore, it is important to analyze not only the numerical changes (attitude change), but to look at how people actually argue for or against a specific kind of (re)distribution. We will take a closer look at the principles referred to by the participants as well as the subjects addressed during the reason-giving stage in the next section.

Table 6.2 Overall attitude changes: treatment and control groups

	No communication	Chat only	Deliberation	Total
Equal distribution/distribution/lottery				
Acceptance before		60.0%	45.0%	50.0%
Acceptance after		45.0%	7.5%	20.0%
Attitude change		−15.0pp	−37.5pp	−30.0pp
N		20	40	60
Equal distribution/redistribution/effort				
Acceptance before	57.5%	65.0%	57.5%	60.0%
Acceptance after	65.0%	47.5%	47.5%	53.3%
Attitude change	7.5pp	−17.5pp	−10.0pp	−6.7pp
N	40	40	40	120
Weaker first/distribution/lottery				
Acceptance before	85.7%	90.0%	82.5%	86.1%
Acceptance after	97.1%	90.0%	100.0%	95.7%
Attitude change	11.4pp	0.0pp	17.5pp	9.6pp
N	35	40	40	115
Weaker first/redistribution/effort				
Acceptance before		73.3%	68.6%	70.0%
Acceptance after		46.7%	74.3%	66.0%
Attitude change		−26.7pp	5.7pp	−4.0pp
N		15	35	50
Mixed/distribution/lottery				
Acceptance before		46.7%	40.0%	41.8%
Acceptance after		26.7%	32.5%	30.9%
Attitude change		−20.0pp	−7.5pp	−10.9pp
N		15	40	55
Mixed/redistribution/effort				
Acceptance before		46.7%	77.1%	68.0%
Acceptance after		46.7%	68.6%	62.0%
Attitude change		0.0pp	−8.6pp	−6.0pp
N		15	35	50

This table summarizes the relative acceptance rates of the proposed distribution procedures before (personal statements) and after (votes for acceptance) the group chat for the various distribution/redistribution, lottery/effort, and communication treatment combinations of each proposed distribution. The third row of each proposed distribution shows the percentage points change between acceptance rates before and after the distribution. Positive values indicate that acceptance rates increased. Negative values indicate that acceptance rates decreased

Before that, however, it is important to discuss how we operationalized need in the experimental design, particularly in relation to the difference between the mixed principle and the weaker first principle. Both principles were designed to satisfy the needs of all players. The mixed principle leads to a situation in which the minimum consumption costs of the least well-off participants are covered, but they do not have a chance to earn a surplus. They leave the game exactly above the debt limit, while the rest of the resource is distributed in proportion to the initial endowments, with the more well-off players receiving more. The weaker first principle leads to a situation in which all members gain a surplus above their minimum consumption costs. The common fund is distributed in a way that leads to more outcome equality, since the common resource is distributed only among the three poorer players, while the two richer players do not get a share of the common fund. Therefore, the mixed and the weaker first principles represent two very different forms of need satisfaction. The results show that acceptance of the mixed principle (need satisfaction as debt avoidance) decreases after deliberation. However, for the weaker first principle (need satisfaction, additional positive payout for the players in need, proximity to outcome equality), acceptance increases after deliberation.

In the following, based on data from the second series of experiments, we will take a closer look at the reasons people give for their choice of how to (re)distribute common resources. The findings are based on a qualitative content analysis of the reasons stated by the participants during the experiment.

6.5 Justifying a Need-Based Distribution

In the second series of experiments (Pritzlaff-Scheele and Zauchner 2019),[9] we studied the interactions (deliberation and vote) between the initial members of a group and a newly arrived member ('immigration scenario'). We also studied the latter's level of participation. In our experimental design, four group members (players 2, 3, 4, 5) took part in an initial task (effort task) and earned unequally distributed initial endowments based on their relative success in the effort task (15/24/35/56; see Fig. 6.1). Following the effort task, participants had to contribute a share of their initial endowments to a common fund of 30 tokens (in proportion to the size of their initial endowments: 1/5/9/15), which led to a distribution of 14/19/26/41. At this point, they were confronted with the arrival of a new group member (player 1). Since player 1 did not participate in the effort task, player 1 had no initial endowment and was unable to contribute to the common fund. Thus, the starting balance of the five members at the beginning of each round was 0/14/19/26/41.

The task was to deliberate and vote on the distribution of the common fund (30 tokens) to all five group members. The redistribution procedure that the group members agreed on was implemented across five subsequent rounds. There was a minimum consumption threshold of 16 tokens per round for each member. If a

[9] The experiments were conducted in May and October 2019. We thank the team of the Vienna Center of Experimental Economics (VCEE), University of Vienna. The experiments were conducted in German. Therefore, the excerpts from the reason-giving stages presented in the following section were translated into English.

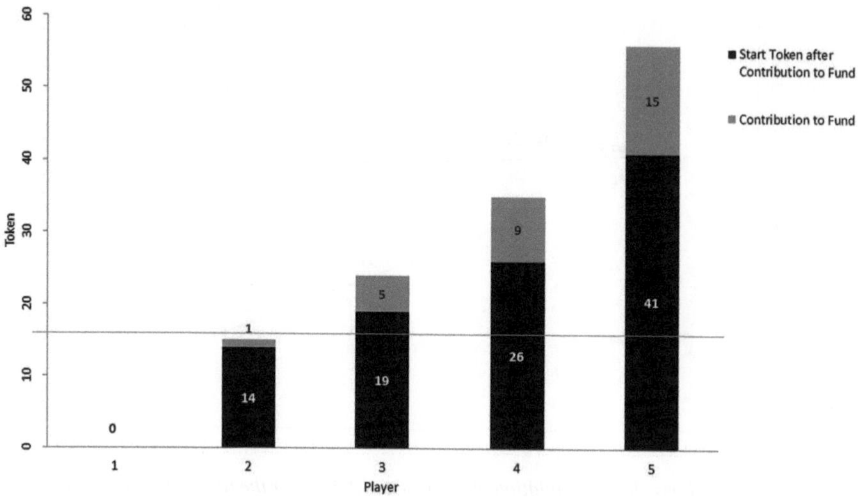

The figure shows contributions (grey bars) and initial endowments after contributions (black bars) of the five group members. The line signifies the minimum consumption (16 tokens) in each round.

Fig. 6.1 Contributions

member ended up with less than 16 tokens per round, the member would run into debt. The surplus above the minimal consumption threshold of 16 tokens (savings) as well as the deficits (debts) per round accumulated. The initial endowments of the subsequent rounds, however, did not change. Figure 6.2 shows the accumulation of savings and debts over the rounds without redistribution.

In all treatment variations, the initial proposal presented to the players was to distribute the common fund equally (6/6/6/6/6). A screen presentation demonstrated to the participants the effects of the proposed equal distribution after five rounds. The groups were informed that should they unanimously accept an equal distribution, it would determine the payouts for the five subsequent rounds. They were also told that if they failed to reach a unanimous agreement, they would get the opportunity to deliberate and vote on an alternative distribution of the 30 tokens.

When a group accepted the equal distribution, the group members were individually asked if they would have still preferred the equal distribution (option 1) over two alternative, hypothetical ways of distributing the 30 tokens. One of these hypothetical alternatives (option 2) was a distribution according to the weaker first principle (21/7/2/0/0), which would have resulted in an outcome distribution of 21/21/21/26/41. The other alternative (option 3) was a distribution according to the mixed principle (16/2/3/4/5), which would have led to an outcome of 16/16/22/30/46.

Whenever group members did not reach a unanimous agreement to accept the equal distribution, the group proceeded to the stage where the members were asked

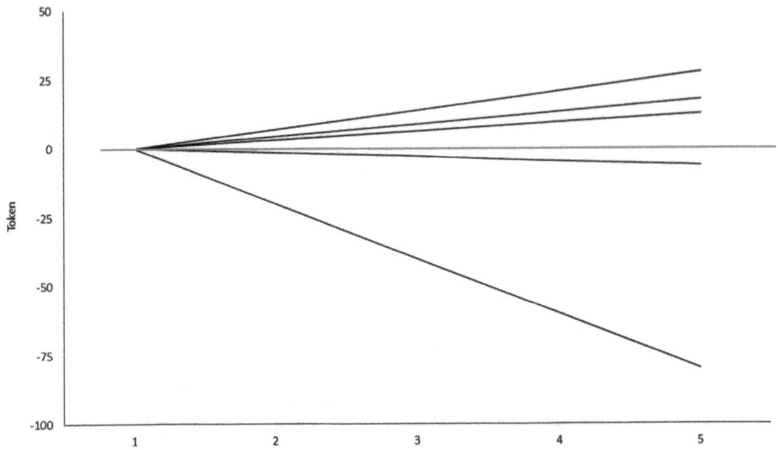

The figure shows the accumulation of savings and debts over the rounds when there is no redistribution. Values above the 'zero' line show how savings accumulate. Values below the 'zero' line show how debts accumulate.

Fig. 6.2 Accumulation of savings and debts

to deliberate and vote on an alternative distribution. The requirement for a decision on an alternative distribution was a simple majority (see Fig. 6.3).

Since the newly arrived member (player 1) did not have the chance to participate in the effort task and therefore was not equipped with an initial endowment, player 1 needed a substantial share of the common fund in order to avoid accruing debts. An equal distribution was not sufficient to cover the minimum consumption costs of player 1. In order to meet the needs of the new member, the group had to reject the proposed equal distribution and propose an alternative distribution that covered the needs of player 1.

Unlike in the first series of experiments, the variation "equal distribution/redistribution/effort" was chosen for all groups. While these parameters were kept constant, the levels of participation in the decision process were varied. In one treatment condition, player 1 was not able to participate in the deliberation nor to vote (no participation); in a second treatment condition, player 1 was able to participate in the deliberation process (reason-giving and chat) and to vote (full participation). In the control condition, player 1 participated in the deliberation (reason-giving and chat) but was not allowed to vote (limited participation).[10]

We expected that the group was more likely to accept an equal distribution when the new member was not allowed to participate in the deliberation process. Moreover, we expected the new member's needs to be met less often when the

[10] We assume that the treatment with no participation rights resembles the real-life constraints on immigrants into a society.

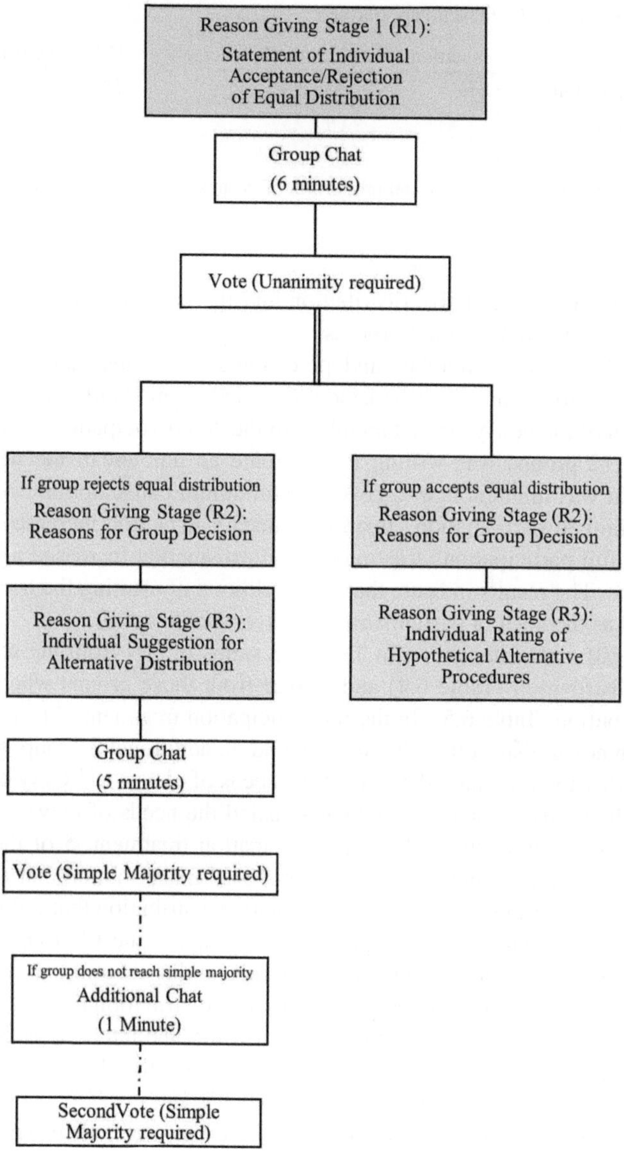

Fig. 6.3 Overview of experimental design: reason-giving stages R1, R2, and R3, chat and vote

Table 6.3 Overall need satisfaction of player 1

	No participation	Limited participation	Full participation	Total
Need satisfaction in %	8.3%	33.3%	58.3%	33.3%
Need satisfaction in *n*	1	4	7	12
N	12	12	12	36

This table summarizes the number and proportion of groups in each participation treatment that satisfied player 1's needs

group agreed on an alternative distribution and the new member was not allowed to participate in the deliberation process.

Table 6.3 shows the number and percentage of groups that satisfied player 1's needs. It shows that need satisfaction varied significantly with the level of participation of the newly arrived member. In the "no participation" treatment, only one of the 12 groups was willing to distribute an amount to the newly arrived member that was high enough to cover the minimum consumption costs of player 1. In the "limited participation" treatment, need satisfaction increased to 4 out of 12. In the "full participation" treatment, need satisfaction increased again to 7 out of 12 groups. The results indicate that the likelihood of meeting the needs of player 1 increased as the level of participation of player 1 increased.

The overall need satisfaction in Table 6.3 stems in part from the acceptance of the equal distribution (Table 6.4) and in part from those groups who rejected the equal distribution (Table 6.5). In the no participation treatment, 8 of the 12 groups accepted an equal distribution (Table 6.4), and an additional 3 groups proposed an alternative distribution that did not meet the needs of player 1.[11] Only one of the 12 groups in the no participation treatment satisfied the needs of player 1 using their alternative distribution. In the limited participation treatment, 5 of the 12 groups accepted the equal distribution, 4 groups proposed a distribution that met the need of player 1, and 3 groups suggested an alternative distribution that did not meet the needs of player 1. In the full participation treatment, 4 of the 12 groups accepted an equal distribution, 7 groups proposed an alternative distribution that met the needs of player 1, and one group proposed an alternative distribution that did not meet the needs of player 1. The results in Table 6.4 show that the intuitive perception of an equal distribution as fair diminishes when player 1 gets the chance to argue against an equal distribution that would not meet player 1's needs.

As shown in Table 6.5, the likelihood of an alternative distribution that met the needs of player 1 increased with the level of participation of player 1. While only 1 of the 4 groups that chose an alternative distribution in the no participation treatment was willing to meet the needs of player 1, 4 of the 7 groups in the limited

[11] Since player 2 needed 2 tokens of the common fund, the needs of player 2 were met by an equal distribution. Hypothetically, there could have been a proposal for an alternative distribution in which the needs of player 1 (16 tokens) would have been met, while the needs of player 2 (2 tokens) would not have been met. However, this case did not happen. The needs of player 2 were met in all treatment variations. We therefore focus on the needs of player 1 in our discussion.

Table 6.4 Acceptance of equal redistribution

	No participation	Limited participation	Full participation	Total
Need satisfaction in %	66.7%	41.7%	33.3%	47.2%
Need satisfaction in *n*	8	5	4	17
N	12	12	12	36

This table summarizes the number and proportion of groups in each participation treatment that accepted the proposed equal distribution

Table 6.5 Need satisfaction of player 1 in the alternative distributions

	No participation	Limited participation	Full participation	Total
Need satisfaction in %	25.0%	57.1%	87.5%	63.2%
Need satisfaction in *n*	1	4	7	12
N	4	7	8	19

This table summarizes the number and proportion of groups in each participation treatment that satisfied player 1's needs in their chosen alternative distributions

participation treatment did the same. In the full participation treatment, 7 out of 12 groups rejected the equal distribution and chose an alternative distribution that met the needs of player 1; only one group that opted for an alternative distribution did not meet player 1's needs.

Again, members of the group were asked to state reasons for their choices at three stages of the experiment. The text data from the reason-giving stages was coded with the main categories "principles" and "addressees"[12] and several subcategories for each, including combinations of different distribution principles and addressees mentioned. In the following, we present the main findings from our qualitative analysis.

As shown in Table 6.6, the overall finding is that while "monistic" reasons based on a single principle like equality, need, or merit can be found, combinations of different principles—in the sense of pluralistic understandings of justice—are quite common. In the reasons stated, participants differentiate between several principles of justice. They refer to various principles in one argument. The level of differentiation presented in the arguments during the reason-giving stages even increases during the process of deliberation. While the number of arguments backed by the principle of equality decreases, the number of arguments based solely on need stays more or less at the same level. The number of arguments that combine need with other principles of distributive justice increases ("combination including need"), while the number of pluralistic arguments without need ("combination without need") stays at the same level.

[12] The category "addressee" denotes any specific individual(s) or groups addressed in participants' stated reasons for their distribution choices. The category includes, but is not limited to, the suggested recipients of the proposed distribution.

Table 6.6 Principles: codings before and after deliberation ($N = 504$)

	Equality (only)	Merit (only)	Need (only)	Fairness (only)	Procedure (only)	Outcome (only)	Other (only)	Not specified	Combin. including need	Combin. without need
Sum	26	13	51	79	20	46	7	38	114	110
R1	11	7	19	34	3	15	4	16	25	34
R2	10	5	14	25	15	12	0	13	36	38
R3	5	1	18	20	2	19	3	9	53	38

Based on 36 groups; in the no participation treatment (12 groups), the newly arrived member (P1) was not allowed to participate in the reason-giving stages. R1, R2, and R3 mark the different stages of reason-giving—before deliberation, after deliberation, and a third stage where participants were asked either to present an alternative distribution of the common fund (if they rejected the initial proposal for an equal distribution) or to compare the equal distribution with two hypothetical alternative distributions (if they accepted the initial proposal for an equal distribution). In the latter situation, the hypothetical alternatives were a "weaker first" distribution and a distribution according to the "mixed" principle

Table 6.7 Addressees: codings before and after deliberation ($N = 504$)

	I (only)	We/all (only)	Player 1 (only)	Other individuals (Only)	Subgroup (only)	Not specified	Combin. including player 1	Combin. without player 1
Sum	26	151	40	1	45	80	86	75
R1	16	51	14	0	15	33	17	22
R2	3	59	17	0	21	23	20	25
R3	7	41	9	1	9	24	49	28

Based on 36 groups; in the no participation treatment (12 groups), the newly arrived member (P1) was not allowed to participate in the reason-giving stages

Table 6.7 shows that the number of arguments that exclusively mention the newly arrived member (player 1) does not increase during the process of deliberation. However, the number of arguments that include player 1 as part of a group of various addressees increases ("combination including player 1"). Again, participants tend to differentiate between several individuals or groups/subgroups in one argument, and the level of differentiation increases during the process of deliberation.

Participants tend to state their suggestions on how to distribute the common fund in a way that includes a reference to the group as a whole ("we"/"all"), or to various individuals or subgroups that constitute the group ("the poorer members"/"the richer members"). They tend to make suggestions from the group's perspective, while suggestions that refer to individual preferences are rather rare. This finding is related to the development of a "we-mode reasoning" as opposed to an "I-mode reasoning" (Schwenkenbecher 2019, 2021). The participants of the deliberative process perform a change of perspective almost from the beginning of the experiment. They discuss redistribution of the common fund from the perspective of the group as a whole (we-mode reasoning) rather than from their individual perspectives. This is shown in Table 6.7, where the number of "we/all" codings (151 in total) plus the number of subgroups or combinations of subjects addressed in the arguments is high, while the number of I-mode reasons is low (26). The actual level of need satisfaction (Tables 6.3 and 6.5 above) shows that participation of the newly arrived member (player 1) in the deliberation process makes a huge difference when it comes to a need-based distribution. When player 1 is not able to participate in the deliberative process, player 1 is seldom considered as part of the "we."

We now take a closer look at the actual reasons presented by the participants in the different treatment variations. Since participants were asked to state their reasons at three different stages of the experiment (R1–R3), we will first present an example from a group in the no participation treatment (group 12) that covers all three stages of the deliberative process. This example also serves to illustrate the way the deliberative process proceeds when player 1 is not included in the deliberation. The group in this example accepts the initial equal distribution option. Afterwards, we will take a closer look at two examples from the full participation treatment (group 14) and the limited participation treatment (group 32) in which the

Table 6.8 Reasons before chat and voting (group 12, no participation treatment, R1)

Player	Reason
Player 2	I am in favor because ... it is the best decision for all participants
Player 3	I am in favor because ... everyone gets their fair share
Player 4	I am in favor because ... because it is better to divide the tokens equally and fairly among the group members
Player 5	I am against it because... the distribution doesn't seem quite fair. Participants with starting balances of 0 tokens have no chance to participate and will only get more into debt. A better redistribution system should be implemented

Table 6.9 Reasons after chat and voting (group 12, no participation treatment, R2)

Player	Reason
Player 2	Everyone has agreed and accepted that it happened that way
Player 3	I agree with the distribution procedure because it pays out a fair and just share to all participants
Player 4	Everyone then gets a fair distribution of the tokens
Player 5	In the procedure, each group member is treated equally regardless of other aspects and receives the same payout. That is why this procedure is particularly fair and just

groups rejected the equal distribution and opted for an alternative distribution that covered the needs of player 1. In these examples, we will focus on the reasons given for a need-based alternative distribution.

Table 6.8 shows the individual reasons given by four participants in a group in the no participation treatment at the beginning of the deliberative process (prior to the first chat, R1). This excerpt shows that during the reason-giving stage R1, immediately after they are presented with the proposal to distribute the common fund equally, three of the four deliberating members are in favor of this proposal and consider it to be fair. Only member 5, the player with the highest initial endowment, argues against an equal distribution and in favor of a distribution that takes the situation of player 1 into account. During the following chat, player 5 is not able to convince the other three participants to change their preferences. The group makes a unanimous decision to accept an equal distribution.

Table 6.9 shows participants' stated reasons for their unanimous acceptance of an equal distribution (R2). The voting behavior as well as the reason presented by player 5 at this stage are rather difficult to interpret, since player 5 initially argued against an equal distribution but then votes in favor of an equal distribution and presents a reason after the vote that supports an equal distribution. Player 5 even characterizes an equal distribution as "particularly fair and just."

Table 6.10 displays participants' stated reasons after they accepted the equal distribution. At this stage, they are asked (hypothetically) if they would still have accepted an equal distribution (option 1) if they could have opted for a weaker first distribution (option 2) or a distribution according to the mixed principle (option 3). As is shown in Table 6.10, player 2 and player 5 would have opted for a

Table 6.10 Reasons after acceptance of equal distribution, choice of hypothetical alternatives (group 12, no participation treatment, R3)

Player	Chosen option (hypothetical)	Reason
Player 2	3	It always has to be a unanimous decision
Player 3	1	It is simply distributed equally and everyone gets a fair share
Player 4	1	I have chosen the procedure equal distribution because everyone gets a fair distribution
Player 5	3	No member of the group is in the negative range and there is still a performance-related payment, however based on a social redistribution so that all participants have a satisfactory income

Option 1 = equal distribution, option 2 = weaker first, option 3 = mixed principle

distribution according to the mixed principle that would have covered the needs of player 1 (in the sense of debt avoidance). Player 2's reason is rather difficult to interpret ("It always has to be a unanimous decision"). Player 5, who argued against an equal distribution at the beginning of the deliberative process, makes the different principles behind his choice transparent. Player 5 is in favor of a need-based redistribution that covers the minimum consumption threshold of player 1 while keeping the surplus performance-related.

Table 6.11 shows excerpts from a group in the full participation treatment (group 14) in which player 1 is able to participate in the reason-giving stage, the chat, and the vote. After group 14 rejected equal distribution with four votes against and one in favor and then gave their reasons for this decision, they arrived at the stage at which they presented their alternative proposals for a distribution. Table 6.11 shows the reasons they give for their individual proposals (R3). The numerical proposals as well as their stated reasons show that they combine need with other distributive principles. At this stage, the individual members are willing to give more than an equal share to player 1, but they are not necessarily willing to meet the needs of player 1 (16 tokens). After another round of communication in the chat, their chosen distribution is 21/7/2/0/0, as proposed by player 4. This distribution, which leads to an outcome distribution of 21/21/21/26/41, meets the needs of players 1 and 2 and even grants them a surplus.

Finally, Table 6.12 presents excerpts from the reason-giving stage R3 of a group in the limited participation treatment. In this group, all five members make an initial proposal that already meets the needs of player 1. As shown in Tables 6.6 and 6.7 above, at this stage of the experiment (R3), the reasons presented by the participants become more differentiated than those presented at the earlier reason-giving stages. It is obvious that the members do not only rely on need as a principle of distribution, but also take criteria like "good performance" and proportionality into account. However, while the group in the full deliberation treatment (group 14, Table 6.11) granted player 1 a sizeable surplus, the group in the limited participation treatment (group 32, Table 6.12) decided to grant player 1 only 1 token of surplus above the minimum consumption costs. Group 32 decided unanimously (without player 1,

Table 6.11 Reasons for proposed alternative distribution (group 14, full participation treatment, R3)

Player	Proposed alternative distribution	Reason
Player 1	18/4/3/3/2	In a rush, this would be a good way for everyone to stay in the positive area and also earn some extra money, even if it would be a minimal extra income
Player 2	10/8/6/4/2	With my indicated distribution the differences are not too big and still it is distributed fairly according to the starting capital
Player 3	14/6/5/4/1	The biggest part would go to player 1, because he has no tokens at all. The other tokens are distributed according to need and also as a kind of reward for those who did well in the test, they are still the best, but the difference between the players is small
Player 4	21/7/2/0/0	If the tokens are distributed like this, we can cover all our minimum living expenses and even save 5 tokens as well
Player 5	10/8/6/4/2	I think the lower the starting capital the more tokens the participant should get. Hence it is fairer

Table 6.12 Reasons for proposed alternative distribution (group 32, limited participation treatment, R3)

Player	Proposed alternative distribution	Reason
Player 1	16/6/4/3/1	Player 1 needs 16 token, player 5 already has a lot, even without tokens. In between, an attempt is made to create a smaller difference
Player 2	17/3/3/3/4	No one should get into debt, but a good performance should still be rewarded
Player 3	20/7/3/0/0	After subtracting the 16 tokens, no one remains under the limit. The goal is that all come out at 5. But I made a mistake and would deduct 1 more from player 3 (me) and give it to player 1
Player 4	16/2/3/4/5	Everyone reaches 16 tokens, the rest is distributed fairly. Since you “sacrifice” more the more you have, it is only fair if you do not lose too much. Therefore 5, 4, 3 for the players who give away more, so that everyone has something
Player 5	16/7/4/2/1	Player 1 needs to be helped!

who was not allowed to participate in the vote) to distribute the fund according to player 2’s proposal (17/3/3/3/4).

Overall, the qualitative results show that while need satisfaction is an important principle that participants refer to when distributing resources, it is only one among several principles. During the process of deliberation, the reasons presented become more and more differentiated and take various principles and addressees into account. The findings support the hypothesis that when a group has to decide on the distribution of a resource, a deliberative process raises the acceptance of needs as a distributive principle. Moreover, our findings support the hypothesis that when arguments and justifications for a need-based distribution are made transparent to members of the deciding group, the initial, 'intuitive" acceptance of strict equality diminishes. Finally, the findings from the second series of experiments support the hypothesis that when people in need are included in the deliberative process and are able to present reasons for a distribution that meets their needs, the acceptance of need-based distribution increases.

6.6 Conclusion

While individuals intuitively accept an equal distribution of resources, an unequal distribution requires some form of justification. In all treatments of both series of our experiments, all group members were informed about the numerical distribution of the initial endowments and the effects of the proposed distribution of the common fund (transparency of information) before they deliberated with each other. However, participants were more likely to accept a distribution that met the needs of all group members when they were presented with reasons for a need-based distribution. Therefore, in addition to mere information disclosure, we find that a specific kind of transparency (transparency of reasons), achieved through deliberation, substantially raises the chances of all participants' needs being satisfied. Moreover, our findings suggest that reason-giving has a substantial effect not only on the acceptance of need-based distribution, but also leads to a decreasing acceptance of strict equality as an "intuitively fair" principle of distribution. Therefore, our findings support the thesis that the recognition of needs "requires specific procedures in which what is recognized as need is also argumentatively identified as what is necessary" (Nullmeier 2020, p. 198). A closer look at the operationalization of need in our experiments, however, also suggests that this is an open-ended process. While the operationalization of need we implemented assumes that needs are satisfied when participants are able to cover their minimum consumption costs (distribution according to the mixed or Boulding-principle), our findings show that a "weaker first" principle, which provides the least well-off with a surplus above their minimum consumption costs, is what people have in mind when distributing resources according to need. Finally, our findings show that it is important that people in need have their say in the deliberative process on how to distribute resources. For their needs to be met, people in need have to be participants in the deliberative process and a member of the deliberating "we."

Acknowledgments In this chapter, we present results from the project "Limits of Proceduralism? Experimental Studies on the Stability of Procedures of Need Determination," which formed a part of the research group FOR 2104 "Need-Based Justice and Distribution Procedures." In this project, we used laboratory group experiments to study the effect of deliberation—and especially reason-giving—as well as participation, in different scenarios of (re)distribution. The research was financed by the German Research Foundation (DFG Grants NU 108/4-1 and PR 1551/1-1). The project was renamed "Needs Within and Across Borders. Experimental Investigations on the

Stability of Transnational Need-Based Distribution Procedures" in funding phase 2 of the FOR 2104 research group (DFG Grants NU 108/4-2 and PR 1551/1-2).

References

Adams, B. (2014): "Reason-Giving in Deliberative Forums", *Journal of Public Deliberation* 10 (2), 1–27.

Almås, I., A. W. Cappelen, E. Ø. Sørensen, and B. Tungodden (2010): "Fairness and the Development of Inequality Acceptance", *Science* 328 (5982), 1176–1178.

Appelbaum, L. D. (2001): "The Influence of Perceived Deservingness on Policy Decisions Regarding Aid to the Poor", *Political Psychology* 22 (3), 419–442.

Asada, Y., R. Urquhart, M. Brown, G. Warner, M. McNally, and A. Murphy (2020): "Troutville: Where People Discuss Fairness Issues", *Canadian Journal of Bioethics/Revue Canadienne de Bioéthicque* 3 (1), 70–82.

Bächtiger, A., J. S. Dryzek, J. Mansbridge, and M. E. Warren (eds.) (2018): *The Oxford Handbook of Deliberative Democracy*. Oxford: Oxford University Press.

Baume, S. (2021): "Transparency in Public Affairs. The Rise of a Successful Political Metaphor", in S. Berger, S. Fengler, D. Owetschkin, and J. Sittmann (eds.): *Cultures of Transparency. Between Promise and Peril*, 17–29. London: Routledge.

Becker, A. (2013): "Accountability and the Fairness Bias: The Effects of Effort vs. Luck", *Social Choice and Welfare* 41 (3), 685–699.

Bock, O., I. Baetge, and A. Nicklisch (2014): "hroot–Hamburg Registration and Organization Online Tool", *European Economic Review* 71, 117–120.

Boulding, K. E. (1962): "Social Justice in Social Dynamics", in: R. B. Brandt (ed.): *Social justice*, 73–92. Englewood Cliffs, NJ: Prentice-Hall.

Brandts, J., L. Gerhards, and L. Mechtenberg (2022): "Deliberative Structures and their Impact on Voting Under Economic Conflict", *Experimental Economics* 25 (2), 680–705.

Chen, D. L., M. Schonger, and C. Wickens (2016): "oTree–An Open-Source Platform for Laboratory, Online, and Field Experiments", *Journal of Behavioral and Experimental Finance* 9 (C), 88–97.

Clark, A. E., and C. D'Ambrosio (2015): "Attitudes to Income Inequality: Experimental and Survey Evidence", in A. B. Atkinson, and F. Bourguignon (eds.): *Handbook of Income Distribution*, vol. 2A, 1147–1208. Amsterdam: Elsevier.

Cooper, D. J., and J. H. Kagel (2015): "Other-Regarding Preferences: A Selective Survey of Experimental Results", in J. H. Kagel, and A. E. Roth (eds.): *The Handbook of Experimental Economics*, vol. 2, 217–289. Princeton: Princeton University Press.

Curato, N., D. M. Farrell, B. Geissel, K. Grönlund et al. (2021): *Deliberative Mini-Publics. Core Design Features*. Bristol: Bristol University Press

Durante, R., L. Putterman, and J. van der Weele (2014): "Preferences for Redistribution and Perception of Fairness: An Experimental Study", *Journal of the European Economic Association* 12 (4), 1059–1086.

Eavey, C. L. (1991): "Patterns of Distribution in Spatial Games", *Rationality and Society* 3 (4), 450–474.

Elster, J. (ed.) (2015): *Secrecy and Publicity in Votes and Debates*. New York: Cambridge University Press.

Fehrler, S., and N. Hughes (2018): "How Transparency Kills Information Aggregation: Theory and Experiment", *American Economic Journal: Microeconomics* 10 (1), 181–209.

Fischbacher, U. (2007): "Z-Tree: Zurich Toolbox for Teadymade Economic Experiments", *Experimental Economics* 10 (2), 171–178.

Fischbacher, U., D. Grammling, and J. Hausfeld (2021): "Redistribution Beyond Equality and Status Quo. Heterogeneous Societies in the Lab", *Thurgau Institute of Economics (TWI) Research Paper Series* No. 123.

Fishkin, J. S. (2009): *When the People Speak: Deliberative Democracy and Public Consultation*. Oxford: Oxford University Press.

Forst, R. (2014): "Two Pictures of Justice", in R. Forst (ed.): *Justification and Critique*, 17–37. Cambridge: Polity Press.

Frohlich, N., and J. A. Oppenheimer (1990): "Choosing Justice in Experimental Democracies with Production", *American Political Science Review* 84 (2), 461–477.

Frohlich, N., J. A. Oppenheimer, and C. L. Eavey (1987): "Choices of Principles of Distributive Justice in Experimental Groups", *American Journal of Political Science* 31 (3), 606–636.

Fung, A. (2013): "Infotopia: Unleashing the Democratic Power of Transparency", *Politics and Society* 41 (2), 183–212.

Giacomini, M., J. Hurley, and D. DeJean (2014): "Fair Reckoning: A Qualitative Investigation of Responses to an Economic Health Resource Allocation Survey", *Health Expectation* 17 (2), 174–185.

Gosepath, S. (2015): "The Principles and the Presumption of Equality", in C. Fourie, F. Schuppert, and I. Wallimann-Helmer (eds.): *Social Equality. On What It Means to Be Equal*, 167–185. Oxford: Oxford University Press.

Greiner, B. (2015): "Subject Pool Recruitment Procedures: Organizing Experiments with ORSEE", *Journal of the Economic Science Association* 1 (1), 114–125.

Gutmann, A., and D. Thompson (1996): *Democracy and Disagreement. Why Moral Conflict Cannot Be Avoided in Politics, and What Should Be Done About It.* Cambridge, MA: The Belknap Press of Harvard University Press.

Habermas, J. (1997): *Between Facts and Norms. Contributions to a Discourse Theory of Law and Democracy* (translated by William Rehg). Cambridge, UK: Polity Press.

Habermas, J. (2003): *Truth and Justification* (translated by Barbara Fultner). Cambridge, UK: Polity Press.

Kelly, E. I. (2021): "Publicity", in H. LaFollette et al. (eds.): *The International Encyclopedia of Ethics*, 2nd ed., vol. 8 (O–P), 5124–5132. Hoboken, NJ: Wiley Blackwell.

Lamm, H., and T. Schwinger (1980): "Norms Concerning Distributive Justice: Are Needs Taken into Consideration in Allocation Decisions?", *Social Psychology Quarterly* 43 (4), 425–429.

Lefgren, L. J., D. P. Sims, and O. B. Stoddard (2016): "Effort, Luck, and Voting for Redistribution", *Journal of Public Economics* 143, 89–97.

Lim, C.-M. (2019): "Public Reason, Compromise within Consensus, and Legitimacy", in M. Knoll, S. Snyder, and. N. Şimsek (eds.): *New Perspectives on Distributive Justice. Deep Disagreements, Pluralism, and the Problem of Consensus*, 225–241. Berlin: De Gruyter.

Luskin, R. C., J. S. Fishkin, and R. Jowell (2002): "Considered Opinions: Deliberative Polling in Britain", *British Journal of Political Science* 32 (3), 455–487.

Mendelberg, T., and C. Karpowitz (2007): "How People Deliberate About Justice: Groups, Gender, and Decision Rules", in S. Rosenberg (ed.): *Deliberation, Participation and Democracy: Can the People Govern*?, 101–129. Basingstoke: Palgrave Macmillan.

Michelbach, P. A., J. T. Scott, R. E. Matland, and B. H. Bornstein (2003): "Doing Rawls Justice: An Experimental Study of Income Distribution Norms", *American Journal of Political Science* 47 (3), 523–539.

Michoń, Piotr (2021): "Deservingness for 'Family 500 +' Benefit in Poland: Qualitative Study of Internet Debates", *Social Indicators Research* 157 (1), 203–223.

Miller, D. (1999):*Principles of Social Justice*. Cambridge, MA: Harvard University Press.

Mollerstrom, J., B.-A. Reme, and E. Ø. Sørensen (2015): "Luck, Choice and Responsibility. An Experimental Study of Fairness Views", *Journal of Public Economics* 131, 33–40.

Myers, C. D., and T. Mendelberg (2013): "Political Deliberation", in D. Sears, L. Huddy, and J. Levy (eds.): *Oxford Handbook of Political Psychology*, 699–734. Oxford: Oxford University Press.

Naurin, D., and C. Reh (2018): "Deliberative Negotiation", in A. Bächtiger, J. S. Dryzek, J. Mansbridge, and M. E. Warren (eds.): *The Oxford Handbook of Deliberative Democracy*, 728–741. Oxford: Oxford University Press.

Nullmeier, F. (2020): "Towards a Theory of Need-Based Justice", in S. Traub, and B. Kittel (ed.): *Need-Based Distributive Justice: An Interdisciplinary Perspective*, 191–208. Cham: Springer Nature.

Nydegger, R. V., and G. Owen (1974): "Two-Person Bargaining: An Experimental Test of the Nash Axioms", *International Journal of Game Theory* 3 (4), 239–249

Ordóñez, L., and B. A. Mellers (1993): "Trade-Offs in Fairness and Preference Judgments", in B. Mellers and J. Baron (eds.): *Psychological Perspectives on Justice: Theory and Applications*, 138–154. Cambridge: Cambridge University.

Paetzel, F., J. Lorenz, and M. Tepe (2018): "Transparency Diminishes Framing-Effects in an Experiment on Voting and Redistribution", *European Journal of Political Economy* 55, 169–184.

Pritzlaff-Scheele, T., and, P. F. Zauchner (2019): *Immigration and Needs-Based Redistribution. Experimental Investigations on the Stability of Attitudes to Sharing Welfare Resources*, unpublished manuscript.

Schwenkenbecher, A. (2019): "Collective Moral Obligations: 'We-Reasoning' and the Perspective of the Deliberating Agent", *The Monist* 102 (2), 151–171.

Schwenkenbecher, A. (2021): *Getting Our Act Together. A Theory of Collective Moral Obligation.* London: Routledge.

Scott, J. T., R. E. Matland, P. A. Michelbach, and B. H. Bornstein (2001): "Just Deserts. An Experimental Study of Distributive Justice Norms", *American Journal of Political Science* 45 (4), 749–767.

Selten, R. (1987): "Equity and Coalition Bargaining in Experimental Three-Person Games", in A. E. Roth (ed.): *Laboratory Experimentation in Economics. Six Points of View*, 42–98. Cambridge: Cambridge University Press.

Setälä, M., and K. Herne (2014): "Normative Theory and Experimental Research in the Study of Deliberative Mini-Publics", in K. Grönlund, A. Bächtiger, and M. Setälä (eds.): *Deliberative Mini-Publics. Involving Citizens in the Democratic Process*, 59–75. Colchester: ECPR Press.

Starmans, C., M. Sheskin, and P. Bloom (2017): "Why People Prefer Unequal Societies", *Nature Human Behaviour* 1, 0082.

Traub, S., C. Seidl, U. Schmidt, and M. V. Levati (2005): "Friedman, Harsanyi, Rawls, Boulding–or Somebody Else? An Experimental Investigation of Distributive Justice", *Social Choice and Welfare* 24 (2), 283–309.

Valero, V. (2022): "Redistribution and Beliefs About the Source of Income Inequality", *Experimental Economics* 25 (3), 876–901.

van Oorschot, W., F. Roosma, B. Meuleman, and T. Reeskens (eds.) (2017): *The Social Legitimacy of Targeted Welfare. Attitudes to Welfare Deservingness*. Cheltenham: Edward Elgar.

Zauchner, P. F., and T. Pritzlaff-Scheelc (2017): "Meeting Needs. An Experimental Study on Need-Based Justice and Inequality", *FOR 2104 Working Paper* 2017–07.

Zimmermann, K., J.-O. Heuer, and S. Mau (2018): "Changing Preferences Towards Redistribution. How Deliberation Shapes Welfare Attitudes", *Social Policy and Administration* 52 (5), 926–982.

Part III
Welfare Consequences of Prioritizing Need-Based Distributions

Chapter 7
Need-Based Justice and Social Utility: A Preference Approach

Andreas Nicklisch

Abstract This chapter examines the economic incentives of need-based income redistribution. We ask whether the outcome obtained in a redistribution system that assigns transfers according to needs leads to efficient resource production and whether the past-transfer outcomes is generally acceptable for the involved parties. In turn, settings with unacceptable distribution procedures are institutionally unfit and cause at the extreme migration to other, more attractive systems. Redistribution does not incur implicit costs, that is, the resource production is not negatively influenced by the subsequent distribution. Oversupply and undersupply of resources required to satisfy the recognized needs do not lead to transfers beyond or short off the needs. Rather decision makers send the required amount to satisfy the need or they send nothing at all. Thus need-based redistribution creates a flexibility regarding the applied fairness norm. If transfers are too high for a society to satisfy all currently accepted need standards, a reevaluation of needs follows leading to lower standards.

7.1 Introduction

In his famous book *Elements of the Philosophy of Right*,[1] the German philosopher Georg Wilhelm Friedrich Hegel states that "what is reasonable is real [. . .]." That is to say, only justifiable entities persist, and the sustainability of an order depends on its acceptance.[2] In our project, we attempt to apply Hegel's principle to distribution

[1] Grundlinien der Philosophie des Rechts (1820, cited according to Knowles 2003).

[2] Hegel has been criticized by other philosophers for how he continues the sentence: "[. . .] and what is real is sensible." Critics argue that Hegel primarily attempts to legitimize an ancient regime and hinders the fight of societal liberation (see Popper 2003).

A. Nicklisch (✉)
University of Applied Sciences of the Grisons, Chur, Switzerland
e-mail: Andreas.Nicklisch@fhgr.ch

B. Kittel, S. Traub (eds.), *Priority of Needs?*,
https://doi.org/10.1007/978-3-031-53051-7_7

procedures. In other words, acceptance by members of a society is of major importance for the survival of a distribution procedure: only distribution procedures acceptable to the members of a society survive in the long run. Procedures deemed unacceptable will lead to all sorts of actions by members to divert resources away from the system, such as black labor or lower labor effort. Both limitations on economic production reduce the efficiency of a society: black labor involves the direct costs of financial control while lower labor effort leads to the indirect costs of extra unworked hours. Those types of costs in turn make unacceptable distribution procedures institutionally unfit and cause—at the extreme—a change of the institutional setting or dismantlement because members migrate to other, more attractive systems (see, e.g., Chugunova et al. 2020). In this chapter, the central question is under which conditions a majority of decision makers choose a distribution system based on need-based justice, which side effects this causes, and which factors increase its acceptance.

7.2 Acceptance and Fairness

The acceptance—and thus in the long run the sustainability—of a distribution system depends largely on the ability of the system to reflect the understandings of fairness of its members. Fairness is a curious concept: people have very specific feelings about what is and is not fair. However, they struggle to specify their beliefs about which conditions determine fairness and which determine unfairness. This creates a substantial problem for social science, since fairness is pivotal for the vast majority of decision makers (see, for instance, Camerer 1999). Therefore, it is crucial for social science to incorporate fairness—economists call this social utility—into their decision algorithms and models for human behavior. Models that do not take fairness into account fail to describe persistent developments in human societies.

What do we know so far about fairness? Overall, fairness seems to subsume many different motives (e.g., Cappelen et al. 2007; Nicklisch and Wolff 2012). There is evidencc that people care both for procedural fairness and distributional fairness. According to the former motive, people like to act in a way that matches how others have treated them (e.g., Rabin 1993; Cox et al. 2007). This covers, on the one hand, being nice to those who have acted generously and, on the other hand, being mean to those who have been greedy. Regarding the latter motive, there is solid evidence that people have a taste for an even distribution of resources (e.g., Fehr and Schmidt 1999; Bolton and Ockenfels 2000). In other circumstances, people prefer a distribution of resources proportional to the effort invested into the production of those resources (e.g., Gill and Stone 2010): those who have invested a lot of work to create a resource may keep more of it than those who have invested little. Finally, as this edited volume shows, there is evidence for the importance of need-based justice. An allocation is just in terms of need-based justice if the resources are distributed according to socially or politically recognized needs.

This chapter summarizes what we know so far about those motives, specifically the little we know about need-based justice and how it relates to other fairness motives. For this, we follow Konow's (2003) taxonomy, introducing briefly the major types of fairness motives and discussing any interdependencies between them. We then discuss our main results regarding the behavioral incentives for need-based redistribution. Finally, we provide evidence suggesting that there is a hierarchy among the motives and how this hierarchy guides people's decisions.

7.3 The Zoo

Most of us dislike isolation and enjoy the company of others. Unsurprisingly, we therefore pay attention to those who surround us. For most of us, social utility is a vital element of the decision process (although it took economists decades to acknowledge this). At its core, social utility assumes that a person draws some utility from the well-being of another person. The utility may be positive (altruism) or negative (resentments), and it decreases the further away the other's utility is from a reference value. The problem is the multitude of reference values that are available: equity, proportionality, reciprocity, and need-based justice define distinct reference values (see, e.g., Cappelen et al. 2007). Shifting the other's income closer to those reference values increases the extent to which the act of altering incomes is viewed as fair.

We should emphasize that all concepts of fairness are embedded in particular contexts (see, e.g., Konow 2001; Konow 2003). That is, while we report predominantly experimental evidence on the importance of certain fairness motives, the different experimental designs emphasize particular aspects of procedural and distributional fairness. For instance, in an environment where people earn their endowments through work, the experimental design usually draws people's attention to differences in effort that participants invest into resource production. Thus, the principle of proportionality according to investments becomes more salient in such a context than in a context where people are simply endowed by the experimenter (e.g., Luccasen and Grossman 2017). In turn, people are typically more inclined to help others when income inequalities reflect differences in luck than when inequalities reflect differences in choices (e.g., Cappelen et al. 2013). Therefore, what we consider a fair distribution of income differs across environments, but also between histories of interactions, and the consequences arising from the new income distribution. Thus, revealed fairness preferences corresponding to certain reference values are strongly shaped by several contextual conditions. There is still an ongoing dispute among economists whether specific fairness motives affect decisions even when they are less salient.

Frohlich et al. (1987) and Frohlich and Oppenheimer (1990) are the first to analyze a larger set of distribution motives. In their experiments, they vary the underlying redistribution procedures to elicit subjects' fairness preferences. The most preferred principle implements a minimum income for the worst-off members in society while redistributing any surplus in proportion to participants' efforts in the production of the resource. After getting similar experimental results, Traub et al. (2009) conclude that most of their subjects preferred a distribution that is equitable enough to prevent protest but still allows some to outperform others.

Gerber et al. (2019) extend Frohlich and Oppenheimer's work by analyzing both theoretical and experimental "voting by feet" between different redistribution systems. Thus, subjects join societies that practice redistribution in line with the subjects' preferred principle. The authors vary the "thickness" of the veil of ignorance behind which people choose their preferred redistribution system (i.e., people do not know, partly know, or fully know their level of productivity before voting). Results show less redistribution than predicted behind the full veil of ignorance and more than predicted when the veil of ignorance is partly lifted. In contrast to the prediction, several redistribution motives coexist simultaneously in the course of the experiment.

Warm Glow

We will begin with a rather extreme version of pro-sociality that focuses on how the act of giving leads to the concept of a "warm glow of giving" (e.g., Andreoni 1989, 1990, 1995). Warm glow of giving refers to the utility that a person i draws from sending money to another person j. That is, j's well-being matters less for i's utility than the fact that i is sending the money: suppose j is guaranteed to receive a fixed income, and i draws extra utility when i partly or fully provides that income. In other words, the utility is egocentric in the sense that the act of giving triggers the pro-social utility component, not the other's change in income. Although warm glow of giving cannot explain all facets of pro-sociality, most economists accept that it has an effect (e.g., Crumpler and Grossman 2008).

Equality

Equality is perhaps the most intuitive reference value for fairness. At its center is the idea that all involved parties in the distribution process are equal and deserve an equal share of the income. Therefore, persons draw utility from an equal distribution of income, even to the extent that person i feels unpleasant when experiencing an advantage. That is, keeping i's income constant, i prefers j have the same amount over j receiving less or more income than i (e.g., Bolton and Ockenfels 2000; Fehr and Schmidt 1999). Despite the appealing simplicity of equality, there is evidence that the preference for equality is rather fragile and less robust when the context changes (Engelmann and Strobel 2004). Thus, it seems that equality plays a role only under very specific conditions.

Equity

Equity relates to the procedure that brings about the outcomes. It argues that a process should not favor a particular person and should provide equal chances for everybody (there are variations on this principle; see the seminal article by Fleurbaey 2010). Any individual may feel free to increase the chance of a favorable outcome for herself through individual effort and talent. Provided that all individuals are initially equipped with the same chances and opportunity, the process and any outcome, even unequal outcomes, are fair.[3] Therefore, a process rendering outcomes proportional to the input people deliver is fair from an equity point of view.

Importantly, motives play an important role in equity-based decision making: a process that does not provide equal chances for everybody cannot yield fair outcomes and requires corrections. In other words, if there are circumstances beyond a person's control reducing their gain, then the process and its outcome is not fair and needs correction. Thus, unequal initial chances justify corrective redistributions. In turn, if an individual is personally responsible for the differences in outcomes, the process and its outcome is fair and no correction is needed (see Konow 2000; Fong 2001).[4]

Reciprocity

Reciprocity is also concerned with procedural fairness. One important factor for procedural fairness are foregone alternatives. That is, suppose a person j assigns another person i two monetary units from a total of ten. i will perceive the fairness of this act very differently depending on if j had the alternative to assign five out of ten units or if j only had the alternative to assign zero out of ten units. i would likely consider the distribution of two units as mean in the former context and as generous in the latter context (Falk et al. 2003). In the former case, i draws utility from giving j a similarly mean distribution in response, whereas in the latter case, i gains utility from giving j a generous distribution. In other words, reciprocity as a fairness principle allows for both punishment and reward.

Needs

Need-based justice is concerned with the satisfaction of recognized needs. In other words, the involved individuals decide on a set of recognized needs that are supported by redistribution from a shared resource. While the process of recognition is an important feature of need-based justice that lays beyond our focus, we will later present stylized facts regarding the preferences for (or against) certain distributions to needy individuals and the incentives created for decision makers by need-based redistribution.[5] For instance, we will ask how much support should be provided to subjects living in poverty when funds are scarce (i.e., when resources are short and may not match the needs of those who give and those who receive)?

Analyzing the incentives for need-based justice is important because it reveals the limits of a redistribution system based on needs. That is, we do not want to reward people who are responsible for their need. Nor do we want to corrupt the system of need-based distribution by creating dependencies for recipients. If the

[3] Cappelen et al. (2010) test experimentally the willingness of participants to equalize income differences in response to various factors causing uneven income distributions. The authors find a significant reduction in support from those who had equal starting positions but ended up being needy. However, these participants receive some minor support nonetheless.

[4] Cappelen et al. (2013) and other researchers refer to this idea as the "theory of entitlements."

[5] One important complement to the studies of our research project is the paper by Alcantud et al. (2022): they analyze the welfare of societies that organize transfers based on need-based justice.

needy constantly meet their needs through redistribution, they may "unlearn" to take the responsibility for earning their required income. In other words, the equity motive mentioned earlier also involves an educational element: it is one thing to compensate inequalities in initial chances; it is another thing to equalize those inequalities that arise from personal choices, particularly if the consequences of support allow recipients to continue to exert little effort in the future.

Thus, this chapter contributes to the search for a sustainable, generally acceptable redistribution system (an earlier example is Schumacher et al. 2017, who analyze the target conflict between altruism and efficiency). That is, our chapter helps to establish under what conditions members of a society deem "a process by which [those] needs are determined as socially or politically recognized" (Nullmeier 2020, p. 198) as generally acceptable. Analyzing these factors may provide important insights for the ongoing debate about the pros and cons of unconditional basic income in Europe (examples include large-scale field experiments in Finland [see Kangas et al. 2021] and the Netherlands and Scotland [see Delsen and Schilpzand 2019]).[6]

7.4 The Objectives

At the core of each fairness *model* is a distribution objective that defines target values for the incomes of each member in a society. The final distribution of incomes ideally implements or at least approaches those target values. For instance, assuming that i is inequality averse, i feels unpleasant when experiencing inequality, whether that inequality is to i's advantage or disadvantage. In this case, the target value equals one nth of the total income, with n denoting here the number of group members (e.g., Bolton and Ockenfels 2000). In turn, suppose i holds reciprocal fairness preferences, while j is unkind to i. In this case, j's ideal income is zero, provided that i can fully determine j's transfer (e.g., Cox et al. 2007). Notice that quite often, target values for different motives coincide. For instance, suppose j offers i a mean offer in the ultimation game that is rejected by i, which leads to zero incomes for both players. By doing so, one may claim that i establishes income equality while also maximizing her negative reciprocity.

While j's subjectively stated needs appear to be a natural starting point for the target values of need-based redistribution, generally acceptable needs, a far more restrictive subset, are more pertinent for real social contexts. Their boundaries are far from easily determined and are very context dependent (see the discussion in Konow and Schwettmann 2016 on dessert). According to Nullmeier (2020,

[6] There are some experimental studies that analyze the incentive effects of unconditional basic income on effort (Haigner et al. 2012) and risk-taking (Füllbrunn et al. 2019). Chapter 8 of this volume offers a discussion on the latter effect and the interplay between need-based justice and risk-taking.

p. 191), recognized "need aims at a necessary and compelling determination of personal demands beyond subjective feelings and desires." Before discussing which incentives of need-based justice prevent their general acceptance, let us assume that we have determined the subset of needs acceptable to all members of society. We can then ask what happens when there is a conflict between different target values and when the shared resources are insufficient for supporting those needs.

That is, what happens when there is a substantial conflict between several fairness motives? Is there a common hierarchy among fairness principles? What happens, for instance, if the resources at i's disposal are less than j's needs?[7] Do we still observe any transfers? And if yes, according to which fairness standards are decision makers making those transfers? Along the same lines, what happens if the minimum income transfer required for j is far less than the resources at i's disposal? Do we observe transfers above j's needs? And if yes, according to which fairness standard are decision makers distributing the surplus? In other words, is there a lexicographical order among the fairness principles?

To answer those questions, we ran a number of experimental studies on redistribution under the condition of minimum income thresholds. In Kienle (2023), the author asks what giving looks like in a context of donations to help others achieve a minimum income requirement. In other words, giving occurs not in a context-free space but serves a specific purpose. Needs are introduced by minimal income requirements such that some transfer recipients require the financial help of others to pass the income threshold that allows recipients to continue on to another stage of the experiment. Kienle approximates the effort exerted to produce the initial endowments by measuring the stress participants experience during the real effort task. For this, she introduces an innovative technique: she computes the change in the heart rates of participants before and during the task. In addition, by altering the distances from the threshold, she tests whether different need gaps trigger different distribution types. She shows that there are predominantly two fairness types, participants who transfer nothing and participants who transfer precisely what is needed for the recipient to pass the threshold. In other words, there is no significant variation in what participants transfer nor any significant heterogeneity in fairness ideals without the income threshold (e.g., Cappelen et al. 2007). Moreover, Kienle (2023) does not observe a combination of fairness considerations such that participants first transfer the amount needed to the recipient and then divide the remaining resources evenly between all. Seemingly, for a majority of participants, there is a strong hierarchical order within the set of target values. When recipients have salient needs, those needs are satisfied, but nothing more.

Kienle (2023) presents two more remarkable results: on the one hand, in line with earlier research (e.g., Kittel et al. 2020), the satisfaction of others' needs appears to be price sensitive. That is, the higher the transfers required to satisfy the needs of the transfer recipient, the lower the likelihood of a transfer. On the other hand,

[7] Notice that Bauer et al. (2022) discuss a similar problem: resources are insufficient to finance the acceptable needs of all potential receivers, while we consider one specific acceptable need.

stress during the production of the initial resources influences the fairness principle underlying participants' transfers. Surprisingly, this influence is not linear in the sense that more stress increases the likelihood of zero transfers, but depends on the gender of the transferring participant: females are less likely than males to give the exact amount needed by the recipient to meet their needs. Overall, women exhibit a less obvious pattern of distribution. While there is a link between the pattern of giving and effort for women, this is not related to their stress levels during rest. In contrast, men exhibit more consistent distribution patterns.

In contrast to price sensitivity, there is little evidence that lowering the economic endowments of those in need lowers their giving: several authors in fact demonstrate that increasing economic pressure on those who are asked to support others in need intensifies their pro-sociality. For instance, Schwirplies (2023) identifies changes in charitable giving in a community in the USA after hurricane Sandy: total donations increase significantly in the immediate aftermath of the hurricane. With respect to the COVID-19 pandemic, an explicit reminder about the crisis makes respondents more willing to prioritize society's problems over their own problems (Cappelen et al. 2021). Even in the immediate aftermath of the lockdown, Shachat et al. (2021) find high rates of altruism (and cooperation and risk aversion). Along the same lines, Ross et al. (2023) demonstrate that self-reported financial affectedness is positively correlated with intensified altruism, while the preference for efficiency deteriorates.

Specifically, Ross et al. (2023) examine inter-temporal distribution decisions on private payments and donations during the coronavirus pandemic. They simultaneously measured individual efficiency concerns, altruism, and time preferences in an online experiment conducted among US residents during different stages of the crisis. Participants are asked to distribute money on different dates and between different recipients—that is, today versus in two weeks and private payouts versus donations—to a charity fighting against the pandemic. To assess participants' affectedness by COVID-19, the authors collected data on participants' employment status and financial situation, as well as their individual vulnerability to COVID-19. They demonstrate that having at least one COVID-19 risk factor and self-reported financial affectedness are negatively correlated with individual preference for efficiency, whereas the same factors have a positive effect on altruism. The results point to an equally important role of personal, financial, and medical insecurity for the willingness to provide support during the crisis.

7.5 Producing the Distribution Mass

A pivotal aspect of any form of redistribution is its potential influence on the production of the redistribution mass. Many economists argue that collecting the resources necessary to finance redistribution leads to inefficiencies: taxation influences labor incentives because labor, unlike leisure, is taxed (e.g., Feldstein 1999; Harberger 1964; Keane and Rogerson 2015; Mirrlees 1971). Thus, redistribution causes implicit costs by potentially decreasing the total labor supply in a society.

Whether redistribution is positive or negative for a society appears unclear a priori. There are confounding negative substitution effects and positive income effects for labor: taxation lowers work incentives in that it makes leisure a more attractive option (the substitution effect); taxation may also increase work effort in that more effort is needed to yield the same net income than without taxation (the income effect).

People reveal considerably lower social preferences when they must earn their endowment for the subsequent interaction (e.g., Oxoby and Spraggon 2008). Chugunova et al. (2022) analyze the potentially negative incentive effect of redistribution with a real effort production of the redistribution mass. There are two types of players, potential senders and potential recipients. Both senders and recipients have to perform a real effort task and receive the same piece rate per solved task. However, the task for potential recipients is considerably more difficult than for potential senders. In some treatment variations, they introduce a subsistence income threshold and a redistribution system that supports disadvantaged members of the society to meet that threshold. In other treatment conditions there is no subsistence income threshold but rather a redistribution system that supports disadvantaged members of the society. Their results show that high-talent taxpayers perform equally well in all conditions. Yet, the less talented ones significantly decrease their performance in response to the introduction of the tax. The negative effect of taxation is mitigated when an income threshold is present, and the tax is spent meaningfully. Thus, there is little evidence of any implicit costs of need-based justice.

An interesting extension is provided by Chugunova et al. (2017). They apply the same experimental setting as in Chugunova et al. (2022) but allow senders to observe the work speed of recipients while performing the real effort task. By introducing transparency of labor, the authors believed that senders' acceptance of transfers would increase. That is, they expected senders to be more accepting of redistribution to help recipients pass the income threshold when they observe that the recipients are working hard to meet that threshold.

Contrary to the authors' expectations, their experimental findings show significantly lower transfers in the transparency treatment. Recall that the task for potential recipients is considerably more difficult than for potential senders, which means that recipients' work is slower (recipients had to add two five-digit numbers per task while senders had to add two three-digit numbers per task; both received the same piece rate per task). Unfortunately, potential senders adapt their own work speed to the observed slow work. As a consequence, there is a significantly lower production of distribution mass and significantly lower transfers by senders. Hence, in this case, transparency does not facilitate, but rather mitigates against, need-based redistribution.

Importantly, Chugunova et al. (2023) demonstrate how fragile the results regarding the distribution mass are. In their study, they analyze how the timing and type of donation decision, relative to the production of disposable income, affect charitable giving. Again, they study the willingness to donate, the amounts donated, and the impact on labor supply in a real-effort online experiment with a subsistence income constraint. The authors find no evidence that the timing of the donation decision affects the propensity to donate or the amounts donated. Along similar lines, Paetzel et al. (2018) find that increasing the transparency of the redistributive consequences diminishes framing effects to a large extent.

However, Chugunova et al. (2023) also observe that committing to donate a fixed absolute amount, as opposed to a share of future earnings, may negatively affect both margins of donation. In turn, they do not find evidence that a commitment in advance has a motivational effect. Rather, their findings suggest that, when soliciting donations before resource production, formulating the donation requests as a share of future earnings rather than fixed absolute amounts may serve as an effective strategy to enhance charitable giving.

7.6 Responsibility for Neediness and the Consequences of Support

Now let us return to the features of need-based income distribution that foster or prevent the general acceptance of need-based justice. Why is the acceptance of a redistribution procedure so crucial for its sustainability? The answer is twofold: on the one hand, redistribution systems supporting needs that are not generally recognized as acceptable lead to all kinds of avoidance actions. These include, for instance, black labor or lower labor effort. Avoidance actions lower the efficiency and the institutional fitness of the redistribution system, thus creating an important disadvantage in the institutional competition between redistribution systems. On the other hand, illegitimate redistribution or even the complete absence of redistribution can cause direct migration between redistribution systems, which may even cause some systems to disappear altogether (see, e.g., Chugunova et al. 2020). Therefore, misleading recognition of needs threatens the sustainability of redistribution systems, while general acceptance by members of the society secures its success and growth in the context of institutional competition.

Kienle and Nicklisch (2023) experimentally test two important aspects of the acceptance of redistribution: the responsibility of the recipient for her neediness and the effects of sufficient support for the recipient. The study extends Kienle's analysis (2023) to the pre-play stage and the aftermath of the transfer decision. That is, the study analyzes a potential moral conflict for those who are asked to support the needy. On the one hand, they may want to help needy people. On the other hand, they may not want to reward low levels of effort or the careless behavior of those who are responsible for their need. In other words, the (strict) egalitarian motive for giving clashes with the libertarian motive.

The study adjusts the design of Kienle (2023) by allowing the recipient to earn an income that is partly or fully under their direct control. As a result, the recipient is partly or fully responsible for their degree of neediness. Experimental results show a significantly higher acceptance rate for income redistribution in favor of recipients who are not responsible for their neediness than for recipients who are responsible (e.g., Cappelen et al. 2010).

In addition, Kienle and Nicklisch (2023) systematically vary the consequences of supporting the needy. Recipients either participate in an additional sequence of the real effort task or participate in a lottery with the same expected payoff. The latter treatment variation is introduced because the equity motive also involves an educational element: when senders consistently finance the laziness of others, their current support may lead to additional future neediness. Senders, in line with other studies, should not want to reward people who are responsible for their need. Nor do we want to corrupt the system of need-based redistribution by creating dependencies on the part of recipients. Recipients may "unlearn" taking responsibility for earning their required income. That is to say, the equity perspective to compensate inequalities in the initial chances, but not those inequalities which arise from personal responsibilities, is of particular importance if the consequences of support "allow" for another misconduct of little effort provision, that is, in the treatment variation with repeated real effort task.

Kienle and Nicklisch (2023) demonstrate two important results: firstly, small reductions in the recipients' effort lead to the same decrease in the likelihood of a transfer as large reductions in effort. In other words, keeping the gap of the neediness constant, both small and large levels of responsibility mitigate against redistribution. Secondly, there is little evidence for the proposition that the educational element matters for the transfers. Neither the likelihood nor the size of the transfers differ significantly between the repeated effort and the lottery treatments. Overall, need-based justice appears to be sensitive to abuse by the recipient, while the consequences of redistribution seem to have little influence.

7.7 On the Superiority of Need-Based Justice

The work of our group could pioneer the systematic analysis of need-based fairness preferences by providing several stylized facts. Overall, it seems that need-based fairness is a crucial fairness motive. When needs are salient, a substantial group of participants decide to give in accordance with this motive (Kienle 2023). Importantly, we do not observe a combination of several fairness motives. Thus, giving does not combine an amount satisfying the needs of the recipient with an amount that shares the remaining resources evenly, for instance. Rather, participants give what is needed to satisfy the needs of the other, or nothing is given. In turn, need-based giving is price-sensitive (Kienle 2023). That is, if the need of the potential recipient increases, giving becomes less likely. Furthermore, the likelihood of support for needy persons is influenced by the responsibility of the recipient for her neediness, but not by the consequences of the support (Kienle and Nicklisch 2023). Finally, the distribution does not incur implicit costs, that is, the production of the distribution mass is not negatively influenced by the subsequent distribution (Chugunova et al. 2022).

Summarizing those stylized facts, a fair division of income involves a trade-off between the utility of own money and the benefits of social utility. If the latter aspect contains potentially several motives, there seems to be a hierarchical order among them. That is, the decision maker targets one specific fairness norm and does not mix several motives. Some norms may be beneficial from a selfish point of view as they require little transfers. Some other norms cause large benefits from creating a lot of social utility but demand large transfers. In the end, i does not choose the most appropriate fairness norm, but the one that maximizes the difference between the "appropriateness" of a norm and the necessary transfers to implement such norm. Need-based fairness seems to be one candidate among many alternative fairness motives. However, our results suggest that it is a very important candidate for many decision makers.

7.8 An Economic Theory of Need-Based Justice?

From an interdisciplinary point of view, economic preferences may appear rather arbitrary as they allow any subjective focal point to be considered as a fairness motive. Crucial milestones like the social deliberation that lead to a common agreement upon fairness candidates are beyond the scope of an economic formalization.[8] Likewise, provided we agreed upon need-based justice being such a candidate, the process of social and political recognition of needs is again not discussed in this type of economic literature.

Nonetheless, it appears crucial for us to integrate also the economic view into a behaviorally informed concept of need-based justice. The reason for this is that economics can inform us substantially about the limits of this concept. Referring to Nullmeier's (2020) ten requirements for the further development of a theory of need-based justice, the earlier summarized evidence shows that needs are limited by the size of the transfer. That is, the acceptance of needs as personal demands beyond subjective feelings and desires deteriorates with the price enclosed to its satisfaction. On the other hand, oversupply and undersupply of resources to satisfy the recognized needs do not lead to transfers beyond or short off the needs. In other words, either decision makers send the required amount to satisfy the need or they send nothing (as this probably equalizes the initial chances at the beginning of the interaction). Importantly, this type of flexibility regarding the applied fairness norm determines another crucial limitation resulting from the price sensitivity for redistribution based on need-based justice within a society. If the burden is too high for a society to satisfy all needs, it may follow the reevaluation of needs, or a systematic shift to another, cheaper fairness concept. The former point may also indicate a flexibility regarding what the decision maker considers as necessary for the participation and inclusion in social life, being able to lead a worthy, valuable,

[8] There are studies that analyze how the social environment shapes the structure of pro-sociality (e.g., Fischbacher and Gächter 2010; Thöni and Gächter 2015). However, this literature explores the importance of pro-sociality, not the acceptance of specific justice principles.

and decent life for the transfer recipient. However, there is no empirical evidence for this claim yet.

The results of the economic experiments demonstrate the importance of procedural justice for the application of need-based justice. Even a slight misconduct that the transfer recipient is responsible for (in the terms measured in reduced effort provision) leads to a similar reduction in the likelihood of receiving a transfer than large misconducts. Small and large degrees of responsibility for neediness mitigates the support: that is to say, equalizing unequal chances of transfer recipients is acceptable, and rewarding the misconduct of recipients is not acceptable. Surprisingly, with regards to this point, transfer senders are focused on the history of the recipient's behavior. The consequences of the support seem to have little influence on the sender's decision making.

At the same time, the flexibility of need-based justice and the social recognition of needs due to its price sensitivity may create a crucial problem for redistribution mechanisms such as unconditional basic income, which are being discussed in several European countries. Despite the lack of acceptance of transfers to recipients who have even a small degree of responsibility for their neediness, the excessive costs of redistribution will lead to a downward adjustment of needs that were once socially recognized and considered acceptable.

Overall, need-based justice is a powerful concept to explain human behavior and a widely accepted normative structure of social interactions and institutions. Its character seems to be monistic. We find little evidence for a pluralistic application of fairness concepts by the decision makers. At the same time, the experimental evidence suggests low implicit costs for redistribution systems based on needs. Most importantly, need-based justice appears to be one of the most accepted systems among citizens. As mentioned at the beginning, only legitimate forms of redistribution survive. The broad acceptance of need-based justice suggests it has the "fitness" needed for the long run. Thus, need-based justice offers an avenue for increasing the sustainability of social order.

Acknowledgments In this chapter, we present results from the project "Justice, Incentives, and (Heterogeneous) Needs in Distribution Processes," which formed a part of the research group FOR 2104 "Need-Based Justice and Distribution Procedures." In this project, Marina Chugunova, Ann-Katrin Kienle, Kai-Uwe Schnapp, and Andreas Nicklisch used laboratory group experiments to study the incentives of redistribution based on individual needs for the production of income. The research was financed by the German Research Foundation (DFG Grants Ni 1610/1–1) and the Swiss National Science Foundation (SNF Grants 100019E_178317/1).

References

Alcantud, J. C. R., M. Mariotti, and R. Veneziani (2022): "Sufficientarianism", *Theoretical Economics* 17 (4), 1529–1557.

Andreoni, J. (1989): "Giving with Impure Altruism: Applications to Charity and Ricardian Equivalence", *Journal of Political Economy* 97 (6), 1447–1458.

Andreoni, J. (1990): "Impure Altruism and Donations to Public Goods: A Theory of Warm-Glow Giving", *Economic Journal* 100 (401), 464–477.

Andreoni, J. (1995): "Warm-Glow versus Cold-Prickle: The Effects of Positive and Negative Framing on Cooperation in Experiments", *The Quarterly Journal of Economics* 110 (1), 1–21.

Bauer, A. M., F. Meyer, J. Romann, M. Siebel, and S. Traub (2022): "Need, Equity, and Accountability: Evidence on Third-Party Distribution Decisions from a Vignette Study", *Social Choice and Welfare* 59 (4), 769–814.

Bolton, G. E., and A. Ockenfels (2000): "ERC: A Theory of Equity, Reciprocity, and Competition", *American Economic Review* 91 (1), 166–193.

Camerer, C. (1999): "Behavioral Economics: Reunifying Psychology and Economics", *Proceedings of the National Academy of Sciences* 96 (19), 10575–10577.

Cappelen, A. W., A. D. Hole, E. Ø. Sørensen, and B. Tungodden (2007): "The Pluralism of Fairness Ideals: An Experimental Approach", *American Economic Review* 97 (3), 818–827.

Cappelen, A. W., E. Ø. Sørensen, and B. Tungodden (2010): "Responsibility for What? Fairness and Individual Responsibility", *European Economic Review* 54 (3), 429–441.

Cappelen, A. W., J. Konow, E. Ø. Sørensen, and B. Tungodden (2013): "Just Luck: An Experimental Study of Risk-Taking and Fairness", *American Economic Review* 103 (4), 1398–1413.

Cappelen, A. W., R. Falch, E. Ø. Sørensen, and B. Tungodden (2021): "Solidarity and Fairness in Times of Crisis", *Journal of Economic Behavior & Organization* 186, 1–11.

Chugunova, M., W. J. Luhan, and A. Nicklisch (2020): "When to Leave Carrots for Sticks: On the Evolution of Sanctioning Institutions in Open Communities", *Economics Letters* 191, 109155.

Chugunova, M., A. Nicklisch, and K. U. Schnapp (2017): "On the Effects of Transparency and Reciprocity on Labor Supply in the Redistribution Systems", *FOR Working Paper* 2017–19.

Chugunova, M., A. Nicklisch, and K. U. Schnapp (2022): "Redistribution and Production with a Subsistence Income Constraint: A Real-Effort Experiment", *FinanzArchiv: Public Finance Analysis*, 78 (1–2), 208–238.

Chugunova, M., A. Nicklisch, and K. U. Schnapp (2023): *The Impact of Timing and Type of Donation Decision on Charitable Giving*, unpublished working paper.

Cox, J. C., D. Friedman, and S. Gjerstad (2007): "A Tractable Model of Reciprocity and Fairness", *Games and Economic Behavior* 59 (1), 17–45.

Crumpler, H., and P. J. Grossman (2008): "An Experimental Test of Warm Glow Giving", *Journal of Public Economics* 92 (5–6), 1011–1021.

Delsen, L., and R. Schilpzand (2019): "Individual Preferences for the Unconditional Basic Income in the European Union", in L. Delsen (ed.): *Empirical Research on an Unconditional Basic Income in Europe*, 29–60. Cham: Springer Nature.

Engelmann, D., and M. Strobel (2004): "Inequality Aversion, Efficiency, and Maximin Preferences in Simple Distribution Experiments", *American Economic Review* 94 (4), 857–869.

Falk, A., E. Fehr, and U. Fischbacher (2003): "On the Nature of Fair Behavior", *Economic Inquiry* 41 (1), 20–26.

Fehr, E., and K. M. Schmidt (1999): "A Theory of Fairness, Competition, and Cooperation", *Quarterly Journal of Economics* 114 (3), 817–868.

Feldstein, M. (1999): "Tax Avoidance and the Deadweight Loss of the Income Tax", *Review of Economics and Statistics* 81 (4), 674–680.

Fischbacher, U., and S. Gächter (2010): "Social Preferences, Beliefs, and the Dynamics of Free Riding in Public Goods Experiments", *American Economic Review* 100 (1), 541–556.

Fleurbaey, M. (2010): "Assessing Risky Social Situations", *Journal of Political Economy* 118 (4), 649–680.

Fong, C. (2001): "Social Preferences, Self-Interest, and the Demand for Redistribution", *Journal of Public Economics* 82 (2), 225–246.

Frohlich, N., J. A. Oppenheimer, and C. L. Eavey (1987): "Choices of Principles of Distributive Justice in Experimental Groups, *American Journal of Political Science* 31 (3), 606–636.

Frohlich, N., and J. A. Oppenheimer (1990): "Choosing Justice in Experimental Democracies with Production. *American Political Science Review* 84 (2), 461–477.

Füllbrunn, S., L. Delsen, and J. Vyrastekova (2019): "Experimental Economics: A Test-Bed for the Unconditional Basic Income?" in L. Delsen (ed.): *Empirical Research on an Unconditional Basic Income in Europe*, 171–199. Cham: Springer Nature.

Gerber, A., A. Nicklisch, and S. Voigt (2019): "The Role of Ignorance in the Emergence of Redistribution", *Journal of Economic Behavior & Organization* 163, 239–261.

Gill, D., and R. Stone (2010): "Fairness and Desert in Tournaments", *Games and Economic Behavior* 69 (2), 346–364.

Haigner, S., W. Höchtl, F. G. Schneider, F. Wakolbinger, and S. Jenewein (2012): "Keep on Working: Unconditional Basic Income in the Lab", *Basic Income Studies* 7 (1), 1–14.

Harberger, A. (1964): "Taxation, Resource Allocation, and Welfare", in NBER and The Brookings Institution (eds.): *The Role of Direct and Indirect Taxes in the Federal Reserve System*, 25–80. Princeton: Princeton University Press.

Kangas, O., S. Jauhiainen, M. Simanainen, and M. Ylikanno (eds.) (2021): *Experimenting with Unconditional Basic Income: Lessons from the Finnish BI Experiment 2017–2018*. Cheltenham: Edward Elgar Publishing.

Keane, M., and R. Rogerson (2015): "Reconciling Micro and Macro Labor Supply Elasticities: A Structural Perspective", *Annual Review of Economics* 7, 89–117.

Kienle, A.-K. (2023): *Dictators Under Pressure: Fairness Norms and Monetary Support to Those in Need*, unpublished working paper.

Kienle, A.-K., and A. Nicklisch (2023): *Responsibility for Needs, Consequences of Support, and the Acceptance to Give*, unpublished working paper.

Kittel, B., S. Neuhofer, and M. Schwaninger (2020): "The Impact of Need on Distributive Decisions: Experimental Evidence on Anchor Effects of Exogenous Thresholds in the Laboratory", *PloS one* 15 (4), e0228753.

Knowles, D. (2003): *Routledge Philosophy Guidebook to Hegel and the Philosophy of Right*. London: Routledge.

Konow, J. (2000): "Fair Shares: Accountability and Cognitive Dissonance in Allocation Decisions", *American Economic Review* 90 (4), 1072–1092.

Konow, J. (2001): "Fair and Square: The Four Sides of Distributive Justice", *Journal of Economic Behavior & Organization* 46 (2), 137–164.

Konow, J. (2003): "Which is the Fairest One of All? A Positive Analysis of Justice Theories", *Journal of Economic Literature* 41 (4), 1188–1239.

Konow, J., and L. Schwettmann (2016): "The Economics of Justice", in C. Sabbagh, and M. Schmitt (eds): *Handbook of Social Justice Theory and Research*, 83–106. New York: Springer.

Luccasen, A., and P. J. Grossman (2017): "Warm-Glow Giving: Earned Money and the Option to Take", *Economic Inquiry* 55 (2), 996–1006.

Mirrlees, J. A. (1971): "An Exploration in the Theory of Optimum Income Taxation", *Review of Economic Studies* 38, 175–208.

Nicklisch, A., and I. Wolff (2012): "On the Nature of Reciprocity: Evidence from the Ultimatum Reciprocity Measure", *Journal of Economic Behavior & Organization* 84 (3), 892–905.

Nullmeier, F. (2020): "Towards a Theory of Need-Based Justice", in S. Traub, and B. Kittel (eds): *Need-Based Distributive Justice: An Interdisciplinary Perspective*, 191–208. Cham: Sringer Nature.

Oxoby, R. J., and J. Spraggon (2008): "Mine and Yours: Property Rights in Dictator Games", *Journal of Economic Behavior & Organization* 65 (3–4), 703–713.

Paetzel, F., J. Lorenz, and M. Tepe (2018): "Transparency Diminishes Framing-Effects in Voting on Redistribution: Some Experimental Evidence", *European Journal of Political Economy* 55, 169–184.

Popper, K. R. (2003): *Die offene Gesellschaft und ihre Feinde II: Falsche Propheten. Hegel, Marx und die Folgen*, 8th. ed. Tübingen: Mohr Siebeck.

Rabin, M. (1993): "Incorporating Fairness into Game Theory and Economics", *American Economic Review* 83 (5), 1281–1302
Ross, J., A.-K. Kienle, and A. Nicklisch (2023): *Sharing the Cake during a Crisis: The Impact of the COVID-19 Pandemic on Intertemporal Altruism and Efficiency Concerns*, unpublished working paper.
Schumacher, H., I. Kesternich, M. Kosfeld, and J. Winter (2017): "One, Two, Many–Insensitivity to Group Size in Games with Concentrated Benefits and Dispersed Costs", *Review of Economic Studies* 84 (3), 1346–1377.
Schwirplies, C. (2023): "Does Additional Demand for Charitable Aid Increase Giving? Evidence from Hurricane Sandy", *Journal of Economic Behavior & Organization* 209, 53–73.
Shachat, J., M. J. Walker, and L. Wei (2021): "How the Onset of the Covid-19 Pandemic Impacted Pro-Social Behaviour and Individual Preferences: Experimental Evidence from China", *Journal of Economic Behavior & Organization* 190, 480–494.
Thöni, C., and S. Gächter (2015): "Peer Effects and Social Preferences in Voluntary Cooperation: A Theoretical and Experimental Analysis", *Journal of Economic Psychology* 48, 72–88.
Traub, S., C. Seidl, and U. Schmidt (2009): "An Experimental Study on Individual Choice, Social Welfare, and Social Preferences", *European Economic Review* 53 (4), 385–400.

Chapter 8
How Sustainable is Need-Based Redistribution?

Stefan Traub, Jan Philipp Krügel, and Meike Benker

Abstract This chapter examines the economic sustainability of need-based income redistribution via the welfare state. We model the welfare state as an insurance device to reduce the variance of lifetime incomes when social inequality results from individual risk-taking, specifically educational investment. Our contract-theoretic model analysis shows that income redistribution can lead to higher efficiency and overall welfare under certain conditions. In this context, need-based redistribution, which includes an explicit means test, is clearly superior to an unconditional basic income. Experimental tests of the model confirm the hypothesis that need-based redistribution is sustainable. From our theoretical and experimental results, we conclude that a lexicographic combination of need-based justice and equity—the Boulding principle—not only reflects the redistribution preferences of the population well, but is also convincing from an ethical perspective.

8.1 Introduction

In the introduction to this edited volume, Kittel and Traub (Chap. 1) outline the premises and implications of a theory of distributive justice based on the *need principle*. The need principle states that the distribution of scarce resources should be governed by the criterion of satisfying socially and politically acknowledged needs. In this respect, distributive justice prevails when all members of society have sufficient means at their disposal to cover their needs. The *need hypothesis* assumes that the more distributional decisions follow the need principle, the more coherent, legitimate, stable, and sustainable the distributional outcomes will be (Traub 2020). In contrast to monistic theories like Rawls' egalitarian theory of justice (Rawls 1971, 1974), need can be combined with other distribution criteria such as equality, equity, and efficiency to form a pluralistic theory of distributive justice (cf. Nullmeier

S. Traub (✉) · J. P. Krügel · M. Benker
Department of Economics, Helmut-Schmidt University Hamburg, Hamburg, Germany
e-mail: traubs@hsu-hh.de; kruegel@hsu-hh.de; benkerm@hsu-hh.de

B. Kittel, S. Traub (eds.), *Priority of Needs?*,
https://doi.org/10.1007/978-3-031-53051-7_8

2020). The purpose of this chapter is to show that the need hypothesis—as part of a pluralistic theory of distributive justice—holds with respect to the sustainability of the distributional outcome when the redistributive welfare state is modeled as an insurance against too much variance in lifetime incomes. This chapter thus also contributes to the "classical" debate on the trade-off between equality and efficiency (cf. Okun 1975).

The research group "Need-based Justice and Distribution Procedures" (2015–2022), of which the authors in this edited volume were members, has predominantly used (laboratory) experimental methods to generate empirical evidence about the need hypothesis. Thus, the project has contributed to a growing literature since the 1970s that empirically addresses questions of distributive justice from different angles (for overviews, see, e.g., Gaertner and Schokkaert 2012; Konow 2001, 2003; Konow and Schwettmann 2016; Traub and Kittel 2020). The first authors to experimentally investigate need as a principle of justice were psychologists Lamm and Schwinger (1980, 1983). Yaari and Bar-Hillel (1984) asked subjects, among other things, to divide fruit as equitably as possible between two individuals who differed in their need for vitamin F. Eighty-two percent of all subjects chose to divide exactly according to need.

The accumulated experimental evidence suggests that normative theories of distributive justice informed by data should be pluralistic and context-dependent (Konow and Schwettmann 2016). This means that a theory of justice should consist of multiple justice criteria whose weights are determined by context in terms of institutional factors and personal characteristics. In this respect, experimental studies tend to support the philosophical concepts of "spheres of justice" (Walzer 1983), "local justice" (Elster 1992), or Miller's (1999) "pluralistic" approach. Along with equality and equity, need emerged here as an essential component of pluralist theories of justice (Konow 2001, 2003). Another regularity is that subjects choose a distributional principle that maximizes average income subject to a minimum income (Frohlich and Oppenheimer 1992). As pointed out by Konow (2003), this corresponds to a combination of different distributional principles, namely Harsanyi's (1955) utilitarianism in the sense of expected utility maximization and Rawls' difference principle. This conception of justice was described by Boulding (1962) years before the experimental studies: "Society lays a modest table at which all can sup and a high table at which the deserving can feast" (p. 83). We call this the *Boulding Principle*.

In the Introduction to this volume, Kittel and Traub also point out that the satisfaction of acknowledged needs "must be economically affordable for the society, both for the preservation of resources and for maintaining incentives to invest and work such that the economy produces a sufficient amount of the necessary resources" (p. 15). We argue both theoretically and based on the results of several experimental studies that need-based redistribution sets positive investment incentives that lead to efficiency gains. We therefore think that need-based redistribution is a (relatively) *sustainable* redistribution policy.

In this chapter, we present from a contract-theoretic perspective the rationale for giving priority to needs based on the sustainability of need-based redistribution.

The starting point of our theoretical analysis is that income inequality—the typical right-skewed income distribution in OECD countries—can partly be explained by individual risk taking. Inequality and risk are thus closely intertwined. In particular, Sinn (1995, 1996) pointed out in his Theory of the Welfare State (TWS) that income redistribution paradoxically can lead to more risk-taking in terms of educational investments and thus greater economic efficiency due to the Domar–Musgrave effect (Domar and Musgrave 1944), which is explained in detail below. We convert Sinn's (more complex) original theoretical considerations into a simple experimentally testable model. In the model, a social planner determines how much of their expected lifetime incomes members of a hypothetical society should invest in education when the outcome is determined by a stochastic process. Three key results derived from the model show how social inequality and efficiency change when a redistributive welfare state is introduced. We then show that the central parameter of Sinn's welfare state corresponds with an unconditional basic income (UBI) and compare this with need-based redistribution in the form of a means-tested benefit. Our theoretical main finding is that need-based redistribution allows for higher efficiency, albeit coupled with greater inequality, and leads to an overall increase in social welfare.

The model has been tested empirically using data from three laboratory-experimental studies. We present the experimental designs and results in detail in this chapter. A distinctive feature is that we adopted a contract-theoretic decision scenario developed by Harsanyi (1953) and Friedman (1953). In this scenario, an involved social planner makes his (educational) investment decisions behind the veil of ignorance (VOI), where the veil guarantees the social planner's impartiality. Our first study (Traub and Krügel 2017) clearly supports Sinn's conjecture that redistribution via the welfare state can lead to an increase in efficiency. Surprisingly, a paradoxical equality-efficiency trade-off can occur in which no redistribution would mean more equality and less efficiency. When needs are taken into account, as in our second study (Benker et al. 2017), traditional measures of risk or inequality do not correctly capture subjects' distributional preferences. It turns out that subjects tolerate a relatively high degree of inequality in the context of need-based redistribution as long as the acknowledged need is covered.[1] We argue that this distributional preference is compatible with the Boulding principle (Boulding 1962; Raphael 1980). Finally, Krügel and Traub (2023) find that there is less discrimination in connection with the solidarity-based satisfaction of needs than is usual in the social-identity literature (cf. Paetzel and Sausgruber 2018).

The rest of the chapter is structured as follows. In Sect. 8.2, we review the relevant literature on redistribution via the welfare state. In the first subsection (Sect. 8.2.1), we briefly address how the stochasticity of personal income gives rise to inequality. Section 8.2.2 then deals with the taxation of risky educational investments. In Sect. 8.2.3, we consider the distribution of lifetime income as a

[1] Traub et al. (2023) study the acknowledgment of needs in a laboratory experiment. They find that the majority of dictators in a dictator game are sensitive to information about the recipients' needs.

social contract. Section 8.2.4 addresses ex-ante heterogeneity and the scope of need-based redistribution. In the last subsection (Sect. 8.2.5) of Sect. 8.2, we derive several research questions. We then outline our theoretical model framework in Sect. 8.3. To test the model and help us answer the research questions, we present three experimental studies in Sect. 8.4. The last section (Sect. 8.5) of this chapter summarizes the results and relates them to the overarching research question of this edited volume, that is, whether and how need should be prioritized as a principle of distributive justice.

8.2 Risk, Redistribution, and the Welfare State

A common definition of the welfare state asserts that it has two main purposes (Barr 2020, p. 8–9). Firstly, the welfare state acts as *social insurance*, which is financed by contributions and insures against income and cost risks such as unemployment, sickness, accident, long-term care, and longevity without prior means testing. Secondly, it acts as *pure (income) redistribution*, which is usually tax-financed and means-tested: "It is generally a benefit of last resort, designed to help individuals and families who are in poverty," whether as social assistance in emergencies or as a substitute for or supplement to social insurance benefits. The latter function is often justified with the normative argument that a more equal society is fairer.

In this section, we deal with the contract-theoretic view of pure income redistribution. This particular perspective assumes that inequality in the personal distribution of income results from individual risk taking, for example, in the course of educational investments. Pure income redistribution reduces the risk of default and may therefore even increase economic efficiency. This stands in contrast to the commonly assumed trade-off between equality and efficiency.

8.2.1 Inequality and the Stochasticity of Personal Income

Studies show that income inequality measured by the Gini coefficient in developed industrialized countries has increased only moderately in the early 2000s (OECD 2011). Atkinson et al. (2009) used tax statistics to show that there has been a significant increase in the share of top earners over the past 30 years. This trend is observable for the English-speaking countries, India and China, but not for continental Europe and Japan. In addition to the Gini coefficient and other measures of dispersion, the skewness of income distribution in particular has increased (Krieger and Traub 2011, 2013). A number of reasons have been given for these developments, from the increasing spread of wages due to technical progress to international financial market developments and a lower effectiveness of tax systems.

A detail related to this development is that the personal income distribution shows a considerable degree of stochasticity. Older studies, e.g., by Jencks (1972) and Lillard and Willis (1978) were only able to explain a fraction of the measured income inequality—Jencks (1972) could explain 12–15%—through individual-specific factors such as family background and education (for an overview see Quadrini and Ríos-Rull 1997). Therefore, the development of personal income distribution is usually modeled by a stochastic process in empirical studies as well as in macro models:[2] "Earnings are best described as being driven by a permanent income shock and a serially correlated transitory shock." (Meghir and Pistaferri 2004, p. 25).

Note that Gibrat (1931) already assumed that inequalities in personal income are created by a multiplicative stochastic process in which the relative change in income is a random variable independent of the past ("law of proportionate effect"). If the central limit theorem applies, then the sum of this effect is asymptotically normally distributed and the income itself is a lognormally distributed random variable, i.e., right-skewed.[3] Modern endogenous growth theory considers human capital or stochastic human capital accumulation instead of income (Romer 1994; Lucas 1988) and thus emphasizes the uncertainty inherent in educational investments (for a literature review see Grochulski and Piskorski 2010).[4]

8.2.2 Educational Investment, Taxation, and the Welfare State

From a microeconomic point of view, uncertain educational investments are made by actors who follow a certain decision calculus, for example, the maximization of expected utility. Numerous authors have examined the effect of proportional and progressive taxes on investment decisions at risk in partial analytic model frameworks and in general equilibrium (Ahsan 1974, 1976; Allingham 1972; Atkinson and Stiglitz 1980; Bamberg and Richter 1984; Domar and Musgrave 1944; Kanbur 1979; Konrad 1991; Sandmo 1977). Diamond et al. (1980), Eaton and Rosen (1980), Varian (1980), and Rochet (1991) developed a theory of optimal income taxation under risk.

---

[2] Cagetti (2003) and Carroll (1997) studied the life-cycle saving behavior of households, modeling the growth rate of income by a stochastic process. Castañeda et al. (2003) showed that US income and wealth inequality can be replicated almost exactly using a model in which the initial endowment of households with effective labor is generated by a Markov process. Huggett and Ventura (1999) examined the growth and welfare effects of various social reforms, e.g., the introduction of a minimum income, whereby labor productivity was exposed to individual stochastic shocks.

[3] For more details and a critique of the stochastic theory, see Mincer (1970), Atkinson (1976), and Sahota (1978).

[4] We use the terms education and human capital as synonyms.

A central result of this literature is the (partial analytical) *Domar–Musgrave effect*: If the state participates equally in the profits and losses of a risky investment through a proportional tax ("full loss compensation"), then the individually optimal investment amount *increases*. This incentive effect means that the tax is avoided by taking higher risks. In an international panel study, Bird (2001) actually found empirical evidence for a positive correlation between redistribution activities and willingness to take risks.

The model-theoretic analysis of the welfare state by Sinn (1995, 1996) is based on the uncertainty of economic decisions and the Domar–Musgrave effect: "While the production of safety is an important function of the welfare state, the Domar-Musgrave effect of increased risk taking may be even more important. Protected by the welfare state, people engage in risky and profitable activities which they otherwise would not have dared to undertake" (p. 496). Sinn further argues as follows: If the individual risks are stochastically independent of each other (iid) and have a positive return on average, then there will be a secure budget surplus for the state. If the tax revenue is distributed to the investors in advance, for example, in the form of a lump-sum transfer, then the optimal investment amount additionally increases due to an income effect (when the investors' preferences exhibit decreasing absolute risk aversion). Furthermore, when individual willingness to take risks increases disproportionally (decreasing relative risk aversion), then redistribution may even increase inequality ("redistribution paradox"). On the other hand, this type of insurance also has a negative incentive effect in the form of moral hazard: "Protected by the welfare state, people may neglect to take necessary care, may take too much risk, and end up in a worse situation than without such protection." (Sinn 1995, p. 497).

8.2.3 The Welfare State as a Social Contract

In his theory, Sinn characterized the welfare state as an insurance device that enables society to decrease the variance in lifetime incomes by means of redistributive taxation. In the words of Sinn, "redistributive taxation and insurance are two sides of the same coin" (Sinn 1995, p. 496). The idea that the distribution of lifetime incomes is generated by individual choices under risk can be traced back to Friedman, who held that it follows from expected utility maximization that "[...] the inequality of income in a society may be regarded [...] as [...] a reflection of deliberate choice in accordance with the tastes and preferences of the members of society rather than simply an 'act of God'" (Friedman 1953, p. 278). Although Kanbur (1979) later showed in a general equilibrium framework that the relationship between risk taking and inequality is not monotonic and that greater diversity in risk preferences does not necessarily contribute to more social inequality, the individualistic approach to social welfare proposed by Friedman has become very influential.

Harsanyi (1953, 1955, 1978) made an important contribution to this literature by demonstrating the equivalence between expected utility maximization and welfare maximization with interpersonally comparable cardinal utility. Harsanyi's utilitarianism postulates that people maximize their utility from behind a veil of ignorance under the assumption that all future income positions are equally likely ("equiprobability model"). Hence, though they are personally involved in shaping the society, people act *ethically* as though they were impartial welfare maximizers.[5] Consequently, the concepts of individual risk aversion and social inequality aversion collapse into each other in the Friedman–Harsanyi framework.

8.2.4 Heterogeneity and the Scope of Need-Based Justice

An open flank of the Harsanyi–Friedman scenario is the assumed representativeness of the impartial observer. There may be no reason to question the result from an ex-post perspective as long as the group members are ex-ante homogeneous in terms of their risk/inequality preference. However, Alesina et al. (2001) and Alesina and Glaeser (2004) argued that greater social fragmentation in a country (e.g., based on ethnic origin, skin color, or religion) correlates with less redistribution. They showed that the United States exhibits both greater fragmentation and less redistribution than Western European countries.

Several studies have shown a negative association between social diversity and the provision of public goods (James 1993; Kuijs 2000; Soroka et al. 2006). Luttmer (2001) showed for the USA that people living in areas with many welfare recipients agree to more redistribution if the welfare recipients have the same skin color or origin as themselves, i.e., the group is more homogeneous overall ("racial group effect"). In an experimental study, Klor and Shayo (2010) found that subjects vote for a redistributive regime that benefits members of their own group, even if it reduces their own payoff (cf. Bernard et al. 2016, Goette et al. 2006, Chen and Li 2009).

Social identity theory explains this behavior. The theory postulates that a person's social identity is determined by membership in a social group. When a person feels she belongs to a group, she benefits from the positive comparison of her own group with a relevant other group (Tajfel and Turner 1979; Akerlof and Kranton 2000). The term *ingroup bias* means that people tend to treat others who belong to their own social group better than those who belong to another group (Tajfel et al. 1971; Brewer 1979; Bourhis and Gagnon 2001). Paetzel and Sausgruber (2018) showed that ingroup bias is more pronounced within the high-performing group when group membership is determined by performance. According to Tajfel and Turner (1979), a person identifies with a group when she feels that she belongs to several characteristics of the group. Guiso et al. (2006) argue that groups develop values and social norms (cultures) that are path-dependent. A number of

[5] The model has provoked a lot of criticism. See, for example, Diamond (1967), Rawls (1971, 1974) and Harsanyi's reply (Harsanyi 1975a,b).

authors identified ingroup social status and outgroup social distance as two variables positively influencing utility (Turner et al. 1987; Shayo 2009; Bernard et al. 2016). According to Lane's (2016) meta-study, discriminatory behavior occurs in about one-third of all laboratory experiments and is more pronounced when group identity is artificially generated and when distributional decisions between ingroup and outgroup are taken into account.

Scholars have also examined heterogeneity in public good experiments. Fisher et al. (1995) formed groups of subjects who benefited differently from the public good. They showed that individuals with high (low) marginal per capita return (MPCR) contributed a lot (little). Ostrom et al. (1994), van Dijk et al. (2002), and Cherry et al. (2005) varied the participants' initial endowments and showed that inequality leads to lower contributions. In contrast, Chan et al. (1996) and Buckley and Croson (2006) found positive effects, and Chan et al. (1999) and Sadrieh and Verbon (2006) found no significant effects of heterogeneous initial endowments. Other studies influenced the composition of the group. Gunnthorsdottir et al. (2007) and Gächter and Thöni (2005) used subjects' ranking according to their contributions in the first round to assemble the groups in the following periods. Burlando and Guala (2005) categorized the participants and then grouped them as homogeneously as possible. De Oliveira et al. (2015) explicitly examined the difference between homogeneous and heterogeneous groups: One free rider in a heterogeneous group was sufficient to significantly reduce contributions and efficiency compared to homogeneous groups consisting of cooperators.

The question remaining is whether a social contract such as the Harsanyi–Friedman framework is sustainable, i.e., may enduringly increase overall economic efficiency, even when there is ex-ante heterogeneity in the form of social identities. The literature shows quite clearly that social identities lead to discrimination against the outgroup. With regard to (need-based) redistribution, scholarship still has to clarify whether the existence of social identities restricts the scope of the welfare state and reduces the potential for efficiency gains.

8.2.5 Summary

The previous discussion has shown that a significant part of lifetime income inequality can be explained by chance, resulting, for example, from risky educational investment choices. As the inequality caused by different investment outcomes accumulates over time, the typical right-skewed income distribution in industrialized countries develops. Following TWS, we interpret the redistributive welfare state as an insurance against failure in educational investments, i.e., to mitigate the effects of being at the bottom of the income distribution. In Friedman and Harsanyi's theoretical framework, every investor is also a social planner because together with her investment she determines the levels of efficiency and inequality in society and, thus, total welfare. Ex-ante heterogeneity may lead to discriminatory behavior toward other social groups and thus limit the scope and efficiency of income redistribution.

Based on the above, we have formulated a set of research questions that we will address in the following sections, first using a theoretical and then an experimental approach:

1. How can the optimal educational investment choice of the social planner be characterized?
2. What is the effect of the welfare state (in terms of Sinn's uniform tax and lump-sum transfer) on the optimal educational investment? Do efficiency, inequality, and welfare change?
3. How can need be incorporated into the model?
4. Does need-based redistribution perform better than the uniform tax plus lump-sum transfer (which later on will be reinterpreted as an UBI that is funded by a flat tax)?
5. How do UBI and need-based redistribution fare when social planners' redistribution preferences are influenced by social identities?

8.3 The Theoretical Argument Illustrated

In this section, we want to address the question of the sustainability of need-based redistribution from a theoretical point of view. Using Sinn's (1995, 1996) TWS, we outline a simple model in which an involved social planner makes a risky investment choice on behalf of a hypothetical society from behind the veil of ignorance. In order to keep the explanation of the model as simple as possible, we use educational investments as a concrete example.

This section has seven subsections. In Sect. 8.3.1, we introduce the notation and model educational success as a random variable. The second subsection (Sect. 8.3.2) derives the social planner's optimal education choice from expected utility maximization. Sections 8.3.3 and 8.3.4 show how redistributive taxation can increase welfare due to the Domar–Musgrave effect and an income effect. In the fifth subsection (Sect. 8.3.5), we incorporate need in the social planner's decision problem. Section 8.3.6 is concerned with the social planner's simultaneous optimal choice of educational investment and tax rate. Here, we also show that the uniform tax plus lump-sum transfer can be interpreted as a UBI that is financed by means of a flat tax. In the final subsection (Sect. 8.3.7), we introduce need-based redistribution, which consists of a proportional tax with a tax exemption limit and a conditional transfer to the needy students. We show that, under the assumptions made, need-based redistribution generates higher welfare than UBI/flat tax. Note that we highlight some central theoretical results. These are reconsidered from an experimental point of view in Sect. 8.4.

8.3.1 Basic Model of Risky Educational Investment

The society consists of an even number of $n = 2 \times N$ identical students, where $N \in \mathbb{N} = \{1; 2; 3; \ldots\}$. Each student $i = 1, \ldots, n$, is initially endowed with an equal lifetime income of $Y_{i,0} = Y_0 = 100$ monetary units, say thaler. The social planner has the opportunity to determine whether and how much each student must invest in a risky project, namely her professional and academic education.

The investment has the characteristics of a "super lottery" (Wagner 1958), which means it will be played exactly $T \in \mathbb{N} = \{1; 2; 3; \ldots\}$ times in a row, like the exams for various vocational training certificates and academic degrees. For simplicity, we assume that at each stage $t \leq T$ of the super lottery, a fair coin toss decides whether the exam was successful or not. Thus, every exam is a Bernoulli experiment with a success probability of $p = 0.5$. The number of successful exams after t rounds is therefore a binomially distributed random variable X with $t + 1$ distinct outcomes $x \in X = \{0, 1, 2, \ldots, t\}$. We set $N = 2^{T-1}$. So, if we assume that the super lottery—the vocational and academic training path—leads to $T = 3$ exams, then there are exactly $n = 2 \times 2^2 = 8$ students.

After all students have more or less successfully completed their vocational and academic training, there are now $T + 1 = 4$ different educational classes in the society, which are formed by the number of passed vocational and academic degrees x. Let $f_X(x)$ denote the relative frequency of having passed x exams. One in eight students ($f_X(0) = 1/8$) has failed all exams, three ($f_X(1) = 3/8$) have failed two exams and passed one exam, three ($f_X(2) = 3/8$) have failed one and passed two, and one student ($f_X(3) = 1/8$) has passed all exams.

A successfully passed exam leads to a positive return $r^+ = 0.6$ on the investment while failure leads to a negative return $r^- = -0.4$. Thus, it is reasonably assumed that education has a positive expected return from the point of view of society as a whole, $E(r) = 0.5 \times 0.6 + 0.5 \times (-0.4) = 0.1 > 0$. Henceforth, such educational investments are called *productive*. Positive expected returns are a necessary condition for the social planner to invest at all if she exhibits *risk aversion*, i.e, her von Neumann–Morgenstern utility function has a concave shape.

8.3.2 Social Planner's Optimal Educational Choice

What absolute share V_0, $0 \leq V_0 \leq 100$ of the students' life time income should the social planner risk for education from an *ex-ante* perspective? The *ex-post* lifetime income of a student with x academic degrees is given by

$$Y_3(x) = 100 + \left((1 + 0.6+)^x (1 - 0.4)^{3-x} - 1\right) V_0 \,, \tag{8.1}$$

which is in increasing order of x, $Y_3(x) = \{100 - 0.784\ V_0;\ 100 - 0.424\ V_0;\ 100 + 0536\ V_0;\ 100 + 3.096\ V_0\}$.

To start, we assume that the social planner has an isoelastic von Neumann–Morgenstern utility function of income $u(\cdot) = ln\ (Y_3(x))$, that is, the utility function exhibits *constant relative risk aversion* (CRRA). The CRRA property means that the relative share of lifetime income invested in education is independent of the level of income (see, e.g., Wakker 2008). Maximizing the expected utility of lifetime income

$$EU = \sum_{x=0}^{3} f_X(x) \ln (Y_3(x)) \tag{8.2}$$

$$= \frac{1}{8} \ln (Y_3(0)) + \frac{3}{8} \ln (Y_3(1)) + \frac{3}{8} \ln (Y_3(2)) + \frac{1}{8} \ln (Y_3(3))$$

with respect to V_0 yields an optimal educational investment of $V_0^\star = 40.73$ thaler.

The vector of the students' education optimized lifetime incomes in the four education classes x is given by $Y_3^\star(x) = \{68.07; 82.73; 121.83; 226.09\}$ thaler. The average lifetime income (weighted by $f_X(x)$) of 113.48 thaler clearly exceeds the initial endowment of 100 thaler. The increase in efficiency, however, goes hand in hand with inequality. The coefficient of variation of the lifetime incomes is 44.4%.

Figure 8.1 depicts the situation of the basic model graphically as a histogram. The figure shows a right-skewed lifetime income distribution caused by the randomness

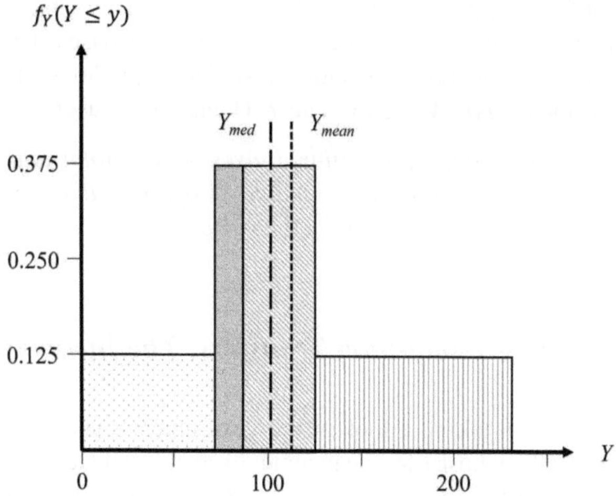

The figure shows a histogram of students' education optimized lifetime incomes Y for four educational classes after passing up to three vocational and academic degrees.

Fig. 8.1 Histogram of Lifetime Incomes

of the success or failure of educational investments. The average return to education exceeds its median of 102.28 thaler.[6]

8.3.3 Introducing Taxes: The Domar–Musgrave Effect

What happens when the government imposes a uniform proportional tax both on profits *and* losses with a tax rate of $0 < \tau < 1$? This means that profits and losses are reduced by the same percentage. Hence, the ex-post lifetime income with proportional tax is given by

$$Y_{3,\tau}(x) = 100 + \left((1+0.6+)^{x}(1-0.4)^{3-x} - 1\right) V_0 \times (1-\tau)\,, \qquad (8.3)$$

and setting, say, $\tau = 0.2$ the optimum educational investment is given by $V^{\star}_{0,\,\tau} = 50.91$ thaler. The students' lifetime incomes remain unchanged, $Y^{\star}_{3,\,\tau}(x) = \{68.07;$ $82.73; 121.83; 226.09\}$, as do average lifetime income and inequality.

Interestingly, the new investment is exactly $1/(1-\tau)$ times the old investment. The reason for this is the uniformity of taxation of profits and losses. The tax reduces the overall risk of the investment, because all positive and negative outcomes of the educational lottery are reduced proportionately, i.e., $Y^{\star}_{3}(x)$ is a mean-preserving spread (Diamond and Stiglitz 1974) of $Y^{\star}_{3,\,\tau}(x)$. Consequently, the marginal utility of income increases and the risk averse social planner raises the investment in inverse proportion to the tax rate until all students' previous utility levels are restored. This is the *Domar–Musgrave effect* (Domar and Musgrave 1944).

Result 1 *Introducing uniform proportional taxes on the profits and losses of educational investment increases the social planner's optimal educational investment, but it does not alter the distribution of lifetime incomes.*

8.3.4 Introducing Lump-Sum Transfers: The Income Effect

In addition, it is worth taking a look at the government's tax revenues. The four "winners" ($x \in \{2; 3\}$) whose lifetime incomes exceed 100 thaler together pay 38.32 thaler in taxes, while the four "losers" ($x \in \{0; 1\}$) whose lifetime incomes fall below 100 thaler get 16.75 thaler from the tax office. Thus, the government has generated a budget surplus of 21.57 thaler. So, as long as the government does not burn the money, but does something useful with it, taxation increases the welfare of the society.

[6] The median is calculated as half the difference between the second and third classes of education.

Result 2 *Uniform proportional taxation of the profits and losses of educational investment increases social welfare.*

It is worthwhile delving further into this result, which is intuitively surprising at first glance but can be attributed simply to the reduction in lifetime-income risk through uniform taxation. Assuming that the government splits the surplus evenly among all students as a lump-sum transfer $\theta = \tau \times \sum_{x=0}^{3} f_X(x)(Y_3(x) - 100)$, students' ex-post income is given by

$$Y_{3,\tau,\theta}(x) = 100 + \theta + \left((1+0.6+)^x (1-0.4)^{3-x} - 1\right) V_0 \times (1-\tau). \qquad (8.4)$$

If the social planner correctly anticipates the transfer θ, the optimum educational investment increases again to $V^{\star}_{0,\tau,\theta} = 52.23$ thaler. The students' lifetime incomes are $Y^{\star}_{3,\tau,\theta}(x) = \{69.96; 85.02; 125.21; 232.35\}$ thaler, and the mean and the coefficient of variation of lifetime income are 116.62 thaler and 44.4%. Accordingly, welfare is the highest with uniform taxation plus lump-sum transfer. Inequality in terms of the coefficient of variation does not change because we assumed that the social planner's von Neumann–Morgenstern utility function has the CRRA property.

The key data of the numerical example are summarized in the upper panel (*No Need Threshold*) of Table 8.1. The table shows, by redistribution type, the optimum educational investment; the lifetime incomes of the four educational levels in increasing order; the students' mean income Y_{mean} as a measure of efficiency; the coefficient of variation of the income distribution as a measure of inequality; the expected utility EU of the social planner as a measure of social welfare; and the equally distributed equivalent lifetime income Y^{EDE} (Atkinson 1970), where $Y^{EDE} = [u(EU)]^{-1} = \exp(EU)$. By definition, the social planner is indifferent between Y^{EDE} (each student receives the same relatively low amount as a lifetime income) and the vector of $Y^{\star}$ that results from the optimal investment (the students receive unequal amounts that are on average higher than Y^{EDE} as their lifetime incomes).

As the last two columns of Table 8.1 show, social welfare in terms of the social planner's expected utility (EU) increases from 4.66 to 4.69 when we move from the situation without redistribution to the situation where the surplus of the uniform tax is redistributed to the students by a lump-sum transfer.

The social welfare consequences of income redistribution are also shown in Fig. 8.2 in a μ-σ diagram (Sharpe 1964). Without redistribution, all available lifetime-income profiles are on the straight *education-market line* passing from Y_0 through $Y_3^{\star}$, where higher efficiency Y_{mean} on the abscissa is associated with greater inequality $cvar$ on the ordinate due to the risk involved in educational investment. In the numerical example, the social planner maximizes welfare by investing 40.73 thaler per student, which results in the lifetime-income profile $Y_3^{\star}$. The equally distributed equivalent lifetime income is $Y_3^{EDE} = 105.85$ thaler. Equivalent income and the education-optimized lifetime-income profile lie on the same social indifference curve with an expected utility (social welfare) of 4.66.

Table 8.1 Educational Investment, Income Redistribution, and Social Welfare

Redistribution Type	Educational Investment thaler	Lifetime Incomes thaler	Y_{mean} thaler	$cvar$ %	EU –	Y^{EDE} thaler
No Need Threshold						
No Redistribution	40.73	{68.07; 82.73; 121.83; 226.09}	113.48	44.4	4.66	105.85
Uniform Tax ($\tau = 0.2$)	50.91	{68.07; 82.73; 121.83; 226.09}	113.48	44.4	4.66	105.85
+ Lump-Sum Transfer ($\theta = 2.77$)	52.23	{69.96; 85.02; 125.21; 232.35}	116.62	44.4	4.69	108.78
Need Threshold 80 thaler						
No Redistribution	25.51	{80.00; 89.18; 113.67; 178.98}	108.44	29.1	4.66	105.13
Uniform Tax ($\tau = 0.2$)	31.89	{80.00; 89.18; 113.67; 178.98}	108.44	29.1	4.66	105.13
+ Lump-Sum Transfer ($\theta = 1.85$)	34.84	{80.00; 90.03; 116.79; 188.14}	111.07	31.1	4.68	107.24
Uniform Tax ($\tau^\star = 0.559$)	75.72	{80.00; 92.02; 124.08; 209.56}	117.23	35.3	4.72	112.11
+ Lump-Sum Transfer ($\theta^\star = 6.18$)						
Means-Tested Benefit ($\tau_N^\star = 0.144$)	100.00	{80.00; 80.00; 131.44; 350.49}	133.10	68.7	4.75	115.92

The table shows, by redistribution type, the optimum educational investment, the lifetime incomes of the four educational levels in increasing order, and the students' mean income Y_{mean} in thaler; it also shows the coefficient of variation ($cvar$) of the income distribution in percent, the expected utility EU of the social planner, and the equally distributed equivalent lifetime income Y^{EDE} in thaler

All lifetime income profiles in the shaded area to the right below the indifference curve increase social welfare. Three distinct cases are possible. Case *I* increases efficiency and decreases inequality and is thus clearly a welfare improvement. Case *II* leads to slightly more inequality, but the increase in mean income has a stronger positive impact on welfare. Case *III* leads to a reduction in both efficiency and inequality, where the latter has a positive effect on welfare. We do not consider case *III* any further, as it would have to be assumed here that the absolute amount of the investment falls despite rising income (increasing absolute risk aversion, IARA).[7]

As outlined above, uniform taxation of the profits and losses of productive educational investments leads to a budget surplus, which is redistributed to students

[7] For empirical evidence supporting IARA, see Eisenhauer (1997).

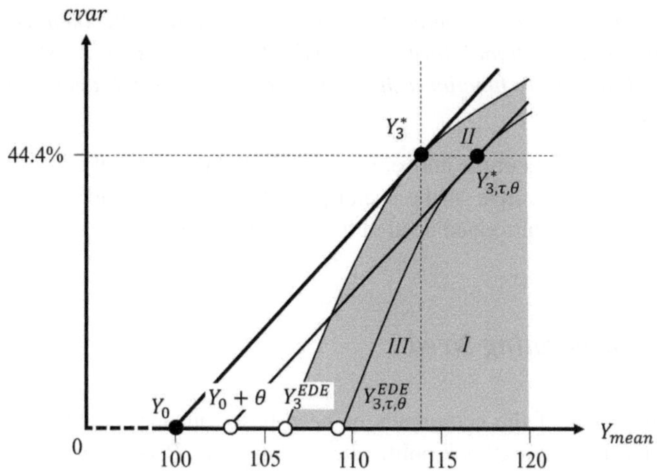

The figure shows the social planner's educational choice in a μ-σ diagram, where Y_{mean} and cvar indicate the efficiency and the inequality (risk) of the educational investment. All feasible investments are located on the straight educational-market lines starting at Y_0 and $Y_0 + \theta$ (lump-sum transfer). The optimum educational investment $Y^\star$ is located at the tangent of the educational-market line with the social indifference curve. Y^{EDE} is the equally distributed income that would be equivalent to $Y^\star$. The shaded area indicates a welfare increase with respect to $Y_3^\star$. Cases I and II (III) show an increase (a decrease) of efficency. Cases I and III (II) show a decrease (an increase) of inequality.

Fig. 8.2 Educational Choice and Income Redistribution in a μ-σ Diagram

as a lump-sum transfer θ. The social planner correctly anticipates this transfer and, therefore, her education-market line shifts to the right by θ (and flattens out a bit for small θ). In the finance literature, it is generally assumed that investors exhibit decreasing absolute risk aversion (DARA), i.e., increase their investments in absolute terms with rising income (for the theoretical argument see Pratt 1965, Arrow 1965; for empirical evidence, see Friend and Blume 1975, Paravisini et al. 2017). If, as assumed, the social planner's utility function also exhibits constant relative risk aversion (CRRA), then the educational investment increases proportionally and inequality remains constant, as marked by $Y^\star_{3,\tau,\theta}$ in the figure.

The shaded area around *II* describes the paradoxical case that income redistribution leads to higher efficiency and *greater* inequality. Sinn (1995, 1996) calls this situation "redistribution paradox." When the social planner's utility function exhibits decreasing relative risk aversion (DRRA), she increases the relative share invested as compared to initial wealth, so there is more inequality in lifetime incomes due to the higher risk associated with her educational choice.

Result 3 *When the social planner correctly anticipates the lump-sum transfer, her additional educational investment will decrease (leave constant, increase) inequality if her utility function exhibits increasing (constant, decreasing) relative risk aversion.*

In the numerical example above, we investigated the optimal educational investment from the perspective of the social planner without considering the students' *needs*. We therefore introduce need in the following subsection.

8.3.5 Incorporating Need

In their overview of the economics of need-based justice, Nicklisch and Paetzel (2020) point out that textbook political economy (e.g., Persson and Tabellini 2000) offers numerous explanations for why, despite their political power, the majority of relatively poor people in modern welfare states refrain from voting for (even) more redistribution (see, e.g., Corneo and Grüner 2002). Some argue that the median voter considers the cost of redistribution in terms of efficiency loss (Meltzer and Richard 1981). Another answer is that voters believe in upward mobility (Benabou and Ok 2001). The theoretical debate mainly focuses on the "big trade-off" (Okun 1975) between equality and efficiency. Surprisingly, need rarely features in this literature even though real-world social policies seem to be mainly driven by a need orientation: "governmental transfers satisfy individual needs that recipients are unable to finance themselves; subsidies are implemented to avoid suffering, and institutional settings such as minimum income, basic income or breadline income [...] reflect considerations of need-based justice in a social contract rather than trying to equalize net wealth within societies" (Nicklisch and Paetzel 2020, p. 162).

Kittel and Traub (2022) point out that in Europe-wide surveys, need-based justice enjoys great empirical support, similar to equity and far ahead of equality (see Hülle et al. 2018, Adriaans et al. 2019). In this respect, the question arises as to why need enjoys such high empirical approval. As hypothesized in the beginning of this chapter, a possible answer to this is that need-based redistribution guarantees every citizen a socially or politically acknowledged minimum and is more *sustainable*, i.e., less inefficient than equality-based redistribution. In the following, we will therefore include need in the social planner's decision calculus. In the section after, we will empirically test the model. This will enable us address the main question of this edited volume, namely whether need should enjoy priority in distributional problems.

As far as we know, there is only one maximization approach in textbook economics that explicitly takes (basic) needs into account, namely the Stone–Geary (Geary 1950; Stone 1954) utility function $U_i = (q_j - \gamma_j)^{\beta_j}$, where the consumption of good j, q_j, only creates utility U_i to household i when it exceeds the minimum consumption level γ_j. The Linear Expenditure System based on the maximization of the Stone–Geary utility function is a standard approach for estimating demand systems (cf. Deaton and Muellbauer 1980). Assuming $\sum_j \beta_j = 1$, we obtain $q_j = \gamma_j + \beta_j/p_j \times (y_i - \sum_k p_k\gamma_k)$ for the j demand functions, where y_i and p_j are income and prices, respectively. Demand can be split into two components: First, the minimum consumption of each good has to be met; second, after subtracting the subsistence income $Y_N = \sum_k p_k\gamma_k$ that is needed to buy the minimum quantities, the household spends the remainder of its income according to its preferences β_j. Diederich et al. (2020) are the first to apply the Stone–Geary approach to decision-making under risk and investigate it in a laboratory experiment (see Chap. 2 in this volume).

We can now continue our numerical example. In what follows, we assume that the social planner believes that no member of society should have less than 80 thalers of lifetime income, because at least 80 thalers are necessary to lead a decent life in terms of being able to consume the minimum quantities γ_j of the goods j. We call $Y_N = 80$ the *need threshold.* As with Nullmeier's (2020) ten theses for a need-based theory of justice, this approach assumes that while goods are scarce, in principle all needs can be satisfied (a situation of *oversupply*, pp. 202–204). It should also be noted that the model is not about *need gaps* and their correction (pp. 204–205), However, acknowledged needs should be satisfied as they are absolute.

The lower panel of Table 8.1 contains the numerical calculations for a need threshold of 80 thaler. The need threshold constrains the social planner's maximization problem so that she chooses to invest only $\tilde{V}_0 = 25.51$ thaler in the initial situation without redistribution. Since the original educational investment of 40.73 thaler was optimal in the situation without a need threshold, welfare in the sense of the equally distributed equivalent income is correspondingly lower (105.13 instead of 105.85 thaler).[8] However, these figures cannot be compared directly with one another because, in the initial situation, the lowest educational class has a lifetime income that falls below the need threshold. Consequently, the utility for those students would be undefined.

Imposing a uniform tax on profits and losses increases the constrained optimum educational investment to 31.89 thaler due to the Domar–Musgrave effect. When the social planner is able to redistribute the budget surplus by means of the lump-sum transfer, she chooses to invest $\tilde{V}_{0,\tau,\theta} = 34.84$ thaler. The students' lifetime incomes are $\tilde{Y}_{3,\tau,\theta}(x) = \{80.00; 90.03; 116.79; 188.14\}$ thaler, the mean income is 111.07 thaler, and the coefficient of variation of lifetime income is 31.1%. It is worth noting that in the case of the lump-sum transfers, inequality increases somewhat because the 80 thaler restriction only applies after taxes and transfers. Thus, the social planner can invest disproportionately more in education despite her CARA preferences.

[8] This difference seems small but of course depends on the assumptions of the numerical example for the curvature of the utility function and the parameters.

8.3.6 Optimal Choice of the Uniform Tax

The question arises as to whether the combination of uniform tax and lump-sum transfer is the best instrument for maximizing welfare if the need threshold is also taken into account as a restriction. In fact, the tax rate τ that generates the surplus used for the lump-sum transfer cannot be increased at will. According to Result 1, risk averse social planners would react with more investments to higher tax rates, and hence, the less successful students would be in an even worse position.

We can easily determine the maximum social welfare generated by the combination of uniform tax and lump-sum transfer by letting the social planner freely choose not only the educational investment V_0 but also τ (and thus θ). The result of this optimization can also be found in the lower panel of Table 8.1. The social planner chooses a significantly higher tax rate of 55.9%, which allows a lump-sum transfer of 6.18 thaler. The educational investment is 75.72%, leading to a higher mean income and greater inequality than the arbitrarily chosen exogenous tax rate of 20%.

Let us take a closer look at the tax scale that is created by $\tau^\star$, $T(Y) = \tau^\star \times (Y - 100) - \theta^\star = 0.559Y - 62.08$. This is a flat tax with marginal tax rate 0.559 on all lifetime incomes $Y > 0$, which is combined with an *unconditional basic income* (UBI) of 62.08 thaler. Note that the UBI is lower than the need threshold because the least successful student has a gross income of 40.64 thaler. Hence, we have $Y_{3,0.559,6.18}(0) = 40.64 \times (1 - 0.559) + 62.08 = 80$ thaler for the poorest student as required. Accordingly, in the following, we interpret Sinn's (1995, 1996) analysis of the welfare state in terms of the introduction of a UBI financed with a flat tax.

8.3.7 Introducing Need-Based Redistribution

As shown in the example in the previous subsection, a relatively high marginal tax rate (of 55.9%) is needed to fund the UBI while helping all students above the need threshold, but the tax rate is constrained from above by Result 1.[9] One way out of this dilemma is *need-based redistribution*, which only transfers money to less successful students if they are actually in need. A central element of need-based redistribution is a *means-tested benefit*, which replaces the UBI.

[9] At this point we do not want to discuss the pros and cons of the UBI because it is not our focus. However, one of the usual criticisms is that its financing requires a very high income tax rate, which would create strong negative incentives, particularly on the labor market (cf. Atkinson 1995).

The means-tested benefit $b(x)$ ensures that none of the less successful students falls below the need threshold of $Y_N = 80$ thaler:

$$b(0) = \begin{cases} 0 & \text{if } 100 - 0.784\ V_0 \geq 80 \\ 80 - 100 - 0.784\ V_0 & \text{otherwise} \end{cases} \tag{8.5}$$

$$b(1) = \begin{cases} 0 & \text{if } 100 - 0.424\ V_0 \geq 80 \\ 80 - 100 - 0.424\ V_0 & \text{otherwise.} \end{cases} \tag{8.6}$$

Their incomes are given by

$$Y_3(0) = 100 - 0.784\ V_0 + b(0) \text{ and} \tag{8.7}$$

$$Y_3(1) = 100 - 0.424\ V_0 + b(1)\ . \tag{8.8}$$

The successful students jointly raise the needed amount $B := b(0) + 3 \times b(1)$ in proportion to their gross lifetime incomes:

$$Y_3(2) = 100 + 0.536\ V_0 - B\frac{100 + 0.536\ V_0}{400 + 4.704\ V_0} \text{ and} \tag{8.9}$$

$$Y_3(3) = 100 + 3.096\ V_0 - B\frac{100 + 3.096\ V_0}{400 + 4.704\ V_0}\ . \tag{8.10}$$

The result, which is also displayed in the last row of Table 8.1, is as follows: For the given parametrization, we get a corner solution with $V^{\star}_{0,N} = 100$ thaler and the social planner imposes a proportional tax with rate $\tau^{\star}_N = 0.144$ on the lifetime incomes of *only* the successful students to finance the means tested benefits $b^{\star}(0) = 58.4$ and $b^{\star}(1) = 22.4$ thaler.[10] The vector of lifetime incomes is given by $Y_{3,N}(x) = \{80.00; 80.00; 131.44; 350.49\}$ thaler. The mean income is 133.10 thaler, and the coefficient of variation is 68.7%.

When comparing the UBI/flat tax with need-based redistribution, the results are clearly in favor of the latter. On the one hand, in comparison to UBI/flat tax, the level of inequality tolerated by the social planner in need-based redistribution is significantly higher (68.7% vs. 35.3%). On the other hand, efficiency is significantly greater (133.10 vs. 117.23 thaler). All in all, welfare in terms of the equally distributed equivalent income is higher under need-based redistribution than under the UBI/flat tax (115.92 vs. 112.11 thaler).

Result 4 *Need-based redistribution enables greater welfare than an unconditional basic income that is financed by a flat tax.*

[10] Since the income of the students is fully taxed when they earn more than the need threshold, $\tau^{\star}_N$ is essentially a proportional income tax with an exemption limit (Freigrenze) of $80/(1 - 0.144) = 93.46$ thaler.

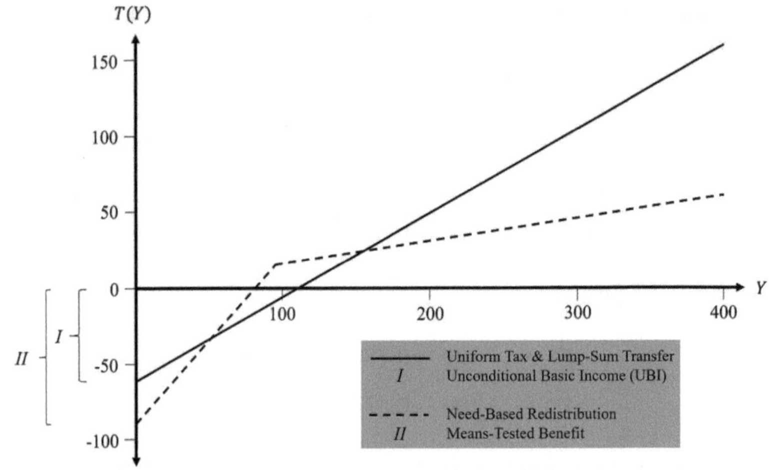

Fig. 8.3 Comparison of Tax Scales

The intuition behind this result is illustrated with the help of Fig. 8.3, which compares the tax scales $T(Y_3)$ of the flat tax and need-based redistribution. Since the UBI benefits all students regardless of their need, it requires a relatively high marginal tax rate to generate enough surplus (496.64 thaler) to fund it. Hence, the tax scale (the solid line in the figure) is very steep. Need-based redistribution merely ensures that no student has less than the need threshold. The tax revenue required for this (125.06 thaler), which is raised only from the successful students, is much lower. The tax scale (the dashed line in the figure) has a transfer withdrawal rate of 1 below the exemption limit and requires a relatively low marginal tax rate for lifetime incomes above the exemption limit, i.e., the tax scale exhibits a flatter slope.

In conclusion, our results show that the welfare state *can* actually contribute to increasing welfare through redistribution in a risky environment. In fact, the welfare state even *has to* redistribute if it does not want to let the "losers" of the "super-lottery" languish below the need threshold. However, the analysis has also shown that the way in which lifetime income is redistributed has an effect on the welfare gain that can be achieved. In our model framework, a UBI financed by a flat tax performs worse than need-based redistribution. To answer this chapter's main research question, need-based redistribution should be given priority to ensure the most sustainable form of income redistribution. However, it should also be mentioned that the model abstracts from all negative incentive effects that could occur *after* redistribution when the veil of ignorance masking the income positions of the members of society is lifted. This could significantly reduce the welfare gains of redistribution. However, we can reasonably assume that the *unconditional* basic income together with a relatively high marginal tax rate of the flat tax would give rise to stronger disincentives than need-based redistribution.

8.4 Experimental Evidence

8.4.1 Experiment #1: Risk Taking in the Welfare State

Traub and Krügel (2017) provide an experimental test of the model of risky educational investment *without* the need-threshold outlined in Sects. 8.3.1, 8.3.2, 8.3.3, and 8.3.4. Previous experimental tests of the Domar–Musgrave effect include Swenson (1989) and King and Wallin (1990), neither of which show a significant effect of the proportional tax scheme on risk-taking. In a series of experimental papers, Fochmann et al. (2012a,b), Ackermann et al. (2013), and Fochmann and Hemmerich (2014) investigate whether risk perception (with a gain-loss framing effect) can explain the findings of Swenson (1989) and King and Wallin (1990). Fochmann and Hemmerich (2014) conclude that the framing of the decision problem plays an important role in the investment decision. Based on their previous studies, they argue that when framing effects are controlled for, investments actually increase, thus providing evidence of the existence of the Domar–Musgrave effect.

8.4.1.1 Experimental Design

The experiment by Traub and Krügel (2017) uses a neutral framing. Any references to the terms "tax" or "transfer" that could give rise to such gain-loss framing effects are completely avoided. Furthermore, the experiment is the first to investigate not only the impact of the uniform proportional tax but also the lump-sum transfer on risk taking, as laid out in the TWS by Sinn (1995, 1996).

Apart from the involved social planner's decision on the level of investment in a risky asset V_0, the experiment additionally involves an elicitation task for distributional preferences (Kerschbamer 2015) and a risk-preference elicitation task (Balafoutas et al. 2013). At the end of the experiment, participants also complete a questionnaire about their sociodemographic characteristics.

The investment task almost exactly resembles the decision problem presented in Sect. 8.3. The authors use a within-subjects design with three different treatments (No Tax, Tax and Lump Sum). They use eight different parametrizations for the positive r^+ and negative r^- return and the tax rate τ in each treatment (see Table 8.2), amounting to $3 \times 8 = 24$ rounds/individual decisions. At the beginning of each round, the subjects receive their initial endowments of $Y_0 = 25$ Euros and are randomly matched to groups of eight ($T = 3$). Their task in each round is to simultaneously and anonymously select their preferred investments V_0, where $0 \leq V_0 \leq 25$.

The experiment combines a random dictator with an involved social planner design as follows. When all eight group members have submitted their investment V_0 for each of the 24 rounds, one round and the decision of one player in this round are randomly chosen to be paid off for the entire group. Then, each group member is randomly assigned to one of the four income positions. That is, one group member

Table 8.2 Round Variation of Parameter Values in Traub and Krügel (2017)

	Var. 1	Var. 2	Var. 3	Var. 4	Var. 5	Var. 6	Var. 7	Var. 8
r^+	0.9	0.9	1	1	0.9	0.9	1	1
r^-	−0.7	−0.7	−0.8	−0.8	−0.6	−0.6	−0.7	−0.7
τ	0.4	0.3	0.3	0.4	0.4	0.3	0.4	0.3

each is assigned to the highest and lowest income positions; three group members each are assigned to the second and third highest income positions. Hence, each player has a certain probability of being the dictator in her group, and each group member has the same ex-ante probability of being assigned to one of the four income positions.

As outlined in the model, in the NO TAX treatment the payoff per point is multiplied by V_0. In the TAX treatment, τ is imposed on both profits and losses. Hence, the payoff per point is multiplied by $V_0(1-\tau)$. In the LUMP SUM treatment, the payoff per point is also multiplied by $V_0(1-\tau)$, and each position receives an additional lump-sum transfer of

$$\theta = \tau V_0 \sum_{x=0}^{3} f_X(x) \left((1+r^+)^x (1+t^-)^{3-x} - 1 \right) . \tag{8.11}$$

Note that, even if the experiment does not specify an explicit need threshold, $25\tau + \theta$ can be interpreted as the unconditional basic income.

8.4.1.2 Results

The experiment was conducted in 2018 at the WISO research lab of the University of Hamburg with 72 subjects. Forty nine (68%) of them were female; 23 (32%) were male. Twenty-four subjects participated in each treatment. One session lasted for 60 minutes. The incentives in the experiment were very high. The highest payoff was 202.10 Euros, the lowest payoff 3.10 Euros, and the average payoff 30.65 Euros.

Figure 8.4 gives a graphical summary of the subjects' investment behavior aggregated over all eight parameter variations per subject. The bars in the upper panel of the figure represent the mean investment by treatment. The investment pattern clearly supports the model. Subjects on average invest the least in NO TAX (5.92 Euros). In TAX, the proportional tax raises the investment to 8.25 Euros, as predicted by the Domar–Musgrave effect.

Observation 1 *A uniform proportional tax on profits and losses increases subjects' investment in a risky asset.*

The figure also shows that subjects invest the most in LUMP SUM (10,76 Euros), which is to be expected due to the income effect.

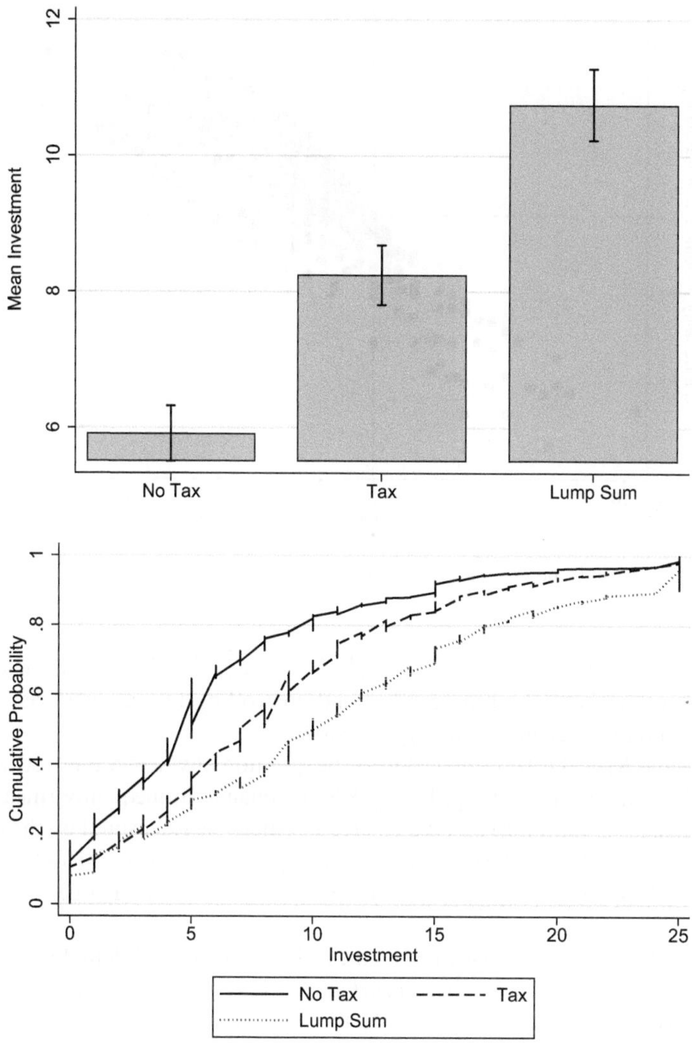

Fig. 8.4 Mean Investment and Cumulative Probability by Treatment in Traub and Krügel (2017)

Observation 2 *A lump-sum transfer further increases subjects' investment in a risky asset.*

The lower panel of the figure additionally shows the cumulative probability distribution of V_0 by treatment. The graph of No Tax visibly and distinctly dominates the graphs of Tax and Lump Sum; the graph of Tax dominates Lump Sum for investments of more than 4 Euros. Their medians are 5, 7, and 10 Euros.

These observations are statistically confirmed by a regression analysis. A random-effects panel Tobit estimation with the investment, V_0, as the dependent

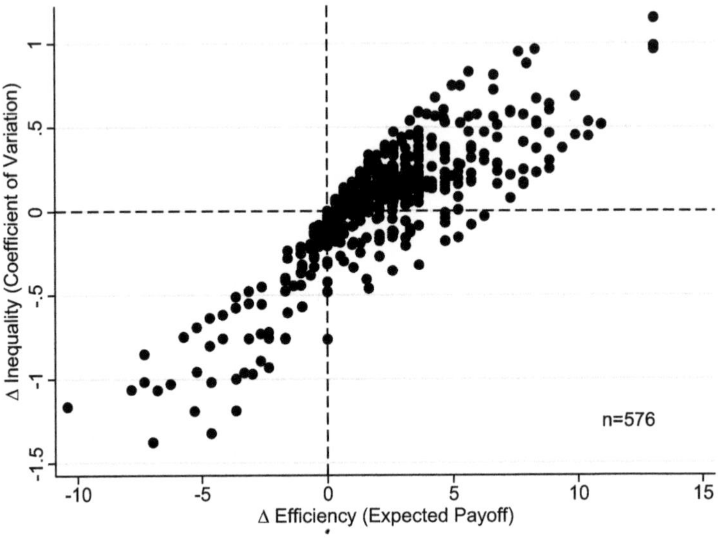

Fig. 8.5 Changes in Inequality and Efficiency in Traub and Krügel (2017)

variable shows that $\bar{V}_0^{\text{NO TAX}} < \bar{V}_0^{\text{TAX}} < \bar{V}_0^{\text{LUMP SUM}}$ holds even when including convariates (such as gender) and controlling for subjects' risk attitude, efficiency preference, and inequality aversion.

Traub and Krügel (2017) also address the question of whether the "redistribution paradox" occurs in this setting. In Fig. 8.5, the change in inequality (measured by the coefficient of variation) and the change in efficiency (measured by the expected payoff) are plotted against each other for a comparison between NO TAX and LUMP SUM. The dots mark $n = 72$ (subjects) $\times$ 8 (rounds) $= 576$ individual observations (cases).

In the 441 cases (76.6%) located to the right of the vertical dotted line, subjects' choices increase efficiency. These cases are in line with decreasing absolute risk aversion (DARA). Among these 441, the 78 cases (13.5%) located below the horizontal dotted line (less inequality; case I in Fig. 8.2) are in line with increasing relative risk aversion (IRRA). The other 363 cases (63.0%), which are located above the horizontal dotted line (more inequality; case II in Fig. 8.2), are also in line with decreasing relative risk aversion (DRRA). There are no cases of constant relative risk aversion (CARA) as assumed by the numerical example. There are, however, 105 cases (18.2%) in the lower left quadrant (case III in Fig. 8.2), where subjects decrease both efficiency and inequality by choosing a lower investment in LUMP SUM. These choices can be explained by increasing absolute risk aversion (IARA). Furthermore, there are 30 cases where subjects never invest and therefore do not change efficiency or inequality.

Observation 3 *Subjects have predominantly DARA and DRRA preferences, i.e., they absolutely and relatively increase their investment in the treatment with uniform* *tax and lump-sum transfer. Therefore, the "redistribution paradox" occurs in the absolute majority of all cases.*

8.4.1.3 Conclusion

The main purpose of the first experiment is to test the TWS. The experimental test clearly supports the model prediction that redistribution via the welfare state can lead to an increase in efficiency. A somewhat surprising result, but one that may also depend on the parameters of the experiment, is that a widespread paradoxical equality–efficiency trade-off occurs in which doing without redistribution means more equality and less efficiency.

8.4.2 Experiment #2: Risk Taking Under Different Welfare-State Regimes

In the previous experiment, we did not take into account the need threshold as we investigated the impact of redistribution on risk taking (as in Sinn's 1995, 1996 original TWS). In the following experiment by Benker et al. (2017), we take into account need and follow the theoretical considerations of Sects. 8.3.5, 8.3.6, and 8.3.7. In particular, we compare the impact of the two different "welfare state regimes"—unconditional basic income financed by flat tax and need-based redistribution—on risk taking when a need threshold has to be taken into account.

8.4.2.1 Experimental Design

As with Traub and Krügel (2017), the experiment uses a neutral framing. It also involves three tasks (the social planner's decision on the investment in a risky asset V_0, an elicitation task for distributional preferences, and a risk-preference elicitation task) and, at the end of the experiment, participants complete a questionnaire about their sociodemographic characteristics.

The investment task almost exactly resembles the decision problem presented in Sect. 8.3. Benker et al. (2017) use a between-subjects design with respect to the need threshold (which is explained below) and a within-subjects design with five different treatments (BASE, NO TAX, TAX, LUMP SUM, and NEED-BASED REDISTRIBUTION). BASE is the same as NO TAX in Traub and Krügel (2017). All other treatments involve a need threshold. NEED-BASED REDISTRIBUTION is implemented along the lines of Sect. 8.3.7. Need is modeled by setting all payoffs that fall short of the need threshold to zero (i.e., these participants receive only a show up fee after the end of the experiment). Subjects are initially endowed with 100 tokens. The need threshold is either 80 tokens (absolute need) or 60% of the mean

Table 8.3 Round Variation of Parameter Values in Benker et al. (2017)

	Basic	High efficiency	High inequality
r^+	0.6	0.7	0.9
r^-	−0.4	−0.4	−0.7

income (relative need).[11] Since these two between-subjects treatments do not lead to different investment behavior, they are pooled in the results. Benker et al. (2017) use three different parametrizations for the positive r^+ and negative r^- return (see Table 8.3). Hence, each subject has to make $5 \times 3 = 15$ investment decisions in the random dictator/involved social planner mode.

The only major difference from the theoretical model is that the subjects in the TAX and LUMP SUM treatments are not free to choose the tax rate. The reason for this is that a two-dimensional optimization task with the additional constraint of the need threshold is too complex for an experiment. Instead, the tax rate is set at $\tau = 40\%$, which is moderate for the financing of an UBI.

8.4.2.2 Results

The laboratory experiment was conducted with 96 student subjects at the WISO-research lab of the University of Hamburg. The experiment was implemented with z-Tree (Fischbacher 2007), and subjects were recruited using hroot (Bock et al. 2014). All subjects played all treatments and parametrizations in a random order. One session lasted for approximately 60 minutes and payoffs ranged from 9 to 53 Euros, with an average payoff of 21 Euro.

Figure 8.6 shows, by treatment, how much the subjects invest in the risky asset on average. A comparison of BASE (30.1%) and NO TAX (25.0%) indicates that the need threshold induces subjects to invest less in order to save fellow players from missing out on a payoff. The bars of NO TAX, TAX (31.2%), and LUMP SUM (49.5%) are qualitatively similar to the first experiment by Traub and Krügel (2017). As expected by the theory, NEED-BASED REDISTRIBUTION leads to significantly higher mean investments (61.9%). These results are robust for subjects' sociodemographic characteristics and additional control variables.

Observation 4 *Need-based redistribution (a means tested benefit that is financed by a proportional tax with an exemption limit) is more efficient than an unconditional basic income financed by a flat tax.*

In all three parametrizations, inequality is significantly greater when the need threshold is met with a means-tested benefit ($cvar = \{0.62, 0.68, 0.87\}$) than with an unconditional basic income ($cvar = \{0.35, 0.39, 0.44\}$). This was to be expected in light of the theory. We do not know the "true" utility function of the

[11] With full investment, i.e. $V_0 = 100$ tokens, both lead to the same need threshold. In total, 60% is also chosen to mirror a common definition of the poverty line.

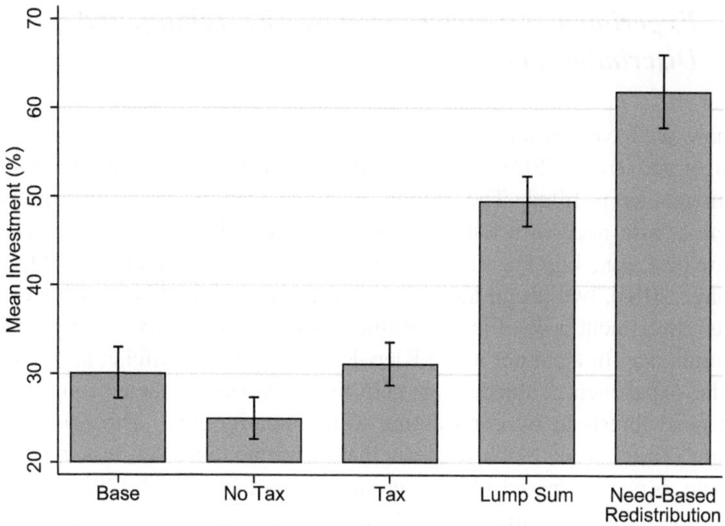

Fig. 8.6 Investment with Need Threshold in Benker et al. (2017)

subjects, and they could not freely choose the tax rate in the LUMP SUM treatment. Hence, we cannot make a welfare comparison that takes efficiency and inequality into account. However, since the effective marginal tax rate on the investment is generally lower than 40% with need-based redistribution, we can reasonably assume that the significantly higher level of efficiency compensates for the lower level of equality.

8.4.2.3 Conclusion

An important conclusion from this study is that when needs are taken into account, traditional measures of risk or inequality do not correctly capture subjects' distributional preferences. Conventional measures such as the coefficient of variation used here (which is based on the variance of incomes) are egalitarian. In fact, it turns out that the subjects tolerate a relatively high degree of inequality of payoffs, especially in the case of need-based redistribution, as long as the acknowledged need is covered. However, this distributional preference is compatible with the Boulding principle of maximizing the average income while taking the minimum income into account (Boulding 1962; Raphael 1980).

8.4.3 Experiment #3: Heterogeneity, Risk Taking, and Discrimination

Until now, we have considered (ex-ante) homogeneous societies. In the experiment by Krügel and Traub (2023), which we present in this subsection, the assumption of homogeneity is lifted. The authors examine identity-based discrimination in connection with need in a risky choice experiment. Based on the social-identity literature (see, e.g., Tajfel et al. 1971, Tajfel and Turner 1979, Shayo 2009, and Klor and Shayo 2010), two group identities are created, which either correlate with the subjects' investment task—the risk attitude—or are completely independent of it—their preference for a painter in the Klee–Kandinsky task (Tajfel et al. 1971).

In the experiment, subjects can help the members of their group to reach a certain need threshold by contributing to a solidarity fund. The Minimal Group Paradigm (Tajfel et al. 1971) suggests that discrimination, i.e., less willingness to contribute, occurs in mixed-identity groups. Krügel and Traub (2023) argue that a differentiation of contributions according to risk attitude can be ethically acceptable when need correlates with risk attitude.

8.4.3.1 Experimental Design

The experiment involves four parts. First, we elicit the risk attitudes of the subjects using an investment task and assign the subjects to two risk groups ("risk averse" and "risk loving"). Second, the participants are divided into two groups ("Klee" and "Kandinsky") based on their preferences for paintings from the famous painters Klee and Kandinsky. After the Klee–Kandinsky task, the subjects are divided into groups of four. The third task again requires an investment and is the main task of the experiment. In each round, participants receive 100 points, which they can (a) keep, (b) invest in a productive risky asset, or (c) contribute to a solidarity fund for the benefit of the other group members. After 10 rounds, each player must have reached a minimum of at least 1200 points. Any shortfall from the 1200 points can be compensated using the solidarity fund (remaining amounts are refunded). If a player does not reach the need threshold of 1200 points even after a transfer from the solidarity fund, she cannot participate in the fourth part of the experiment. In the fourth part, all subjects who reach at least 1200 points can participate in a real-effort task to earn additional money.

There are six treatments. In RISK/HOM and RISK/HET, subjects are matched into groups of four according to their risk group. In MIN/HOM and MIN/HET, subjects are matched based on the results of the minimal group assignment task. In MAX/HOM and MAX/HET, subjects are matched based on the results of the minimal group assignment task. In addition, to maximize consolidation of the group identities, the homogenous groups play an additional game against each other. In homogeneous treatments, the groups are composed of four identical players with respect to risk attitude or group identity. In heterogeneous treatments, the groups are composed of two risk averse and two risk loving subjects in the risk treatments and of two Klee and two Kandinsky individuals in the minimal and maximal group treatments.

8.4.3.2 Results

We ran the experiment in 2022 at the WISO-research lab of the University of Hamburg. We conducted 18 sessions with 372 subjects. The experiment was programmed in z-Tree (Fischbacher 2007). Recruiting was done with hroot (Bock et al. 2014).

The main purpose of the experiment is to find out whether subjects believe that there is less solidarity in heterogeneous than homogeneous groups. We therefore ask each individual how many points they believe will be contributed to the solidarity fund by other group members. We do this after the group assignment, at the beginning of the ten rounds of the group investment task.

Figure 8.7 displays the result of the belief elicitation task by risk attitude. A comparison of risk-averse (upper panel) and risk-loving (lower panel) subjects shows that risk-averse subjects have a greater faith in the generosity of their group members than risk-loving subjects. This is not surprising because risk-averse subjects invest less and are therefore more dependent on transfers from the solidarity fund. However, the comparison between the respective HOM and HET treatments is crucial for answering the research question. We do not see any significant effects here. Thus, the group composition does not affect the beliefs about contribution behavior. In other words, we find neither differentiation according to risk group nor discrimination according to identity in subjects' beliefs.

Krügel and Traub (2023) also check the subjects' actual individual contribution behavior and find some weak evidence for differentiation according to risk group. Risk-averse subjects lower their solidarity contribution in heterogeneous groups, which is ethically justifiable because the risk-loving group members invest more and are simultaneously less likely to need the solidarity fund. Conversely, risk-loving subjects increase their solidarity contributions. Such effects cannot be observed in the discrimination treatments.

Observation 5 *We do not see any differentiation or discrimination with regard to subjects' beliefs about other group members' contribution behavior. In terms of actual contribution behavior, there is weak evidence for differentiation with respect to risk attitudes, which is ethically justifiable.*

8.4.3.3 Conclusion

The study by Krügel and Traub (2023) suggests that there is less discrimination in connection with the solidarity-based satisfaction of needs than is usual in the social identity literature (cf. Paetzel and Sausgruber 2018). In order to be sure of

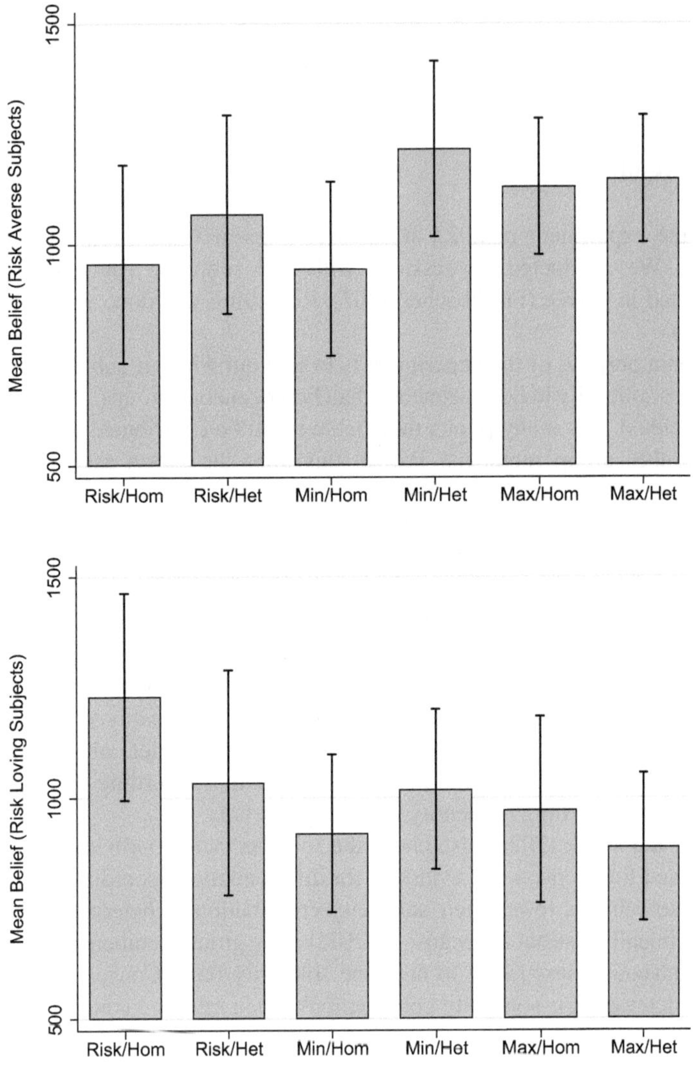

Fig. 8.7 Beliefs about Contributions to the Solidarity Fund in Krügel and Traub (2023)

this conclusion, however, the same design would have to be tested again with a varying need threshold or without any need threshold at all.[12] The latter would mean that the solidarity fund is used for pure redistribution. The systematically different

[12] This has been done in a laboratory experiment by Kittel et al. (2022), which is reported in Chap. 4 of this edited volume.

contributions of the risk-averse and risk-loving subjects in the mixed risk group treatments are rational and ethical.

8.5 Summary and Conclusion

The typical right-skewed shape of the personal income distribution in OECD countries can be explained quite well with the help of stochastic theories of income distribution, i.e., by chance. According to these theories, lifetime income inequality results from individual investment decisions, e.g., in education. Thus, income inequality is also an expression of the individual propensity to take risk. In this sense, the redistributive welfare state can be understood as an insurance device that reduces the variance of lifetime incomes. Sinn (1995, 1996) has drawn attention in his Theory of the Welfare State (TWS) to the fact that income redistribution, because of the reduction of lifetime-income risk, can lead to more productive investment in education and therefore to higher efficiency.

In this chapter, we addressed the sustainability of pure income redistribution in the welfare state. First, we examined whether redistribution can actually lead to efficiency gains, as postulated in the TWS, and is thus economically sustainable. Second, after having shown that the redistribution mechanism proposed by Sinn is close to an unconditional basic income (UBI) financed by a flat tax, we compared its welfare properties with need-based redistribution. By need-based redistribution, we mean a prioritization of the need principle in the sense that the welfare state sees its primary task as first covering all politically acknowledged needs. Specifically, this means that the less-successful needy receive a means-tested transfer that is raised through a (proportional) tax on the incomes of the more-successful "rich," which allows them to live a decent life. As pointed out by Bauer et al. (2023), means-tested benefits are an essential element of the liberal and the conservative welfare state (cf. Esping-Andersen 1990). Typical examples are the U.S. Medicaid program, which only helps individuals and families with insufficient income, and Germany's former Arbeitslosengeld II (replaced by the Bürgergeld as of 2023), which applies strict means testing at the household level ("Bedarfsgemeinschaft").

We structured our considerations of the sustainability and possible superiority of need-based redistribution over an UBI along five concrete research questions (see Sect. 8.2.5). We answered these questions both theoretically, using a model of the welfare state adapted to these issues, and empirically, using three laboratory experiments. The model and experiments applied a contract-theoretic perspective, in the sense of Friedman (1953) and Harsanyi (1953), to the welfare state. According to this perspective, the prevailing inequality is an expression of a social contract that simultaneously determines the individual educational investment and the level of income redistribution. The impartiality of the social planner who sets the contract is guaranteed by the fact that she makes her decision behind the veil of ignorance (VOI).

First, we characterized how the involved social planner (or a subject in the experiment) makes welfare-maximizing educational investment decisions. Second, we showed that the Domar–Musgrave effect and the additional income effect triggered by the UBI do indeed lead to the efficiency increase expected by Sinn. Somewhat surprising is the experimental result that a significant fraction of laboratory societies become more unequal as a result of income redistribution. Sinn had predicted this "redistribution paradox" in cases where investors exhibit decreasing relative risk aversion (DRRA). Whether the paradox can be transferred to the "real world" outside the laboratory is doubtful, however, as financial market studies tend to point to constant or increasing relative risk aversion (IRRA). Third, we explicitly incorporated a need threshold into the model and showed that Sinn's redistribution mechanism is equivalent to a UBI that is funded by a flat tax. Fourth, from both a theoretical and an experimental perspective, the welfare comparison clearly favored need-based redistribution. The driving factor here is that, in contrast to the UBI, relatively low marginal tax rates on the incomes of the "rich" are necessary because only those who are actually needy, i.e., who pass the means test, receive a transfer. It is also noteworthy that the social planner or the average participant in the experiment is willing to forgo equality measured by the variance of incomes in favor of higher efficiency. Fifth, we examined how ex-ante heterogeneity in the form of social identities affects the scope of need-based redistribution. Overall, we found less discrimination against the out-group than is common in such experiments. However, the results are weak and require validation through further research.

Nullmeier (2020, p. 206) argues in favor of an *integrated and strong pluralistic theory of need-based justice*: "Need is applied as a central criterion for distributive justice in experimental settings. Need is also mentioned as one of the few criteria of justice in normative theories. Need is, therefore, an indispensable part of any theory of justice. An integrated theory of need-based justice can be developed as part of a strong pluralistic theory of justice." Our theoretical and experimental results argue in favor of such an *integrated* theory (Nullmeier 2020, p. 193), which develops normative justice principles that at least partly reflect the actual justice conceptions of lay people. In our setting, subjects act as impartial social planners whose distributional decisions are free of self-interest. Moreover, the idea of meeting basic needs that everyone can lead a decent life enjoys very high approval in surveys, which speaks in favor of a *strong pluralistic* theory (Nullmeier 2020, p. 197) that gives need a priority position independent of the context. In the context of our study, i.e., pure income redistribution via the welfare state, we find a combination of need-based justice and the equity principle, in which priority is given to meeting needs, as assumed at the beginning of this edited volume. Such a preference for a lexicographic combination of need and equity as guiding principles for income (re-) distribution can be seen as a stylized fact of the empirical and experimental social choice literature and has already been described by Boulding (1962). Means-tested benefits have therefore prevailed in most welfare states so far, despite all the debates about the unconditional basic income.

Of course, the chosen model and experimental studies have weaknesses. The model neglects any negative incentives to ex-post moral hazard that arise from the insurance function of redistribution. At the very least, however, it can be assumed that these would be (even) more important in the case of a UBI than in the case of means-tested benefits. There are other arguments for and against means-testing, such as the stigmatization of beneficiaries and the high direct (administrative) cost of social assistance, which we could not address here in our admittedly narrow economic view of the welfare state. Moreover, the prioritization of need also assumes that there is scope and capacity for redistribution in the first place. That is, the theory is only applicable to situations of *oversupply* (Nullmeier 2020, p. 202).

Acknowledgments This chapter has been written as part of the DFG Research Group 2104 "Need-based Justice and Distributive Procedures", Project D2 "Need-based Justice as a Social Contract" (reference TR 458/6–2). This funding is gratefully acknowledged. We thank all members of FOR 2104 for making such a project possible.

References

Ackermann, H., M. Fochmann, and B. Mihm (2013): "Biased Effects of Taxes and Subsidies on Portfolio Choices", *Economics Letters* 120, 23–26.

Adriaans, J., P. Eisnecker, and S. Liebig (2019): "A Comparison of Earnings Justice throughout Europe: Widespread Approval in Germany for Income Distribution According to Need and Equity", *DIW Weekly Report* 44/45, 397–404.

Ahsan, S. M. (1974): "Progression and Risk-taking", *Oxford Economic Papers* 26 (3), 318–328.

Ahsan, S. M. (1976): "Taxation in a Two-period Temporal Model of Consumption and Portfolio Allocation", *Journal of Public Economics* 5 (3–4), 337–352.

Alesina, A., and E. Glaeser (2004): *Fighting Poverty in the US and Europe*. Oxford: Oxford University Press.

Alesina, A., E. Glaeser, and B. Sacerdote (2001): "Why Doesn't the United States Have a European-Style Welfare State?", *Brookings Papers on Economic Activity* 2, 187–254.

Allingham, M. G. (1972): "Risk Taking and Taxation", *Zeitschrift für Nationalökonomie* 32 (2–3), 203–224.

Akerlof, G. A., and R. E. Kranton (2000): "Economics and Identity", *Quarterly Journal of Economics* 115, 715–753.

Arrow, K. J. (1965): *Aspects of the Theory of Risk Bearing*. Helsinki: Yrjo Jahnsson Lectures.

Atkinson, A. B. (1970): "On the Measurement of Inequality", *Journal of Economic Theory* 2 (3), 244–263.

Atkinson, A. B. (1976): *The Personal Distribution of Incomes*. London: Allen and Unwin.

Atkinson, A. B. (1995): *Public Economics in Action: The Basic Income/Flat Tax Proposal.* Oxord: Oxford University Press.

Atkinson, A. B., T. Piketty, and E. Saez (2009): "Top Incomes in the Long-Run of History", *NBER Working Papers* 15408.

Atkinson, A. B., and J. E. Stiglitz (1980): *Lectures on Public Economics*. New York: McGraw-Hill.

Balafoutas, L., M. Kocher, L. Putterman, and M. Sutter (2013): "Equality, Equity and Incentives: An Experiment", *European Economic Review* 60, 32–51.

Bamberg, G., and W. F. Richter (1984): "The Effects of Progressive Taxation on Risk-Taking", *Journal of Economics* 44 (2), 93–102.

Barr, N. (2020): *The Economics of the Welfare State* (6th ed). Oxford: Oxford University Press.

Bauer, M. A., A. Diederich, S. Traub, and A. Weiss (2023): "When the Poorest Are Neglected–A Vignette Experiment on Need-Based Distributive Justice", *SSRN Working Paper* 4503209.

Benabou, R., and E. A. Ok (2001): "Social Mobility and the Demand for Redistribution: the POUM Hypothesis", *Quarterly Journal of Economics* 116 (2), 447–487.
Benker, M., J. P. Krügel, and S. Traub (2017): "Risk Taking Under Different Welfare-State Regimes", *FOR 2104 Discussion Paper* No. 2017–11.
Bernard, M., F. Hett, and M. Mechtel (2016): "Social Identity and Social Free-Riding", *European Economic Review* 90, 4–17.
Bird, E. J. (2001): "Does the Welfare State Induce Risk-Taking?", *Journal of Public Economics* 80 (3), 357–383.
Bock, O., I. Baetge, and A. Nicklisch (2014): "hroot: Hamburg Registration and Organization Online Tool", *European Economic Review* 71, 117–120.
Boulding, K. E. (1962): "Social Justice in Social Dynamics", in E. B. Brandt (ed.): *Social Justice*, 73–92. Prentice Hall, Englewood Cliffs, N.J.
Bourhis, R. Y., and A. Gagnon (2001): "Social Orientations in the Minimal Group Paradigm", in R. Brown, and S. Gaertner (eds.): *Intergroup Processes: Blackwell Handbook in Social Psychology* (Vol. 4), 89–111. Oxford: Blackwell.
Brewer, M. B. (1979): "In-Group Bias in the Minimal Intergroup Situation: A Cognitive-Motivational Analysis", *Psychological Bulletin* 86, 307–324.
Buckley, E., and R. Croson (2006): "Income and Wealth Heterogeneity in the Voluntary Provision of Linear Public Goods", *Journal of Public Economics* 90 (4), 935–955.
Burlando, R. M., and F. Guala (2005): "Heterogeneous Agents in Public Goods Experiments", *Experimental Economics* 8 (1), 35–54.
Cagetti, M. (2003): "Wealth Accumulation over the Life Cycle and Precautionary Savings", *Journal of Business and Economic Statistics* 21 (3), 339–353.
Carroll, C.D. (1997): "Buffer-Stock Saving and the Life Cycle/Permanent Income Hypothesis", *Quarterly Journal of Economics* 112 (1), 1–55.
Castañeda, A., J. Diaz-Giménez, and J.-V. Rios-Rull (2003): "Accounting for the U.S. Earnings and Wealth Inequality", *Journal of Political Economy* 111 (4), 818–857.
Chan, K., S. Mestelman, R. Moir, and R. A. Muller (1996): "The Voluntary Provision of Public Goods under Varying Income Distributions", *Canadian Journal of Economics* 29 (1), 54–69.
Chan, K., S. Mestelman, R. Moir, and R. A. Muller (1999): "Heterogeneity and the Voluntary Provision of Public Goods", *Experimental Economics* 2 (1), 5–30.
Chen, Y., and S. X. Li (2009): "Group Identity and Social Preferences", *American Economic Review* 99 (1), 431–457.
Cherry, T. L., S. Kroll, and J. F. Shogren (2005): "The Impact of Endowment Heterogeneity and Origin on Public Good Contributions: Evidence from the Lab", *Journal of Economic Behavior and Organization* 57 (3), 357–365.
Corneo, G., and H. P. Grüner(2002): "Individual Preferences for Political Redistribution", *Journal of Public Economics* 83 (1), 83–107.
Deaton, A., and J. Muellbauer (1980): *Economics and Consumer Behavior*. Cambridge: Cambridge University Press.
De Oliveira, A. C. M., R. T. Croson, and C. Eckel (2015): "One Bad Apple? Heterogeneity and Information in Public Good Provision", *Experimental Economics* 18 (1), 116–135.
Diamond, P. A. (1967): "Cardinal Welfare, Individualistic Ethics, and Interpersonal Comparison of Utility: Comment", *Journal of Political Economy* 75 (5), 765.
Diamond, P. A., L. J. Helms, and J. A. Mirrlees (1980): "Optimal Taxation in a Stochastic Economy", *Journal of Public Economics* 14 (1), 1–29.
Diamond, P. A., and J. E. Stiglitz (1974): "Increases in Risk and Risk Aversion", *Journal of Economic Theory* 8, 337–360.
Diederich, A., M. Wyszynski, and S. Traub (2020): "Need, Frames, and Time Constraints in Risky Decision-Making", *Theory and Decision* 89 (1), 1–37.
Domar, E. D., and R. A. Musgrave (1944): "Proportional Income Taxation and Risk-Taking", *The Quarterly Journal of Economics* 58, 388–422.
Eaton, J., and H. Rosen (1980): "Optimal Redistributive Taxation and Uncertainty", *Quarterly Journal of Economics* 95 (2), 357–364.

Eisenhauer, J. G. (1997): "Risk Aversion, Wealth, and the DARA Hypothesis: A New Test", *International Advances in Economic Research* 3 (1), 46–53.

Elster, J. (1992): *Local Justice. How Institutions Allocate Scarce Goods and Necessary Burdens.* New York: Sage.

Esping-Andersen, G. (1990): *The Three Worlds of Welfare Capitalism.* Princeton: Princeton University Press.

Fischbacher, U. (2007): "z-Tree: Zurich Toolbox for Ready-Made Economic Experiments", *Experimental Economics* 10 (2), 171–178.

Fisher, J. R., M. Isaac, J. W. Schatzberg, and J. M. Walker (1995): "Heterogeneous Demand for Public Goods: Behavior in the Voluntary Contributions Mechanism", *Public Choice* 85 (3), 249–266.

Fochmann, M., and K. Hemmerich (2014): "Real Tax Effects and Tax Perception Effects in Decisions on Asset Allocation", *SSRN Working Paper* 2435935.

Fochmann, M., D. Kiesewetter, and A. Sadrieh (2012a): "Investment Behavior and the Biased Perception of Limited Loss Deduction in Income Taxation", *Journal of Economic Behavior & Organization* 81, 230–242.

Fochmann, M., D. Kiesewetter, and A. Sadrieh (2012b): "The Biased Effect of Aggregated and Disaggregated Income Taxation on Investment Decisions", *Journal of Institutional and Theoretical Economics* 168, 519–546.

Friedman, M. (1953): "Choice, Chance, and the Personal Distribution of Income", *Journal of Political Economy* 61 (4), 277–290.

Friend, I., and M. Blume (1975): "The Demand for Risky Assets", *American Economic Review* 65, 900–922.

Frohlich, N., and J. A. Oppenheimer (1992): *Choosing Justice. An Experimental Approach to Ethical Theory.* Berkely: University of California Press.

Gächter, S., and C. Thöni (2005): "Social Learning and Voluntary Cooperation among Like-Minded People", *Journal of the European Economic Association* 3 (2–3), 303–314.

Gaertner, W., and E. Schokkaert (2012): *Empirical Social Choice: Questionnaire-experimental Studies on Distributive Justice.* Cambridge: Cambridge University Press.

Geary, R. C. (1950): "A Note on 'A Constant-Utility Index of the Cost of Living", *Review of Economic Studies* 18 (1), 65–66.

Gibrat, R. (1931): *Les Inégalités Économiques.* Paris: Recueil Sirey.

Goette, L., D. Huffman, and S. Meier (2006): "The Impact of Group Membership on Cooperation and Norm Enforcement: Evidence Using Random Assignment to Real Social Groups", *American Economic Review* 96, 212–216.

Grochulski, B., and T. Piskorski (2010): "Risky Human Capital and Deferred Capital Income Taxation", *Journal of Economic Theory* 145 (3), 908–943.

Guiso, L., P. Sapienza, and L. Zingales (2006): "Does Culture Affect Economic Outcomes?", *Journal of Economic Perspectives* 20 (2), 23–48.

Gunnthorsdottir, A., R. Vragov, and K. McCabe (2007): "The Meritocracy as a Mechanism to Overcome Social Dilemmas", *MPRA Paper* No. 2454.

Harsanyi, J. C. (1953): "Cardinal Utility in Welfare Economics and the Theory of Risk-Taking", *Journal of Political Economy* 61, 434–435.

Harsanyi, J. C. (1955): "Cardinal Welfare, Individualistic Ethics, and Interpersonal Comparisons of Utility", *Journal of Political Economy* 63 (4), 309–321.

Harsanyi, J. C. (1975a): "Nonlinear Social Welfare Functions: Do Welfare Economists Have a Special Exemption from Bayesian Rationality?", *Theory and Decision* 6, 311–332.

Harsanyi, J. C. (1975b): "Can the Maximin Principle Serve as a Basis for Morality? A Critique of John Rawls's Theory", *American Political Science Review* 69, 594–606.

Harsanyi, J. C. (1978): "Bayesian Decision Theory and Utilitarian Ethics", *American Economic Review (Papers and Proceedings)* 68, 223–228.

Hülle, S., S. Liebig, and M. J. May (2018): "Measuring Attitudes toward Distributive Justice: The Basic Social Justice Orientations Scale", *Social Indicators Research* 136 (2), 663–692.

Huggett, M., and G. Ventura (1999): "On the Distributional Effects of Social Security Reform", *Review of Economic Dynamics* 2 (3), 498–531

James, E. (1993): "Why do Different Countries Choose a Different Public-Private Mix of Educational Services?", *Journal of Human Resources* 28 (3), 571–592.

Jencks, C. (1972): *Inequality: A Reassessment of the Effect of Family and Schooling in America.* New York: Basic Books.

Kanbur, S. M. (1979): "Of Risk Taking and the Personal Distribution of Income", *Journal of Political Economy* 87 (4), 769–797.

Kerschbamer, R. (2015): "The Geometry of Distributional Preferences and a Non-parametric Identification Approach: The Equality Equivalence Test", *European Economic Review* 76, 85–103.

King, R. R., and D. E. Wallin (1990): "Individual Risk Taking and Income Taxes: An Experimental Examination", *Journal of the American Taxation Association* 12, 26–38.

Kittel, B., M. Schwaninger, and R. Szendrő (2022): "Need-based Justice Beyond Social Ties: Experimental Evidence on the Scope of the Need Principle". *FOR 2104 Working Paper* 2022–03.

Kittel, B., and S. Traub (2022): "Bedarfsgerechtigkeit oder unbedingtes Grundeinkommen? Ergebnisse aus Laborexperimenten", in Nonhoff, M., S. Haunss, T. Klenk, and T. Pritzlaff-Scheele (2022): *Gesellschaft und Politik verstehen. Frank Nullmeier zum 65. Geburtstag*, 157–172. Frankfurt: Campus.

Klor, E. F., and M. Shayo (2010): "Social Identity and Preferences over Redistribution", *Journal of Public Economics* 94 (3–4), 269–278.

Konow, J. (2001): "Fair and Square: The Four Sides of Distributive Justice", *Journal of Economic Behavior and Organization* 46, 137–164.

Konow, J. (2003): "Which is the Fairest One of All? A Positive Analysis of Justice Theories", *Journal of Economic Literature* 41, 1188–1239.

Konow, J., and L. Schwettmann (2016): "The Economics of Justice", in Sabbagh C., and M. Schmitt (eds.): *Handbook of Social Justice Research*, 83–106. Heidelberg: Springer.

Konrad, K. (1991): "Risk Taking and Taxation in Complete Capital Markets", *Geneva Papers on Risk and Insurance Theory* 16, 167–177.

Krieger, T., and S. Traub (2011): "Wie hat sich die intragenerationale Umverteilung in der staatlichen Säule des Rentensystems verändert?/Has Intragenerational Redistribution Become Less Important in Pension Systems' Public Pillar?", *Jahrbücher für Nationalökonomie und Statistik* 231 (2), 266–287.

Krieger, T., and S. Traub (2013): "The Bismarckian Factor", *CESifo DICE Report* 11 (1), 64–66.

Krügel, J. P., and S. Traub (2023): "Heterogeneity, Risk-Taking and Discrimination: An Experimental Study", *FOR 2104 Working Paper* 2023–03.

Kuijs, L. (2000): "The Impact of Ethnic Heterogeneity on the Quantity and Quality of Public Spending", *IMF Working Paper* 00/49, Washington: International Monetary Fund.

Lane, T. (2016): "Discrimination in the Laboratory: A Meta-analysis of Economics Experiments", *European Economic Review* 90, 375–402.

Lamm, H., and T. Schwinger (1980): "Norms Concerning Distributive Justice: Are Needs Taken into Consideration in Allocation Decisions?", *Social Psychology Quarterly* 43 (4), 425–429.

Lamm, H., and T. Schwinger (1983): "Need Consideration in Allocation Decisions: Is it Just?", *Journal of Social Psychology* 119 (2), 205–209.

Lillard, L. A., and R. J. Willis (1978): "Dynamic Aspects of Earning Mobility", *Econometrica* 46 (5), 985–1012.

Lucas Jr., R. E. (1988): "On the Mechanics of Economic Development", *Journal of Monetary Economics* 22 (1), 3–42.

Luttmer, E. F. P. (2001): "Group Loyalty and the Taste for Redistribution", *Journal of Political Economy* 199, 500–528.

Meghir, C., and L. Pistaferri (2004): "Income Variance Dynamics and Heterogeneity", *Econometrica* 72 (1), 1–32.

Meltzer, A. H., and S. F. Richard (1981): "A Rational Theory of the Size of Government", *Journal of Political Economy* 89 (5), 914–927.

Miller, D. (1999): *Principles of Social Justice*. Cambridge: Harvard University Press.

Mincer, J. (1970), "The Distribution of Labor Incomes: A Survey with Special Reference to the Human Capital Approach", *Journal of Economic Literature* 8 (1), 1–26.

Nicklisch, A., and F. Paetzel (2020): "Need-Based Justice and Distribution Procedures: The Perspective of Economics", in S. Traub, and B. Kittel (eds.): *Need-Based Distributive Justice*, 161–189. Cham: Springer.

Nullmeier, F. (2020): "Towards a Theory of Need-Based Justice", in S. Traub, and B. Kittel (eds.): *Need-Based Distributive Justice*, 191–208. Cham: Springer.

OECD (2011): *Divided We Stand: Why Inequality Keeps Rising*. Paris: OECD.

Okun, A. M. (1975): *Equality and efficiency: The Big Tradeoff*. Washington, D. C.: Brookings Institution Press.

Ostrom, E., R. Gardner, and J. Walker (1994): *Rules, Games, and Common-Pool Resources*. Ann Arbor: University of Michigan Press.

Paetzel, F., and R. Sausgruber (2018): "Cognitive Ability and In-Group Bias: An Experimental Study", *Journal of Public Economics* 167, 280–292.

Paravisini, D., V., R. Rappoport, and E. Ravina (2017): "Risk Aversion and Wealth: Evidence from Person-to-Person Lending Portfolios", *Management Science* 63 (2), 279–297.

Persson, T., and G. Tabellini (2000): *Political Economics: Explaining Economic Policy*. Cambridge: MIT press.

Pratt, J. W. (1965): "Risk Aversion in the Small and in the Large", *Econometrica* 32 (1/2), 122–136.

Quadrini, V., and J.-V. Ríos-Rull (1997): "Dimensions of Inequality: Facts on the US Distributions of Earnings, Income, and Wealth", *Federal Reserve Bank of Minneapolis Quarterly Review* 21 (2), 3–21.

Raphael, D. D. (1980): *Justice and Liberty*. London: Athlone Press.

Rawls, J. (1971): *A Theory of Justice*. Cambridge: Harvard University Press.

Rawls, J. (1974): "Some Reasons for the Maximin Criterion", *American Economic Review (Papers and Proceedings)* 64, 141–148.

Rochet, J.-C. (1991): "Incentives, Redistribution and Social Insurance", *Geneva Papers on Risk and Insurance Theory* 16 (2), 143–165.

Romer, P. M. (1994): "The Origins of Endogenous Growth", *Journal of Economic Perspectives* 8 (1), 3–22.

Sadrieh, A., and H. A. Verbon (2006): "Inequality, Cooperation, and Growth: An Experimental Study", *European Economic Review* 50, 1197–1222.

Sahota, G. S. (1978): "Theories of Personal Income Distribution: A Survey", *Journal of Economic Literature* 16 (1), 1–55.

Sandmo, A. (1977): "Portfolio Choice, Asset Demand and Taxation: Comparative Statics with Many Assets", *Review of Economic Studies* 44 (2), 369–379.

Sharpe, W. F. (1964): "Capital Asset Prices: A Theory of Market Equilibrium under Conditions of Risk", *The Journal of Finance* 19 (3), 425–442.

Shayo, M. (2009): "A Model of Social Identity with an Application to Political Economy: Nation, Class, and Redistribution", *American Political Science Review* 103, 147–174.

Sinn, H.-W. (1995): "A Theory of the Welfare State", *Scandinavian Journal of Economics* 97, 495–526.

Sinn, H.-W. (1996): "Social Insurance, Incentives and Risk Taking", *International Tax and Public Finance* 3, 259–280.

Soroka, S., K. Banting, and R. Johnston (2006): "Immigration and Redistribution in a Global Era", in S. Bowles, P. Bardhan, and M. Wallerstein (eds.): *Globalization and Egalitarian Redistribution*, 261–288. Princeton: Princeton University Press.

Stone, R. (1954): "Linear Expenditure Systems and Demand Analysis: An Application to the Pattern of British Demand", *Economic Journal* 64 (255), 511–527.

Swenson, C. W. (1989): "Tax Regimes and the Demand for Risky Assets: Some Experimental Market Evidence", *Journal of the American Taxation Association* 11, 54–76.

Tajfel, H., M. G. Billig, R. P. Bundy, and C. Flament (1971): "Social Categorization and Intergroup Behaviour", *European Journal of Social Psychology* 1 (2), 149–178.

Tajfel, H., and J. Turner (1979): "An Integrative Theory of Intergroup Conflict", in W. G. Austin, and S. Worchel (eds.): *The Social Psychology of Intergroup Relations*. Monterey: Brooks-Cole.

Traub, S. (2020): "Perspectives for a Theory of Need-based Distributive Justice", in S. Traub, and B. Kittel (eds): *Need-Based Distributive Justice: An Interdisciplinary Perspective* 1–20. Cham: Springer Nature.

Traub, S., and B. Kittel (eds.) (2020): *Need-Based Distributive Justice: An Interdisciplinary Perspective*. Cham: Springer Nature.

Traub, S., and J. P. Krügel (2017): "Risk Taking and the Welfare State: Some Experimental Evidence", *FOR 2104 Discussion Paper* 2017–1.

Traub, S., M. Schwaninger, F. Paetzel, and S. Neuhofer (2023): "Evidence on Need-Sensitive Giving Behavior: An Experimental Approach to the Acknowledgment of Needs", *Journal of Behavioral and Experimental Economics* 105, 102028.

Turner, J. C., M. A. Hogg, P. J. Oaks, S. D. Reicher, and M. S. Wetherell (1987): *Rediscovering the Social Group: A Self-Categorization Theory*. Oxford: Blackwell.

van Dijk, F., J. Sonnemans, and F. van Winden (2002): "Social Ties in a Public Good Experiment", *Journal of Public Economics* 85, 275–299.

Varian, H. R. (1980): "Redistributive Taxation as Social Insurance", *Journal of Public Economics* 14 (1), 49–68.

Wagner, H. M. (1958): "Advances in Game Theory", *American Economic Review* 48, 368–387.

Wakker, P. P. (2008): "Explaining the Characteristics of the Power (CRRA) Utility Family", *Health economics* 17 (12), 1329–1344.

Walzer, M. (1983): *Spheres of Justice. A Defense of Plurality and Equality*. New York: Basic Books.

Yaari, M. E., and M. Bar-Hillel (1984): "On Dividing Justly", *Social Choice and Welfare* 1, 1–24.

Part IV
Differentiation

Chapter 9
Need and Street-Level Bureaucracy: How Street-Level Bureaucrats Understand and Prioritize Need

Kai-Uwe Schnapp

Abstract Because the government is responsible for the social welfare of its citizens on behalf of society, it writes laws, establishes procedures, and hires individuals to implement social policy at the local level. This local implementation requires street-level bureaucrats (SLBs) to objectify individual needs and exercise discretion in addressing them. In this chapter, I will show how the individual norms and values of SLBs play a role in the process of objectification at the street level and how differences in conceptions and attitudes among SLBs shape individual street-level decision-making. I will also show how education, societal debates, such as those inspired by court rulings, as well as the work environment of SLBs, shape how they view need and deservingness and how they see their role in the welfare system. As a result, the government must not only draft welfare laws. It must also explain its intentions and ensure that SLBs in the welfare system have the space to continually reflect on the normative foundations of their work if they are to properly take on the state's responsibility for the welfare of its more needy citizens.

9.1 Introduction

In the middle of the twentieth century, after the end of World War II, the United Nations issued the Universal Declaration of Human Rights (UDHR). It first and foremost establishes the civil liberties, freedom of thought, and religion, and safeguards for every individual that comes with the rule of law. Article 22, however, also explicitly talks about social rights:

> Everyone, as a member of society, has the right to social security and is entitled to realization, through national effort and international cooperation [. . .], of the economic, social, and cultural rights indispensable for his dignity and the free development of his personality. (UN General Assembly 1948)

K.-U. Schnapp (✉)
Faculty of Business, Economics and Social Sciences, Universität Hamburg, Hamburg, Germany
e-mail: kai-uwe.schnapp@uni-hamburg.de

B. Kittel, S. Traub (eds.), *Priority of Needs?*,
https://doi.org/10.1007/978-3-031-53051-7_9

Societies at large and governments in particular are defined as responsible for ensuring the basic social well-being of their citizens as a way to realize distributive justice. And many nation-states that (re)wrote their constitutions after the adoption of the UDHR explicitly mention social rights and thus the responsibility of government for distributive justice (Daly 2019).

When a government takes on responsibility for distributive justice as a prerequisite for the basic social well-being of all its citizens, it has to answer the following questions: What do citizens need? Who deserves to be helped? Who gets what and how much? Traub (2020, p. 5) understands the process of answering these questions as objectification: A process in which a society develops an objective understanding of individual need. Objectification of need takes place at different levels of government. General need levels are usually defined at the national level through law-making, as are the rules defining who is eligible for welfare state measures (Nullmeier 2020, p. 140). The implementation of these rules, however, usually takes place at the local level. Here, street-level bureaucrats (SLBs), as Lipsky (1980, p. 3) famously named them, adapt the legal provisions to individual members of society and their individual situations of need. It is exactly this level of objectification as street-level decision-making that I am interested in this chapter. I am especially interested in the individual attitudes of SLBs toward need and deservingness.

Why is this a relevant focus? The general decisions about who gets what are made by law, but the details of what matters to individuals in a society are decided at the local or, as Lipsky would have it, at the street level. Although the goal of welfare state policy is to provide assistance that is tailored to individual situations of need, neither the law nor administrative rules have the capacity to efficiently regulate every detail of every individual case. Hence, SLBs are given discretion to judge individual welfare cases and develop individually fitting welfare solutions (Frederickson 2010; Grimm and Plambeck 2013; Lipsky 1980; Maynard-Moody and Musheno 2003; Zacka 2017). In the implementation of welfare state policy, SLBs translate the abstract legal definition of who gets what into concrete individualized decisions. This translation necessitates properly reacting to a plethora of individual need constellations.

Discretion means that SLBs individually make judgments and take decisions that directly affect the recipients of government aid. With discretion, the following question arises: Which rules will SLBs' use to guide their judgments and decisions. Of course, their procedures have to follow certain laws and regulations. But, as stated above, laws and regulations are not a sufficient basis for appropriate decisions. There needs to be room to adjust their decisions to individual circumstances. So what guides SLBs when filling this discretionary space? There are different sets of norms, values, and attitudes that guide this decision-making at the level of the individual SLB. Those can be, e.g., general public service norms such as the norm of impartial treatment of everyone, or general societal norms like reciprocity and solidarity. These general norms are of course not effective as such. They need to be turned into individually held norms, values, and beliefs that are relevant for street-level administrative decision-making. As individually held norms, they "act as filters that regulate how bureaucrats make use of their discretionary power" (Zacka 2017, p. 12).

This situation confronts the government with a principal-agent problem (Lane 2005, Chapters 2 and 5; McCubbins et al. 1987). Since SLBs require discretion to be effective implementers of the law, there is room for bureaucratic drift: SLBs may not implement exactly what a legislative authority intended but may instead add their interpretation of what the proper level of support is in any given case. In addition to legal stipulations on levels of support, SLBs are also subject to the core governmental norm of impartiality. Again, "the government" or "the legislative authority" is not around everywhere to make sure that all law is executed impartially. While the government can try to monitor street-level implementation to some extent, it also needs to trust SLBs to faithfully interpret and impartially execute the substance of the law. It is therefore relevant to understand how SLBs think about need and deservingness as well as other principles of justice because these attitudes are likely to affect their decision-making.

To summarize, individual welfare cases are dealt with and decided upon by street-level bureaucrats. These SLBs need to be able to apply discretion to appropriately react to the large variety of individual need situations and to what they perceive as individual deservingness. Hence, when interpreting and acting upon the law, SLBs' individually held norms have an impact on their actual street-level actions. In this article, I therefore address the following research questions:

What norms and values do SLBs hold that are relevant to their work? How do these norms and values compare to abstract public service norms or general societal norms and values? And what are the effects of these attitudes at the decision-making stage?

To address these questions, I will first start with a brief literature review. I will then synthesize the results of two empirical studies carried out under the auspices of the DFG Research Group "Need-Based Justice and Distribution Procedures." In one study, Brian Dietrich and I interviewed SLBs in German job agencies, asking about their understanding of need and deservingness, their perception of the discretionary space they possess, and the perceptions they have of their clients. In the second study, Brian Dietrich, Michael Jankowski, Markus Tepe, and I conducted survey experiments with public servants and respondents from the general population. These experiments were designed to discover which deservingness norms are effective in hypothetical welfare decisions.[1]

In this chapter, I will proceed as follows. First, I will look at how the literature discusses distributive justice with a focus on the concepts of *need* and *deservingness*. The purpose of this reflection is to provide a sensitizing understanding (Blumer 1954, pp. 7–9) of these concepts for the interpretation of the interview data. I will then provide a brief overview of the concepts of *discretion* and *impartiality*.

[1] Throughout this chapter, I will use "we" whenever I directly refer to the process and results of the joint work with Brian Dietrich, Michael Jankowski, and Markus Tepe. I will use "I" when I refer to ideas that developed on the basis of this joint work while writing this text.

In addition to sensitizing to these concepts, this will show in more detail what judgments need to be made by SLBs and where in the process of interpreting the law individual norms and values are likely to become important. It will also highlight the importance of the civil service norm of impartiality for discretionary decision-making. The next part of the chapter reviews and synthesizes our work on those norms and values based on interviews with German job agency workers as well as the abovementioned survey experiments. I will close with a summary and some policy implications of our research.

9.2 Need and Deservingness

9.2.1 *What Do They Need?*

Konow (2003) and Miller (1976) suggest distinguishing between three principles of distributive justice: equity, equality, and need. Equity posits recognizing each person's actions and qualities so that those who contribute more to the commonwealth should receive more. Equality postulates that every citizen is entitled to the same amount of resources as any other. The need principle states that every citizen should have enough resources to participate at some minimum level in the everyday social, political, and economic life of society.

In this volume, Kittel and Traub (p. 2) describe the equity principle as "liberal in the sense of allowing each individual to decide how much to contribute [. . .] and thus to autonomously determine her share." They critically remark that the equity principle has no provisions for those who cannot provide for themselves. Regarding Article 22 of the UDHR, a strict application of the equity principle is very likely to violate the social rights mentioned therein. The application of the equity principle will not lead to moral equality (Gosepath 2003, p. 288) concerning "the economic, social and cultural rights indispensable for [a person's—KUS] dignity and the free development of his personality" (UN General Assembly 1948). The equity principle therefore cannot provide a system of redistribution that ensures that every human being can live with dignity. This is especially true when equity is understood as a strict quid-pro-quo. If someone ought to reciprocate but cannot due to individual circumstances, then that person will not receive the means for a dignified life. What is needed is a more open understanding of reciprocity, that is, reciprocity according to one's ability: Those who are not able to reciprocate still deserve and get the means for a dignified life. In this sense, Boulding interpreted society as a big family "from whose table not even the humblest of her members shall be excluded" (Boulding 1962, p. 83). While a strict application of equity cannot ensure this outcome, in the real world of SLBs, the equity principle may still have currency. It may be relevant, for example, in considerations of how deserving different people are of societal help, as I will argue in the section on deservingness below. Therefore, it will be relevant to look for equity-related arguments and actions in the empirical observations we collect.

The principle that has been most intuitively understood as fairness, at least since the French Revolution, is the equality principle. For a democratic welfare state under the rule of law, it is obvious that equality before the law and equality in democratic processes are inviolable principles. Regarding basic social security, the potential of the concept seems to be more mixed. If understood as strict economic equality, the equality principle becomes potentially illiberal and implies a tendency toward heavy state interventions in vested individual material rights (Frankfurt 2015, p. 9). It may therefore stand in contrast to many provisions in modern constitutions as well as in the UDHR that guarantees everyone the right to personal freedom and self-determination. The equality principle may also lead to some need not being adequately met. For example, a person living with a very serious illness needs much more than her equal share to fulfill her basic need (Frankfurt 2015, pp. 34ff). Importantly, the focus on equality is misguided insofar as it focuses on the question of comparative wealth instead of asking whether a person has enough in comparison to her own standards, as Frankfurt (2015) argues. He even asserts that a focus on equality may have alienating effects (2015, p. 12). Instead of making a comparative assessment of a person's economic or social status, he advocates for the principle of having "enough," asserting that having a "sufficient amount" to sustain oneself is the crucial factor. He also argues that it is not inequality as such that is objectionable, but its possible consequence that some people have too little (Frankfurt 2015, pp. 40–41, also see Kittel and Traub in this volume, p. 8) In this understanding, economic inequality is unethical if it leads to poverty and suffering. Hence, the challenge for distributive justice is not to give the same to all but to make sure that everyone has enough. This means, according to Frankfurt, having so much that it is reasonable to be content with the number of resources, especially the money, one possesses (Frankfurt 2015, p. 48). Differences in individual wealth beyond this level are acceptable when they do no harm (p. 36–38) and as long as excessive wealth is prevented (p. 5).

Given these arguments, the equality principle does not seem to be the ideal principle to ensure distributive justice either. Frankfurt presents an important argument as to why it still enjoys broad support in society. "The very concept of having an equal share", he writes, "is itself considerably more transparent and intelligible than the concept of having enough," and "a theory of equality is much easier to articulate than a theory of sufficiency" (Frankfurt 2015, p. 15). He finally claims that these characteristics of the equality principle lead to a situation where the sufficiency principle is under-researched and under-specified (ibid.), a position that Miller (1999) and Sen (2009) support. For all these reasons, it is plausible to expect that the equality principle will be found in the value set of SLBs.

While a basic justification for the sufficiantarian position has been given above, an important question remains: When is it reasonable to be content? or What is sufficient to fulfill a person's need? Frankfurt gives an initial answer to this question: "A contented person regards having more money as inessential to his being satisfied with his life" (Frankfurt 2015, p. 53). But, when can a person be satisfied with her life? I will interpret Gosepath's (2015) focus on the conditions that make a dignified life possible as such a criterion. Thus, if a person can live with dignity, she has reason to be satisfied with her life. A system of redistribution (a welfare system) must then ensure that every person can live with dignity. Need would then be defined as what is necessary for a dignified life. But, we still need an answer to the question of what is needed to live such a life. According to Fraser, there is and can be no universal understanding of this. Consequently, the answer to this question must be socially constructed specifically for different social contexts (Fraser 1989). Need must be objectified in the words of Traub (2020, p. 5). What this means is very nicely illustrated by Adam Smith's reference to the value of leather shoes in the England of his time, which even the poorest person needs (Smith 1976, pp. 869–870, also see Kittel and Traub in this volume, p. 12). In light of Gosepath's argument on dignity, I define it as follows: If a creditable person has a reason to be ashamed, she cannot live a dignified life. If in a given time and age something is needed to not be ashamed, people ought to possess this good or service to be able to live a dignified life. According to Smith's quote, that something was leather shoes in his time (and in his perception). The possession of a smartphone may be a contemporary correlate to Smith's "leather shoes."

Nussbaum introduced the idea of capabilities to express that it is participation in society as such and the freedom to choose one's actions that are important. For her, "[...] all [the people in a nation—KUS] should get above a certain threshold level of combined capability, in the sense not of coerced functioning but of substantial freedom to choose and act" (Nussbaum 2011, p. 5). It is not difficult to see how Nussbaum's argument connects to dignity. Not having the freedom to choose and act and not being equally respected does obviously imply at least diminished dignity, if not a total lack of it (also see Sen 1988, pp. 272–274, 276–279). Doyal and Gough add "physical survival" as a precondition for the successful experience of personal autonomy and based on that suggest the following intermediate need to secure physical survival: (1) nutritional food and clean water, (2) protective housing, (3) a non-hazardous work environment, (4) a non-hazardous physical environment, (5) safe birth control and child-bearing, and (6) appropriate health care. They further argue that (1) a secure childhood, (2) significant primary relationships, (3) physical security, (4) economic security, and (5) appropriate education are the intermediate needs that must be fulfilled for human autonomy (Doyal and Gough 1991, pp. 157–158).[2]

As stated above, article 22 of the UDHR makes safeguarding the dignity of people the responsibility of states and thus governments. A very stringent wording of this responsibility can be found in the German Constitution (Barak 2013, pp. 369–370):

[2] There is a great number of philosophers and social theorists who define and justify "lists of needs" as well as discuss concepts such as "autonomy and social relations" and a "decent life." An instructive overview can be found in Siebel and Schramme (2020).

> Human dignity shall be inviolable. To respect and protect it shall be the duty of all state authority (Basic Law of the Federal Republic of Germany, Article 1, Sentence 1).

Dignity is treated here as an absolute right, something that cannot be limited by any law, the government, or the constitution itself, and "all state authority" is obliged to protect the dignity of all citizens (Barak 2013, pp. 369–370). This has been strongly emphasized in the decision of the German Constitutional Court (the Bundesverfassungsgericht) on sanctions used to make welfare clients more cooperative. In its decision, the Court forbids sanctions that deduct more than 30% of the cash transfers prescribed by social law. It based this decision on the following guiding principles:

> The human dignity that forms the basis of the claim [to a dignified minimum standard of living—KUS] is available to all and is not lost even through allegedly "undignified behavior" (Sanktionen im Sozialrecht, 5.11.2019, Guiding Principles).

It added later in the verdict:

> The independent securing of a person's existence is not a condition for his or her being entitled to human dignity; rather, creating the conditions for a self-reliant life is part of the state's duty to protect under Article 1 (1) sentence 2 of the Basic Law (Sanktionen im Sozialrecht, 5.11.2019, Paragraph 123).

Hence, the state and the government are there to protect "the autonomy of the individual will, the freedom of choice, and the freedom of man to act as a free creature" (Barak 2021, p. XX). Barak's formulation and that of the Constitutional Court link directly to Nussbaum's capabilities approach, on the one hand, and to German welfare law, on the other. German welfare law is geared toward enabling "Teilhabe." "'Teilhabe' means comprehensive inclusion in the essential processes and institutions of society" (Nullmeier 2015, p. 102). "Teilhaben" as a verb means being an active and valued part of society, being able to participate politically, economically, and socially. Forst adds that people have to be treated "not as objects, but as subjects" of the welfare process (Forst 2015, p. 51).[3] Hence, SLBs who implement welfare state policy are the ones tasked with protecting the dignity of their clients and enabling their social and political participation. In doing so, they objectify need against the backdrop of abstract principles and, to refer back to Fraser (1989), to a concrete historical and societal context. It is therefore likely that SLBs will provide justifications or take particular positions when asked about their understanding of need and the role of the state in its fulfillment.

[3] This comprehensive understanding is not captured by the English terms "participate" and "participation." To be precise, it would have to be "comprehensive political, economic, and social participation as a valued member of society." In the remainder of this text I will use "social and political participation" for the German "Teilhabe".

9.2.2 Who Is Deserving of Help?

"Who are the worthy?" is the title of a chapter in Maynard-Moody and Musheno's book on street-level bureaucrats (2003). Their preliminary answer is based on interviews with different types of SLBs in the USA, namely police officers, teachers, and social workers. According to the authors, SLBs regard their citizen-clients as worthy of help when they "have genuine needs, are of good character, and are motivated to respond to treatment" (p. 106). They also assert that "street-level workers are making normative judgments about who gets what from government" (Maynard-Moody and Musheno 2003, p. 106). In the literature, one finds at least two sources of norms that could guide those judgments. One source is sociocultural norms held by members of a given society. The other source is norms specific to public service. I will briefly review both to sensitize for the empirical work below.

Drawing on a historical overview of perceptions of the welfare state and especially its clients, van Oorschot (2000) describes five criteria for deservingness that are present in people's attitudes toward the poor and help for the poor. He refers to them as the CARIN criteria. They are (1) control, (2) attitude, (3) reciprocity, (4) identity, and (5) need (van Oorschot 2000, p. 36). *Control* refers to a (poor) person's responsibility for her situation or the level of control she can exert over this situation. *Attitude* asks how a poor person responds to help offered to her and understands a certain type of attitude as appropriate, e.g., compliance and gratefulness. *Reciprocity* refers to whether a poor person has contributed to society in exchange for help. This reciprocity can be material, like contributions to the social security system, or behavioral, like cooperative behavior in interactions with welfare bureaucracies. Such cooperative behavior includes being forthcoming with information and documents, being punctual at appointments, etc. *Identity* refers to how socially distant a person perceives themselves to be from the poor person. The question asked is whether a poor person belongs to the same or a similar group as the respondent. The criteria for this sameness are not clearly defined, but regularly used ones are ethnicity, culture, family ties, etc.[4] Finally, *need* refers to the amount of support and reasons for support, e.g., health condition, being disabled, and the existence of dependent children (for all five criteria see van Oorschot 2000, p. 36; van Oorschot and Roosma 2017, pp. 13–14). Deservingness understood this way has been shown to explain support for and opposition to social benefits among citizens and politicians alike (Gee et al. 2017; Reeskens and van der Meer 2019; Reeskens and van Oorschot 2013; van Oorschot 2000; van Oorschot and Roosma 2017).

---

[4] The argument is similar to the sociological homophily argument made by McPherson et al. (2001) with regard to social networks. People tend to connect more easily with or support people who share certain social characteristics with them. Furthermore, to my understanding, the CARIN argument is a priori oriented toward the insiders of national welfare systems (Miller 2016, p. 27). People, who are not eligible for support within a national welfare system, are thus a priori not even part of the consideration.

According to studies of general population attitudes toward welfare recipients, people use the CARIN criteria as deservingness criteria. Jilke and Tummers (2018) have developed a set of criteria directly geared toward analyzing SLBs' decision-making. The authors call their criteria "deservingness cues" (p. 226) to indicate that they are principles SLBs use, often unwittingly, to understand and evaluate situations in which they have to make decisions. These cues refer to the person's need for help (need deservingness), whether the person has earned help (earned deservingness), and the efficiency and effectiveness of giving help to the person (resource-deservingness) (Jilke and Tummers 2018, p. 226ff). Need deservingness means that "clients are seen as worthy of investing time and resources because they are perceived to be in need of help" (Jilke and Tummers 2018, p. 231), e.g., as a consequence of career shocks beyond their control, educational or health disadvantages. Charity and altruism are motives to help in the case of need deservingness. Earned deservingness means that "clients are seen as worthy [of help—KUS] because they have shown high effort" (Jilke and Tummers 2018, p. 231) to manage their situation (also Gee et al. 2017). This effort can include activities prior to the need situation as well as efforts undertaken while already in need. The underlying motive for support under earned deservingness is perceived reciprocity on the part of the needy person, or at least a serious attempt to act reciprocally. A classic example of earned deservingness is somebody who diligently worked her whole adult life only to find herself unemployed shortly before retirement. Finally, resource-deservingness means that "clients are seen as worthy [...] because they are perceived to be successful in terms of bureaucratic success criteria" (Jilke and Tummers 2018, p. 231). The underlying motive here is giving someone the chance to use limited (government) resources efficiently and effectively. An exemplary case of a resource-deserving person is someone with a solid educational and professional background who is unemployed. If such a person just needs a bit of additional training in order to quickly find a new job, this person would be seen as resource-deserving. Examples of the application of all three cues can be found throughout the interview excerpts in Maynard-Moody and Musheno (2003), though the authors do not categorize their examples in these terms.

Oorschot's criteria and the cues by Jilke and Tummers are closely related, with two exceptions: Resource-deservingness does not play an obvious part in the CARIN criteria while identity as a criterion for deservingness is not at all visible in Jilke and Tummer's cues. I will briefly discuss both later in this section. Before that, I will map the rest of the criteria/cues onto each other.

Need deservingness (Jilke and Tummers 2018) and the level of need (van Oorschot 2000) are similar concepts—they both refer to people not having enough resources and needing (solidary) help from society. Earned deservingness is related to the equity principle. However, I mean here a soft understanding of equity as the concept is not an absolute quid pro quo but rather a willingness to reciprocate according to one's abilities. This, as outlined earlier, makes it similar to earned deservingness (Jilke and Tummers 2018) and reciprocity (van Oorschot 2000). People in need earn the support of society when they reciprocate in a socially acceptable manner, e.g., diligently use educational or job opportunities. In this understanding, attitude (van Oorschot 2000) also overlaps with reciprocity and thus earned-deservingness. Having the "right" attitude, e.g., being cooperative in the welfare process or being thankful, is interpreted as effort on the part of the welfare client, thus earning her a supportive attitude from decision-makers. Control (van Oorschot 2000) is a more complicated concept as it has different connotations when absent and when present. When people in need have no control over their situation, they are likely to be perceived straightforwardly as persons in need. Control is no longer relevant, and need deservingness takes over. However, when a person in need has control, this diminishes the perceived relevance of the observed need. This perception brings the principle of equity into play, which then justifies society offering less help then objectively needed.

From the perspective of distributive justice, resource-deservingness is an obvious outlier as a deservingness cue. This cue points at administrative efficiency and effectiveness as norms guiding administrative action (Frederickson 2010, p. 10), not distributive justice. However, to better understand and contextualize the reasoning of SLBs when they make justice-related judgments, I will characterize how SLBs think about efficiency and effectiveness.

The normative evaluation of identity as a deservingness criterion is altogether different: Treating claimants differently based on ascriptive criteria is discrimination. This runs against all principles of distributive justice discussed above, including those given in the UDHR. One may normatively argue that a person should be grateful for society's help and therefore make differences between claimants based on their gratefulness, though this is contested. One may also argue that a person's responsibility for being in need (control) should play a role in distributive justice and therefore make differences between claimants based on control, though this is contested. It is not, however, possible to justify street-level decision-making based on ascriptive criteria like ethnicity, nationality, or belonging to a certain family. Such criteria are illegitimate as the basis for making differences between claimants as the public service has to be impartial vis-a-vis all constituents (Frederickson 2010; Rothstein and Teorell 2008; Svara and Brunet 2020, pp. 355–356). Therefore, identity does not and cannot feature in the administration-oriented cues suggested by Jilke and Tummers (2018).

Impartiality reflects a societal commitment to equality (Mendus 2008, p. 423). As Barry (1989) argues, in the public sphere, a society's moral and legal rules are usually required to be impartial. Impartiality here means "that in deciding how to allocate the resource, we ignore all personal attributes [...] that are irrelevant to the problem at hand" (Moreno-Ternero and Roemer 2006, p. 1419). In the private sphere, individuals are entitled to show more concern for family members than for strangers, for example (Mendus 2008, p. 427). However, individuals who occupy public service positions are strictly required to act impartially while in those roles (Mendus 2008, p. 427). In the context of social welfare, impartiality requires that administrative discretion in allocating welfare benefits is free from discrimination. An impartial welfare system will treat everyone equally under equal circumstances (Rothstein and Teorell 2008) but act upon differences where circumstances require differential treatment to achieve similar outcomes. Frederickson (2010) similarly argues that unequal cases must be treated unequally in order to achieve socially equitable outcomes. Public servants, therefore, need to differentiate, for example, between parents and people without children to achieve the intended outcome of helping and supporting individuals in a way that suits their individual need. After all, that is why discretion is a regular feature of administrative action—so that SLBs can judge individual welfare cases as they see fit and develop individually suitable welfare solutions (Frederickson 2010; Grimm and Plambeck 2013; Lipsky 1980; Maynard-Moody and Musheno 2003; Zacka 2017). Differences made based on ascriptive criteria like age, gender, ethnicity, and religion, however, do not lead to more appropriate policy responses to individual need. They lead to discrimination. This is corroborated by comprehensive anti-discrimination and equal-opportunity laws that are in place in many developed democracies (OECD 2015).

Despite this normative basis, the literature suggests that impartiality is not a given in street-level bureaucracy. There is evidence that identity matters in the public service. Reeskens and his coauthors (Reeskens and van der Meer 2019; Reeskens and van Oorschot 2013), for example, show that foreign origin is among the three most important conditions for reduced welfare solidarity. Pfaff et al. (2021) provide evidence in support of religious discrimination among civil servants in the American public school system. Grohs et al. (2016) sent requests to German municipal administrations while varying the sender's gender and ethnic background (Turkish and German). Their results indicate that German administrators do not commit systematic ethnic discrimination, but they find a tendency for positive discrimination when ethnicity and gender stereotypes interact. Conducting a conjoint experiment among German welfare offices, Hemker and Rink (2017) found that response rates did not vary across the treatment conditions. However, the response quality was significantly lower for requests from non-natives. Therefore, ensuring an impartial public service is an ongoing challenge (Herd and Moynihan 2018; Meier 2019).

In conclusion, public servants are normatively expected to be impartial vis-a-vis their clients in the fulfillment of their duties. Empirical research, however, shows that public servants can act in ways that are discriminatory. Public servants also follow deservingness cues based on identity, which contravene the principle of impartiality. I therefore pay particular attention to whether SLBs raise identity-related arguments in the interview data.

9.3 Norms Guiding SLBs' Decision-Making and Their Effects

In this section, I will review and integrate the results of two empirical studies we conducted to investigate conceptions of need and other justice principles relevant to German public servants in general and SLBs in welfare administrations in particular.

Surveys are insufficient for describing and understanding processes of social recognition. The close inspection of "everyday interactions, and social practices within institutions and organizations are also required" (Nullmeier 2020, p. 198). We therefore conducted qualitative interviews with caseworkers at German Jobcenters to ask them about the norms they hold, what their understanding of need and deservingness is, and how they discuss these principles and related issues. We took a qualitative approach in order to delve more deeply into the complex world of norms and values guiding SLBs in their everyday work. However, this approach has its limitations when it comes to exploring norms of impartiality and deservingness. Since prejudice and discrimination are possible issues here, direct questions are likely to elicit socially desirable responses that mask their true attitudes. So, to gauge the impartiality of SLBs' real decisions, whether or not there is discrimination, and how the different deservingness norms play out in welfare decisions, we designed a survey experiment that limits as much as possible socially desirable responses. By using both interviews and surveys, we can better understand the respective attitudes of SLBs and their consequences.

9.3.1 Distributive Justice, Need, and Deservingness in SLBs' Thinking

In what follows, I discuss the norms and values that drive SLBs in their everyday decision-making as a first step in this chapter toward an empirically grounded theory of need-based justice. I will briefly characterize the guided interviews we conducted with SLBs in German Jobcenters and then report our findings regarding their thinking about distributive justice, need, and deservingness.

We first used a qualitative method to reconstruct SLBs' conceptions of fairness, need, and deservingness. Our data include 37 semistructured expert interviews with employees of German employment offices (Jobcenter) conducted between March and July of 2021.[5] Jobcenters are the central institutions in Germany that provide social welfare to welfare claimants. They are responsible for job placements, job (re)qualification, and basic social security services. In mid-2021, the German Jobcenters provided services to about 4.6 million people (Bundesagentur für Arbeit 2021, p. 22).

Given their close and direct contact with welfare recipients, SLBs in Jobcenters are the most important street-level actors in the context of social welfare and the recognition of need in Germany. Conceptions of need and deservingness, whether implicit or explicit, are of particular relevance in their daily practice and consequently for the people they serve. For these reasons, we chose SLBs in job agencies as the target group for our research.

[5] The sample includes 20 female and 17 male respondents. The average age at the time of the survey was 46.6 years (youngest: 30 years, oldest: 62 years). Employees had been in their jobs for an average of 8.6 years.

To analyze the data, we applied interpretive content analysis by Mayring (2015), which combines deductive and inductive categorizations. After the end of the fieldwork, the interviews were transcribed by an external transcription agency. The data were then analyzed using MAXQDA Analytics Pro 2022.[6]

Deservingness in the World of Welfare SLBs

In our search for conceptions of need and need-based justice, we found that SLBs in German Jobcenters primarily argue and legitimize their actions based on the principle of equity or the principle of equality. Most SLBs reveal their conceptions of need when explicitly asked. However, need seems to have a supplementary character rather than being the primary driver of their decision-making. In the following, I report on these findings in more detail.

Equity-oriented SLBs take a very explicit position that clients need to do something to be seen as worthy of support from the Jobcenter and, through the Jobcenter, from society. These SLBs explicitly expect some form of reciprocity from their clients before they fully dedicate resources to them. However, perceptions of what constitutes appropriate reciprocity vary widely. At the very demanding end of the spectrum is the expectation that clients will, for example, accept job offers or additional training without complaint, regardless of quality and personal suitability, as illustrated by the following quote:

> Those who simply don't feel like turning up, who just don't want to, don't deserve to get paid here. [...] Those people should just do any of these auxiliary tasks that have a social value and otherwise there is nothing. (Interview 18, item 43)[7]

At the other end of the spectrum, expectations of reciprocity are much softer. We observe, for example, that efforts to cooperate properly with an SLB in a Jobcenter are interpreted as sufficient to make a client deserving of help. Similarly, activities that are seen as contributing to society, such as caring for children or the elderly in one's own family, are interpreted by SLBs as reciprocity:

> Well, I have single parents with four or five children. [...] Here, I really say that they don't need to provide any extra services. (Interview 24, Pos. 47)

The above quote goes on to say that this assessment changes when children stop being dependent on their parents. Then, according to the SLB, the "normal" expectations of labor market integration apply.

Obviously, arguments about control are also equity-oriented, as discussed above with reference to van Oorschot (2000). When people are responsible for the situation of hardship in which they find themselves, the equity-oriented type of SLB is much less willing to provide unwavering and comprehensive support. Having control but not using it properly is apparently interpreted as not reciprocating adequately, or not

[6] For more detail, see Dietrich and Schnapp (2023).

[7] All quotes from interviews were translated using DeepL and then edited by the author.

contributing one's fair share to the overall good of society. As Siebel and Schramme (2020, p. 37) put it, "self-inflicted need gaps are unworthy of being filled."

However, there are categories of people who are perceived as need deserving a priori, without any expectation of contribution or reciprocity. These are groups of people who structurally lack control over their welfare situation. Children are an obvious case, but so are people who are chronically ill or have certain mental health conditions. In the latter case, SLBs often expressed that such individual conditions need to be addressed before the respective clients can be asked to contribute in the labor market.

People who are perceived as having no ability to reciprocate or contribute can even counteract the effects of SLBs' equity-oriented attitude toward clients who are perceived as in control of their situation. In the following quotation, an SLB discusses a client and father of small children whose conduct had breached specific rules in such a way that they were considering pausing his welfare payments. However, because the SLB was concerned about the impact of this sanction on the client's children, they refrained from this practice:

> Yeah, and that we actually take into account what the overall structure of a family is like. If I cut a dad's benefits, will he then take the money intended for his children? So, it makes no sense for me to cut his benefits. It's only the little children who suffer afterward [...]. And that's why it would be wrong to implement a penalty here. (Interview 1, item 77)

SLBs' decision-making processes involve intricate calculations that consider various factors, including clients' social contexts (Nullmeier 2020, p. 205). This dilemma is highlighted nicely in the quotation above. While equity-oriented thinking remains an important consideration, a strict application of the principle of equity may harm those who are dependent on the client and themselves have no control over their situation. In such cases, a client in control, but with dependents may even be "saved" from the consequences of a strict expectation of reciprocity. The quotation demonstrates how detailed knowledge of a situation is a prerequisite for proper decision-making, how discretion enables SLBs to react to specific circumstances, and how normative judgments interact with these factors to shape the outcome of an individual welfare decision.

In summary, equity-focused SLBs look primarily for reciprocity and some form of social contribution from their clients. In fact, they expect clients to act reciprocally, to have the right attitude, and to actively use any control they do have. This focus implies thinking about deservingness primarily as earned deservingness. However, most SLBs do not use abstract concepts to describe their perspectives. Most refer to concrete acts of reciprocity such as cooperation, having the right attitude, and caring for children. The most explicit reference to more abstract principles is to say things like "it is only fair to do this" or "it is only fair to ask for this," where "this" always refers to an act of reciprocity or contribution. These observations are very similar to Maynard-Moody and Musheno (2003, esp. pp. 104–106) findings on SLBs in social services, schools, and the police in the United States of America.

Furthermore, SLBs' implicit understanding of equity is not a proportional one. The position taken is not that those who contribute more should receive more. SLBs' interpretation of equity is rather dichotomous, asking whether someone contributes at all and therefore deserves support or whether they contribute nothing and therefore forfeit their right to support. Clients' contributions can either be those they make in the present (i.e., by being cooperative, taking part in trainings without complaint, etc.) or those they make before the situation of need arises (e.g., using their control to try to better their situation). Finally, there are people such as the elderly, the sick, and, of course, children, who are never expected to reciprocate, but who are always seen as deserving of support because they are interpreted as structurally not being in control of their situation.

We observe a very different attitude in equality-oriented SLBs: Here, the idea prevails that everyone is entitled to some basic support from society to enable them to live a dignified life. In other words, equality-oriented SLBs see every member of society as equally deserving of some basic help regardless of their having contributed to society or reciprocated societal help. In addition, these SLBs point to the fact that Germany is a very rich society with a rich government and that both can tolerate "dragging along" some people who, for various reasons, do not contribute. The following quotes from our interviews illustrate this position:

> So, even if someone is not willing to contribute at all, we actually have to, [...] not for legal reasons, but for moral reasons, we have to [help]. Because otherwise, we don't need a social system. So basically, I think we actually have to pull everyone along for moral reasons because we are a community. (Interview 34, pos 71)

> Yes, these are cases for an unconditional basic income. These people [...] we just drag them along as a society. And actually, man, we are such a rich country, we should actually be able to do that. (Interview 34, pos. 62–63, similarly Interview 33, pos. 87 and Interview 17, item 69)

So, deservingness is not an important concept for equality-oriented SLBs. All members of society are seen as equally deserving of basic support from society, regardless of their contribution or reciprocity. I also want to emphasize the contextual component evident in these quotes. The position of being willing to help everyone, regardless of their efforts, is almost always linked to the claim that Germany is a very rich society that can easily afford to provide unconditional help at a basic level. However, none of the SLBs interviewed argued that justice as equality means an equal distribution of resources, as was suggested in Sect. 9.2.1 above. Equality for our respondents means an equal right to basic support, regardless of one's own efforts. It does not mean a right to an equal share of society's resources.

For equity-oriented SLBs, however, deservingness is important. They expect clients to contribute if they are in control of their situation, i.e., if they are generally able to go to work, get further training, etc. SLBs provide support when they observe this form of reciprocity. However, even in the eyes of this group of SLBs, there are clients who are deserving simply because they are in need and who do not have to contribute. These clients include children and adults with conditions that temporarily or permanently prevent them from giving back and contributing to society.

In sum, there are two types of SLBs. The first is equity-oriented. For these SLBs, deservingness is important. They recognize need in some cases but expect most clients who are able to reciprocate to earn their support. Thus, SLBs "exempt" certain people from expectations of reciprocity only when they perceive them as need-deserving. The second is equality-oriented. For this type, everyone is entitled to some basic support from society. In other words, everyone who comes to them is interpreted as need-deserving. There is no place in the thinking of this type of SLBs for people having to earn deservingness to get supported.

I have so far empirically covered control, reciprocity, and attitude (van Oorschot 2000), as well as need and earned deservingness (Jilke and Tummers 2018), in the thinking of SLBs. In the literature discussed in Sect. 9.2.2, I identified two more concepts, namely resource deservingness and identity, which are thought to explain SLBs' disposition regarding supporting people in need and how they perceive them as deserving of help. For both of these concepts, my argument was that they do not fit easily into a distributive justice perspective on deservingness. I have also argued that the two concepts may nevertheless influence how SLBs evaluate clients and respond to client characteristics. Therefore, I will briefly report on the empirical evidence we found with respect to these concepts.

There are indeed arguments by respondents that point at the concept of resource deservingness. However, they rarely use such arguments. And when SLBs do use them, they do so not quite in the way Jilke and Tummers (2018) defined the concept. These authors expect SLBs to see clients as resource-deserving when helping them requires little administrative effort. Yet, what we see in our interviews is a different argument. SLBs tend to save their time when dealing with those clients that they believe are unlikely to change their behavior. In this situation, particularly equality-oriented SLBs provide the material support to which clients are entitled, but beyond that leave such clients to their own devices. The time saved is then spent with clients who are judged as making an effort to change their situation but may require some additional effort on the part of the SLB. This is a kind of efficiency argument: SLBs increase their effort when they expect that effort to be effective, but save their efforts when they believe it will not be effective.

We did not find any evidence for the influence of identity in our interviews. While some SLBs admit to feeling sympathy or antipathy toward a client, there is no mention in their interviews of ascriptive criteria or other identity-based distinctions being responsible for those feelings. Yet, the results of the conjoint experiments reported below show that identity does sometimes play a role in how people think and act. This suggests that we have missed something in our guided interviews. One reason for this discrepancy could be socially desirable response behavior in the interviews, which we were able to bypass in the conjoint experiment. I will therefore return to the issue of identity in Sect. 9.3.2 and in the discussion.

First, however, I will outline how we reconstructed what need substantively means to welfare SLBs. In the next section, I will show what SLBs believe welfare clients are entitled to, what SLBs think they actually need, and what level of support SLBs consider "enough."

Need in the World of Welfare SLBs

There are two questions that we must answer in order to understand what people should be entitled to. First, we must answer the question of what purpose that entitlement should serve. The answer could be, for example, to ensure a dignified life or social and political participation ("Teilhabe"). Second, we must determine what exactly is needed to achieve a dignified life or appropriate social and political participation. The majority of SLBs listed concrete goods and services that they consider to be necessary to fulfill basic need.

SLBs' lists were usually less abstract than those found in the literature (Doyal and Gough 1991; Gosepath 2015; Nussbaum 2011). They included concrete goods and services that clients require in their daily lives, rather than abstract principles. For example, most SLBs did not use phrases like "need to have access to means of communication" or "need to be able to take part in societal communication at a currently accepted and necessary level." Rather, they simply stated that access to the internet and access to a mobile phone should be guaranteed by the state. The more general principles behind their lists of goods became visible, however, when SLBs justified them. For example, in referring to the need for a mobile phone, they pointed out that clients needed to be able to have the conversations necessary to take part in everyday life or, more concretely, to apply for jobs, etc. Another example is the very specific reference to "a cup of coffee" (see the quote from interview 5, point 41 below). It is clear in the context of the interview that the SLB is talking about enabling a client to sometimes do things that are common or standard in our society. She does not frame that in abstract terms but uses the very concrete example of a cup of coffee while meeting someone in a café.

Comparing the list-based conceptions of different SLBs, we find an implicit hierarchy of goods and services to which they believe everyone in a society is entitled. This hierarchy moves from the provision of very basic goods and services to extended social and political participation. The level of *basic need* refers to the provision of shelter, food, clothing, and health services. All respondents believe that everyone in a society is entitled to this level of need satisfaction. However, there is a small group of SLBs who limit even this physical understanding of need. This group is sometimes also willing to deprive clients of cash transfers as a sanction or simply to limit what goods the money can be spent on. They argue that clients can meet their physical need for food with food vouchers instead of cash transfers, and that even with just vouchers "*there still is something in the fridge at the end of the month* [emph. KUS]" (Interview 23, item 103). These SLBs are often aware of the fact that with this "treatment," they are depriving clients of the ability to freely decide for themselves how to use the resources provided by the welfare state, and thus, to practice a "self-reliant life" in the words of the Constitutional Court. The following quote demonstrates this reasoning:

> That's a bit of disenfranchisement, but I would say, for example, that we should go more for food vouchers and less for cash benefits. That people don't have the opportunity to buy cigarettes and alcohol and all that kind of thing. (Interview_18, item 33).

Such SLBs accept this restriction as an unavoidable cost of getting the client to be more cooperative and therefore explicitly contravene the Constitutional Court's decision on sanctions.

There is also much agreement among SLBs on the second level of need satisfaction, which is *basic social and political participation*.[8] This level includes the ability to use basic infrastructure services such as public transport or means of communication such as telephones and the internet, but also basic access to education and training. All of this is nicely summed up in the following quote:

> [...] a basic provision does not include a huge villa—yes, that is clear, [...] but a decent, normal flat [...], that is, one that can also be heated, where warm tap water is normally available [...] and then of course food anyway. [...] Means of transport must be made possible to some extent, that is the person must be able to get to the prospective employer, must perhaps be able to go shopping by bus or whatever. Communication must be guaranteed to a large extent, that is telephone or internet connection, for which the costs must perhaps be taken into account. Everything around education and school, in particular, has to be guaranteed [...]. (Interview 15, item 35)

Compared to the previous two levels, a smaller number of SLBs agree that having sufficient resources for *extended social and political participation* is a reasonable entitlement. Extended social and political participation means being able to use sports clubs and cultural facilities such as theaters and cinemas, museums, and zoos. According to our respondents, it should also include having a coffee in a museum or something to eat when visiting a zoo. Respondents describe this belief in the following terms:

> There are opportunities, and I think everyone should have them, for example, to do reduced sports. [...] Yes, well, exercise, further education, public transport, and culture. Discounted admission to museums, theatres and movies. (Interview 25, item 3)

> But that you just say, okay, I'm going to meet someone in a café [...], and then I can afford a cup of coffee [...]. There might be an extra budget or something so that people are not so isolated because of their tight budget. (Interview 5, item 41)

The second quote in particular is about enabling greater participation and giving people a degree of autonomy and self-determination in the sense of Nussbaum (2011). The activities of having a coffee and visiting cultural institutions are not understood as a means to an end—they are themselves the end: Self-determined participation in public life.

The following quote shows a slightly different interpretation of extended social and political participation and also of the question of what is instrumental and what is an ultimate goal.

> I believe that this is social participation and it gives people the opportunity [...] to become part of the whole. If I tell someone that they can go to the zoo or the stadium for free once a

[8] As outlined in Sect. 9.2.1, "social and political participation" refers to the German concept of "Teilhabe," a term used in the German welfare law.

Table 9.1 Need Levels

	Need level	Example
	comprehensive social and political **participation**	autonomy and freedom of action, larger amenities and comforts
	extended social and political **participation**	access to sports and cultural activities, the ability to pay for minor amenities and comforts, a limited degree of autonomy
	basic social and political **participation**	education, mobility (public transport), communication (internet, telephone)
	basic need	food, shelter, clothing, medical care

Source: Based on Dietrich and Schnapp 2023, Abbildung 1

> year, then they have had fun, but we probably won't solve anything. But if I give someone the opportunity to play soccer in a sports club without it costing him anything, [...] then that leads to someone participating, someone building up a network, having social contacts, and so on and so forth. (Interview_4, item 39)

We can clearly see that "becoming part of the whole" and "building networks", i.e., increasing the social embeddedness of people, are interpreted here as the ultimate goal, while financing sports, movies, or a cup of coffee is only instrumental to reach this goal.

The final level of need satisfaction is *comprehensive social and political participation.* It includes an even higher level of self-determination and freedom of action. Clients should be given the means to freely shape their lives and participate in things that are considered "normal" in society. For example, clients should be able to freely plan for leisure time, including, e.g., short trips or even simple holidays at a nearby seaside resort.

> Well, I think a holiday has to be part of it, [...] you have to be able to go on a trip somehow. (Interview 6, item 55).

Table 9.1 summarizes the different levels of need.

Interim Summary

So, what norms and values drive SLBs in their everyday decision-making? Our interviews revealed that SLBs either focus on equality- or equity-related norms of distributive justice. In developing perspectives on how to work with their clients, they do not neatly distinguish between principles of distributive justice and dimensions of deservingness. These concepts are closely intertwined in the SLBs' everyday thinking and actions. However, deservingness as such is primarily an issue for equity-oriented SLBs. Equality-oriented SLBs, on the other hand, do not ask the question "Who is deserving?" because, in their normative worldview, everyone is.

With respect to what constitutes need, we observed different views. These views, when aggregated across SLBs, lead to a hierarchical picture of need. On one end of the spectrum, we find a very basic understanding of need as physical need, as described by Doyal and Gough (1991). On the other end, there is a very broad and complex understanding of need. Here SLBs aim to enable welfare recipients to participate in the everyday undertakings of society, including not only education and communication but also, for example, basic leisure activities. The focus is on enabling people to live in dignity (Gosepath 2003) and to give them freedom of choice and action (Nussbaum 2011, p. 24).

Only a small number of SLBs we interviewed interpreted comprehensive social and political participation as a need that society and thus the state must fulfill. Many SLBs rather take positions that are in line with Boulding (1962) and Frankfurt (2015): Society has to meet a basic level of need beyond which fairness should be based on performance-related differences between people. Above established thresholds of need, SLBs mostly understand fairness as allowing someone to use resources in proportion to their own contribution. Accordingly, many SLBs believe that there are legitimate differences in wealth between the working population and those receiving welfare. The latter should not be better off than working people.

In the following section, I will review the results from our conjoint experiment that address the deservingness discussion from a second perspective. In doing so, I will focus particularly on identity as a deservingness cue, since we did not learn anything about this issue in our guided interviews.

9.3.2 *Effects of Norms and Attitudes Held by SLBs: A Conjoint Experiment*

To systematically test deservingness criteria from the literature and uncover how impartial real welfare decisions are, we conducted an online survey with a paired conjoint experiment (Hainmueller et al. 2014) that simulates discretionary decisions in a welfare context. Respondents had to choose between two fictional welfare recipients with exceptional need. The fictional characters vary on a set of attributes that reflect their deservingness in terms of the CARIN criteria (van Oorschot 2000) and the deservingness cues outlined by Jilke and Tummers (2018). Legally, both recipients are equally entitled to financial support to meet their exceptional need. However, at the time of the decision, the case manager's budget is only sufficient to support one person. After being provided with details on a pair of clients, respondents are asked to decide which of the two welfare recipients should receive financial assistance. The decision setting is repeated eight times, with the characteristics of the recipients randomized in each new round.

In the conjoint experiment, we use eight attributes to describe the clients who apply for financial assistance (see Table 9.2). The first three attributes provide information about the candidates' need, control, and attitude/reciprocity. As the CARIN

Table 9.2 Individual Attributes Used to "Construct" Welfare Applicants of Different Types

		Attribute	Values
Deservingness	Need	Household Composition	1 Adult, 2 Adults, 2 Adults + 1 Child, 1 Adult + 2 Children, 2 Adults +3 Children
	Earned	Reason for Unemployment	Disabled due to accident, Bankruptcy of the employer, Voluntary dismissal, Fired for wrongdoing
		Supportive Behavior	Low, Medium, High
Identity		Ethnic Background	Germany, France, Romania, Turkey, Syria, Vietnam
Supplementary Attributes		*Gender*	*Male, Female*
		Age	*23 years, 36 years, 48 years, 57 years*
		Education Level	*Unskilled, Vocational Training, Technical College, University*
		Duration of Unemployment	*0.5 years, 1 year, 1.5 years, 3 years*

Source: Based on Dietrich et al. (2023, Tab. 1)

criteria overlap with the deservingness cues described by Jilke and Tummers, these attributes cover need and earned deservingness at the same time. The fourth attribute is related to identity (the "I" in CARIN). To increase the realism of the choice situation, we added a supplementary set of attributes to our vignettes (see Table 9.2). These were four attributes that are commonly known to SLBs when interacting with their clients: age, gender, education, and duration of unemployment.

Our online survey reached 1,937 individuals from the German population, of whom 352 self-identified as working in the public sector. In addition, we surveyed 510 students from a College for Public Administration and 127 from a College for Social Work. In what follows, I present results for the two student groups and the group of public servants within the general population.[9]

Findings

Figure 9.1 reports results for the deservingness criteria as well as the effect of identity for all groups of respondents. In the first panel, I plot household composition as a measure of perceived need deservingness. It is obvious that all groups of respondents react strongly to the perceived need, with strong differences across treatments and moderate differences across respondent groups. Household composition is the strongest determining factor. Singles and childless couples are unlikely to receive financial support from respondents, while lone parents and families with three children are comparatively more likely to receive support. Social work students show the most decisive response with a much higher probability of

[9] For more details, see Dietrich et al. (2023).

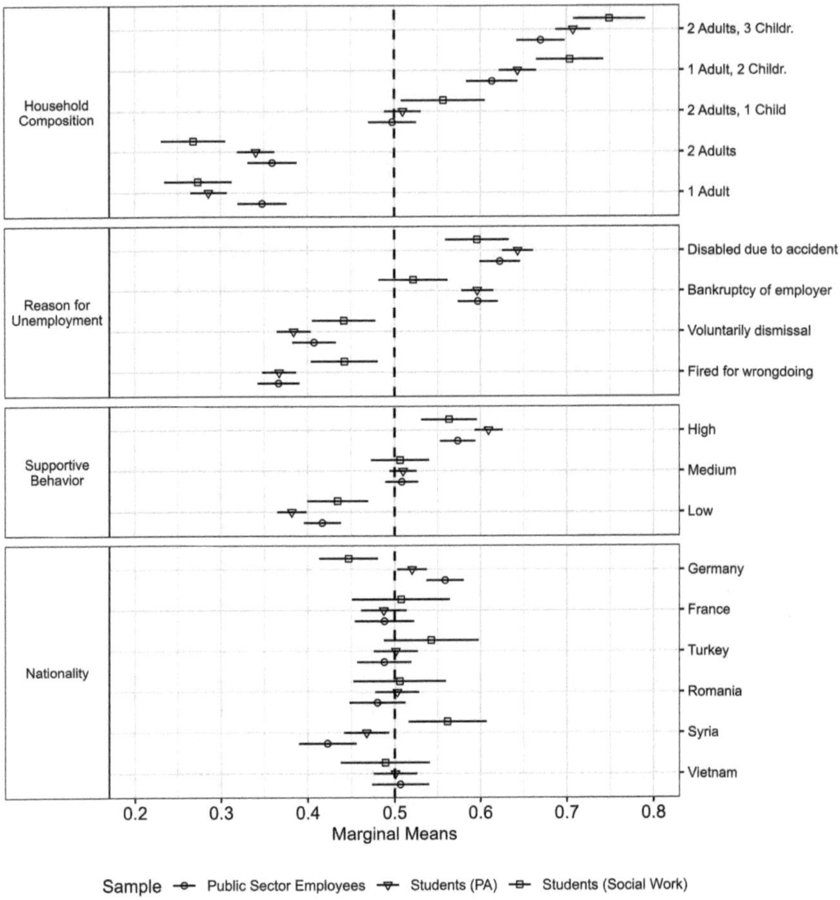

Note: The figure shows the marginal means of the 4 substantively important treatments. Marginal means greater than 0.5 indicate an above-average probability of being chosen for financial assistance. Marginal means under 0.5 indicate a below-average probability. The horizontal lines are 95% confidence intervals. Source: Based on data of Dietrich et al. (2023).

Fig. 9.1 Deservingness Criteria for Civil Servants in the General Population and Two Student Populations

supporting families with more than one child and, at the opposite end of the scale, being highly restrictive with households without children. Public servants from the general population show the weakest response or the least differentiation with respect to need. But even in this group, there is a very clear pattern of responding to the perceived need deservingness of the fictional clients.

We also find clear patterns for the response to earned deservingness, although these responses are somewhat weaker than those to need deservingness. Involuntary unemployment of a fictional client increases the likelihood of support from respondents. All groups of respondents have a significantly higher likelihood of helping clients who became unemployed because of an accident or due to their employer going bankrupt than helping clients who became unemployed by choice. Social work students again stand out, but this time because of their less decisive responses. They are less likely to help when clients lose a job due to misconduct or voluntary resignation, but at a lower rate than other groups (the differences are not significant at the 95%-level). I will return to this observation shortly, but will first look at client interaction as the third deservingness criterion in the experiment.

Client interaction behavior as the third dimension of earned deservingness also has a clear impact on all groups of respondents. Highly cooperative behavior leads to a significantly higher likelihood of receiving financial assistance than low cooperation (lack of reciprocity). It seems that respondents are sanctioning lack of reciprocity. While cooperative behavior in client interactions is rewarded by all groups, social work students are the least "punitive" when clients are uncooperative, i.e., are not reciprocating.

I will now briefly interpret these results in light of the findings from the guided interviews presented in Sect. 9.3.1 I attribute the differences observed between social work students and the other groups of respondents to a stronger orientation toward equality among social work students. Unfortunately, we do not have data on these attitudes from our survey. However, given that the School of Social Work is a Protestant college, i.e., an institution where the concept of charity is highly valued, it is plausible to find a stronger equality orientation among these students than among the other groups of respondents. A stronger orientation toward equality as the focal concept of distributive justice implies, according to the discussion above, understanding everyone in need as equally deserving. Assuming this interpretation is true, that would also mean that social work students were less or not at all likely to apply earned deservingness in their decision-making.

This leaves us with identity as the last substantively relevant item tested in the experiment. Though there is clearly evidence of identity-related differentiation in the literature (see Sect. 9.2.2), I was not able to find any signs of that in the guided interviews. This makes observing identity-related decision criteria in the conjoint experiment all the more important.

The attribute "ethnic background" contains different nationalities that vary in their alleged cultural proximity to the majority (German) community. We use France as the country of origin of a fictional recipient with high cultural proximity to Germany. Immigrants of Turkish origin represent the largest migrant population in Germany. Although large parts of this population live in Germany for three or more generations, recent research shows that they are still perceived as culturally very different from the majority population (Diehl et al. 2013). Immigrants from Romania experience numerous culturally loaded stereotypes in Germany and are also supposed to represent a culturally more distant group than Turkish people. Finally, Syria and Vietnam are the two countries of origin with the highest cultural distance from Germany. While Syria could have taken this position alone, we used Vietnam as a comparison group to examine whether a Muslim background influences decision-making.

If identity is important in our respondents' thinking, then this should show up in their responses to fictional clients' countries of origin. This response is plotted in the fourth panel of Fig. 9.1. The fourth panel shows the weakest effects of all the panels, and most effects are not statistically significant. But two countries of origin stand out: Germany and Syria. Respondents from the public sector in the general population survey and public administration students seem to slightly favor German clients while at the same time being significantly less likely to give the requested financial assistance to clients of Syrian origin. Social work students show an inverse pattern. They slightly disadvantage people with a German background and positively discriminate against Syrians and people of Turkish origin (where the latter effect is not significant).

The results for members of the public sector and public administration students are consistent with the empirical literature, as discussed in Sect. 9.2.2. At the same time, this means that SLBs' observed behavior is not in line with the expectations of impartiality we have of public officials. The results for social work students are unexpected given the available empirical literature: This group is less likely to give financial assistance to clients of German origin while slightly favoring people from Syria. This finding needs to be examined further, as in our project we did not collect the data needed to validly interpret this observation.

Interim Summary
Empirical results show that deservingness criteria have effects on the (potential) decisions people make in welfare contexts. The strongest driver for differentiating between clients is need deservingness, but attributes of earned deservingness are almost as important. Identity, as a normatively undesirable deservingness criterion, also plays a role. We find a tendency of positive discrimination for Germans and discrimination against Syrians among public servants sampled from the general population and in the group of public administration students. We find the inverse pattern in social work students. It bears mentioning that the identity-based effects are smaller than the effects of need and earned deservingness.

The observations on need and earned deservingness are consistent with the findings from the guided interviews. The statistical analysis corroborates that perceptions of need and deservingness are relevant in SLBs' decision-making. The results on identity show that we missed an important aspect of SLBs' attitudes in the guided interviews. The fact that we find the potential to discriminate against certain welfare clients based on their identity and despite their need shows, as Herd and Moynihan (2018) and Meier (2019) have pointed out, that ensuring an impartial public service remains a challenge.

9.4 Discussion and Conclusion

Nullmeier (2020) presented 10 theses on the further development of a theory of need-based justice in the last chapter of "Need-based Distributive Justice: An Interdisciplinary Perspective" (Traub and Kittel 2020). In this discussion, I will revisit the research results presented above through the lens of these theses to show how our results contribute to a positive theory of need-based justice.

In the introduction to this chapter, I wrote that in the Universal Declaration of Human Rights, societies in general and governments in particular are defined as responsible for the basic social well-being of their citizens. Starting from there, I briefly outlined how governments fulfill this obligation by creating welfare laws and implementing them. In addition, I briefly explained why SLBs using discretion is an inevitable part of this implementation process and then asked what else beyond the law is guiding SLBs' use of discretion.

In the context of a theory of need-based justice, this is an important question. According to Nullmeier (2020, p. 198), such a theory needs to make reference to the process by which need is socially and politically recognized. While taking law-making and the setup of welfare institutions for granted, this research focused on the individual role of SLBs in objectifying need (Kittel and Traub in this volume, p. 13) and especially on the SLBs' understanding of deservingness and need as important influences in this process of objectification.

Equity and Equality in SLBs' Thoughts About Deservingness
In our search for conceptions of need, we found that SLBs in German Jobcenters first ask whether a client is deserving of societal support before determining the substance of their need. With respect to deservingness, SLBs argue and legitimize their positions based on the principle of equity or the principle of equality.

Deservingness proper is an issue primarily for equity-oriented SLBs. In this regard, they distinguish between two types of clients. On the one hand, there are clients who are in control of their situation. When that is the case, SLBs often interpret need gaps as self-inflicted and possibly deny societal support to such clients (Nullmeier 2020, p. 204). What equity-oriented SLBs expect from clients with control over their situation, according to the interviews, is a minimum amount of reciprocity in the process of receiving help and some form of contribution to society. In other words, if for an SLB "the origins of need gaps are decisive for the role that need plays as a criterion of justice" (Nullmeier 2020, p. 204), then clients who they perceive as having control over their situation, and thus as being responsible for their situation of need, have to earn solidary help from society rather than being entitled to it. On the other hand, according to equity-oriented SLBs, there are clients who are not in control of their need situation, such as children and people with disabilities. Such clients are perceived as deserving help without any preconditions.

When SLBs are equality-oriented, they perceive everyone as being equally entitled to some of society's resources, independently of what they contribute. This understanding of equality is not a distributional one, but one of being equally entitled as a member of society to have one's basic need met. Equality-oriented SLBs strongly agree with the argument of the German Constitutional Court that the government cannot cut 100% of welfare payments as a sanction without depriving people of the basic support they unconditionally deserve as human beings. In line with this argument, equality-oriented SLBs logically have no use for the concept of deservingness. They see everyone in need as deserving of society's help because it is society's responsibility to support all of its members who are in need. Different conceptions of deservingness do not make sense from this perspective, nor does the understanding that support must be "earned."

These differing positions among SLBS are usually well-known to them. They are also aware, and actively discuss in the interviews, that the equity-oriented position is sometimes not in line with the Constitutional Court's thinking on this issue. As this hints at broader societal discussions on this matter, I will return to this topic in more detail later, after a brief summary of SLBs' construction of need levels.

A Hierarchy of Need

"The core element of the concept of need", according to Nullmeier (2020, p. 204), "is the notion of something that is necessary, compelling, imperative, indispensable, essentially required—something that goes beyond mere desires or preferences and takes precedence over desires" (Nullmeier 2020, p. 191). The SLBs in our interviews share this view. They seem to also agree with Boulding that there should be a social minimum (Boulding 1962, p. 83) or a floor constraint as observed by Frohlich and Oppenheimer (1990) in their experiments. Yet, "it is one thing to establish the principle of social minimum, it is quite another thing to determine where this minimum shall be set" (Boulding 1962, p. 83).

In our interviews, we found that SLBs had different reference points for answering the question of what constitutes the minimum. Some SLBs opted for a subjective definition, basing their understanding of a sufficient provision of welfare on how satisfied their clients were with "what they have." Some SLBs were even amazed at how little some clients needed to be satisfied. Others provided their own list of goods needed to cover basic need.

Differences in opinion between SLBs are to some extent explained by how important certain general principles are to them. The more SLBs are concerned with concepts like dignity, self-determination, autonomy, and self-reliance, the higher the level of goods and services they see as necessary for the state and society to provide even "the humblest of their members" (Boulding 1962, p. 83). Hence, across SLBs we see a hierarchical pattern of what is perceived as a "legitimate need." The spectrum ranges from very basic physical need to quite abstract need that, if fulfilled, enable welfare recipients to participate socially and politically ("Teilhabe") in the "normal" undertakings of their society. These include not only education and communication but also certain levels of leisurely activity. Thus, while "hierarchies of needs or comprehensive lists of basic needs [...] do not offer indications as to when needs can be regarded as satisfied" (Nullmeier 2020, p. 200), SLBs obviously have their personal interpretation of what is sufficient and rely on this individual understanding while objectifying individual need.

A Social Debate on Need

Observing the reality of need objectification in welfare administrations reveals that "deciding which criteria of justice to apply in a situation" depends partly "on the individual characteristics of the persons acting or judging" (Nullmeier 2020, p. 205). Observing this reality also shows that SLBs as a group reflect the complexity of the philosophical and social science debates about need levels and need satisfaction. Individually, most SLBs are unwittingly "strong pluralists" (Nullmeier 2020, p. 196). That means "they focus not on all, but a subset of justice principles" (ibid.) as guiding principles of their day-to-day work. Most of them individually have a favorite narrative with respect to deservingness, mostly based on equality or equity, which they combine with a particular understanding of what a person needs. As a group, however, SLBs seem to exhibit a pluralistic conception of need, as on aggregate, I find all justice principles represented in SLBs' thinking.

With this pluralistic thinking, SLBs reflect ongoing societal debates about what constitutes a just welfare system. This is nicely summarized in the following quote:

> There was once [...] Mr. Dübel, who was shown and portrayed on TV. And he was a totally satisfied unemployed person who had rabbits (laughs) in his apartment and took care of them, that was his whole life. And he didn't want to work, he didn't want to. And [...] that was probably a relatively big discussion, caused a lot of hatred. And there are people who are triggered by that, also here among the colleagues. So many people in Germany are triggered and upset when someone doesn't want to work but still wants money. [...]. I realize that it doesn't upset me that much, and I always think, [...] these people are content with what they have, and we can easily take them along as a society. (Interview_34, pos. 62–63)

Following the German Constitutional Court's decision against the use of monetary sanctions within the welfare system, discussions about entitlements and the welfare state have only intensified, as many of our interviews show. It illustrates Fraser's (1989) observation that the meaning of distributive justice is actively and continuously being constructed by societies. Yet, there are limits set for this construction by, e.g., constitutions and the UDHR. The Constitutional Court's ruling and justification of this ruling are examples of that. The dissatisfaction we observed among some SLBs with this ruling points to the fact that the normative basis for the Constitutional Court's ruling is not equally shared by everyone working in the welfare system. This could be interpreted as the need to discuss this normative basis more extensively within welfare state institutions. The goal of such a discussion being to develop a better understanding of the absolute position of dignity within the Basic Law of Germany (Barak 2013, p. 196), and of the ensuing obligation of all state authority to protect the dignity of all citizens, e.g. by securing the provision for basic need for all (needy) citizens.

The differences in attitudes among SLBs also have practical consequences in their day-to-day decision-making. I raised the question in the introduction of how the attitudes of SLBs affect their individual-level welfare decisions, given the scope they have for discretion. The conjoint experiments showed that certain characteristics of clients related to their perceived need and deservingness did indeed influence the decisions made by our respondents. The qualitative interviews provide clues as to the reasons for these differences. As our respondents reported in their actual treatment of clients in addition to their attitudes, I find that their thinking has direct consequences for their treatment of clients. This highlights that the characteristics of SLBs within the system, and not just the clients' characteristics, can have a significant impact. If clients encounter SLBs who are equality-oriented, then they are likely to receive broadly supportive treatment. If clients encounter SLBs who are equity-oriented, then it makes a difference how much control clients are perceived to have over their situation and how reciprocal their actions are perceived to be. And these "situational, social and personal characteristics together determine the extent to which the principle of need is met" (Nullmeier 2020, p. 205).

Practical Consequences
So, what are the practical consequences of our research? As the government is responsible for the social well-being of its citizens, it writes relevant laws, establishes procedures, and hires people to take care of the local implementation of social policy. Local implementation of social policies implies that SLBs are significantly responsible for the objectification of individual need and require discretion to be able to successfully cater to that need. As demonstrated above, individual norms and values do matter in this process. This raises questions about the origins of decision-makers' principles. As the different responses to need between social work and public administration students suggest, education is likely to make a difference. Societal discourse inspired, e.g., by court rulings and their justifications, also matters. Finally, SLBs' job environment, the house culture, as well as discussions among SLBs form how they view need and deservingness and how they view their role in the welfare system. Thus, governments should not only write the laws. They should also explain their intentions clearly to the public and make sure that SLBs administrating welfare claimants continuously have the space to discuss the concrete technicalities and normative foundations of their work (Durant and Rosenbloom 2020; Rosenbloom 2005; Svara and Brunet 2005, 2020). In other words, the process of socially constructing need understandings, levels, and thresholds should be actively orchestrated to support the development of a common understanding among those who implement need-oriented social policy on a day-to-day basis.

Open Research Questions
That said, questions still remain about street-level objectification and street-level fulfillment of need. As Nullmeier asserts, "there can be no theory of need-based justice without reference to a process by which needs are determined as socially or politically recognized" (Nullmeier 2020, p. 198). In this chapter, I first and foremost looked at the attitudinal conditions of this process of objectifying and politically recognizing need. Future research will have to determine more precisely how SLBs make those decisions and the influence of their individual normative beliefs. In addition, more work is needed to understand how SLBs' individual characteristics, such as type and level of education, affect their behavior and how their own life experiences, e.g., of social hardship, shape how they perform their roles. Furthermore, while this chapter investigated individual attitudes toward need and deservingness, there was no space to address the interaction of these attitudes. Future research could explore in more depth how these different attitudes interact in specific cases. In particular, the chapter leaves open questions about the consistency of SLBs' normative convictions. Are equity-oriented SLBs more restrictive than equality-oriented SLBs with respect to their understandings of need satisfaction?

How do SLBs' understandings of their roles as caseworkers, welfare workers, and public servants interact with these attitudes? And finally, how do SLBs understand or interpret the discretionary space left to them? Do they see themselves as having discretion to begin with and, if so, how do they fill and reflect on this room to maneuver? And, finally, what effects do these factors have at the level of individual decision-making, i.e., at the level where need is objectified through an administrative process?

Acknowledgments This research was funded by the Deutsche Forschungsgemeinschaft as part of the DFG Research Group 2104 (FOR 2104) "Need-based Justice and Distribution Procedures" (project code Schn 1282/5-1).

References

Barak, A. (2013): "Human Dignity: The Constitutional Value and the Constitutional Right", *Proceedings of the British Academy* 192, 361–380.

Barak, A. (2021): "Foreword", in E. Daly (ed.): *Dignity Rights: Courts, Constitutions, and the Worth of the Human Person*, XIX–XXII. Philadelphia: University of Pennsylvania Press.

Barry, B. (1989): *Justice as Impartiality*. Oxford: Oxford University Press.

Basic Law for the Federal Republic of Germany, as amended September 29th 2020 (BGBl. I S. 2048). https://www.gesetze-im-internet.de/englischgg/

Blumer, H. (1954): "What Is Wrong With Social Theory?", *American Sociological Review* 19 (1), 3–10.

Boulding, K. E. (1962): "Social Justice in Social Dynamics", in K. E. Boulding, W. K. Frankena, P. A. Freund, A. Gewirth, and G. Vlastos (eds.): *Social Justice*, 73–92. Englewood Cliffs: Prentice Hall.

Bundesagentur für Arbeit (2021). *Blickpunkt Arbeitsmarkt–Monatsbericht zum Arbeits- und Ausbildungsmarkt* (Juni 2021). Nürnberg: Bundesagentur für Arbeit.

Daly, E. (2019): *Das Konzept der Würde*. Rosa-Luxemburg-Stiftung. Online-Publikationen. https://www.rosalux.de/publikation/id/40131/das-konzept-der-wuerde.

Diehl, C., V. A. Andorfer, Y. Khoudja, and K. Krause (2013): "Not In My Kitchen? Ethnic Discrimination and Discrimination Intentions in Shared Housing among University Students in Germany", *Journal of Ethnic and Migration Studies* 39, 1679–1697.

Dietrich, B., M. Jankowski, K.-U. Schnapp, and M. Tepe (2023): *Differentiation or Discrimination? Discretionary Decision-making of Street-level Bureaucrats FOR 2104 Working Paper* 2023-01.

Dietrich, B., and K.-U. Schnapp (2023): "Bedarfskonzepte und Gerechtigkeitsvorstellungen bei Mitarbeitenden örtlicher Sozialverwaltungen", *Zeitschrift für Sozialreform* 69 (1), 31–55.

Doyal, L., and I. Gough (1991): *A Theory of Human Need*. Houndmills: Macmillan.

Durant, R. F., and D. H. Rosenbloom (2020): "Response to James Svara and James Brunet Regarding Social Equity", *American Review of Public Administration* 50 (4–5), 358–359.

Forst, R. (2015): "Die erste Frage der Gerechtigkeit", in O. Meinefeld, D. Jugel, S. Schönfelder, and P. Siller (eds.): *Inklusion: Wege in die Teilhabegesellschaft; Konzeption und Bearbeitung*. Frankfurt/New York: Campus Verlag.

Frankfurt, H. G. (2015): *On Equality*. Princeton: Princeton University Press.

Fraser, N. (1989): "Talking About Needs: Interpretive Contests as Political Conflicts in Welfare-State Societies", *Ethics* 99 (2), 291–313.

Frederickson, H. G. (2010): *Social Equity and Public Administration: Origins, Developments, and Applications*. Armonk: M. E. Sharpe.

Frohlich, N., and J. A. Oppenheimer, (1990): "Choosing Justice in Experimental Democracies with Production", *American Political Science Review* 84 (2), 461–477.

Gee, L. K., M. Migueis, and S. Parsa (2017): "Redistributive Choices and Increasing Income Inequality: Experimental Evidence for Income as a Signal of Deservingness",*Experimental Economics* 20 (4), 894–923.

UN General Assembly (1948): *Universal Declaration of Human Rights* (217 (III) A). https://www.un.org/en/about-us/universal-declaration-of-human-rights

Gosepath, S. (2003): "Verteidigung egalitärer Gerechtigkeit", *Deutsche Zeitschrift für Philosophie* 51 (2), 275–297.

Gosepath, S. (2015): "The Principles and the Presumption of Equality", in C. Fourie, G. F. Schuppert, and I. Wallimann-Helmer (eds.): *Social Equality. On What It Means to Be Equal*, 167–185. Oxford: Oxford University Press.

Grimm, N., and J. Plambeck (2013): *Zwischen Ermessen und Vermessen: Mitarbeiterinnen und Mitarbeiter des Hamburger Jobcenters als wohlfahrtsstaatliche Akteure*. Hamburg: Hamburger Institut für Sozialforschung. https://www.diakonie-hamburg.de/export/sites/default/.content/downloads/Fachbereiche/ME/Zwischen-Vermessen-und-Ermessenweb.pdf

Grohs, S., C. Adam, and C. Knill (2016): "Are Some Citizens More Equal than Others? Evidence from a Field Experiment", *Public Administration Review* 76, 155–164.

Hainmueller, J., D. J. Hopkins, and T. Yamamoto (2014): "Causal Inference in Conjoint Analysis: Understanding Multidimensional Choices via Stated Preference Experiments", *Political Analysis* 22 (01), 1–30.

Hemker, J., and A. Rink (2017): "Multiple Dimensions of Bureaucratic Discrimination: Evidence from German Welfare Offices", *American Journal of Political Science* 61 (4), 786–803.

Herd, P., and D. P. Moynihan (2018): *Administrative Burden: Policymaking by Other Means*. New York: Russell Sage Foundation.

Jilke, S. R., and L. Tummers (2018): "Which Clients are Deserving of Help? A Theoretical Model and Experimental Test", *Journal of Public Administration Research and Theory* 28 (2), 226–238.

Konow, J. (2003): "Which Is the Fairest One of All? A Positive Analysis of Justice Theories", *Journal of Economic Literature* 41 (4), 1188–1239.

Lane, J.-E. (2005): *Public Administration and Public Management: The Principal-Agent Perspective*. New York: Routledge.

Lipsky, M. (1980): *Street-Level Bureaucracy: Dilemmas of the Individual in Public Services*. New York: Russell Sage Foundation.

Maynard-Moody, S., and M. Musheno (2003): *Cops, Teachers, Counselors*. Ann Arbor: University of Michigan Press.

Mayring, P. (2015): *Qualitative Inhaltsanalyse. Grundlagen und Techniken* (12th rev. ed.). Weinheim: Beltz.

McCubbins, M. D., R. Noll, and B. R. Weingast (1987): "Administrative Procedures as Instruments of Political Control", *Journal of Law, Economics, and Organization* 3, 243–277.

McPherson, M. J., L. Smith-Lovin, and J. M. Cook (2001): "Birds of a Feather: Homophily in Social Networks", *Annual Review of Sociology* 27, 415–444.

Meier, K. J. (2019): "Theoretical Frontiers in Representative Bureaucracy: New Directions for Research", *Perspectives on Public Management and Governance* 2 (1), 39–56.

Mendus, S. (2008): "Impartiality", in J. S. Dryzek, B. Honig, and A. Phillips (eds.): *Oxford Handbook of Political Theory*, 423–435). Oxford: Oxford University Press.

Miller, D. (1976): *Social Justice*. Oxford: Oxford University Press.

Miller, D. (1999). *Principles of Social Justice*. Cambridge: Harvard University Press.

Miller, D. (2016). *Strangers in Our Midst. The Political Philosophy of Immigration*. Cambridge: Harvard University Press.

Moreno-Ternero, J. D., and J. E. Roemer (2006): "Impartiality, Priority, and Solidarity in the Theory of Justice", *Econometrica* 74 (5), 1419–1427.

Nullmeier, F. (2015): "Inklusive Sozialpolitik und die Entwicklung des Teilhabegedankens", in O. Meinefeld, D. Jugel, S. Schönfelder, and P. Siller (eds.): *Inklusion: Wege in die Teilhabegesellschaft; Konzeption und Bearbeitung*, 92–104. Frankfurt/New York: Campus Verlag.

Nullmeier, F. (2020): "Towards a Theory of Need-Based Justice", In S. Traub, and B. Kittel (eds.): *Need-based Distributive Justice: An Interdisciplinary Perspective*, 191–208. Cham: Springer Nature.

Nullmeier, F., T. Pritzlaff-Scheele, K.-U. Schnapp, and M. Tepe (2020): "Collective Decisions on Need-based Distribution: A Political Science Perspective", in S. Traub, and B. Kittel (eds.): *Need-based Distributive Justice: An Interdisciplinary Perspective*, 133–156. Cham: Springer Nature.

Nussbaum, M. C. (2011): *Creating Capabilities. The Human Development Approach*. Cambridge: Belknap Press.

OECD (2015): *Managing a Diverse Public Administration and Effectively Responding to the Needs of a More Diverse Workforce*. Paris: OECD.

Pfaff, S., C. Crabtree, H. L. Kern, and J. B. Holbein (2021): "Do Street-Level Bureaucrats Discriminate Based on Religion? A Large-Scale Correspondence Experiment among American Public School Principals", *Public Administration Review* 81 (2), 244–259.

Reeskens, T., and T. van der Meer (2019): "The Inevitable Deservingness Gap: A Study Into the Insurmountable Immigrant Penalty in Perceived Welfare Deservingness", *Journal of European Social Policy* 29 (2), 166–188.

Reeskens, T., and W. van Oorschot (2013): "Equity, Equality, or Need? A Study of Popular Preferences for Welfare Redistribution Principles Across 24 European Countries", *Journal of European Public Policy* 20 (8), 1174–1195.

Rosenbloom, D. (2005): "Taking Social Equity Seriously in MPA Education", *Journal of Public Affairs Education* 11 (3), 247–252.

Rothstein, B., and J. Teorell (2008): "What Is Quality of Government? A Theory of Impartial Government Institutions", *Governance* 21 (2), 165–190.

Sanktionen im Sozialrecht (2019): 1 BvL 7/16 (Bundesverfassungsgericht November 5, 2019). https://www.bundesverfassungsgericht.de/e/ls20191105 1bvl000716.html

Sen, A. K. (1988): "Freedom of Choice: Concept and Content", *European Economic Review* 32 (2–3), 269–294.

Sen, A. K. (2009): *The Idea of Justice*. Cambridge: Belknap Press.

Siebel, M., and T. Schramme (2020): "Need-Based Justice from the Perspective of Philosophy", in S. Traub, and B. Kittel (eds.): *Need-based Distributive Justice: An Interdisciplinary Perspective*, 21–58. Cham: Springer Nature.

Smith, A. (1976): "An Inquiry Into the Nature and Causes of the Wealth of Nations (1776)", in R. H. Campbell, and R. S. Skinner (eds.): *The Glasgow Edition of the Works and Correspondence of Adam Smith*, vol. II. Oxford: Oxford University Press.

Svara, J. H., and J. R. Brunet (2005): "Social Equity Is a Pillar of Public Administration", *Journal of Public Affairs Education* 11 (3), 253–258.

Svara, J. H., and J. R. Brunet (2020): "The Importance of Social Equity to Prevent a Hollow Public Administration", *American Review of Public Administration* 50 (4–5), 352–357.

Traub, S. (2020): "Perspectives for a Theory of Need-Based Distributive Justice", in S. Traub, and B. Kittel (eds.): *Need-based Distributive Justice: An Interdisciplinary Perspective*, 1–20. Cham: Springer.

van Oorschot, W. (2000): "Who Should Get What, and Why? On Deservingness Criteria and the Conditionality of Solidarity Among the Public", *Policy and Politics* 28 (1), 33–48.

van Oorschot, W., and F. Roosma (2017): "The Social Legitimacy of Targeted Welfare and Welfare Deservingness", in W. van Oorschot, F. Roosma, B. Meuleman, and T. Reeskens (eds.): *The Social Legitimacy of Targeted Welfare: Attitudes toward Welfare Deservingness*, 3–33. Cheltenham: Edward Elgar.

Zacka, B. (2017): *When the State Meets the Street: Public Service and Moral Agency*. Cambridge: Belknap Press.

Chapter 10
Justice Principles, Prioritization in the Healthcare Sector, and the Effect of Framing

Adele Diederich and Marc Wyszynski

Abstract Prioritizing who to provide healthcare services seems unavoidable under conditions of scarce resources. Triage is one of the best-known approaches for establishing the criteria for healthcare allocation. Here we utilize justice distribution principles, i.e., equity, equality, and need as prioritization criteria and investigate the effects of attribute framing on healthcare allocation decisions. In particular, we discuss psychological theory and previous research on framing effects in terms of delivering and withholding services. We also present recent empirical findings demonstrating that framing influences people's preferences for justice distribution principles in healthcare.

10.1 Introduction

While building an informed theory of need-based justice in Chap. 2, we applied a psychological approach to the question of transparency, i.e., the effects of providing complete information relevant to distribution decisions and judgments. In particular, we investigated the effect of presenting information in different but objectively equivalent ways, i.e., framing effects, on judgments and decisions when identifying need. In that chapter, need was the sole distribution criterion. To meet Nullmeier's third thesis toward a theory of need-based justice "Pluralistic theories of social justice can be distinguished from monistic theories. Need-based justice is listed in all pluralistic theories of justice as one of three, four or five central criteria of social justice." (Nullmeier 2020, p. 193), we abandon the monistic view of distributive justice and adopt a pluralistic one. That is, in addition to need, we consider other principles of distributive justice for the fair allocation of resources.

A. Diederich (✉)
Department of Psychology, Carl von Ossietzky University Oldenburg, Oldenburg, Germany
e-mail: adele.diederich@uni-oldenburg.de

M. Wyszynski
University of Bremen, Bremen, Germany
e-mail: m.wyszynski@uni-bremen.de

B. Kittel, S. Traub (eds.), *Priority of Needs?*,
https://doi.org/10.1007/978-3-031-53051-7_10

In psychology, the pluralistic view of distributive justice has become the rule rather than the exception. Although early models and empirical work in social psychology primarily focused on equity as the sole distribution principle (Adams 1965; Homans 1958; Walster et al. 1973), Deutsch (1975) and others soon recognized that other principles may well play a role in determining distribution outcomes. For instance, a fair allocation of resources may also occur according to needs, ability, effort, accomplishments, reciprocity, a specified minimum threshold (Deutsch 1975, p. 139), and other principles. Deutsch (1975) focused on three main principles of equity, equality, and need, which he considered *equally* important. Although scholars have since regarded the three principles as equally important, the equity principle has received by far the most attention in research. In particular, formal models were developed that only accounted for equity; need was treated as just an add-on (Diederich 2020). The list of proposed justice principles was extended over time, and, depending on the discipline, relabeled or reinvented. Sabbagh et al. (1994), for instance, refined and disaggregated the three "main" principles into the following: arithmetic equality, equality of results, and equality of opportunities; primary needs and secondary needs (in line with Murray 1938; requirement of Thesis 1 of Nullmeier 2020); and equity in terms of effort, contribution, and ability. Note that they differentiate between distribution principles and distributive rules, which are the subprinciples. Leventhal (1976) complemented the three principles with additional ones such as the promise rule and the legality rule, which, however, he did not discuss further, and instead lumped together and labeled as *other*. Leventhal proposed a weighted additive model to determine a person's deserved outcome. Note that both Deutsch and Leventhal called the equity principle a *contribution* principle. Other proposed principles are *entitlement* (Liebig and Sauer 2016; Lerner 1975; Miller 1979) and *accountability* (Konow 1996, 2001). See Konow (2003) and Törnblom and Kazemi (2015) for a summary and comprehensive list of principles. In this chapter, we include equity, equality, need, and others (similar to Leventhal 1976, in our research, we label any additional principles besides the three main principles as "other").

Furthermore, Nullmeier's second thesis emphasizes that empirical research is essential for the development of a theory of need-based justice (Nullmeier 2020, p. 193). Accordingly, we apply empirical tests to study need-based distribution in the context of healthcare services. Distributing healthcare services to patients according to some criteria is common practice in medicine, with the severity of the disease as a crucial criterion for being treated first (triage). However, there are many more criteria that have been discussed in research and in practice to determine who gets the service and who gets the service first. This is known as prioritization in medicine.

This chapter is organized as follows. We first summarize the major debates regarding prioritization in medicine and will focus on the aforementioned distributive justice criteria. We then summarize findings from several studies that investigate the general public's opinions about and attitudes toward healthcare distribution principles. Finally, we show how the framing of survey items and questions can affect opinions about the distribution principles.

10.2 Prioritizing Healthcare Services

Physicians have always prioritized patients. Patients usually experience the consequences of this in terms of waiting times. In Germany, scientific discourse and public discussions about prioritizing healthcare services started relatively late in comparison to other countries like the Scandinavian countries, Israel, the United Kingdom, New Zealand, and the Netherlands (Diederich et al. 2009). While the specific reasons for these discussions are different for each country, fairness featured prominently in all of them.

Without going into all aspects of prioritization (see e.g., Cochrane 2016), one important reason for the cautious discussion in Germany was the fact that citizens confused prioritization with rationing of healthcare services. That is, many citizens believed a patient would not get the service at all rather than simply having to wait for it. In December 2020, during the COVID-19 pandemic, this changed drastically. Now, almost all German citizens understand what prioritization means: A rank order of who should be vaccinated first according to some criteria, including preexisting health conditions (sickest first; need), age (oldest first; equity), and system importance (people working in important positions first, e.g., healthcare professionals, police, and emergency forces; equity). Even the term triage, invented long before the nineteenth century, is familiar to many as a list of criteria according to which patients are treated first, second, etc., or not at all. In early 2022, the distribution of PCR (polymerase chain reaction) tests to detect COVID-19 infections was prioritized, again according to some criteria. Obviously, once criteria for distribution are proposed, they are contested, for example, with respect to fairness.

In the following, we briefly summarize the academic debate on the criteria we included in our empirical study. In particular, we consider equity in terms of age; personal responsibility for health outcomes; social responsibility, including instrumental value, of a person (responsibility for family members and people working in system-important positions); socioeconomic status; the healthcare needs of a person; and equality in terms of chance. Note that we leave out economic criteria like costs of a treatment, which are at the heart of health economics.

10.2.1 Equity

Walster, Berscheid, and Walster's equity theory (Walster et al. 1973), a modification of Adam's inequity theory (Adams 1965), is one of the most influential approaches in social justice research. A perceived fair distribution exists (always in relation to another person) when the ratio of a person A's output (O_A) and input (I_A) is the same as the ratio for person B's output (O_B) and input (I_B), that is

$$\frac{\mathrm{O}_A}{\mathrm{I}_A} = \frac{\mathrm{O}_B}{\mathrm{I}_B}. \tag{10.1}$$

Outcomes may be positive (e.g., rewards, payments) or negative (e.g., punishments, costs). In the current healthcare context, an output may be, for instance, the position on the waiting list. Input includes sociodemographic characteristics such as education, intelligence, experience, training, skill, seniority, age, sex, ethnic background, social status, and degree of effort (Adams 1965, p. 193). We include age, personal responsibility, instrumental value, and socioeconomic status as specifications of equity and discuss them briefly.

10.2.1.1 Age

Scientists and practitioners have for decades debated the age of the patient as a criterion for fair healthcare allocation. Age is one of the most controversially discussed criteria in philosophy, health economics, and medicine. Some debates are primarily concerned with whether elderly patients should be prioritized above younger ones or vice versa, or whether age should play a role at all when allocating healthcare resources, and how such decisions can be made in a (morally) justifiable way. Others focus on whether the biological age of a patient is more important than the chronological age (for a discussion including theoretical positions such as utilitarian ageism, fair inning, time-specific prioritarianism, and the prudential lifespan perspective see, e.g., Williams 1997, Fleck 2016, Bognar 2016, and Watters 2016).

Economic and justice research predominantly focuses on efficiency and equity. They investigate how and what type of age weight functions (e.g., single-peaked functions for relative weights, flat for equity weights) can be incorporated in the quality adjusted life year (QALY) measure used in economic evaluations of healthcare programs (Tsuchiya 1999; Tsuchiya et al. 2003; Williams 1997). The results of most of these studies suggest that lower weight should be given to older people (e.g., Busschbach et al. 1993; Dolan et al. 2005; Johannesson and Johansson 1996; Rodríguez and Pinto 2000). That is, the elderly should be given a lower priority when distributing healthcare services. However, the body of empirical studies is inconclusive: there are arguments for "younger first," "older first," and "age is irrelevant" (e.g., Williams 1997; Tsuchiya 1999; Diederich 2011, 2016a; Sabik and Lie 2008). Interestingly, middle-aged people, the ones who contribute most to the healthcare system through their health insurance premiums are considered the group with the lowest priority (Diederich 2016a). Note that during the COVID-19 pandemic, the German government decided that the elderly should receive vaccinations first.

10.2.1.2 Personal Responsibility

Personal responsibility for maintaining good health is another highly debated criterion for prioritizing healthcare services. In Germany, taking responsibility for one's own health is a legal principle, which includes an obligation to co-pay for treatments when injuries are self-inflicted (see Schmidt 2007). Cappelen and Norheim (2005) cite World Health Organization (WHO) studies showing that among the ten leading risk factors contributing to the burden of disease in high-income countries, seven can be directly attributed to unhealthy lifestyles. These are tobacco (first), blood pressure (second), alcohol (third), high cholesterol (fourth), being overweight (fifth), low fruit and vegetable intake (sixth), and physical inactivity (seventh). These factors, which are all related to unhealthy lifestyles, may also be interrelated and influence each other.

Liberal egalitarians support the idea that society should carry only those healthcare expenditures that result from factors outside one's personal control, such as genetic dispositions, whereas costs that arise from the individual's choices should be partly or fully carried by the sick via taxes, co-payments, or additional insurances to guarantee a fair allocation of scarce medical resources (Cappelen and Norheim 2005; Olsen 1997, 2017). During the COVID-19 pandemic, some German public health stakeholders (e.g., physicians, health insurances, and politicians) proposed that willingly unvaccinated patients should pay (part of) the costs for their medical treatments if they contract COVID-19 (see, e.g., Bruche 2021; Menke 2021). However, the proposal was not implemented because it received little support from politicians and the public.

Surveys conducted with convenience and representative samples found that the majority of participants endorse co-payments for healthcare services in general when patients live an unhealthy lifestyle, e.g., smoking, excessive alcohol consumption, extreme sports, illegal drugs consumption, and unhealthy diet. For details see, Diederich and Schreier (2010), Diederich et al. (2012), Diederich (2016a), Myllykangas et al. (1996), and Stumpf et al. (2014). Studies that have investigated posteriotization of patients, that is, giving some a lower priority due to their lifestyle, have found both support for (e.g., Ryynänen et al. 1999) and rejection of these measures (e.g., Bowling 1996). Scholars have found that participants, when presented with specific healthcare services such as organ transplantation, joint replacement, and heart surgery, show low support for posteriotizing patients with risky health behavior (e.g., Krütli et al. 2016; Nord et al. 1995; Rogge and Kittel 2016), with the exception of smokers and drinkers (Charny et al. 1989).

10.2.1.3 Social Responsibility

Instrumental value and social responsibility describe a person's role in society. Instrumental value expresses the individual's usefulness to society, system importance, or professional responsibility like supervising several employees (Krütli et al. 2016). Social responsibility is associated with having responsibility for children, other family members, or the community at large (Rogge and Kittel 2016). Acceptance of social responsibility as a criterion for prioritization depends mainly on the type of role. For instance, community service, having an executive position, having public responsibilities, and the like, according to studies, do not receive much support as criteria for prioritization. However, acceptance is high for roles involving family support, particularly when children are involved (e.g., Diederich et al. 2012, Wegener et al. 2010, Krütli et al. 2016, Nord et al. 1995, Rogge and Kittel 2016, Stumpf et al. 2014, Tymstra and Andela 1993, for different scenarios and results).

10.2.1.4 Socioeconomic Status

Socioeconomic status (SES) is a composite measure consisting of various indicators related to income, occupation, and sometimes education. Scholars have proposed various scales to measure SES (see Oakes and Rossi (2003), for a historical overview and newer developments). For instance, the "Winkler-Index" (Winkler and Stolzenberg 1999) is widely used in Germany. It is a three-dimensional, additive, non-weighted social class index that uses academic/vocational education, monthly net household income, and current/last occupation as indicators. Several studies have investigated the acceptance of SES (or aspects of it) as a prioritization criterion. The empirical results are mixed. The upshot of it is that better-off citizens should not receive priority. When subjects do accept prioritization according to SES, they prefer the prioritization of poorer people above wealthier people (see, e.g., Diederich et al. 2012, Wegener et al. 2010, Krütli et al. 2016, Myllykangas et al. 1996, Pinho and Pinto Borges 2018, Ryynänen et al. 1999, for various studies and results).

Note that the last three criteria, personal responsibility, social responsibility, and SES, are composite measures. Each component may serve as an ingredient of a person's input (denominator) in the equity ratio.

10.2.2 Equality

Equality as a principle of distributive justice has received the most attention in philosophy, strongly influenced by Rawls (1971). In its simplest form, the principle says that every person should have the same level of material goods and services (Lamont and Favor 2017). In the context of healthcare service allocation, Cookson and Dolan (1999) suggest that equality may be established by minimizing inequality. This is, for instance, the argument of the fair innings and related perspectives (see section on age above). Another implementation of the equality principle in healthcare is random selection of patients for treatment, for example, by a lottery (e.g., Lamont and Favor 2017; Sabbagh 2001; Waring 2004). This method, however, is not supported by a majority of respondents in surveys. When tested across different healthcare scenarios, such as heart disease treatments, organ transplantation, joint replacement, treatment for life-threatening illness, and more, the acceptance rate was consistently low to very low (Mossialos and King 1999; Wegener et al. 2010; Krütli et al. 2016; Diederich 2016a).

There is a recent example of a real-life application of this rule in the allocation of an expensive and scarce medicine: In 2020, the pharmaceutical corporation Novartis used a lottery to give away 100 doses of the gene therapy "Zolgensma". Zolgensma is a very expensive therapy (roughly 2,000,000 Euro per dose; Dyer 2020) to treat spinal muscular atrophy (Type I and II), a rare disease with a high mortality rate (the vast majority of patients die before the age of 2; see e.g., Birnkrant et al. 1998; Hirtz et al. 2005).

Other scarce healthcare resources such as dialysis, treatments against AIDS, and multiple sclerosis medicines have also been allocated in the past by using lotteries (see Waring 2004, for an overview).

10.2.3 Need

Need in distributive justice research is hardly studied on its own terms. Although scholars mostly study it in combination with other principles (see also the third thesis on pluralistic and monistic theories of distributive justice in Nullmeier 2020), describe it as in competition with equity and equality, or ignore it altogether (Diederich 2020), it plays a major role in the practice of healthcare. There are three particularly common oeprationalizations of need (Hurley 2000). The first operationalizes severity of the illness, the urgency of the intervention, or how life-threatening the illness is as a measure for need (e.g., "Rule of Rescue"; Jonsen 1986; McKie and Richardson 2003; Hauck et al. 2004). This corresponds with "the core element of the concept of need" that Nullmeier describes in his first thesis for a theory of need-based justice (Nullmeier 2020, p. 191).

The second operationalization of need refers to an individual's "capacity to benefit" (also referred to as "need gap"; Nullmeier 2020, p. 192) from the use of particular healthcare services (Culyer and Wagstaff 1993). Two conditions must be met to acknowledge the existence of need: (1) there is a capacity to benefit, i.e., a treatment that must be effective in the achieving a specific objective, and (2) the objective itself must be accepted by society as being "worthwhile" (Culyer and Wagstaff 1993; Hauck et al. 2004; Hurley 2000). On the social and political recognition of needs, see Part II of this volume. Accordingly, an individual does not necessarily have to be ill to be in need (preventive measures) or to be in need when ill (no effective measures available; Culyer and Wagstaff 1993). The third operationalization of need includes the amount of healthcare expenditures required before exhausting the capacity to benefit (Culyer and Wagstaff 1993; Hauck et al. 2004). Thus, need is defined "as the expenditure required to effect the maximum possible health improvement or, equivalently, the expenditure required to reduce the individual's capacity to benefit to zero." (Culyer and Wagstaff 1993, p. 436). One example is a new medical treatment that is cheaper but of the same efficacy as an existing one. Expenditures, and therefore the need for them, would be lower for the same benefit.

Moreover, independent from its definition, distributing healthcare services according to need requires that people with the same need receive equal services (in quantity and quality) and that people with higher needs are given (proportionally) higher priority than people with lower needs (Culyer and Wagstaff 1993; Hauck et al. 2004; Hurley 2000). Some elements of the German step-by-step plan for prioritizing the COVID-19 vaccinations (the government prioritized COVID-19 vaccinations based on risk of severe disease, risk of transmission, and availability of vaccine) are examples of a need-based distribution of healthcare resources. Accordingly, people who have a high risk of hospitalization or death due to a COVID-19 infection (e.g., the elderly and/or those with preexisting conditions) were given the highest priority for vaccinations. Another example is prioritizing PCR tests (polymerase chain reaction test) for detecting COVID-19 infections. PCR tests are considered the "gold standard" for COVID-19 diagnostics (Robert Koch-Institut 2022). Due to a high incidence rate of new COVID-19 cases at the beginning of 2022, the PCR testing labs were overwhelmed. To reduce the workload of laboratories, PCR tests were only distributed to particular groups such as patients at high risk.

10.2.4 Other Criteria

Scholars have proposed many other criteria in addition to the ones described above. Some of them are closely related to medical practice, such as therapeutic benefit, therapeutic effectiveness (e.g., Diederich and Salzmann 2015; Friedrich and Schöne-Seifert 2013; Pinho and Pinto Borges 2018; Schöne-Seifert et al. 2012; Stumpf et al. 2014; Winkelhage et al. 2013), and evidence-based medicine (e.g., Diederich and Salzmann 2015; Niessen et al. 2000; Rudan et al. 2010; Stumpf et al. 2014). Others are more situational, such as waiting time and the "first come first served" rule (e.g., Egan and Kotloff 2005; Krütli et al. 2016; Mariotti et al. 2014; Oedingen et al. 2020; Pinho and Pinto Borges 2018), or relate to an economic context, such as cost of treatment, cost-effectiveness, and reciprocity (e.g., Diederich and Salzmann 2015; Krütli et al. 2016; McKie et al. 2009; Pinho and Pinto Borges 2018; Stumpf et al. 2014).

In studies, the majority of respondents preferred treatments that are more effective and beneficial over other criteria, e.g., costs of treatment or reciprocity and support evidence-based medicine (see e.g., Diederich and Salzmann 2015; Stumpf et al. 2014; Pinho and Pinto Borges 2018; Schöne-Seifert et al. 2012). Waiting time and the "first come, first served rule" typically refer to the time a patient waits to receive a particular treatment. Participants tend to prefer shorter waiting times for more urgent medical conditions and longer waiting times for less urgent ones (Oedingen et al. (2020); see the previous section of this chapter). However, when clearly distinguished from other criteria (e.g., when urgency is not a factor), most respondents disagree with waiting time as a criterion (Pinho and Pinto Borges 2018). Criteria that relate to healthcare costs are mostly not accepted. In particular, treatment costs and also cost-effectiveness are not supported by the public as fair criteria for healthcare service allocation (e.g., Diederich and Salzmann 2015; McKie et al. 2009; Pinho and Pinto Borges 2018; Stumpf et al. 2014). Similarly, voluntary payments to societal services in the past ("reciprocity") are strongly rejected as grounds for prioritization in healthcare.

10.3 Legitimizing Priority Setting in Healthcare

Priority setting[1] (which is practiced by policymakers) has practical implications for medical staff and patients, particularly when it comes to the reform of healthcare systems to reduce costs (see e.g., Ham 1997; Sabik and Lie 2008).

A common approach taken by policymakers is to adopt a utilitarian framework that seeks to maximize societal health benefits by making healthcare services more cost-effective. However, as many have argued, including healthy and unhealthy citizens in the policy of setting priorities is vital for making legitimate health policy decisions (Bowling 1996; Bruni et al. 2008; Diederich and Schreier 2009; Diederich 2016b; Diederich and Salzmann 2015; Mossialos and King 1999). Including the public's expectations, perspectives, preferences, and values about prioritization procedures is essential for allocating healthcare services in ways that will be accepted as fair (e.g., Daniels 2007; Daniels and Sabin 2002). As stated in the WHO's Ljubljana charter on reforming healthcare in Europe, "health care reforms must address citizens' needs, taking into account, through the democratic process, their expectations about health and health care" (World Health Organization Regional Office for Europe 1996, p. 2). That is, it is in line with democratic ideals to ensure participation of the public in the making of priority setting policies (Bruni et al. 2008, p. 15).

Many of the studies summarized above focus on one specific criterion for prioritizing healthcare, e.g., age. Participants were often given only binary response options (agree/not agree) or one-dimensional rating scales. Even when several criteria were included in a study, they were often presented in isolation, which did not allow for any comparisons or trade-offs. Of course, participants agreeing to different criteria at similar rates or giving them similar rating scores could mean that those criteria are equally important for distributing healthcare services (which contradicts the assumptions of Deutsch 1975). Having equal weights for different criteria is perfectly compatible with pluralistic theories of justice (third thesis of Nullmeier 2020), but can create acute problems when trying to prioritize patients for

[1] In contrast to prioritization, which is the specific act of ordering items based on predefined criteria, priority setting is the process of establishing a systematic approach to determine importance across various healthcare interventions.

healthcare services. While equal weighting of a few different criteria is feasible (see the equal prioritization of "age" and "health situation" in Germany's COVID-19 vaccination scheme), equal weighting of all criteria logically leaves the decision-maker in an impossible situation.

The Public's Acceptance of Multiple Healthcare Distribution Principles

In the following, we briefly summarize the results of studies that include the aforementioned justice principles. As previously mentioned, we omit studies focused on the cost of treatment as a criterion.

Findings of the International Social Justice Project (Wegener et al. 2010) showed that, across samples from different countries, equity (operationalized as social responsibility and instrumental value) and equality (lottery) receive very similar acceptance rates. However, monetary contribution as an application of equity is accepted to a much lesser extent (see also Mossialos and King 1999).

Other studies investigate attitudes toward various criteria that are specifications of the equity principle and include need in their analyses (capacity to benefit, Stumpf et al. 2014; severity of disease, Diederich et al. 2012; degree of urgency, Ryynänen et al. 1999). These studies show that compared to equity, need is one of the most accepted principles (Ryynänen et al. 1999; Stumpf et al. 2014), or even the most accepted principle (Diederich et al. 2012), for distributing healthcare services.

Pinho and Pinto Borges (2018) and Krütli et al. (2016) compare attitudes toward healthcare allocation criteria, including equity (various forms), equality (lottery), and need (capacity to benefit and risk of life in Pinho and Pinto Borges; sickest first in Krütli et al.). In both studies, need is the most accepted principle of the three. However, the acceptance of equality and equity differed between the studies: in Pinho and Pinto Borges (2018), a distribution according to equality is more accepted than most equity criteria, and in Krütli et al. (2016), respondents prefer equity over equality.

Conjoint analysis is a particularly effective method for eliciting a person's preference order for particular criteria. Conjoint analyses have rarely been used in research on preferences for healthcare resource distribution criteria. In the following, we outline a few of the rare exceptions.

The Eurotransplant kidney allocation system (ETKAS)[2] was one of the first algorithms that tried to distribute kidneys justly. It provides a point-score system that takes into account five criteria (De Meester et al. 1998): two are medical (Human Leukocyte Antigens, HLA, mismatches, and the chance of a good HLA match),

[2] ETKAS was installed in 1996 and emerged from the XCOMB model by Wujciak and Opelz (1993a,b). Since then, it has been modified many times. We do not consider the modified versions here.

one is social (waiting time), one is organizational (the distance between donor and transplant program), and one is political (the international exchange balance).

The result of the simulation, i.e., the weights of the criteria, became the basis for German law on organ allocation ("Transplantationsgesetz", see Schreiber and Haverich 2000). To investigate what physicians, specifically those who perform kidney transplant surgery, consider a fair distribution of the treatment, Diederich (2001) performed a conjoint analysis with 33 physicians. Overall, the physicians' evaluations agree with the law that the two medical and the social criteria with the HLA mismatches should be the most important criteria and that waiting times should be the second most important criterion.

Furthermore, in their conjoint analyses, Winkelhage and Diederich (2012) and Wirsik et al. (2009) include several criteria that are constituents of the equity principle (e.g., age, health behavior, and SES) and the need principle (the former study consideres severity of illness while the latter considers capacity of benefit, i.e., "improvement in health" and "quality of life"). Participants in both studies evaluate need as the most important criterion (together with age).

As part of our empirical study below, we conducted a conjoint analysis that includes equity (health behavior and instrumental value) and need (severity of illness, mortality risk). Moreover, we offered respondents the opportunity to discard the ranking they indicated in the conjoint task and choose an equality-based allocation (lottery) instead. The study shows that need is clearly the most important criterion. Only a few respondents discarded their selection in favor of an allocation based on a lottery.

Whenever a study comparing attitudes toward multiple healthcare distribution principles included the need principle, need turned out to be one of the most or the most accepted principle for prioritizing healthcare services. People accept the equity and the equality principle to a lower extent. The acceptance rate for equity, in particular, often depends on its operationalization.

10.4 Framing Effects in Justice Judgments

Involving the general public in judgments about prioritization usually requires tools such as questionnaires and surveys. How the items and questions are constructed and phrased may influence participants' responses (see e.g., Gächter et al. 2009; Guyatt et al. 1999; Kragt and Bennett 2012). As shown in Chap. 2, a person's choices and judgments may depend on whether the task or question is framed positively (gain) or negatively (loss). Positive frames lead to a more favorable answer than negative frames. As we discussed in Chap. 2, numerous experiments across many disciplines with a variety of decision scenarios have shown framing effects, i.e., preference shifts and preference reversals.

Surprisingly few studies have been conducted in the context of justice judgments. In Törnblom's (1988) framework for allocation processes, outcome allocations are either presented positively or negatively and may be accomplished in three different ways: delivery, withholding, and withdrawal (for a summary of the approach see Diederich 2020). To test whether people prefer to use identical or different justice principles depending on the framing of the outcome allocation, Törnblom and Ahlin (1998) conducted a vignette study describing a nuclear test that could result in people suffering radiation exposure. They found that the positive–negative framing influenced fairness considerations for equity (rated fairer in the negative than in the positive frame) and equality (rated fairer in the positive than in the negative), but not for need. The framing of the mode of allocation (i.e., delivering vs. withholding) had an impact on fairness ratings for equity and need when outcomes were positive (rated fairer in the withholding framing than in the delivering framing).

Utilizing Törnblom's classification framework, Gamliel and Peer (2006) showed framing effects on justice judgments in three vignettes related to working environments. Participants rated the fairness of positive and negative frames with respect to five allocation principles (ability, effort, tenure, need, and equality) using a 6-point rating scale. In the delivering scenario, need received, on average, the highest ratings, both for positive and negative frames. The positive–negative framing influenced the fairness ratings of all principles (except equality) depending on the scenario described. For all framing effects, participants rated the corresponding principle as fairer in the positive than in the negative frame.

Framing Effects in Justice Judgments on Healthcare Allocation

To the best of our knowledge, there are only two framing studies focused on attitudes to justice principles in healthcare resource allocation. Gamliel and Peer (2010) conducted two experiments offering questionnaires to undergraduate students. In experiment 1, the task was to rate the "perceived fairness" of four positively/negatively framed distribution criteria on a 7-point Likert scale: (1) Merit ("patients who are least/most responsible for their condition would receive/not receive the resource"); (2) tenure ("patients who had been waiting the longest/shortest time would receive/not receive the resource"); (3) need ("patients who most/least need the resource would receive/not receive it"); and (4) equality ("patients who won/lost a random draw would receive/not receive the resource"). They were embedded in three health scenarios: heart transplants, lung transplants, and AIDS vaccinations.

They found framing effects for merit, need, and tenure (data collapsed across scenarios). The perceived fairness of these principles was higher in positively framed situations (i.e., to deliver healthcare resources to certain patients) than in negatively framed situations (i.e., to not deliver healthcare resources to other patients). Furthermore, overall fairness ratings were highest for need, followed by equality, then tenure, and last merit. In their second experiment, Gamliel and Peer included three negatively and positively framed distributive justice criteria, merit, tenure, and equality, and two health scenarios, heart transplantation and AIDS vaccination. They constructed ten statements that reflect different psychological states: cognitive (e.g., "I think the decision is fair"), affective (e.g., "I feel good about this decision"), and behavioral (e.g., "I would donate a small amount of money to an organization aimed at promoting such decisions"). The task was to rate the agreement with the 10 items provided for each of the 12 conditions (2 frames, 2 health scenarios, 3 justice criteria) on a 7-point Likert scale. Note that they used a between-subjects design for presenting the 12 conditions (i.e., each participant received 1 of the 12 conditions with 10 items to rate their level of agreement). As for their first experiment, framing effects were observed for merit and tenure but not for equality. Furthermore, on average, equality received the highest fairness ratings and merit the lowest.

Diederich (2016a) conducted an online survey study on priority setting with female physicians (members of the Ärztinnenbund; see Diederich et al. (2015), for details). Of the more than 1,500 members, about half of them participated. One topic was concerned with personal responsibility for health outcomes (see above). Four scenarios (related to alcohol, exercise, weight, and smoking) were framed positively, i.e., rewarding patients for healthy behavior by partially refunding health insurance costs or negatively, i.e., penalizing patients for unhealthy behavior by demanding co-payment for healthcare services. We observed two preference reversals (for alcohol and exercise) but, interestingly, they went in opposite directions. For alcohol, the proportions of agreement were smaller in the positive frame than in the negative frame, and the opposite was true for exercise. For the remaining two scenarios (weight and smoking), we observed preference shifts. The agreement was larger than 0.5 for both the positive and negative frames, but these were also in opposite directions: For weight, there were lower levels of agreement in the positive frame than in the negative frame, while for smoking, there were greater levels of agreement in the positive frame than in the negative frame.

For the remainder of this section, we report preliminary data from a recent study we conducted in the context of the research group FOR 2104. For an online survey experiment involving 485 participants, we constructed six health scenarios: heart transplant, artificial respiration, treatment against unusual infection, treatment against COVID-19, vaccination against unusual infection, and vaccination against COVID-19. Each scenario was framed in terms of delivering a specified treatment (positive frame) or withholding the treatment (negative frame). Furthermore, each scenario and frame included statements related to the distributive justice principles of need, equality, equity, and waiting time. We further divided equity into personal responsibility, instrumental value, and social security payments a patient has made in the past. To match the respective frame, the statements included antagonistic word pairs such as most/least responsible and longest/shortest waiting time, similar to Gamliel and Peer (2010). Table 10.1 shows one example statement for each principle presented in the deliver framing and the withhold framing.

The task of one group of participants was to rate each statement with respect to their perceived fairness on a 5-point Likert scale. The other group rated each statement in terms of perceived justice. Because no difference was observed between these treatments, data were collapsed for the analysis. For comparison, we performed a similar statistical analysis on averaged ratings within each condition

Table 10.1 Distribution Principles and Healthcare Allocation Statements Framed Positively (Delivery Framing) and Negatively (Withhold Framing)

Principle	Deliver framing	Withhold framing
Equality: *Lottery*	Patients who have *won* a lottery receive the resource	Patients who have *lost* a lottery do not receive the resource
Need: *Urgency*	Patients who need the resource the *most* receive it	Patients who need the resource the *least* do not receive it
Other: *Waiting time*	Patients who wait the *longest* time for the resource receive it	Patients who wait the *shortest* time for the resource do not receive it
Equity: *Instrumental value*	Patients *most* important to maintain essential public services or facilities (e.g., medical care, child care, grocery stores, police) receive the resource	Patients *least* important to maintain essential public services or facilities (e.g., medical care, child care, grocery stores, police) do not receive the resource
Personal responsi-bility	Patients *least* responsible for their condition receive the resource	Patients *most* responsible for their condition do not receive the resource
Social security payments	Patients who paid *most* to the social security system (e.g., health insurance premium) in the past year receive the resource	Patients who paid *least* to the social security system (e.g., health insurance premium) in the past year do not receive the resource

and framing effect size (Cohen's d, Cohen 1988) as it was done in Gamliel and Peer (2010).

We observed framing effects for all scenarios: Statements in a positive frame (deliver) got higher mean fairness ratings than in a negative frame (withhold).

In the heart transplant and artificial respiration scenarios, need received the highest fairness ratings followed by equity (waiting time), equity (personal responsibility), and equality (Table 10.2). Similar to Gamliel and Peer (2010), we found small to medium framing effects (according to the classification of Cohen 1988) for need and waiting time (the "other" principle) in both scenarios, but not for equity (personal responsibility) and equality. Moreover, when comparing equity and the other healthcare resource distribution principles (i.e., personal responsibility and waiting time) in the artificial respiration scenario, a special constellation emerges: Fairness ratings for waiting time were much lower in the withhold frame than in the deliver frame, indicating a framing effect; ratings for personal responsibility, however, were not affected by the framing of the scenario. That is, subjects rated waiting time much fairer than personal responsibility in the deliver frame, but the difference between them is smaller in the withhold frame.

In the treatment against an unusual infection and COVID-19 scenarios, need received the highest fairness ratings, followed by equity (personal responsibility), equity (instrumental value), equality, and finally, equity (amount of payments made to the social system in the past). We observed small-to-medium effects (see Cohen 1988) of framing for need and equity (instrumental value) in both scenarios (Table 10.3). As for the heart transplant and artificial respiration scenarios, ratings for equity (personal responsibility) and equality were not affected by the receive-

Table 10.2 Average Ratings per Principle and Frame for the Heart Transplant and Artificial Respiration Scenarios

Scenario	Frame	Equality *(Lottery)*	Need *(Urgency)*	Other *(Waiting time)*	Equity *(Personal responsib.)*
Heart transplant	Receive (SD)	2.36 (1.22)	4.23 (0.85)	3.88 (0.83)	3.09 (1.15)
	Withhold (SD)	2.34 (1.20)	3.97 (0.81)	3.37 (0.98)	3.14 (1.08)
	ES (*d*)	0.02	0.31***	0.57***	−0.05
Artificial respiration	Receive (SD)	2.20 (1.23)	4.43 (0.79)	3.54 (0.94)	3.05 (1.15)
	Withhold (SD)	2.25 (1.21)	4.00 (0.85)	2.90 (0.96)	3.06 (1.13)
	ES (*d*)	−0.04	0.53***	0.68***	−0.01

SD standard deviations, *ES (d)* effect size (Cohen's *d*)
Significance level: *$p < 0.05$, **$p < 0.01$, ***$p < 0.001$

withhold framing; the same applies to equity (amount of payments made to the social system in the past).

In the vaccination against unusual infection and COVID-19 scenarios, need received the highest fairness ratings, followed by equity (instrumental value), then equality, and finally equity (amount of payments made to the social system in the past). Again, small-to-medium effects (see Cohen 1988) of framing occur for ratings of the need and equity (instrumental value) principles (Table 10.4). However, framing affects ratings of the need principle only in the vaccination against unusual infection scenario. In the other scenario, i.e., vaccination against COVID-19, ratings of the need principle were not different between the frames. The reason why we could not observe any framing effects in that particular scenario might be due to the different labeling of the disease, i.e., unusual infection vs COVID-19 (framing in its loose form, see Kühberger 1998), which may have influenced the ratings for the different distribution principles.

To summarize, framing of the scenarios affected participants' justice ratings of the principles for healthcare resource distribution. In particular, ratings depended on whether the distribution of a specific healthcare resource is framed as delivering or withholding it. For example, participants in our study rated the need, waiting time, and equity (instrumental value) principles as fairer in the deliver frame than they did in the withhold frame. We observed no framing effects for attitudes toward the equality principle and other operationalizations of the equity principle (i.e., personal responsibility and payments made to the social system). Another framing, rather in a loose sense, is labeling of the disease being treated. Giving a disease different names (e.g., unusual infection vs. COVID-19) may further affect the fairness ratings of certain distribution principles. Moreover, framing effect sizes may also depend on factors such as item construction, analysis methods, and effects related to "unpacking" (Tversky and Koehler 1994) a statement.

Table 10.3 Average Ratings per Principle and Frame for the Treatment Against Unusual Infection and COVID-19 Scenarios

Scenario	Frame	Equality *(Lottery)*	Need *(Urgency)*	Equity *(Instrument. value)*	Equity (*Personal responsib.*)	Equity (*Social payments*)
Treatment	Receive (SD)	2.61 (1.40)	4.41 (0.69)	2.82 (1.20)	3.13 (1.27)	1.64 (0.91)
Unusual	Withhold (SD)	2.42 (1.32)	4.15 (0.77)	2.37 (1.20)	3.37 (1.11)	1.62 (0.94)
	ES (*d*)	0.14	0.36**	0.38**	−0.21	0.02
COVID-19	Receive (SD)	2.28 (1.2)	4.33 (0.85)	3.01 (1.25)	3.11 (1.29)	1.63 (0.95)
	Withhold (SD)	2.36 (1.28)	4.02 (0.83)	2.28 (1.06)	3.37 (1.08)	1.52 (0.81)
	ES (*d*)	−0.06	0.37**	0.63***	−0.22	0.13

SD standard deviations, *ES (d)* effect size (Cohen's *d*)
Significance level: $^{*}p < 0.05$, $^{**}p < 0.01$, $^{***}p < 0.001$

Table 10.4 Average Ratings per Principle and Frame for the Vaccination Against Unusual Infection and COVID-19 Scenarios

Scenario	Frame	Equality *(Lottery)*	Need *(Urgency)*	Equity *(Instument. value)*	Equity *(Social payments)*
Vaccination Unusual	Receive (SD)	2.50 (1.31)	4.43 (0.77)	3.27 (1.23)	1.71 (0.99)
	Withhold (SD)	2.24 (1.18)	4.18 (0.75)	2.79 (1.20)	1.75 (1.01)
	ES (*d*)	0.21	0.33**	0.41**	−0.041
COVID-19	Receive (SD)	2.13 (1.06)	4.09 (0.96)	3.61 (1.21)	1.70 (0.95)
	Withhold (SD)	2.25 (1.18)	4.18 (0.81)	3.06 (1.17)	1.58 (0.83)
	ES (*d*)	−0.11	−0.10	0.46***	0.13

SD standard deviations, *ES (d)* effect size (Cohen's *d*)
Significance level: *$p < 0.05$, **$p < 0.01$, ***$p < 0.001$

10.5 Concluding Remarks

Establishing fairness in healthcare prioritization procedures is one major concern for distributive healthcare policies (see e.g., Cappelen and Norheim 2006; Nord et al. 1999; Williams 1997). Combining normative principles of distributive justice and attitudes from the public toward certain criteria might improve the legitimacy and the public's acceptance of prioritization procedures. Moreover, incorporating empirical results in normative theories will support the development of more "realistic" theories of justice (Nullmeier 2020).

As outlined in this chapter, multiple operationalizations of distributive justice principles are required for establishing a fair healthcare resource prioritization. These include more specific operationalizations of equity, equality, need, and other distributive justice principles (cf., "Pluralistic and Monistic Theories", Nullmeier 2020).

Prioritization according to equity means relating a person's output to their input such as personal responsibility (e.g., health behavior), instrumental value (e.g., people working in system important positions), or socioeconomic status (e.g., ability to pay). Equality, i.e., the "to each the same" principle, is often applied as a lottery distribution. The application of need in the context of healthcare resource distribution usually refers to the urgency of the intervention or severity of the illness. That is, healthcare resources are distributed first to patients who need the resources the most. According to this definition, receiving the resources is often indispensable for the survival of the patient, which corresponds to the core element of the concept of need (Nullmeier 2020). Hence, need in the context of healthcare prioritization can be clearly distinguished from other conceptions such as desire, interest, and preference. Other principles usually relate to the situational context. Applications of such alternative principles include, for example, the time a person has to wait for a treatment (waiting time). Participants' attitudes toward different operationalizations of the principles depend on various factors. Among them are specific applications of criteria, domains, situational contexts, global events related to health (e.g.,

COVID-19 pandemic), sample compositions, and framing of the survey items. In particular, public support for prioritizing healthcare services according to the equity principle varies greatly depending on these factors. Participants support equality when patients receive equal treatment and reject it when the resource is distributed according to a (fair) lottery draw. The public consistently supports the need principle in all its forms, i.e., urgency of intervention, severity of illness, extent of threat to life, and capacity to benefit. Hence, need is considered as the most important distribution principle in healthcare. However, in other domains, e.g., hierarchically structured organizations, cooperatives, and the labor market, other principles such as equity, equality, and entitlement receive greater support than need (see, e.g., Diederich 2020; Jost and Kay 2010; Liebig and Sauer 2016; Törnblom and Ahlin 1998).

Presenting healthcare distribution scenarios in a positive or negative frame affects people's attitudes toward prioritization criteria. Whether or not framing effects occur depends significantly on the principles, their operationalization, the situational context, and other factors such as specific domains and current global events. However, people perceive prioritization based on these principles as fairer in positive (i.e., receiving the service) than in negative (i.e., not receiving the service) frames, especially when it comes to the need principle. Moreover, the name of the disease mediates any framing effects: the latter are present when the disease is called "unusual infection," and they disappear when the name of the same disease is changed to "COVID-19."

The findings reviewed and reported in this chapter based on practical applications of pluralistic theories of distributive justice show how people relate different principles to each other in the domain of healthcare prioritization. By demonstrating the impact of factors such as positive–negative framings and the labeling of diseases on attitudes toward distribution principles, this chapter shows the relevance of transparency when making judgments on distribution problems. That is, increasing transparency, e.g., by providing information in more than one way (framing), may help to improve the methods (e.g., surveys and questionnaires) used to involve the general public in political decisions on resource allocations, such as prioritization in healthcare.

Acknowledgments The chapter presents results from the project "Framing in need determination," funded by the German Research Foundation (DFG) (DI506 13–2). It was part of the DFG research group FOR 2104 "Need-based Justice and Distributive Procedures."

References

Adams, J. S. (1965): "Inequity in Social Exchange", in L. Berkowitz (ed.): *Advances in Experimental Social Psychology*, vol. 2, 267–299. New York: Academic Press.

Birnkrant, D. J., J. F. Pope, J. E. Martin, A. H. Repucci, and R. M. Eiben (1998): "Treatment of Type I Spinal Muscular Atrophy with Noninvasive Ventilation and Gastrostomy Feeding", *Pediatric Neurology* 18 (5), 407–410

Bognar, G. (2016): "Priority Setting and Age", in E. Nagel, and M. Lauerer (eds.): *Prioritization in Medicine: An International Dialogue*, 163–177. Cham: Springer.

Bowling, A. (1996): "Health Care Rationing: The Public's Debate", *British Medical Journal* 312 (7032), 670–674.

Bruche, J. (2021): *Corona: Müssen Ungeimpfte höhere Krankenkassenbeiträge zahlen? Welle der ungeimpften CoViD-19-Patienten schwappt in Krankenhäuser*. Südwestrundfunk. https://www.swr.de/swraktuell/baden-wuerttemberg/braucht-es-krankenkassentarife-fuer-ungeimpfte-100.html

Bruni, R. A., A. Laupacis, and D. K. Martin (2008): "Public Engagement in Setting Priorities in Health Care", *Canadian Medial Association Journal* 179 (1), 15–18.

Busschbach, J. J. V., D. J. Hessing, and F. T. De Charro (1993): "The Utility of Health at Different Stages in Life: A Quantitative Approach", *Social Science and Medicine* 37 (2), 153–158.

Cappelen, A. W., and O. F. Norheim (2005): "Responsibility in Health Care: A Liberal Egalitarian Approach", *Journal of Medical Ethics* 31, 476–480.

Cappelen, A. W., and O. F. Norheim (2006): "Responsibility, Fairness and Rationing in Health Care", *Health Policy* 76 (3), 312–319.

Charny, M. C., P. A. Lewis, and S. C. Farrow (1989): "Choosing Who Shall not Be Treated in the NHS", *Social Science and Medicine* 28 (12), 1331–1338.

Cochrane, J. R. (2016): "Fundamental Evaluation Criteria in the Medicine of the Twenty-First Century", in E. Nagel, and M. Lauerer (eds.): *Prioritization in Medicine: An International Dialogue*, 11–37. Cham: Springer.

Cohen, J. (1988): *Statistical Power Analysis for the Behavioral Sciences*, 2nd ed. New York: Routledge.

Cookson, R., and P. Dolan (1999): "Public Views on Health Care Rationing: A Group Discussion Study", *Health Policy* 49 (1–2), 63–74.

Culyer, A. J., and A. Wagstaff (1993): "Equity and Equality in Health and Health Care", *Journal of Health Economics* 12 (4), 431–457.

Daniels, N. (2007): *Just Health: Meeting Health Needs Fairly*. New York: Cambridge University Press.

Daniels, N., and J. Sabin (2002): *Setting Limits Fairly: Can We Learn to Share Medical Resources?* Oxford: Oxford University Press.

De Meester, J., G. G. Persijn, T. Wujciak, G. Opelz, and Y. Vanrenterghem (1998): "The New Eurotransplant Kidney Allocation System–Report One Year After Implementation", *Transplantation* 66 (9), 1154–1159.

Deutsch, M. (1975): "Equity, Equality, and Need: What Determines which Value Will Be Used as the Basis of Distributive Justice?", *Journal of Social Issues* 31 (3), 137–149.

Diederich, A. (2001): "A Rational Reconstruction of Expert Judgments in Organ Allocation: A Conjoint Measurement Approach", *Analyse and Kritik* 23 (2), 245–261.

Diederich, A. (2011): "Einstellungen zu Priorisierungen in der medizinischen Versorgung", in A. Diederich, C. Koch, R. Kray, and R. Sibbel (eds.): *Priorisierte Medizin: Ausweg oder Sackgasse der Gesundheitsgesellschaft?*, 13–38. Wiesbaden: Gabler.

Diederich, A. (2016a): "Age and Personal Responsibility as Prioritization Criteria? The View of the Public and of Physicians", in E. Nagel, and M. Lauerer (eds): *Prioritization in Medicine: An International Dialogue*, 241–257. Cham: Springer.

Diederich, A. (2016b): "What Health Care Services Does the Public Want and Who Should Decide? Ask Them!", *Israel Journal of Health Policy Research* 5, 47.

Diederich, A. (2020): "Identifying Needs: The Psychological Perspective", in S. Traub, and B. Kittel (eds.): *Need-Based Distributive Justice: An Interdisciplinary Perspective*, 59–89. Cham: Springer Nature.

Diederich, A., G. du Bois, and D. Dörr (2015): "Einstellungen zu Priorisierungen in der medizinischen Versorgung: Ergebnisse einer Befragung des Deutschen Ärztinnenbundes (DÄB)", *FOR 655 Working Paper* 40/2015.

Diederich, A., D. Salzmann (2015): "Public Preferences Regarding Therapeutic Benefit, Costs of a Medical Treatment and Evidence-Based Medicine as Prioritization Criteria", *Journal of Public Health* 23 (3), 137–148.

Diederich, A., and M. Schreier (2009): "Kriterien der Priorisierung aus gesellschaftlicher Sicht", *Zeitschrift für Evidenz, Fortbildung und Qualität im Gesundheitswesen* 103 (2), 111–116.

Diederich, A., and M. Schreier (2010): "Zur Akzeptanz von Eigenverantwortung als Posteriorisierungskriterium", *Bundesgesundheitsblatt-Gesundheitsforschung-Gesundheitsschutz* 53 (9), 896–902.

Diederich, A., J. Swait, and N. Wirsik (2012): "Citizen Participation in Patient Prioritization Policy Decisions: An Empirical and Experimental Study on Patients' Characteristics", *PLOS ONE* 7 (5), e36,824

Diederich, A., J. Winkelhage, M. Schnoor, and M. Schreier (2009): "Priorisierung. Öffentlicher Diskurs erforderlich", *Deutsches Ärzteblatt* 106 (14), A654–656.

Dolan, P., R. Shaw, A. Tsuchiya, and A. Williams (2005): "QALY Maximisation and People's Preferences: A Methodological Review of the Literature", *Health Economics* 14 (2), 197–208.

Dyer, O. (2020): "Health Ministers Condemn Novartis Lottery for Zolgensma, the World's Most Expensive Drug", *British Medical Journal* 368, m580.

Egan, T. M., and R. M. Kotloff (2005): "Pro/Con Debate: Lung Allocation Should Be Based on Medical Urgency and Transplant Survival and not on Waiting Time", *CHEST* 128 (1), 407–415.

Fleck, L. (2016): "Just Caring: Fair Innings and Priority Setting", in E. Nagel, and M. Lauerer (eds.): *Prioritization in Medicine: An International Dialogue*, 197–216. Cham: Springer.

Friedrich, D. R., and B. Schöne-Seifert (2013): "Wirksamkeit und Nutzen bei der Priorisierung medizinischer Leistungen", in B. Schmitz-Luhn, and A. Bohmeier (eds.): *Priorisierung in der Medizin: Kriterien im Dialog*, Kölner Schriften zum Medizinrecht, 31–36. Heidelberg: Springer.

Gächter, S., H. Orzen, E. Renner, and C. Starmer (2009): "Are Experimental Economists Prone to Framing Effects? A Natural Field Experiment", *Journal of Economic Behavior & Organization* 70 (3), 443–446.

Gamliel, E., and E. Peer (2006): "Positive versus Negative Framing Affects Justice Judgments", *Social Justice Research* 19 (3), 307–322.

Gamliel, E., and E. Peer (2010): "Attribute Framing Affects the Perceived Fairness of Health Care Allocation Principles", *Judgment and Decision Making* 5 (1), 11–20.

Guyatt, G.H., D. J. Cook, D. King, G. R. Norman, S. L. Kane, and C. van Ineveld (1999): "Effect of the Framing of Questionnaire Items Regarding Satisfaction with Training on Residents' Responses", *Academic Medicine* 74 (2), 192–194.

Ham, C. (1997): "Priority Setting in Health Care: Learning from International Experience", *Health Policy* 42 (1), 49–66.

Hauck, K., P. C. Smith, and M. Goddard (2004): "The Economics of Priority Setting for Health Care: A Literature Review", *HNP discussion paper* 28878. Washington: The International Bank for Reconstruction and Development/The World Bank.

Hirtz, D., S. Iannaccone, J. Heemskerk, K. Gwinn-Hardy, R. Moxley, and L. P. Rowland (2005): "Challenges and Opportunities in Clinical Trials for Spinal Muscular Atrophy", *Neurology* 65 (9), 1352–1357.

Homans, G. C. (1958): "Social Behavior as Exchange", *American Journal of Sociology* 63 (6), 597–606.

Hurley, J. (2000): "An Overview of the Normative Economics of the Health Sector", in A. J. Culyer, and J. P. Newhouse (eds.): *Handbook of Health Economics*, vol. 1, 55–118. Amsterdam: Elsevier.

Johannesson, M., and P. O. Johansson (1996): "The Economics of Ageing: On the Attitude of Swedish People to the Distribution of Health Care Resources Between the Young and the Old", *Health Policy* 37 (3), 153–161.

Jonsen, A. R. (1986): "Bentham in a Box: Technology Assessment and Health Care Allocation", *Journal of Law, Medicine and Ethics* 14 (3–4), 172–174.

Jost, J. T., and A. C. Kay (2010): "Social Justice: History, Theory, and Research", in: *Handbook of Social Psychology*, vol. 2, 1122–1165, 5th ed. Hoboken, NJ: Wiley.

Konow, J. (1996): "A Positive Theory of Economic Fairness", *Journal of Economic Behavior & Organization* 31 (1), 13–35.

Konow, J. (2001): "Fair and Square: the Four Sides of Distributive Justice", *Journal of Economic Behavior & Organization* 46 (2), 137–164.

Konow, J. (2003): "Which is the Fairest One of All? A Positive Analysis of Justice Theories", *Journal of Economic Literature* 41 (4), 1188–1239.

Kragt, M. E., and J. W. Bennett (2012): "Attribute Framing in Choice Experiments: How Do Attribute Level Descriptions Affect Value Estimates?", *Environmental and Resource Economics* 51 (1), 43–59.

Krütli, P., T. Rosemann, K. Y. Törnblom, and T. Smieszek (2016): "How to Fairly Allocate Scarce Medical Resources: Ethical Argumentation under Scrutiny by Health Professionals and Lay People", *PLOS ONE* 11 (7), e0159,086.

Kühberger, A. (1998): "The Influence of Framing on Risky Decisions: A Meta-Analysis", *Organizational Behavior and Human Decision Processes* 75 (1), 23–55.

Lamont J., and C. Favor (2017): "Distributive Justice", in E. N. Zalta (ed.): *The Stanford Encyclopedia of Philosophy*, winter 2017. Stanford University. https://plato.stanford.edu/archives/win2017/entries/justice-distributive/

Lerner, M. J. (1975): "The Justice Motive in Social Behavior: Introduction", *Journal of Social Issues* 31 (3), 1–19.

Leventhal, G. S. (1976): "Fairness in Social Relations", in J. Thibaut, J. T. Spence, and R. C. Carsob (eds.): *Contemporary Topics in Social Psychology*, 211–239. Morristown: General Learning Press.

Liebig, S., and C. Sauer (2016): "Sociology of Justice", in C. Sabbagh, and M. Schmitt (eds.): *Handbook of Social Justice Theory and Research*, 37–59. New York: Springer.

Mariotti G., et al. (2014): "Waiting Time Prioritisation for Specialist Services in Italy: The Homogeneous Waiting Time Groups Approach", *Health Policy* 117 (1), 54–63.

McKie, J., and J. Richardson (2003): "The Rule of Rescue", *Social Science and Medicine* 56 (12), 2407–2419.

McKie, J., R. Hurworth, J. Richardson, and B. Shrimpton (2009): "Treatment Costs and Priority Setting in Health Care: A Qualitative Study", *Australia and New Zealand Health Policy* 6, 11.

Menke, F. (2021): *Provokanter Corona-Vorschlag: Ungeimpfte zur Kasse bitten*. Westdeutscher Rundfunk. https://www1.wdr.de/nachrichten/themen/coronavirus/ungeimpfte-corona-kosten-102.html

Miller, D. (1979): *Social Justice*. Oxford: Oxford University Press.

Mossialos, E., and D. King (1999): "Citizens and Rationing: Analysis of a European Survey", *Health Policy* 49 (1), 75–135.

Murray, H. (1938): *Explorations in Personality*. Oxford: Oxford University Press.

Myllykangas, M., O. P. Ryynänen, J. Kinnunen, and J. Takala (1996): "Comparison of Doctors', Nurses', Politicians' and Public Attitudes to Health Care Priorities", *Journal of Health Services Research and Policy* 1 (4), 212–216.

Niessen, L. W., E. W. M. Grijseels, and F. F. H Rutten (2000): "The Evidence-Based Approach in Health Policy and Health Care Delivery", *Social Science and Medicine* 51 (6), 859–869.

Nord, E., J. Richardson, A. Street, H. Kuhse, and P. Singer (1995): "Maximizing Health Benefits vs Egalitarianism: An Australian Survey of Health Issues", *Social Science and Medicine* 41 (10), 1429–1437.

Nord, E., J. L. Pinto, J. Richardson, P. Menzel, and P. Ubel (1999): "Incorporating Societal Concerns for Fairness in Numerical Valuations of Health Programmes", *Health Economics* 8 (1), 25–39.

Nullmeier, F. (2020): "Towards a Theory of Need-Based Justice", in S. Traub, and B. Kittel (eds.): *Need-Based Distributive Justice: An Interdisciplinary Perspective*, 191–208. Cham: Springer Nature.

Oakes, J. M., and P. H. Rossi (2003): "The Measurement of SES in Health Research: Current Practice and Steps Toward a New Approach", *Social Science and Medicine* 56 (4), 769–784.

Oedingen, C., T. Bartling, M. L. Dierks, A. C. Mühlbacher, H. Schrem, and C. Krauth (2020): "Public Preferences for the Allocation of Donor Organs for Transplantation: Focus Group Discussions", *Health Expectations* 23 (3), 670–680.

Olsen, J. A. (1997): "Theories of Justice and their Implications for Priority Setting in Health Care", *Journal of Health Economics* 16 (6), 625–639.

Olsen, J. A. (2017): *Principles in Health Economics and Policy*. Oxford: Oxford University Press.

Pinho, M., and A. Pinto Borges (2018): "A Three-Country Survey of Public Attitudes Towards the Use of Rationing Criteria to Set Healthcare Priorities Between Patients", *International Journal of Ethics and Systems* 34 (4), 472–492.

Rawls, J. (1971): *A Theory of Justice*. Cambridge: Harvard University Press.

Robert Koch-Institut (2022): Hinweise zur Testung von Patienten auf Infektion mit dem neuartigen Coronavirus SARS-CoV-2. https://www.rki.de/DE/Content/InfAZ/N/Neuartiges_Coronavirus/Vorl_Testung_nCoV.html

Rodríguez, E., and J. L. Pinto (2000): "The Social Value of Health Programmes: Is Age a Relevant Factor?", *Health Economics* 9 (7), 611–621.

Rogge, J., and B. Kittel (2016): "Who Shall not Be Treated: Public Attitudes on Setting Health Care Priorities by Person-Based Criteria in 28 Nations", *PLOS ONE* 11 (6), e0157,018.

Rudan, I., L. Kapiriri, M. Tomlinson, M. Balliet, B. Cohen, and M. Chopra (2010): "Evidence-Based Priority Setting for Health Care and Research: Tools to Support Policy in Maternal, Neonatal, and Child Health in Africa", *PLOS Medicine* 7 (7), e1000,308.

Ryynänen, O. P., M. Myllykangas, J. Kinnunen, and J. Takala (1999): "Attitudes to Health Care Prioritisation Methods and Criteria among Nurses, Doctors, Politicians and the General Public", *Social Science and Medicine* 49 (11), 1529–1539.

Sabbagh, C. (2001): "A Taxonomy of Normative and Empirically Oriented Theories of Distributive Justice", *Social Justice Research* 14 (3), 237–263.

Sabbagh, C., Y. Dar, and N. Resh (1994): "The Structure of Social Justice Judgments: A Facet Approach", *Social Psychology Quarterly* 57 (3), 244–261.

Sabik, L. M., and R. K. Lie (2008): "Priority Setting in Health Care: Lessons from the Experiences of Eight Countries", *International Journal for Equity in Health* 7, 4.

Schmidt, H. (2007): "Personal Responsibility for Health–Developments under the German Health-care Reform 2007", *European Journal of Health Law* 14 (3), 241–250.

Schöne-Seifert, B., D. R. Friedrich, and A. Diederich (2012): "'Leistungsbeschränkungen in der Medizin nach Maßgabe von Nutzen-Schwellen: Akzeptanz in der deutschen Bevölkerung?", *Zeitschrift für Evidenz, Fortbildung und Qualität im Gesundsheitswesen* 106 (6), 426–434.

Schreiber, H. L., and A. Haverich (2000): "Richtlinien für die Warteliste und für die Organvermittlung", *Deutsches Ärzteblatt* 97 (7), A 385–386.

Stumpf, S., S. Hecker, and H. Raspe (2014): "Kriterien für die Priorisierung medizinischer Leistungen im Licht eines regionalen Surveys–Ergebnisse und methodologische Fragen", *Das Gesundheitswesen* 76 (4), 221–231.

Törnblom, K. (1988): "Positive and Negative Allocations: A Typology and a Model for Conflicting Justice Principles", *Advances in Group Processes* 5, 141–168.

Törnblom, K., and E. Ahlin (1998): "Mode of Accomplishing Positive and Negative Outcomes: Its Effect on Fairness Evaluations", *Social Justice Research* 11 (4), 423–442.

Törnblom, K., and A. Kazemi (2015): "Distributive Justice: Revisiting Past Statements and Reflecting on Future Prospects", in R. S. Cropanzano, and M. L. Ambrose (eds.): *The Oxford Handbook of Justice in the Workplace*, 15–50. Oxford: Oxford University Press.

Tsuchiya, A. (1999): "Age-Related Preferences and Age Weighting Health Benefits", *Social Science and Medicine* 48 (2), 267–276.

Tsuchiya, A., P. Dolan, and R. Shaw (2003): "Measuring People's Preferences Regarding Ageism in Health: Some Methodological Issues and some Fresh Evidence", *Social Science and Medicine* 57 (4), 687–696.

Tversky, A., and D. J. Koehler (1994): "Support Theory: A Nonextensional Representation of Subjective Probability", *Psychological Review* 101 (4), 547–567.

Tymstra, T., and M. Andela (1993): "Opinions of Dutch Physicians, Nurses, and Citizens on Health Care Policy, Rationing, and Technology", *Journal of the American Medical Association* 270 (24), 2995–2999.

Walster, E., E. Berscheid, and G. W. Walster (1973): "New Directions in Equity Research", *Journal of Personality and Social Psychology* 25 (2), 151–176.

Waring, D. R. (2004): *Medical Benefit and the Human Lottery: An Egalitarian Approach to Patient Selection*. Dordecht: Springer.

Watters, S. M. (2016): "Fair Innings as a Basis for Prioritization: An Empirical Perspective", in E. Nagel, and M. Lauerer (eds.): *Prioritization in Medicine: An International Dialogue*, 179–196. Cham: Springer.

Wegener, B., D. Mason, and International Social Justice Project (ISJP) (2010): *International Social Justice Project, 1991 and 1996*. Interuniversity Consortium for Political and Social Research. https://doi.org/10.3886/ICPSR06705.v2

Williams, A. (1997): "Intergenerational Equity: An Exploration of the 'Fair Innings' Argument", *Health Economics* 6 (2), 117–132.

Winkelhage, J., and A. Diederich (2012): "The Relevance of Personal Characteristics in Allocating Health Care Resources–Controversial Preferences of Laypersons with Different Educational Backgrounds", *International Journal of Environmental Research and Public Health* 9 (1), 223–243.

Winkelhage, J., M. Schreier, and A. Diederich (2013): "Priority Setting in Health Care: Attitudes of Physicians and Patients", *Health* 5 (4), 712–719.

Winkler, J., and H. Stolzenberg (1999): "Der Sozialschichtindex im Bundes-Gesundheitssurvey", *Das Gesundheitswesen* 61 (Sonderheft 2), S178–S183.

Wirsik, N., A. Diederich, and M. Schreier (2009): "Coinjont-Analyse: Prätest zur Evaluation von patientenbezogenen Merkmalen und dem Einfluss von Proxies auf die Bildung der Rangfolge", *FOR 655 Working Paper* 22/2009.

World Health Organization Regional Office for Europe (1996): *The Ljubljana Charter on Reforming Health Care in Europe*. Technical documents. https://apps.who.int/iris/handle/10665/347612

Wujciak, T., and G. Opelz (1993a): "Computer Analysis of Cadaver Kidney Allocation Procedures", *Transplantation* 55 (3), 516–521.

Wujciak, T., and G. Opelz (1993b): "A Proposal for Improved Cadaver Kidney Allocation", *Transplantation* 56 (6), 1513–1517.

Chapter 11
Conclusion: Elements of a Theory of Need-Based Justice

Bernhard Kittel and Stefan Traub

Abstract This chapter aggregates the results of the disciplinary and mostly experimental sub-projects of the research group "Need-Based Justice and Distribution Procedures" into an empirically informed normative theory of need-based justice. Its elements include a concept of need, the identification of need, the recognition of need, and the consequences of need-based redistribution. The chapter also critically discusses the results in relation to the normative criteria of consistency, legitimacy, and sustainability. As a central result, we present a distributive principle for prosperous societies based on reciprocal solidarity—the Lexineed principle—which, within the framework of a strong pluralistic theory of distributive justice, gives priority to the satisfaction of recognized needs over all other principles of justice.

11.1 The Concept of Need

This chapter derives core elements of an empirically informed theory of need-based justice from the theoretical considerations and experimental findings presented in the previous ten chapters. The theory has a core and three key layers, which are presented in this and the following three sections: the *concept of need*, the *identification* of needs, the *recognition* of needs, and the welfare *consequences* of need-based redistribution (see Fig. 11.1). In that order, the latter three layers represent the micro, meso, and macro levels of the argument. They are also each supplemented by normative requirements, namely *consistency*, *legitimacy*, and *sustainability*. At the micro level, which refers to the cognitive layer of the need concept, individuals must identify a situation as being one of need. Such a need

B. Kittel
Department of Economic Sociology, University of Vienna, Wien, Austria
e-mail: bernhard.kittel@univie.ac.at

S. Traub (✉)
Department of Economics, Helmut-Schmidt University, Hamburg, Germany
e-mail: traubs@hsu-hh.de

B. Kittel, S. Traub (eds.), *Priority of Needs?*,
https://doi.org/10.1007/978-3-031-53051-7_11

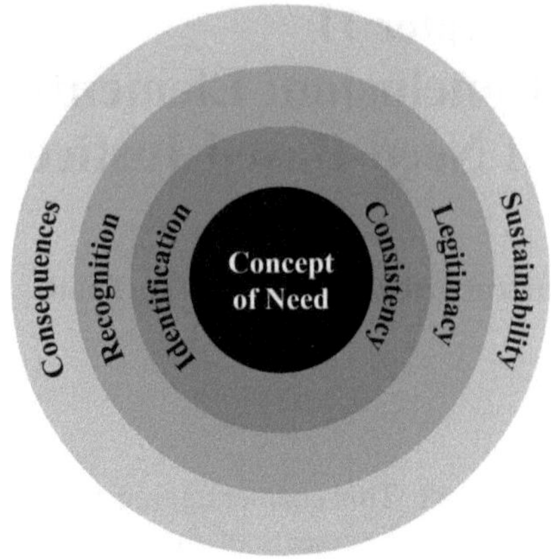

Fig. 11.1 Elements of a Theory of Need-Based Justice

judgment must be consistent in the sense of being description invariant. At the meso level, social and political organizations have to recognize that expressed individual need as legitimate. The macro layer consists of the societal and economic consequences of decisions, which must be sustainable in the long run.

In the first chapter of this volume, we asked the following research question: "Why prioritize needs?" We argued that need is the principle that best fits notions of distributive justice in the welfare states of the twenty-first century. In this chapter, we answer this question in light of the preceding studies. We first revisit the concept of need. Then we argue that reciprocal solidarity is a prerequisite for the recognition and satisfaction of needs, i.e., the establishment of need-based justice. Next, we commit to a concept of *recognized need* that deliberately refrains from objectifying needs through lists and hierarchies of categorical needs. We argue that what is needed by members of a society should be revealed through an intersubjective process of mutual understanding. Sections 11.2, 11.3, and 11.4 then deal with need identification and recognition as well as the welfare consequences of need-based redistribution. Section 11.5 is dedicated to the differentiation of individual and collective assessments of need claims in the process of need recognition. In Sect. 11.6, we synthesize the four elements into an informed theory of need-based justice and discuss the properties of the theory in terms of Nullmeier's ten theses outlined on p. 18 in Chap. 1. The chapter ends with concluding remarks in Sect. 11.7.

11.1.1 Need-Based Justice as Reciprocal Solidarity

In the volume *Need-Based Distributive Justice: An Interdisciplinary Perspective*, Kittel (2020) emphasizes that need-based justice requires consideration of the circumstances of the members of a community and a shared understanding of what is necessary. This is most likely, but not exclusively, achieved in a solidary community built on reciprocity of social relations (Liebig and Sauer 2016). Along these lines—and in contrast to equality and equity as principles of distributive justice—the literature often associates the reciprocal recognition of claims with status equality (Fraser 2000, pp. 113–115) and satisfaction of needs with affective relationships (e.g., Deutsch 1975).

However, it would be highly problematic for a theory of *distributive justice* to make close social relations such as in a family, a neighborhood, or a club a prerequisite for the satisfaction of needs, because the scope of such a theory would be too limited (cf. Nullmeier 2020, p. 206; also see Thesis 9 on p. 18 of this volume). Contrary to such concerns, the review of the psychological literature on distributional justice by Diederich reveals that close social "relationship is not a necessary condition for need considerations" (Diederich 2020, p. 80). Indeed, the idea of solidarity based on reciprocity can also be found in Miller's (1995, 2013, 2016) work, who argues that solidarity in the welfare state is created through a common national identity.

Tying need-based justice to the nation state inevitably leads to a *non-universalist* concept of need. For reciprocal solidarity exists only between individuals who feel connected by a common language, ethnicity, religion, etc., and common historical and cultural experiences (Gellner 1983).[1] However, this limitation on the scope of the need principle, which differentiates between insiders and outsiders,[2] seems to be acceptable from a normative point of view in the context of welfare states; it may even be seen as an advantage, because each welfare state can develop its own understanding of what is necessary given the respective circumstances. The welfare state thus guarantees the mutual satisfaction of recognized needs and creates a symmetrical and reciprocal relationship between equals (Gouldner 1960; Blau 1964). However, when the recognition of needs is unidirectional, as it is between the populations of differently developed states, other principles of distribution apply that are based on humanitarian solidarity rather than social justice (Miller 1999).

[1] Alesina et al. (2001) and Alesina and Glaeser (2004) argue that higher social fragmentation of a country (e.g., by ethnicity, skin color, and religion) correlates with lower redistribution. They show that the United States has both higher fragmentation and less redistribution than Western European countries. Several studies have demonstrated a negative relationship between social diversity and the provision of public goods (James 1993; Kuijs 2000; Soroka et al. 2006). Luttmer (2001) showed for the USA that people living in areas with many welfare recipients agree to more redistribution if the welfare recipients have the same skin color or origin as themselves, i.e., the group is more homogeneous overall (racial group effect).

[2] In an experimental study, Klor and Shayo (2010) found that subjects systematically vote for a redistributive regime that benefits members of their own group, even if this reduces their own payoff. Social identity theory explains this behavior. It posits that a person's social identity is co-determined by membership in a social group. When a person feels that she belongs to a group, she derives benefits from comparing her own group positively with a relevant other group (Tajfel and Turner 1979; Akerlof and Kranton 2000). This *ingroup bias* ensures that people tend to treat others who belong to their own social group better than those who belong to a different group (for a meta-analysis of economic experiments see Lane 2016).

11.1.2 Objectification of Needs

These basic considerations about reciprocal solidarity and the scope of need-based justice indicate that an informed theory of need-based justice must be based on a normatively convincing, evidence-supported and operational concept of need. In principle, a theory of distributive justice can be understood as a model that defines three arguments for its *scope*, *shape*, and *currency* (Page 2006, pp. 50ff). These arguments "answer the question *who* [scope] should get *how much* [shape] of *what* [currency]?" (Siebel and Schramme 2020, p. 23). The currency of need-based justice is need, or more accurately, the satisfaction of socially or politically recognized needs. But what exactly is a recognized need?

In *Need-Based Distributive Justice. An Interdisciplinary Perspective*, Traub (2020, p. 3) asked "[w]hy has need been treated with so much reservation and scepticism in the literature?" Reviewing the voluminous theoretical and empirical literature on distributive justice from the disciplines of economics, philosophy, political science, psychology, and sociology showed that, depending on the discipline and perspective, "need may refer to motives that drive behavior (Lewin 1926), physiological basic needs (Galtung 1980), subjective feelings of deprivation (Runciman 1966), or [...] a requirement for certain human capabilities and functionings in order to be able to live a 'decent life' " (ibid. p. 4). Moreover, we argued that need is usually accorded a more fundamental role than other prominent justice principles like equality and equity (for an overview, see Sabbagh and Schmitt 2016)—but above all, it is more controversial. In our opinion, this controversy has one main focus, namely the *objectification* of needs.

Needs must be neatly distinguished from wants or *desires*. Desires are—even if the individual limits herself to what she considers "realistic" desires (Runciman 1966)—in principle unlimited. Since resources are finite, any attempt to achieve a state of justice by satisfying all desires would be doomed to failure (Vlastos 1962; Miller 2007a; Brock 2012). Thus, it is questionable whether society should be guided by the satisfaction of individual desires, i.e., whether they have *moral significance*. In this context, "having enough" can refer to the fundamentals of human existence, what makes it possible to live a "decent life" in a society, or something else that is morally significant. The controversy of need-based justice hence lies primarily in determining what constitutes human existence, a decent life, or some other criterion.

An obvious way to deal with the dilemma of the potential unlimitedness of desires and the limitedness of resources would be to restrict desires to an "objective" set of needs that are granted moral significance. The instrumental need statement "Mr. Smith's family needs beverages and food for X" constitutes to a desire when X refers to champagne and caviar for the New Year's Eve party. It constitutes a categorical, absolute, or intrinsic need when X refers to basic food items like water, bread, and vegetables for the maintenance of physical health. However, the objectification of need requires procedures and criteria (cf., e.g., Brock 2005; Thomson 2005; Weale and Craig 1998; Wringe 2005). One way to accomplish this task is by delegation to experts. In Rowntree's famous study of poverty in York in 1899 (Rowntree 1901), the physiologist Wilbor Atwater determined how many calories a person needs to maintain her ability to work, launching the Basic Needs Approach to absolute poverty measurement. The social and behavioral sciences have produced numerous variants of this kind of objectification through lists and hierarchies of morally significant needs, from Maslow's (1943) famous Theory of Human Motivation to Sen's (1985, 1999), and Nussbaum's (1988, 2001) versions of the Capabilities Approach. The latter replaced the consumption-oriented Basic Needs Approach in the United Nations Human Development Program (a comprehensive literature review is provided in the relevant disciplinary chapters of Traub and Kittel 2020).

A recurring motive of these lists of basic needs and capabilities, based on expert knowledge of what is necessary, is their organization into hierarchies according to their necessity. More basic needs such as food and shelter are given higher moral significance than, e.g., social and personal autonomy needs. Indeed, in a vignette study with an online sample, Bauer et al. (2023) show that participants perceive a clear hierarchy (in descending order) of needs from "survival" to "decency" to "belonging" and to "autonomy," thus granting more resources to the more needy person in each case. Even if it is obvious that the immediate protection against physical suffering through hunger or cold has a higher moral significance than the realization of personal autonomy, and therefore should be realized first, the focus on basic needs alone falls short. Bauer et al. (2023, p. 3) emphasize that "there are basic needs beyond the biological minimum not to be ignored just because existence comes first." Psychological research shows that social needs contribute to people's mental well-being (e.g., Deci and Ryan 2000; Ryan and Deci 2000). In addition to physical existence, humans are also social beings, which makes it important to ask what needs arise from membership in social communities (Miller 2007b; Brock and Miller 2019).

In summary, "[. . .] the needs that are normatively salient, especially in political distribution, are those that are necessary, indispensable, or inescapable, given the kinds of creatures that we are and the requirements for functioning in *social* settings" (Brock and Miller 2019, emphasis added). The satisfaction of these normatively significant needs serves to avoid harm, or in positive terms, to foster a decent life (cf., e.g., Frankfurt 1984; Wiggins 1998; Miller 1999). This is in line with Nullmeier's thesis that the core of the concept of need is the notion of something that is "necessary, compelling, imperative, indispensable, essentially required—something that goes beyond mere desires or preferences and takes precedence over desires" (Nullmeier 2020, p. 191; see Thesis 1 on p. 18 of this volume) *and* his statement that the satisfaction of needs in the welfare state *is not limited* to mere survival (ibid., p. 201).

How can the needs that the welfare state should meet be determined (if not directly through experts)? We argue, in line with Miller (1999), that need is socially or politically recognized in an intersubjective process (Thesis 5). This process of need *recognition* is based on the experiential values of the members of a solidary community about what is necessary for leading a decent life in any particular time, place, and personal circumstance (Thesis 6). This does not preclude the incorporation of expertise, e.g., in the form of an econometric model, in which expenditure systems are used to identify typical consumption patterns of households in the lower-income percentiles (see, e.g., Geary 1950; Stone 1954; Deaton and Muellbauer 1980; Almås 2012). Note that such an approach, which measures need by the ordinary consumption patterns of a society, distinguishes need-based justice from purely *comparative* concepts of justice ("why does person A have more than person B, and how can this be justified?") by the fact that the *non-comparative aspect* ("does person A have enough in order to …?") is in the foreground (cf. Siebel and Schramme 2020, pp. 23ff).

In the sense of the economic demand theory just quoted, recognized need is a certain quantity—a kind of threshold or minimum consumption—of a resource that is considered necessary for living a decent life. An individual gains utility from the consumption of the resource only when this threshold is reached. Since need-based justice as an expression of reciprocal solidarity is tied to common identities, this threshold is identified and objectified for particular groups of people and varies across time and place (Thesis 9). Since the intersubjective understanding of what a satisfiable need is, is based on common experience and actual consumption patterns, one could speak of a theory of aggregated *revealed preferences* about socially acceptable minimum consumption, i.e., about what constitutes a decent life in a given society. Such a theory must, of course, meet certain normative requirements, which will be discussed in the following sections.

An issue related to the determination of the minimum consumption threshold is how to deal with the *scarcity* of resources. A resource may or may not be sufficient to cover the needs of all members of that group. When the resource is smaller than the sum of thresholds of all members of the community, the distribution problem becomes one of deciding whose needs will be satisfied and whose will not. When the failure to satisfy individual need implies serious harm, assuming that everyone individually prefers to live a decent life, need satisfaction becomes a zero-sum game between the members of the community. Put otherwise, in such situations, needs cannot be differentiated from pure self-interest and the notion of need-based justice loses its moral significance. More interesting for a theory of need-based justice are conditions where the available resources are larger than the sum of all thresholds, and it is possible in principle to satisfy all needs, i.e., situations of *oversupply* (Thesis 9). In this case, decision-makers can cover their own needs and subsequently consider the satisfaction of others' needs as one of several options. Thus, we can ask under which conditions needs are satisfied.

Finally, there is the question of how recognized needs are adjusted to changing resources (cf. Nullmeier 2020, pp. 202–204). Since recognized need is not based on a predetermined catalog of categorical needs but on aggregated revealed preferences, we can assume that the threshold value is variable, but the recognized need can never exceed the available resources. Whether the alignment of needs is disproportionate, proportionate, or subproportionate to the change in resources that determine the usual consumption behavior is a purely empirical question.

Definition (Recognized Need) Recognized need is a threshold for a minimum level of consumption that can be fulfilled with the available resources and that represents the result of an intersubjective understanding of what is necessary to lead a decent life in a certain society characterized by reciprocal solidarity and bound by a common identity.

The definition of recognized need summarizes our previous considerations on the concept of need. For a theory of distributive justice based on recognized needs to be normatively convincing, we argue that the abovementioned three *requirements* of consistency, legitimacy, and sustainability must be fulfilled. The next three sections therefore contain, on the one hand, our theoretical considerations regarding these normative requirements and, on the other hand, the empirical results of our research project, which show whether such a theory of need-based justice that rests on revealed distributional preferences is also convincing from a normative point of view.

Specifically, the three sections address the following questions:

1. We need to answer how individual need *identification* works and how certain distributions are recognized as sufficient for satisfying given needs. Related to the positive question of identification is the normative question of the *consistency* of need judgments. The consistency of individual need judgments has its counterpart in rational choice theory, where it is assumed that the rationality of the underlying preference order can be inferred from the observed choices ("revealed preferences"; see, e.g., Varian 2006). Does a concept of distributive justice based on recognized need lead us to expect consistent judgments of need? Consistency in terms of individual rationality, i.e., completeness and transitivity (cf. Mas-Collel et al. 1995, pp. 6ff), is not only an important normative property of individual (distributional) preferences (cf. Andreoni and Miller 2002) but a fundamental property of social decision functions that aggregate individual distributional preferences (cf. Gaertner 2006, p. 6–9).
2. This leads to the second question of how collective (i.e., social or political) need *recognition* works, i.e., how communities objectify needs by developing an intersubjective understanding of what constitutes a decent life. Answering this question is also about the descriptive input and output *legitimacy* of need-based (re)distribution (see, e.g., Scharpf 1999, 2009). The creation of distributive justice through the political recognition and satisfaction of needs requires institutions that must be democratically legitimized. In terms of input legitimacy, all citizens, including those who represent a minority opinion, must know that their interests are adequately represented in the course of decision-making. In terms of output legitimacy, the actual solutions to problems must also correlate with the common interests of the citizens (see Kraus 2004, pp. 559–571).
3. It is a truism that only what has been earned beforehand can be (re)distributed. Even institutions endowed with great legitimacy fail to provide welfare in the long run if the negative incentive effects they exert lead to the erosion of the basis of prosperity. Consequently, it is necessary to examine the welfare *consequences* of need-based redistribution, i.e., whether the need principle

resolves the perceived conflict between equity and efficiency in a way that is economically *sustainable*.[3]

The first three parts of this volume therefore dealt with the identification and consistency, the recognition and legitimacy, and the consequences and sustainability of need-based redistribution. Part four looked at specific manifestations of need-based distribution in the health sector and in the provision of welfare, which illuminate processes of differentiation that qualify the recognition of needs.

11.2 The Identification of Needs

One of the most fundamental axioms of rational choice theory—so fundamental that it is hardly mentioned—is the axiom of extensionality (Arrow 1982), also known as *description invariance* (Tversky and Kahneman 1986). The choice of an alternative should depend only on the available alternatives, not on their description. "A *frame* is an individual's fundamental representation of a general type of situation, event, or act, which is based on prior individual, social, and cultural experiences and learning" (Traub 1999, pp. 36–37, emph. add.; also see Tversky and Kahneman 1981, p. 453). The *framing* of choice alternatives, e.g., as losses or gains relative to a reference point, leads, as a vast literature shows, to *framing effects*, i.e., to inconsistent choices. These framing effects occur systematically and do not disappear due to learning and monetary incentives (cf., e.g., Kahneman and Tversky 1984; Traub 1999; Kühberger 1998, 2023).

The opinions people form about social policy issues depend on frames and are influenced by framing (cf. Callaghan and Schnell 2009; Wenzelburger and Hörisch 2016). Bruckmüller et al. (2017) show in an experimental study that the perception of global inequality and the intention to address it depend on the verbal description of the problem in terms of the reference country (which was either a poor or a rich country). In a laboratory experiment, Lorenz et al. (2017) and Paetzel et al. (2018) show that framing the vote about redistribution as a mathematically equivalent decision about a minimal income increases the preferred level of redistribution.

In Chap. 2 of this volume, Adele Diederich emphasizes that individual frames are also relevant in the identification of needs. Framings influence the perception and interpretation of the decision situation and thus prestructure individual choices. She distinguishes *internal* framings (Fischer 1997) from *external* framings (Kühberger 1998). Internal framings are based on personal characteristics, experiences, or normative persuasions, while external framings refer to the way in which the decision problem is presented.

---

[3] The magnitude of the indirect costs of (redistributive) taxation has been the subject of much theoretical and empirical work (e.g., Ballard et al. 1985; Ballard 1988; Stantcheva 2021). The trade-off between equity and efficiency is at the core of political economy models (e.g., Meltzer and Richard 1981; for an experimental test, see Tepe et al. 2021a).

Diederich focuses on decisions under risk when answering the research question of whether framing affects the consistency of individual need identification. Her experiments involve gain frames and loss frames (for details about the experimental designs, see Sect. 2.3.1.1). She establishes an interesting theoretical link between need, the Stone–Geary utility function originating from economic demand theory (Geary 1950; Stone 1954), and the foraging theory originating from behavioral biology (Stephens 1981; Stephens and Charnov 1982). In this experiment, need represents a certain quantity—a kind of threshold or minimum consumption—of an important resource. Utility is provided and biological survival becomes possible only when this threshold value is reached or exceeded.

In Diederich's incentivized laboratory experiments, "survival" means reaching a payoff or the next round (where additional earnings can be obtained). Although the economic demand theory and the foraging theory make different basic assumptions, both predict that subjects will be relatively risk seeking when the need gap is large and become more risk averse as the need gap decreases. The expected framing effects emerge in the form of preference reversals and preference shifts, which result from the fact that subjects in the loss frame are more willing to take risks than in the gain frame. Indeed, it also appears that subjects with greater need are more risk seeking. In fact, when need is great, this effect becomes so large that the framing effect disappears.

The aforementioned experiments focus on the identification of one's own needs and the resulting risk-taking behavior. In contrast, Diederich et al. (2018) investigate how subjects decide for others within the framework of the famous Asian-Disease Paradigm (see Sect. 2.3.2). Interestingly, here it is the case that greater need (being more affected by a disease) leads to less risk-taking. Diederich concludes that "in domains where risk-taking is viewed negatively (such as health), choices for others are less risky than choices for oneself" (p. 41). Moreover, in line with previous research on the "identifiable victim effect" (e.g., Jenni and Loewenstein 1997; Kogut and Ritov 2005a,b), Wyszynski et al. (2020) show in a novel "need" dictator game (see Sect. 2.3.3) in which the dictator's own risk behavior affects a needy "recipient," that subjects become more need-sensitive when the recipient is identifiable (when a picture is shown or the person is sitting in the same room).

In addition, Diederich also develops in Sect. 2.5.2 a dynamic dual process model for decisions under risk that integrates need. In the "fast" intuitive system 1, prospect theory (Kahneman and Tversky 1979) applies, allowing for framing effects. In the "slow" rational system 2, expected utility theory applies. The results show that need can lead to an initial bias, or choice probability bias, in favor of the riskier alternative.

In Chap. 3, Alexander Max Bauer and Mark Siebel report results from several vignette experiments, which aimed at determining how need information affects individual justice evaluations under certainty. As is common in empirical social choice (Gaertner and Schokkaert 2012), the subject always assumes the position of an impartial observer when she states her justice evaluations or determines what she considers to be the fairest allocation. Thus, although the decision context (certainty vs. risk) and experimental approach are very different, the results of both projects support and complement each other.

For example, Bauer and Siebel show in Sect. 3.3.1 that the absolute justice evaluation of an allocation of living space is concave, which is consistent with the usual economic assumption of positive and diminishing marginal utility. However, when the same housing allocation is framed either as a need gap or a need surplus, the justice evaluation function exhibits a sigmoid shape, i.e., it is convex below and concave above the reference point of exact need satisfaction. Thus, this study also reveals a possible "dark side" of need identification in the context of framing: Convexity has the consequence that "injustice can be reduced to a greater amount by helping those who have only slightly less than they need than by helping those who have the least" (p. 79). On the other hand, data analysis shows that need leads to a convergence of justice evaluations, i.e., facilitates a normative consensus on what is distributively just, which is encouraging for the objectification of need through a process of intersubjective understanding as discussed in the following section.

In a second experiment, Bauer et al. (2022) study the sensitivity of justice evaluations to information about need levels, individual productivity, and accountability for one's own need (for details, see Sect. 3.3.2). The general result is that just allocations are pulled toward need and productivity levels, but the compensation granted for higher need or lower productivity is only partial. Moreover, if high needs or low productivity is attributable to the person in need, average allocations are smaller. *Accountability* for one's own need, or lack of resources, is thus a factor in identifying need.

The study on different kinds of needs mentioned above and presented in more detail in Sect. 3.3.3 complements this finding: The less important a need, the greater the discount that less productive people have to accept on their needs. If, on the other hand, physical survival or the preservation of health is at stake, then accountability does not play a significant role. This study is also of interest in terms of framing. The four kinds of need, "Survival," "Decency," "Belonging," and "Autonomy," are each represented graphically and described by accompanying text, with the text framed either positively ("enablement frame") or negatively ("avoidance frame"). The verbal framing here is clearly dominated by the neutral graphical representation of the need, so that framing effects do not occur (for details see Bauer et al. 2023).

These observations of individual need judgments and evaluations provide a fairly consistent foundation for the systematization of individual assessments of a person's own and others' needs. People care for others; they respond, at least in what they say, to the urgency and severity of others' needs, others' efforts, and contributions to the satisfaction of their needs; and they hold others accountable for failure to avoid getting into situations of need. Thus, need satisfaction is not unconditional but seems to depend on the situation in which needs appear. Framing effects especially play a role in the identification of needs that are considered less important, which can lead to inconsistent judgments and decisions. However, framing effects can be counteracted by a neutral presentation of the situation.

In the second section of Chap. 3, Bauer and Siebel also explore how measures of need and need-based justice can improve the identification of need. They propose three measures that characterize unjust distributions. That is, (i) the lower the absolute or relative satisfaction of need, (ii) the greater the extent to which existing need gaps could be eliminated by transfers, or (iii) the greater the resources available to be used for oversupply, the more unjust a distribution. Because these new measures of need-based justice are based on axiomatic considerations similar to those commonly used in inequality and poverty measurements, they have the potential to increase the consistency of identification and recognition of need. For example, the measure of need-based justice proposed by Traub et al. (2017) would be immune to the undesirable effect of prioritizing the satisfaction of smaller needs over the satisfaction of larger needs, as described in Sect. 3.3.1, because of its *sensitivity* to larger need gaps.

Overall, these experimental and theoretical contributions also show that *transparency* and *expertise* can contribute to consistent need identification. Transparency here means providing all necessary information about need in a form that is as neutral as possible and does not trigger framing effects. Expertise means supporting the identification of need by axiomatic measures of need or need-based justice.

11.3 The Recognition of Needs

We distinguish between *social* and *political* recognition of needs. Social recognition takes place through interactions between peers in small groups. We speak of political recognition when it takes place in larger structured social groups such as a nation-state and is delegated to democratic institutions. As with need identification, we assume that the process of need recognition is facilitated by transparency and expertise. While transparency in need identification focuses on the complete and neutral presentation of the situation to be evaluated, transparency here is additionally thought to ensure the *legitimacy* of distributional decisions through a better information base and greater citizen participation (Norris 2011; Smith 2009). We refer to this as *social objectification*. Participation is associated with the search for argumentative procedures (as opposed to the contestation of interests). This approach finds its normative grounding in deliberative democratic theory (Habermas 1992; Dryzek 1990, 2002; Elster 1998; Cohen 2009, 2010) and its realization in a plethora of new deliberative and discursive procedures that also apply to distributional decisions such as public budgeting (Fishkin and Laslett 2003; Smith 2009).[4]

The attempt to increase transparency, the degree of participation, and the argumentative quality of democratic decisions is often combined with the increased inclusion of expertise as a procedure of *factual objectification*. Deliberative procedures with expert participation are seen as ways of increasing transparency and

[4] However, transparency is also viewed critically for theoretical (e.g., Etzioni 2010) and empirical reasons (e.g., de Fine Licht 2011).

information and as a way of democratizing expertise (Fischer 2009; Landwehr 2009). At the same time, empirical evidence shows that political debates are being shifted to advisory bodies (e.g., Mayntz et al. 2008; Siefken 2007; Weingart and Lentsch 2008). This is usually justified by the need to objectify the debate by providing a scientific basis for assessments of the state of affairs (Collins and Evans 2007; Bogner 2005). However, the value of expert panels can be seen precisely in dissent (Bogner and Menz 2010).

Bernhard Kittel studies *social* need recognition in Chap. 4. Assuming that needs must be articulated by or on behalf of a person in need in order to be socially relevant, he reports on studies of the conditions under which need claims are recognized by others. As Kittel notes, to recognize a need claim "implies that it is considered salient and consequential: that is, 'A's need *must* be satisfied' " (p. 98, emphasis added). Thus, it is through its recognition that a need acquires its moral significance. Kittel also points out that the moral obligation that accompanies the recognition of an expressed and identified need includes real *transfers* for the benefit of the needy, i.e., a redistribution between the recognizers and the needy in favor of the needy.

In their laboratory experiments, Kittel and his coauthors first establish that decision-making dyads embedded in groups of three allocate shares of a resource to group members who are not in the dyad (the "third players"), which is a clear indication of the presence of social values at the group level, and that needs are indeed a relevant criterion in distributive decisions. Kittel et al. (2020) then show that satisfaction of third players' needs declines with the size of their needs, whereby the allocation that conforms to the equal distribution among all group members is a critical threshold. Need claims above this threshold, which imply that the claimant should receive a larger share than at least one member of the dyad, are rarely satisfied.

This decline in need satisfaction is moderated by the *transparency* of claims (Kittel et al. 2021). When a claim is justified by exogenous information about its veracity, the willingness to satisfy a claim above the equal share increases, whereas it decreases when no such information is available.[5] Transparent needs also lead to lower allocations when an individual's need threshold is low. Finally, Kittel and coauthors show that social proximity induced by common experiences, which generate an insider–outsider differentiation among the participants, raises the probability of coalition formation between those who are more proximate. Such dyads are less likely to satisfy the needs of outsiders when these needs are above the equal share.

As mentioned above, the recognition of needs implies the moral obligation to transfer resources. The resulting conflict between self-interest and need-based justice is accordingly also found in the laboratory experiments outlined here. Kittel

[5] Traub et al. (2023) show in a dictator game with information about the recipient's need that the dictator's giving increases significantly when the need claim matches objectively verifiable facts of the recipient's situation.

concludes that "[...] self-interest is constantly present as a motive, which activates as soon as one's own allocations become lower than allocations to others or even risk falling below one's own need threshold." (p. 120).

Comparable conflicts between justice and self-interest, or conditions in which unfavorable inequality weighs more heavily than favorable inequality, are well known in the literature on social preferences (Fehr and Schmidt 1999, 2006). However, while the experimental designs presented here generate a strong substitution relationship between one's payoff and one's personal sense of fairness (cf. Bowles and Polania-Reyes 2012), especially in close social relationships, there is more likely to be at least some complementarity between self-interest and need recognition. Thus, although Kittel and coauthors create particularly difficult test conditions for social need recognition, the subjects' distribution decisions are clearly oriented to the establishment of need-based justice.

In Chap. 5, Markus Tepe and Nils Springhorn present laboratory experimental research focusing on the *political* recognition of needs in two well-established political economy models, namely the Meltzer–Richard model (Meltzer and Richard 1981) and the Baron–Ferejohn model (Baron and Ferejohn 1989). Two previous studies mentioned earlier (Lorenz et al. 2017; Paetzel et al. 2018) already examined the question of how *transparency* affects the political recognition of needs in these models. Tepe and Springhorn find that framing a redistributive decision problem in terms of a minimum income produces a greater acceptance of redistribution than framing the problem in terms of an equivalent linear tax rate (equivalence framing) in the context of the Meltzer–Richard model. This effect remains robust even when subjects can communicate with each other via a tool and exchange information about the appropriate tax rate or minimum income. However, the effect of equivalence framing is significantly attenuated when subjects have access to a calculator, which allows them to assess the effects of their choices and thus to factually objectify their decisions.

Furthermore, in line with the results of Bauer et al. (2022, 2023) on accountability and need-based redistribution, Tepe and Springhorn find that variation in productivity due to luck is more likely to be equalized than variation due to performance (Tepe et al. 2021b). When redistribution leads to a loss of efficiency (which, compared to the experimental design of Kittel and coauthors, further increases the costs resulting from the moral obligation to redistribute), the willingness to recognize need decreases significantly, as expected (Tepe et al. 2021a).

Using the Baron–Ferejohn model extended to include need, Springhorn (2021) experimentally shows that need is displaced as a distributional criterion by equality when exogenous demand thresholds are set too low. This is not surprising, since in distributional experiments with unearned initial endowments, the equal distribution—the equal-split allocation—serves as a natural reference point (cf. Yaari and Bar-Hillel 1984; Dawid and Dermietzel 2006; Andreoni and Bernheim 2009).

Tepe and Paetzel (2022) use the Baron–Ferejohn model to examine the effect of social identities on need-based justice (for details, see Sect. 5.5.2). Using the minimal group paradigm (Tajfel and Turner 1979), they test whether and how social categorization affects the scope of the need principle. The study shows that group polarization produces in-group favoritism. The authors conclude that the problem of exclusive need-based justice calls for a solution by institutional design and suggest that "policymakers could design democratic allocation regimes in which ascribed features and social identity remain unknown to decision-makers" (p. 138). However, this would limit the transparency of the objectification of need and thus its legitimacy. It can thus be concluded that heterogeneity complicates the political recognition of need and can lead to a dilemma between scope and legitimacy. Even if there may be normatively convincing reasons for need *differentiations* within social groups, as shown in Chap. 10 using the example of health care, *discriminatory* behavior would be a serious problem for the establishment of need-based justice, as the example of street-level bureaucrats in Chap. 9 reveals.

Tepe and coauthors also turn to the question of whether *expertise* influences the process of political recognition of need (see Sect. 5.6.4). In one experiment, subjects must negotiate the allocation of resources in the presence of exogenous demand thresholds. Recognition of needs is found to be high and to increase with increasing resource availability, but the presence of an additional uninvolved player who makes a distributional proposal at the outset tends to lead to more self-serving proposals. Based on the findings compiled in this section, Tepe comes to a rather negative assessment (see p. 143): "[I]t cannot be concluded that expertise, whether grounded in knowledge or authority, will likely lead to allocations more in line with needs." He therefore emphasizes the responsibility of the individual, "...of engaging in political dialogue about the validity of need claims and the mutual recognition of needs."

Nullmeier (2020, p. 198) emphasizes that the recognition of needs "requires specific procedures in which what is recognized as need is also argumentatively identified as what is necessary." In the studies discussed in Chaps. 4 and 5, subjects are limited in their possibilities to express reasons for their proposals. In Chap. 6, we focus on these reasons, which are explicitly elicited in the experiments. Tanja Pritzlaff-Scheele, Patricia Zauchner, and Frank Nullmeier study the effect of deliberation on the recognition and satisfaction of needs.

The three authors argue that need-based distribution—except in rare cases—differs from equal distribution and is more complex and therefore requires a special argumentative justification (cf., e.g., Michelbach et al. 2003; Gosepath 2015, pp. 177–179). They adopt the Habermasian view of deliberation as a special kind of communication that requires the exchange of arguments. In their group negotiation experiments, they then investigate the influence of these arguments on the voting outcome, i.e., the *deliberation effect*.

Set in a laboratory framework, subjects have equal need thresholds and receive unequal initial endowments of tokens. They have to collectively decide whether they accept the default, which is one of three treatment variations, or depart from this proposal and agree on a different distribution of a given number of additional tokens. In one treatment, the default is to allocate the same amount to all group members, which would result in vastly unequal outcomes and therefore not meet the needs of two out of the five members. The other two treatments implement a "weaker first" principle and a mixed proposal, which satisfies the need thresholds of all group members and distributes the remainder according to previous effort (a variant of the "Boulding principle", see Boulding 1962 and Traub et al. 2005). In one treatment, subjects communicate via chat and take part in reason-giving stages. As compared to the control treatments, deliberation reduces the acceptance of the equal and the mixed proposals and raises the approval of the "weaker first" solution.

In a second experiment, Zauchner et al. (2019) use a similar experimental setup, but here the initial endowments of the original group members are generated by a real-effort task. Moreover, an additional player ("immigrant"), who did not contribute to the group effort, joins the group. Across treatments, the extent of the outsider's involvement in the decision process is systematically varied. It turns out that the likelihood that the outsider's needs are satisfied increases with the group members' ability to express reasons and the outsider's participation in the vote.

On the basis of their quantitative and qualitative analyses of the deliberation processes, Pritzlaff-Scheele, Zauchner, and Nullmeier conclude that "when a group has to decide on the distribution of a resource, a deliberative process raises the acceptance of needs as a distributive principle. Moreover, our findings support the hypothesis that when arguments and justifications for a need-based distribution are made transparent to members of the deciding group, the initial, 'intuitive' acceptance of strict equality diminishes" (p. 173). Instead, the acceptance of need-based redistribution increases when the needy persons are included in the deliberation process and can give reasons for satisfying their needs.

While the identification of needs focuses on the non-comparative aspect of need-based justice, i.e., whether someone has enough to live a decent life, the recognition of needs adds a comparative perspective. The findings presented in Chaps. 4, 5, and 6 suggest that people are aware of the moral obligation to make transfers when they recognize needs socially or politically. Since justice is always weighed against self-interest, people also pay attention to relative allocations. More precisely, they are reluctant to recognize and satisfy need claims that result in distributive outcomes that disadvantage themselves or cause substantial inefficiency. Even though the equal distribution of resources is a strong focal point, the deliberation process itself and the participation of those in need in the process shift the individual and collective distributional preferences in favor of recognizing and meeting needs.

11.4 The Welfare Consequences of Need-Based Redistribution

In addition to the identification and recognition of needs, the repercussions of need-based redistribution on individual behavior must also be considered. Although all members of modern democratic societies are endowed with equal political rights, the less well-off do not take advantage of majority rule to level economic inequality (Corneo and Gruener 2000). A rational argument for this restraint could be that redistribution comes with direct (administrative) and—most importantly—indirect (incentive-based) costs. That is, society seems to be confronted with a trade-off between pursuing social goals and the efficiency goal (Barr 1998). The experimental results discussed in the previous sections have shown that people also make such trade-offs with respect to need-based redistribution. That is, what is perceived as a morally significant need claim, and therefore associated with an obligation to transfer resources, is also weighed against the costs that arise for oneself and for one's own solidarity community. In Chap. 7, Andreas Nicklisch expresses this fact as follows: "Analyzing the incentives for need-based justice is important because it reveals the *limits* of a redistribution system based on needs. That is, we do not want to reward people who are responsible for their need. Nor do we want to corrupt the system of need-based distribution by creating dependencies for recipients" (p. 183, emphasis added).

Nicklisch and his coauthors study the incentive effects of need-based redistribution in terms of labor supply in experiments with real-effort tasks. Kienle (2023) measures the stress subjects feel while performing the real-effort task when they have to reach a certain threshold in order to advance to the next round of the experiment. Successful subjects can help those in need move to the next round through financial transfers. First, the study finds that successful subjects either make no transfer or give exactly the amount needed to advance to the next round. That is, apart from need and self-interest, other fairness motives such as equality do not play a role here (in contrast to previously described experiments without real effort, where the natural reference point is the equal distribution). Second, especially for male participants, perceived stress (i.e., their own effort) correlates negatively with willingness to give.

The indirect costs of redistribution are explicitly examined in the experiments of Chugunova et al. (2017, 2022, 2023). The details of the experimental designs are also given in Sect. 7.5. Highly and less productive players are considered. In the control treatment, the highly productive players do not reduce their effort when a redistributive tax in favor of the less productive players is introduced, while the less productive players exert less effort, as expected. However, the negative incentive effect on the less productive players is significantly mitigated if there is a need threshold. Unfortunately, when the highly productive players observe the lower effort of the less productive players, they reduce their own effort, which reduces the possibility of fostering need-based justice. In addition, the more productive players prefer to transfer a certain proportion of their own earnings to the less productive ones as opposed to a fixed amount, supporting previous findings on the comparativity of need recognition.

Finally, Nicklisch discusses how responsibility affects the outcome legitimacy of need-based redistribution and warns that illegitimate distribution systems are unsustainable and self-defeating (cf. Chugunova et al. 2020). Kienle and Nicklisch (2023) show experimentally (using the extended experimental design of Kienle 2023) that responsiblity for one's own need significantly reduces the willingness to transfer. However, the motive of "educating" transfer recipients to behave responsibly (in the future) does not play a significant role.

In Chap. 8, Stefan Traub, Jan Philipp Krügel, and Meike Benker investigate the sustainability of need-based redistribution from a contract-theoretic perspective. The starting point of their theoretical and experimental analysis is that social inequality can partly be explained by individual risk taking. Sinn (1995, 1996) has argued that the welfare state can be seen as an insurance device to reduce the variance of lifetime incomes. So, in contrast to Chap. 7, which is about incentives in the labor market, Chap. 8 is about decisions under risk, specifically educational investment. The question is what impact need-based redistribution has on individual human capital investment and overall efficiency.

The theoretical analysis (see Sect. 8.3) shows that the redistributive welfare state reduces the individual risk of human capital investment, makes education more attractive, and therefore—assuming that there are no other negative incentive effects—increases overall efficiency. When need in the sense of a minimum income is taken into account in the model, need-based redistribution allows for higher inequality compared to a universal basic income while leading to higher welfare overall due to the significant increase in efficiency.

The predictions of the theoretical model are fully supported by two laboratory experiments (Traub and Krüge 2017; Benker et al. 2017). The average investment in education and thus overall efficiency (in terms of the average earnings of the subjects) is highest when there is a welfare state with need-based redistribution. Here, need-based redistribution means first testing who falls below the exogenously determined minimum income after realizing the risk and then having the successful investors provide the necessary transfers to support those in need in proportion to their payoffs. The authors of Chap. 8 conclude "[. . .] that the subjects tolerate a relatively high degree of inequality of payoffs, especially in the case of need-based redistribution, as long as the acknowledged need is covered. However, this distributional preference is compatible with the Boulding principle of maximizing the average income while taking the minimum income into account (Boulding 1962; Raphael 1980)" (p. 221).

Chapter 8 therefore sheds light on an aspect of the recognition of needs that is particularly relevant in the welfare state, namely checking the validity of need claims. While this is relatively easy using social control in smaller solidary communities, large, structured (welfare) states need an institutionalized mechanism. Therefore, means-testing is an integral part of the welfare state. Unlike the universal basic income, means-testing allows resources to be focused on those truly in need and thereby results in fewer negative incentive effects. There are, however, also arguments against means testing, such as the stigmatization of beneficiaries and the high direct (administrative) cost of social assistance. Another aspect that arises from the institutionalization of need recognition and its delegation to bureaucrats is the resulting discretionary power, which is examined by Kai-Uwe Schnapp in Chap. 9.

11.5 Differentiating Need

A recurrent theme throughout the previous sections is the observation that recognizing needs does not occur without scrutiny of the need claims. Decision-makers clearly differentiate between various conditions that give rise to needs and sanction claims that do not appear well-founded or that are considered excessively high by allocating less or no resources to the claimant. In this section, before we synthesize the four elements discussed in the preceding sections into an informed theory of need-based justice and a corresponding principle of justice, namely "lexineed," we will address the problems of differentiation of need that arise from practical examples presented in Part IV of this volume of the application of need-based justice in welfare provision and health care.

As noted by Kai-Uwe Schnapp in Chap. 9, "objectification of need takes place at different levels of government" (p. 236). Implementation of the national rules about who is eligible for social assistance is usually delegated to the local level, where street-level bureaucrats (SLBs) make case-by-case decisions. The legislator (principal) expects the SLBs (agents) to carry out the mandate to establish need-based justice in an *impartial*, i.e., non-discriminatory, manner. This is where Schnapp comes in, using survey experiments to investigate whether bureaucrats actually act impartially and whether the criterion of deservingness plays a role in their decisions when they *differentiate* between welfare recipients.

Schnapp reports that "[m]any SLBs [...] take positions that are in line with Boulding (1962) and Frankfurt (2015): Society has to meet a basic level of need beyond which fairness should be based on performance-related differences between people. Above established thresholds of need, SLBs mostly understand fairness as allowing someone to use resources in proportion to their own contribution" (p. 254). In a large conjoint experiment, Dietrich et al. (2023) show that (i) need deservingness in terms of household size has a strong positive effect on the likelihood of receiving financial support; (ii) "earned" deservingness in terms of not being responsible for one's own financial distress and being cooperative also has a positive effect; and (iii) depending on which group of respondents is considered, discrimination according to the nationality of the person in need may occur (including discrimination against one's own—German—nationality). Schnapp concludes from his investigations that "the process of socially constructing need understandings, levels, and thresholds should be actively orchestrated [by national governments] to support the development of a common understanding among those who implement need-oriented social policy on a day-to-day basis" (p. 262).

There are sectors of the welfare state, such as health care, where even if there is a high fundamental willingness to recognize needs, it is impossible to meet them due to scarcity and the indivisibility of resources, i.e., the moral obligation cannot be directly implemented. Organ donation is one example. In principle, there is no reason to withhold an organ from a patient, but usually too few organs are donated, resulting in long waiting lists. Adele Diederich discusses such situations and the role of need in *prioritizing* healthcare services in Chap. 10.

Reviewing the literature on prioritization in health care, Diederich concludes that "the application of need in the context of healthcare resource distribution usually refers to the urgency of the intervention or severity of the illness. That is, healthcare resources are distributed first to patients who need the resources the most. According to this definition, receiving the resources is often indispensable for the survival of the patient which corresponds to the core element of the concept of need (Nullmeier 2020)" (p. 283). Moreover, she notes that "[t]he public consistently supports the need principle in all its forms, i.e., urgency of intervention, severity of illness, extent of threat to life, and capacity to benefit. Hence, need is considered as the *most important* distribution principle in healthcare" (p. 284, emphasis added). Even in the case of scarce resources, need remains the first criterion for achieving distributive justice in health care by *differentiating* among the needy, as far as possible, according to the urgency of their needs.

11.6 Need-Based Justice and the "Lexineed" Principle

At the core of our informed theory of need-based justice is the concept of *recognized need* defined in Sect. 11.1. This definition is in line with Nullmeier's Thesis 1 that need is something necessary, which goes beyond a desire; Thesis 5 that need must be socially or politically recognized by legitimate procedures; Thesis 6 that methods of objectification of need claims must be based on transparent procedures and may involve experts; and Thesis 7 that situations of oversupply should be considered.

The two elements that ensure the application of the need principle in the short term are need *identification* and need *recognition*. In the sense of Nullmeier's Thesis 2, the identification and the recognition of need do not only have a positive-empirical side, i.e., how need satisfaction actually works in social groups and the welfare state, but also a normative-prescriptive side, how need satisfaction should work. A thorough analysis of the relevant literature and our own contributions discussed in the previous chapters show that the identification of need, especially with regard to framing effects, can be made more *consistent* through transparent, i.e., neutral, accounts and by drawing on expertise, e.g., econometric methods and axiomatic measures of need-based justice. This also helps prevent undesirable policy recommendations, such as addressing injustice by prioritizing the needs of those less in need. At the same time, the recognition of need gains *legitimacy* through transparency, both in the sense of neutral information provision and in the sense of a high level of participation, including those in need themselves.

Recognition of need places a moral obligation on the solidary community or society to transfer resources to the needy persons. As noted by Nullmeier in Thesis 8, however, this also creates an obligation for (potentially) needy persons to contribute to the minimization of their needs through their personal behavior. Indeed, most of the experimental studies presented in this chapter underscore that the recognition of needs by others strongly depends on the needy person's *responsibility* for her neediness. Here, there are also clear hierarchies in which responsibility plays a greater role for needs that are rated as less important. Overall, it is not surprising that people make a trade-off between self-interest or efficiency and the establishment of need-based justice. This, together with means testing delegated to state institutions, also guarantees the *sustainability* of need-based redistribution in the long term.

As explained with regard to the scope of need-based justice, the principle of need refers to social groups and nation-states that are linked by a common identity and can expect reciprocal behavior from their members. However, *differentiations* can occur according to situational, social, and personal characteristics (Thesis 9). As Diederich's chapter on health care has shown, these differentiations are sometimes necessary because not all recognized needs can be met at the same time due to shortages. Prioritization of those in acute need is an empirically relevant and legitimate form of differentiation. In contrast, as observed by Kai-Uwe Schnapp, *discrimination* according to irrelevant criteria such as migration background when using discretionary powers in the recognition of need requires clear countermeasures by governments.

Since our conclusions are based primarily on laboratory and survey experiments, it is worthwhile comparing them with the extensive experimental literature on distributional preferences. Many prior distributional experiments were designed to test elements of Rawls' (1971) theory of distributive justice, in particular the *maximin* principle, and compare it to other distributional principles such as equality, equity, desert, and need. This research consistently revealed that the dominant distributional principle is maximization of average income subject to a minimum income, a surprising regularity that inspired the research project underpinning this volume (Frohlich et al. 1987a,b; Frohlich and Oppenheimer 1990, 1992; Lissowski et al. 1991; Bond and Park 1991; Jackson and Hill 1995; de la Cruz-Doña and Martina 2000; Oleson 2001; Michelbach et al. 2003; Traub et al. 2005, 2009). As pointed out by Konow (2003), this constitutes a combination of competing distributional principles, namely Harsanyi's (1955) utilitarianism in the sense of expected utility maximization and Rawls' maximin principle. Long before this body of experimental research developed, Boulding (1962) had already suggested such a concept of justice: "Society lays a modest table at which all can sup and a high table at which the deserving can feast" (p. 83). Raphael (1980) formulated a similar principle: "Justice, then, is thought to require a basic minimum of equal satisfactions [...] Above that line, room is left for individuals to do as they think fit" (p. 54).

To capture such a pattern of distributional preferences, a *pluralist* theory of distributive justice is needed that combines different principles of justice depending on the context (see Thesis 2). Konow and Schwettmann (2016) have highlighted the pluralism and context dependence of fairness ideals in their survey on the economics of justice (also see Konow 2001, 2003; Nicklisch and Paetzel 2020). However, in light of our experimental results, we argue for a *strong* pluralistic theory of distributive justice in which need is always combined with other distributive principles depending on the situation (see Thesis 4). For example, in the experiments where initial endowments are exogenously allocated, need is often combined with equality, where the equal split serves as a reference point. By contrast, in the experiments where initial endowments had to be earned or were the result of an individual's risk-taking behavior, need was combined with equity.

Finally, we argue for a strong pluralistic theory of need-based justice in which need should not only always play a role but also be *prioritized* (Thesis 10). This is a logical consequence of the definition of need as something indispensable that has moral significance. A theory of distributive justice that is not based on the priority of the satisfaction of recognized needs can therefore be neither normatively nor empirically convincing in the scope of social relations based on *reciprocity*. Neither equity nor equality ensures that all who are involved in a distributive decision will get enough to survive.

Analogous to Rawls' principle of maximin justice (maximizing the utility of the worst-off in society), we therefore propose a "Lexineed" principle, where the prefix "Lexi" refers to the lexicographical order postulated between priority for satisfying needs and other principles of justice.

Proposition (The Lexineed Principle) In order to maximize social welfare, the establishment of distributive justice requires that all socially or politically recognized needs must be satisfied with the available resources as a matter of priority before other justice goals can be pursued with the remaining resources.

Prioritizing the need principle does not, however, imply a *carte blanche* for need claims. The proviso that needs must be socially or politically recognized lays the definition of needs in the hands of the community addressed by a claim. Need recognition can be conceptualized as a circular process, as depicted in Fig. 11.2. What is identified as an individual need depends on the standards that are considered sustainable in the community. Only identified needs qualify for social or political recognition. And only recognized needs are put to the test of sustainability. Thus, if the economy can sustain a certain level of need satisfaction, this level becomes the

Fig. 11.2 The Circular Process of Need Recognition

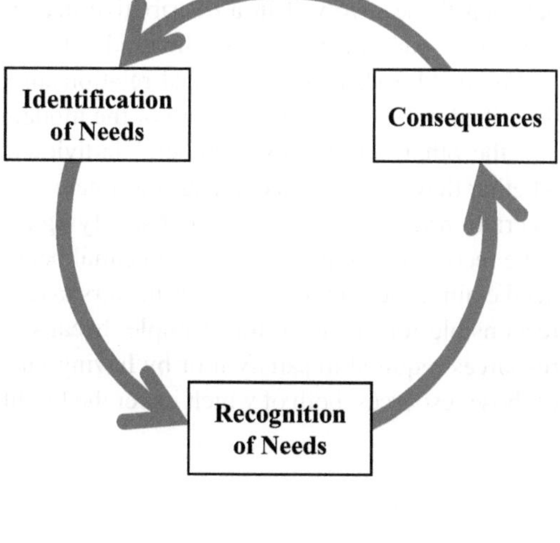

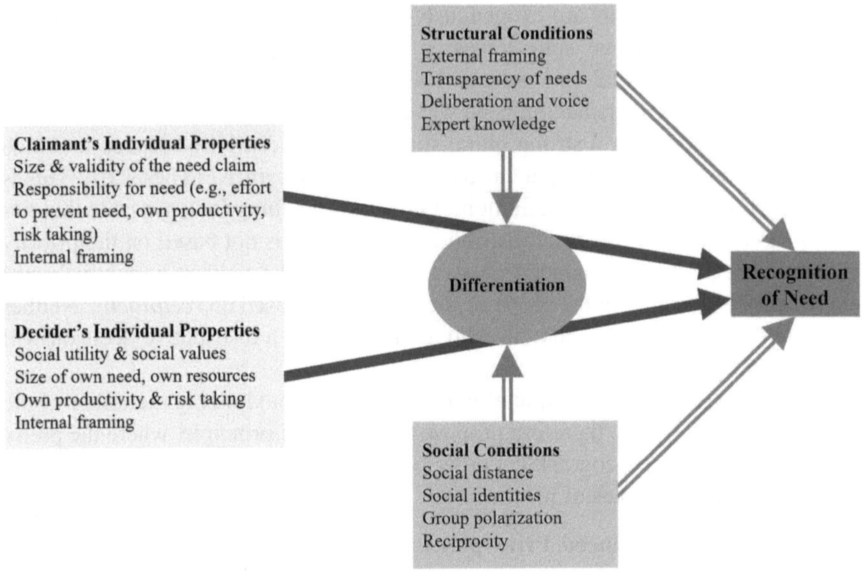

Fig. 11.3 A Causal Model of Need Recognition

standard in the community and serves as a reference for the identification of new claims, which, in turn, must be recognized in the community as legitimate and stand the test of economic sustainability.

Hence, even when the recognized needs are clearly defined and circumscribed, the recognition of a specific need is not self-evident, but depends on various aspects of the situation in which the claim is uttered, that is, decision-makers differentiate between needs. These situational factors include the personal conditions of the claimant, such as the size of her need or her own efforts to satisfy the need or overcome the need condition; personal conditions of the decision-maker, such as her social values and preferences; social conditions, such as the social distance between those involved in a distributive decision; and structural conditions, such as the transparency of needs or the mode of decision-making.

Figure 11.3 sketches the causal relationships that are suggested by the projects described in this volume. The core of the model consists of the effects of claimants' and the other community members' individual properties when the latter decide whether they recognize a claim as legitimate or not. An individual claim comes with a certain price tag and must aim at satisfying a particular need that either is known to be recognized or that has some potential being recognized. When recognizing the need claim as legitimate, decision-makers take into account whether the claimant is responsible for the need, for example, because of insufficient effort to produce the resources required to satisfy it or by having taken excessive risks in the production of those resources, both of which lower the likelihood that the claim will be satisfied.

Likewise, if the claimant is judged not to have made a sufficient effort to prevent the need, then the likelihood of need satisfaction is smaller.

However, factors not under the claimant's control but influencing the decision to satisfy a need as part of the deciders' properties will also influence the decision to recognize a need. The more decision-makers are motivated by social values and the more they consider the satisfaction of a need beneficial for the community as a whole, the more willing they will be to consider a need claim. But decision-makers also compare their own productivity and risk-taking behavior to that of the claimant, which lowers the likelihood of need satisfaction if it turns out that the claimant is less productive and cautious than the decision-maker. In addition, the internal frame that decision-makers adopt depends on their previous experiences, normative values, and habits, which will also contribute to the assessment of the claim.

The effect of these individual factors is both amended and moderated by contextual factors. We distinguish between structural and social factors, which serve as social mechanisms that bring about a social order in the form of a particular distributive solution.[6] Structural factors refer to the rules underlying decision processes or, put otherwise, the way in which the decision problem is presented to decision-makers. External framing captures properties of the choice situation, and transparency refers to the information that is available to decision-makers. Deliberation focuses on the depth of public reflection and the ability of individuals to participate in the decision-making process, whereas expert knowledge introduces the distinction between negotiations among interested parties and unaffected participants with greater knowledge of the issue.

Social factors refer to the social position of individuals in their relational networks. These factors include the social distance between claimants and decision-makers, the social identity of involved actors, and the extent to which claimants and decision-makers belong to different groups. Group characteristics are based on ascriptive criteria, such as gender, sex, ethnicity, and religion, which become salient in particular decision situations. Furthermore, the satisfaction of needs is based on reciprocal relationships. These in turn are based on the expectation that neediness is a temporary condition. Every support is thus matched by a certain effort on the part of the person in need to escape neediness.

The experiments reported in this volume suggest that structural and social factors directly influence the recognition of needs, but also indirectly moderate the effect of claimants' and decision-makers' properties on the recognition of needs. The sketch of the model in Fig. 11.3 may serve as an orientation for further, more detailed explorations of the conditions of need recognition. The reported results are sufficiently strong to suggest that such explorations will not be in vain.

[6] At this point, we draw on a conceptualization proposed by Simpson and Willer (2015).

11.7 Concluding Remarks

The reported findings are one step in a cumulative process of understanding the psychological, social, political, and economic processes underlying the recognition of needs, as well as the philosophical reflections that both motivate these analyses and are motivated by them. The results call for experimental replications and elaborations, for field experiments that bring the analysis closer to natural social settings, and for empirical research to determine the generalizability beyond the laboratory.

The satisfaction of needs as a social problem is as old as humanity, and controversies over the distribution of needed resources, or resources perceived as needed, have been a major source of social conflict, revolutions, and war throughout history. At the same time, the satisfaction of needs in terms of human capabilities is considered the most fundamental principle of justice as it is an indispensable condition of human dignity. If a society fails to satisfy human needs, the classical principles of distributive justice—equity and equality—quickly erode together with other fundamental conditions of peaceful coexistence and social order, such as the rule of law and democracy. As a result, failure to satisfy needs may eventually lead to the replacement of the open society by arbitrariness and despotism (Popper 1945).

A theory of justice based solely on need, however, would necessarily be incomplete because it cannot give guidance on how to proceed when all recognized needs are satisfied. Nevertheless, any theory that disregards need can only be a partial theory because no other principle alone—equity, equality, efficiency, entitlement, or whatever else might be proposed—can provide a convincing foundation for its application. Thus, a theory of justice must necessarily be pluralistic, and needs must be an integral element of such a theory. Meaningful combinations of principles that have been discussed in this volume include the combination of needs and equality and needs and equity.

Sabbagh and Schmitt (2016, p. 1) emphasize in their introduction to the *Handbook of Social Justice Theory and Research* that "[t]he notion of justice is salient both in social life and in scholarly traditions throughout history." Since ancient times, the normative-philosophical analysis of justice has been at the forefront of the debate about what constitutes social justice, which was revived in the 1970s by scholars such as Rawls (1971) and Miller (1976). In the social and behavioral sciences, an empirically oriented tradition of justice research has developed since the end of the Second World War, which has been supplemented by experimental research on justice and distribution preferences since the end of the twentieth century. Our interdisciplinary research project "Need-Based Justice and Distribution Procedures" contributes to research on social justice by merging normative and empirical-experimental perspectives on the establishment of distributive justice in welfare states into an empirically informed normative theory of need-based justice.

The Lexineed principle, which states that distributive justice must first be achieved by satisfying recognized needs before other distribution principles can be applied, is an expression of mutual solidarity linked to shared identities. It commits those who recognize need to actually satisfy it. However, as society is less forgiving of those who are seen as "responsible" for their situation, it also contains an obligation for those who express need to act "responsibly." As we explained in the first chapter, we propose thinking of the twenty-first century as the age of need-based justice. Modern welfare states in principle provide sufficient resources for all citizens to live a decent life, and the political process of recognizing need, complemented by means-testing of welfare entitlements, keeps the efficiency losses of achieving distributive justice within reasonable bounds.

Thus, a crucial moment in the recognition of needs is the differentiation of need claims, which results from the weighing of the multitude of conditions that give rise to an individually specific need. Need-based justice represents, in this sense, simultaneously a general principle of equality, human dignity, that sets a universal standard for the recognition of claims within a defined community, and a strictly individualistic notion of the contents of the claim.

Most welfare states in Europe have been exposed to mass migration for some time. Although most Western countries are probably in a state of surplus, our findings underscore the importance of a common social identity for the sustenance of solidarity. Immigration is a serious challenge for the acceptance of need-based distributive justice in European societies. The data from the European Social Survey discussed in Chap. 1 suggest that the most widely accepted conception of distributive justice is to satisfy needs and distribute the remainder according to merit. But, at a closer look, our studies have also shown that need satisfaction as such is not unconditional either, because allocations to needy persons depend on various personal and situational characteristics. Most notably, the general expectation is that the needy exert some effort to escape the need or reciprocate in some other way. Recognizing the various causes and reasons for migration, this means that the conditions for contributing to the host society must be created, for example, in the form of work permits. As shown in Chap. 9, even trained street-level bureaucrats demand some minimum form of reciprocity. Effort on part of the needy to attain self-sufficiency, however, may be the most difficult demand for migrants to fulfill in view of the various restrictions on labor market access that they face. The need to reconcile these opposing demands faced by migrants highlights the importance of encompassing democratic deliberation for a peaceful and solidary society.

References

Akerlof, G. A., and R. E. Kranton (2000): "Economics and Identity", *Quarterly Journal of Economics* 115, 715–753.

Alesina, A., and E. Glaeser (2004): *Fighting Poverty in the US and Europe*. Oxford: Oxford University Press.

Alesina, A., E. Glaeser, and B. Sacerdote (2001): "Why Doesn't the United States Have a European-Style Welfare State?", *Brookings Papers on Economic Activity* 2, 187–254.

Almås, I. (2012): "International Income Inequality: Measuring PPP Bias by Estimating Engel Curves for Food", *American Economic Review* 102 (2), 1093–1117.

Andreoni J., and B. D. Bernheim (2009): "Social Image and the 50–50 Norm. A Theoretical and Experimental Analysis of Audience Effects", *Econometrica* 77 (5), 1607–1636.

Andreoni, J., and J. Miller (2002): "Giving According to GARP: An Experimental Test of the Consistency of Preferences for Altruism", *Econometrica* 70, 737–57.

Arrow, K. (1982): "Risk Perception in Psychology and Economics", *Economic Inquiry* 20, 1–9.

Ballard, C. L. (1988): "The Marginal Efficiency Cost of Redistribution", *American Economic Review* 78 (5), 1019–1033.

Ballard, C. L., J. B. Shoven, and J. Whalley (1985): "General Equilibrium Computations of the Marginal Welfare Costs of Taxes in the United States", *American Economic Review* 75 (1), 128–138.

Baron, D. P., and J. A. Ferejohn (1989): "Bargaining in Legislatures", *American Political Science Review* 83 (4), 1181–1206.

Bauer, A. M., F. Meyer, J. Romann, M. Siebel, and S. Traub (2022): "Need, Equity, and Accountability, Evidence on Third-Party Distribution Decisions from a Vignette Study", *Social Choice and Welfare* 59, 769–814.

Bauer, A. M., J. Romann, M. Siebel, and S. Traub (2023): "Winter is Coming–How Laypeople Think About Different Kinds of Needs", *SSRN Working Paper* 4383555.

Barr, N. A. (1998): *The Economics of the Welfare State*. Stanford: Stanford University Press.

Benker, M., J. P. Krügel, and S. Traub (2017): "Risk Taking Under Different Welfare-State Regimes", *FOR 2104 Discussion Paper* No. 2017–11.

Blau, P. M. (1964): *Exchange and Power in Social Life*. New York: Wiley.

Bogner, A. (2005): *Wozu Experten? Ambivalenzen der Beziehung von Wissenschaft und Politik*. Wiesbaden: VS Verlag für Sozialwissenschaften.

Bogner, A., and W. Menz (2010): "How Politics Deals with Expert Dissent: The Case of Ethics Councils", *Science, Technology, and Human Values* 35, 888–914.

Bond, D., and J.-C. Park (1991): "An Empirical Test of Rawls's Theory of Justice: A Second Approach, in Korea and the United States", *Simulation und Gaming* 22 (4), 443–462.

Boulding, K. E. (1962): "Social Justice in Social Dynamics", in: R. B. Brandt (ed.): *Social justice*, 73–92. Englewood Cliffs, NJ: Prentice-Hall.

Bowles, S., and S. Polania-Reyes (2012): "Economic Incentives and Social Preferences: Substitutes or Complements?", *Journal of Economic Literature* 50 (2), 368–425.

Brock G. (2005): "Needs and Global Justice", *Royal Institute of Philosophy Supplements* 57, 51–72.

Brock, G. (2012): "Needs and Distributive Justice", in G. F. Gaus and F. D'Agostino (eds.): *The Routledge Companion to Social and Political Philosophy*, 444–455. New York: Routledge.

Brock, G., and D. Miller (2019): "Needs in Moral and Political Philosophy", in Zalta, E. N. (ed.): *The Stanford Encyclopedia of Philosophy*. Stanford: Metaphysics Research Lab.

Bruckmüller, S., G. Reese, and S. E. Martiny (2017): "Is Higher Inequality Less Legitimate? Depends on How You Frame It!", *British Journal of Social Psychology* 56 (4), 766–781.

Callaghan, K., and F. Schnell (2009): "Who Says What to Whom: Why Messengers and Citizen Beliefs Matter in Social Policy Framing", *Social Science Journal* 46 (1), 12–28.

Chugunova, M., W. J. Luhan, and A. Nicklisch (2020): "When to Leave Carrots for Sticks: On the Evolution of Sanctioning Institutions in Open Communities", *Economics Letters* 191, 109155.

Chugunova, M., A. Nicklisch, and K. U. Schnapp (2017): "On the Effects of Transparency and Reciprocity on Labor Supply in the Redistribution Systems", *FOR Working Paper* 2017–19.

Chugunova, M., A. Nicklisch, and K. U. Schnapp (2022): "Redistribution and Production with a Subsistence Income Constraint: A Real-Effort Experiment", *FinanzArchiv: Public Finance Analysis*, 78 (1–2), 208–238.

Chugunova, M., A. Nicklisch, and K. U. Schnapp (2023): *The Impact of Timing and Type of Donation Decision on Charitable Giving*, unpublished working paper.

Cohen, J. (2009): *Philosophy, Politics, Democracy: Selected Essays*. Cambridge: Harvard University Press.

Cohen, J. (2010): *The Arc of the Moral Universe and other Essays*. Cambridge: Harvard University Press.

Collins, H., and R. Evans (2007): *Rethinking Expertise*. Chicago: University of Chicago Press.

Corneo, G., and H. P. Gruener (2000): "Social Limits to Redistribution", *American Economic Review* 90 (5), 1491–1507.

Dawid H., and J. Dermietzel (2006): "How Robust Is the Equal Split Norm? Responsive Strategies, Selection Mechanisms and the Need for Economic Interpretation of Simulation Parameters", *Computational Economics* 28 (4), 371–397

Deaton, A., and J. Muellbauer (1980): *Economics and Consumer Behavior*. Cambridge: Cambridge University Press.

Deci, E. R, and R. M. Ryan (2000): "The "What" and "Why" of Goal Pursuits: Human Needs and the Self-determination of Behavior", *Psychological Inquiry* 11 (4), 227–268.

de Fine Licht, J. (2011): "Do We Really Want to Know? The Potentially Negative Effect of Transparency in Decision Making on Perceived Legitimacy", *Scandinavian Political Studies* 34 (3), 183–204.

de la Cruz-Doña, R., and A. Martina (2000): "Diverse Groups Agreeing on a System of Justice in Distribution: Evidence from the Philippines", *Journal of Interdisciplinary Economics* 11, 35–76.

Deutsch, M. (1975): "Equity, Equality, and Need: What Determines which Value Will Be Used as the Basis of Distributive Justice?", *Journal of Social Issues* 51 (3), 137–149.

Diederich, A. (2020): "Identifying Needs: The Psychological Perspective", in S. Traub, and B. Kittel (eds.): *Need-Based Distributive Justice: An Interdisciplinary Perspective*, 59–89. Springer Nature: Cham.

Diederich, A., M. Wyszynski, and I. Ritov (2018): "Moderators of Framing Effect in Variations of the Asian Disease Problem: Time Constraint, Need, and Disease Type", *Judgment and Decision Making* 13 (6), 529–546.

Dietrich, B., M. Jankowski, K.-U. Schnapp, and M. Tepe (2023): "Prioritizing Exceptional Social Needs. The Role of Discrimination And Client Deservingness in State Employees' and Citizens' Discretionary Behavior", *FOR 2104 Working Paper* 2023–01.

Dryzek, J. S. (1990): *Discursive Democracy: Politics, Policy, and Political Science*. Cambridge: Cambridge University Press.

Dryzek, J. S. (2002): *Deliberative Democracy and Beyond: Liberals, Critics, Contestations*. Oxford: Oxford University Press.

Elster, J. (ed.) (1998): *Deliberative Democracy*. Cambridge: Cambridge University Press.

Etzioni, A. (2010): "Is Transparency the Best Disinfectant?", *Journal of Political Philosophy* 18, 389–404.

Fehr, E., and K. M. Schmidt (1999): "A Theory of Fairness, Competition, and Cooperation", *Quarterly Journal of Economics* 114 (3), 817–868.

Fehr, E., and K. M. Schmidt (2006): "The Economics of Fairness, Reciprocity and Altruism—Experimental Evidence and New Theories", in S.-C. Kolm and J. M. Ythier: *Handbook of the Economics of Giving, Altruism and Reciprocity*, vol. 1, 615–691. Amsterdam: Elsevier.

Fischer, F. (2009): *Democracy and Expertise. Reorienting Policy Inquiry*. Oxford: Oxford University Press.

Fischer, K. (1997): *Tun oder lassen? Die Rolle von Framing-Prozessen für die Wahl von Handlungen oder Unterlassung in Entscheidungssituationen*. Frankfurt/Main: Peter Lang.

Fishkin, J. S., and P. Laslett (eds.) (2003): *Debating Deliberative Democracy*. Oxford: Blackwell.

Frohlich, N., and J. A. Oppenheimer (1990): "Choosing Justice in Experimental Democracies with Production", *American Political Science Review* 84 (2), 461–477.

Frohlich, N., and J. A. Oppenheimer (1992): *Choosing Justice. An Experimental Approach to Ethical Theory*. Berkeley: University of California Press.

Frohlich, N., J. A. Oppenheimer, and C. L. Eavey (1987a): "Laboratory Results on Rawls's Distributive Justice", *British Journal of Political Science* 17 (1), 1–21.

Frohlich, N., J. A. Oppenheimer, and C. L. Eavey (1987b): "Choices of Principles of Distributive Justice in Experimental Groups", *American Journal of Political Science* 31 (3), 606–636.

Frankfurt, H. (1984): "Necessity and Desire", *Philosophy and Phenomenological Research* 45 (1), 1–13.

Frankfurt, H. G. (2015): *On Equality*. Princeton: Princeton University Press.
Fraser, N. (2000): "Rethinking Recognition", *New Left Review* 3, 107–120.
Gaertner, W. (2006): *A Primer in Social Choice Theory*. Oxford: Oxford University Press.
Gaertner, W., and E. Schokkaert (2012): *Empirical Social Choice: Questionnaire-Experimental Studies on Distributive Justice*. Cambridge: Cambridge University Press.
Galtung, J. (1980): "The Basic Needs Approach", in K. Lederer, J. Galtung, and D. Antal (eds.): *Human Needs. A Contribution to the Ongoing Debate*, 55–125, Cambridge: Oelschlager, Gunn and Hain.
Geary, R. C. (1950): "A Note on 'A Constant-Utility Index of the Cost of Living'", *The Review of Economic Studies* 18 (1), 65–66.
Gellner, E. (1983): *Nations and Nationalism*. Oxford: Blackwell.
Gosepath, S. (2015): "The Principles and the Presumption of Equality", in C. Fourie, F. Schuppert, and I. Wallimann-Helmer (eds.): *Social Equality. On What It Means to Be Equal*, 167–185. Oxford: Oxford University Press.
Gouldner, A. W. (1960): "The Norm of Reciprocity: A Preliminary Statement", *American Sociological Review* 25, 161–178.
Habermas, J. (1992): *Faktizität und Geltung. Beiträge zur Diskurstheorie des Rechts und des demokratischen Rechtsstaats*. Frankfurt/M.: Suhrkamp.
Harsanyi, J. C. (1955): "Cardinal Welfare, Individualistic Ethics, and Interpersonal Comparisons of Utility", *Journal of Political Economy* 63 (4), 309–321.
Jackson, M., and P. Hill (1995): "A Fair Share", *Journal of Theoretical Politics* 7 (2), 169–179.
James, E. (1993): "Why do Different Countries Choose a Different Public-Private Mix of Educational Services?", *Journal of Human Resources* 28 (3), 571–592.
Jenni, K., and G. Loewenstein (1997): "Explaining the Identifiable Victim Effect", *Journal of Risk and Uncertainty* 14 (3), 235–257.
Kahneman, D., and A. Tversky (1979): "Prospect Theory: An Analysis of Decision under Risk", *Econometrica* 47, 263–291.
Kahneman, D., and Tversky, A. (1984): "Choices, Values, and Frames", *American Psychologist* 39 (4), 341–350.
Kienle, A.-K. (2023): *Dictators Under Pressure: Fairness Norms and Monetary Support to Those in Need*, unpublished working paper.
Kienle, A.-K., and A. Nicklisch (2023): *Responsibility for Needs, Consequences of Support, and the Acceptance to Give*, unpublished working paper.
Kittel, B. (2020): "Need-based Justice: A Sociological Perspective", in S. Traub and B. Kittel (eds.): *Need-based Distributive Justice: An Interdisciplinary Perspective*, 91–131. Cham: Springer Nature.
Kittel, B., S. Neuhofer, and M. Schwaninger (2020): "The Impact of Need on Distributive Decisions: Experimental Evidence on Anchor Effects of Exogenous Thresholds in the Laboratory", *PLoS ONE* 15 (4), 0228753.
Kittel, B., S. Neuhofer, and M. Schwaninger (2021): "The Dark Side of Transparent Needs. An Experiment on Information and Need-Based Justice", *FOR 2104 Working Paper* 2021–04.
Klor, E. F., and Shayo, M. (2010): "Social Identity and Preferences over Redistribution", *Journal of Public Economics* 94 (3), 269–278.
Kogut T., and I. Ritov (2005a): "The 'Identified Victim' Effect: An Identified Group, or just a Single Individual?", *Journal of Behavioral Decision Making* 18 (3), 157–167.
Kogut T., and I. Ritov (2005b): "The Singularity Effect of Identified Victims in Separate and Joint Evaluations", *Organizational Behavior and Human Decision Processes* 97 (2), 106–116.
Konow, J. (2001): "Fair and Square: The Four Sides of Distributive Justice", *Journal of Economic Behavior und Organization* 46, 137–164.
Konow, J. (2003): "Which is the Fairest One of All? A Positive Analysis of Justice Theories", *Journal of Economic Literature* 41, 1188–1239.
Konow, J., and L. Schwettmann (2016): "The Economics of Justice", in C. Sabbagh, and M. Schmitt (eds.): *Handbook of Social Justice Research*, Heidelberg: Springer, 83–106.

Kraus, P. A. (2004): "Die Begründung demokratischer Politik in Europa. Zur Unterscheidung von Input-und Output-Legitimation bei Fritz W. Scharpf", *Leviathan* 32 (4), 558–567.
Kühberger, A. (1998): "The Influence of Framing on Risky Decisions: A Meta-Analysis", *Organizational Behavior and Human Decision Processes* 75 (1), 23–55.
Kühberger, A. (2023): "A Systematic Review of Risky-Choice Framing Effects", *EXCLI Journal* 22, 1012–1031.
Kuijs, L. (2000): "The Impact of Ethnic Heterogeneity on the Quantity and Quality of Public Spending", *IMF Working Paper* 00/49, Washington: International Monetary Fund.
Landwehr, C. (2009): *Political Conflict and Political Preferences: Communicative Interaction between Facts, Norms and Interests*. Colchester: ECPR Press.
Lane, T. (2016): "Discrimination in the Laboratory. A Meta-analysis of Economic Experiments", *European Economic Review* 90, 375–402.
Lewin, K. (1926): "Vorsatz, Wille und Bedürfnis", *Psychologische Forschung* 7, 330–385.
Liebig, S., and C. Sauer (2016): "Sociology of Justice", in C. Sabbagh and M. Schmitt (eds.): *Handbook of Social Justice Theory and Research*, 37–59. Berlin: Springer.
Lissowski, G., T. Tyszka, and W. Okrasa (1991): "Principles of Distributive Justice Experiments in Poland and America", *Journal of Conflict Resolution* 35 (1), 98–119.
Lorenz, J., F. Paetzel, and M. Tepe (2017): "Just Don't Call It a Tax! Framing in an Experiment on Voting and Redistribution", *Journal of Experimental Political Science* 4 (3), 183–194.
Luttmer, E. F. P. (2001): "Group Loyalty and the Taste for Redistribution", *Journal of Political Economy* 199, 500–528.
Mas-Collel, A., Whinston, M. D., and Green, J. R. (1995): *Microeconomic Theory*. New York: Oxford University Press.
Maslow, A. H. (1943): "A Theory of Human Motivation", *Psychological Review* 50, 370–396.
Mayntz, R., F. Neidhardt, P. Weingart and U. Wengenroth (ed.) (2008): *Wissensproduktion und Wissenstransfer—Wissen im Spannungsfeld von Wissenschaft, Politik und Öffentlichkeit*. Bielefeld: transcript Verlag.
Meltzer, A. H., and Richard, S. F. (1981): "A Rational Theory of the Size of Government", *Journal of Political Economy* 89 (5), 914–927.
Michelbach, P. A., J. T. Scott, R. E. Matland, and B. H. Bornstein (2003): "Doing Rawls Justice: An Experimental Study of Income Distribution Norms", *American Journal of Political Science* 47 (3), 523–539.
Miller, D. (1976). *Social Justice*. London: Oxford University Press.
Miller, D. (1995): *On Nationality*. Oxford: Clarendon Press.
Miller, D. (1999): *Principles of Social Justice*. Cambridge, MA: Harvard University Press.
Miller, D. (2007a): *Human Rights, Basic Needs, and Scarcity*, Working Paper SJ007, Centre for the Study of Social Justice and Department of Politics and International Relations.
Miller, D. (2007b): *National Responsibility and Global Justice*. Oxford: Oxford University Press.
Miller, D. (2013): *Justice for Earthlings. Essays in Political Philosophy*. Cambridge: Cambridge University Press.
Miller, D. (2016): *Strangers in Our Midst. The Political Philosophy of Immigration*. Cambridge, MA: Harvard University Press.
Norris, P. (2011): Democratic Deficit: Critical Citizens Revisited, Cambridge: Cambridge University Press.
Nicklisch, A., and F. Paetzel (2020): "Need-Based Justice and Distribution Procedures: The Perspective of Economics", in S. Traub, and B. Kittel (eds.): *Need-Based Distributive Justice: An Interdisciplinary Perspective*, 161–189. Cham: Springer Nature.
Nullmeier, F. (2020): "Towards a Theory of Need-based Justice", in S. Traub and B. Kittel (eds.): *Need-based Distributive Justice: An Interdisciplinary Perspective*, 191–208. Cham: Springer Nature.
Nussbaum, M. (1988): "Nature, Function, and Capability: Aristotle on Political Distribution", in: *Oxford Studies in Ancient Philosophy*, 145–184 (sup. vol.). Oxford: Clarendon Press.
Nussbaum, M. (2001): *Women and Human Development*. Cambridge: Cambridge University Press.

Oleson, P. E. (2001): *An Experimental Examination of Alternative Theories of Distributive Justice and Economic Fairness*. Disseration. Ann Arbor, Michigan.
Paetzel, F., J. Lorenz, and M. Tepe (2018): "Transparency Diminishes Framing-Effects in Voting on Redistribution: Some Experimental Evidence", *European Journal of Political Economy* 55, 169–184.
Page, E. A. (2006): *Climate Change, Justice and Future Generations*. Cheltenham: Edgar Elgar.
Popper, K. R. (1945): *The Open Society and its Enemies*. London: Routledge.
Raphael, D. D. (1980): *Justice and Liberty*. London: Athlone Press.
Rawls, J. (1971): *A Theory of Justice*. Cambridge, MA: Harvard University Press.
Rowntree, S. (1901): *Poverty: A Study of Town Life*. London: Macmillan.
Runciman, W. G. (1966): *Relative Deprivation and Social justice: Study Attitudes Social Inequality in 20th Century England*. London: Routledge.
Ryan R. M., and E. L. Deci (2000): "Self-Determination Theory and the Facilitation of Intrinsic Motivation, Social Development, and Well-Being", *American Psychologist* 55 (1), 68–78.
Sabbagh, C., and M. Schmitt (eds.) (2016): *Handbook of Social Justice Theory and Research*. Heidelberg: Springer.
Scharpf, F. W. (1999): *Regieren in Europa: Effektiv und demokratisch?* Frankfurt, M.: Campus Verlag.
Scharpf, F. W. (2009): "Legitimacy in the Multilevel European Polity", *European Political Science Review* 1 (2), 173–204.
Sen, A. (1985): *Commodities and Capabilities*. Amsterdam: North-Holland.
Sen, A. (1999): *Development as Freedom*. Oxford: Oxford University Press.
Siebel, M., and T. Schramme (2020): "Need-Based Justice from the Perspective of Philosophy", in S. Traub and B. Kittel: *Need-Based Distributive Justice. An Interdisciplinary Perspective*, 21–58. Cham: Springer.
Siefken, S. T. (2007): *Expertenkommissionen im politischen Prozess—Eine Bilanz zur rot-grünen Bundesregierung 1998–2005*. Wiesbaden: VS Verlag für Sozialwissenschaften.
Simpson, B., and R. Willer (2015): "Beyond Altruism: Sociological Foundations of Cooperation and Prosocial Behavior", *Annual Review of Sociology* 41, 43–63.
Sinn, H.-W. (1995): "A Theory of the Welfare State", *Scandinavian Journal of Economics* 97, 495–526.
Sinn, H.-W. (1996): "Social Insurance, Incentives and Risk Taking", *International Tax and Public Finance* 3, 259–280.
Smith, G. (2009): Democratic Innovations: Designing Institutions for Citizen Participation, Cambridge: Cambridge University Press.
Soroka, S., K. Banting, and R. Johnston (2006): "Immigration and Redistribution in a Global Era", in S. Bowles, P. Bardhan and M. Wallerstein (eds.): *Globalization and Egalitarian Redistribution* 261–288. Princeton: Princeton University Press.
Springhorn, N. (2021): "Bargaining According to the Baron-Ferejohn Model, Taking into Account Need", *FOR2104 Working Paper* 2021–06.
Stantcheva, S. (2021): "Understanding Tax Policy: How Do People Reason?", *Quarterly Journal of Economics* 136 (4), 2309–2369.
Stephens, D. W. (1981): "The Logic of Risk-Sensitive Foraging Preferences", *Animal Behaviour* 29 (2), 628–629.
Stephens, D. W., and E. L. Charnov (1982): "Optimal Foraging: Some Simple Stochastic Models", *Behavioral Ecology and Sociobiology* 10 (4), 251–263.
Stone, R. (1954): "Linear Expenditure Systems and Demand Analysis: An Application to the Pattern of British Demand", *Economic Journal* 64 (255), 511–527.
Tajfel, H., and Turner, J. (1979): "An Integrative Theory of Intergroup Conflict", in: W. G. Austin and S. Worchel (eds.): *The Social Psychology of Intergroup Relations*, 55–65. Monterey: Brooks-Cole.
Tepe, M., and F. Paetzel (2022): *Social Identity in Coalition Bargaining. An Experimental Analysis*, unpublished manuscript.

Tepe, M., F. Paetzel, J. Lorenz, and M. Lutz (2021a): "Efficiency Loss and Support for Income Redistribution: Evidence from a Laboratory Experiment", *Rationality and Society* 33 (3), 313–340.

Tepe, M., P. Vanhuysse, and M. Lutz (2021b): "Merit, Luck and Taxes. Societal Reward Rules, Self-Interest and Ideology in a Real-Effort Voting Experiment", *Political Research Quarterly* 74 (4), 1052–1066.

Thomson G. (2005): "Fundamental Needs", in S. Reader (ed.): *The Philosophy of Need*, 175–186. Cambridge: Cambridge University Press.

Traub, S. (1999): *Framing Effects in Taxation: An Empirical Study Using the German Income Tax Schedule*. Heidelberg: Physica.

Traub, S. (2020): "Perspectives for a Theory of Need-Based Distributive Justice", in S. Traub and B. Kittel (eds.): *Need-Based Distributive Justice: An Interdisciplinary Perspective*, 1–20. Cham: Springer Nature.

Traub, S., A. M. Bauer, M. Siebel, N. Springhorn, and A. R. Weiss (2017): "On the Measurement of Need-Based Justice", *FOR 2104 Working Paper* 2017–12.

Traub, S., B. Kittel (eds.) (2020): *Need-Based Distributive Justice: An Interdisciplinary Perspective*. Cham: Springer Nature.

Traub, S., and J. P. Krügel (2017): "Risk Taking and the Welfare State: Some Experimental Evidence", *FOR 2104 Discussion Paper* 2017–1.

Traub, S., M. Schwaninger, F. Paetzel, and S. Neuhofer (2023): "Evidence on Need-Sensitive Giving Behavior: An Experimental Approach to the Acknowledgment of Needs", *Journal of Behavioral and Experimental Economics* 105, 102028.

Traub, S., C. Seidl, and U. Schmidt (2009): "An Experimental Study on Individual Choice, Social Welfare, and Social Preferences", *European Economic Review* 53, 385–400.

Traub, S., C. Seidl, U. Schmidt, and M. V. Levati (2005): "Friedman, Harsanyi, Rawls, Boulding—or Somebody Else? An Experimental Investigation of Distributive Justice", *Social Choice and Welfare* 24 (2), 283–309.

Tversky, A., and D. Kahneman (1981): "The Framing of Decisions and the Psychology of Choice", *Science* 211 (4481), 453–458.

Tversky, A., and D. Kahneman (1986): "Rational Choice and the Framing of Decisions", *Journal of Business* 59, S251–S278.

Varian, H. R. (2006): "Revealed Preference", in M. Szenberg, L. Ramrattan, and A. A. Gottesman (eds.): *Samuelsonian Economics and the Twenty-First Century*, 99–115. New York: Oxford University Press.

Vlastos, G. (1962): "Justice and Equality", in R. B. Brandt (ed.): *Social Justice*, 31–72. Englewood Cliffs, NJ: Prentice Hall.

Weale, A., and E. Craig (1998): "Needs and Interests", in *Routledge Encyclopedia of Philosophy*, 752–755. London: Routledge.

Weingart, P., and J. Lentsch (2008): *Wissen—Beraten—Entscheiden—Form und Funktion wissenschaftlicher Politikberatung in Deutschland*. Weilerswist: Velbrück Wissenschaft.

Wenzelburger, G., and Hörisch, F. (2016): "Framing Effects and Comparative Social Policy Reform: Comparing Blame Avoidance Evidence from Two Experiments", *Journal of Comparative Policy Analysis: Research and Practice* 18 (2), 157–175.

Wiggins, D. (1998): "What is the Force of the Claim that One Needs Something?", in G. Brock (ed.): *Necessary Goods. Our Responsibilities to Meet Others' Needs*, 33–56. Lanham: Rowman and Littlefield.

Wringe, B. (2005): "Needs, Rights, and Collective Obligations", in S. Reader (ed.): *The Philosophy of Need*, 187–207. Cambridge: Cambridge University Press.

Wyszynski, M., A. Diederich, and I. Ritov (2020): "Gamble for the Needy! Does Identifiability Enhance Donation?", *PLOS ONE* 15, e0234336

Yaari M, and M. Bar-Hillel (1984): "On Dividing Justly", *Social Choice and Welfare* 1 (1), 1–24.

Zauchner, P. F., T. Pritzlaff-Scheele, and F. Nullmeier (2019): *Immigration and Needs-Based Redistribution. Experimental Investigations on the Stability of Attitudes to Sharing Welfare Resources*, unpublished manuscript.

MIX
Papier aus verantwortungsvollen Quellen
Paper from responsible sources
FSC® C105338

If you have any concerns about our products,
you can contact us on
ProductSafety@springernature.com

In case Publisher is established outside the EU,
the EU authorized representative is:
Springer Nature Customer Service Center GmbH
Europaplatz 3, 69115 Heidelberg, Germany

Printed by Libri Plureos GmbH
in Hamburg, Germany